FROM MARRIAGE TO THE MARKET

FROM MARRIAGE
TO THE MARKET

The Transformation of
Women's Lives and Work

Susan Thistle

University of California Press   Berkeley Los Angeles London

University of California Press
Berkeley and Los Angeles, California

University of California Press, Ltd.
London, England

© 2006 by The Regents of the University of California

Library of Congress Cataloging-in-Publication Data

Thistle, Susan.
    From marriage to the market : the transformation of women's
lives and work / Susan Thistle.
        p.   cm.
    Includes bibliographical references and index.
    ISBN-13: 978-0-520-24590-7 (cloth : alk. paper),
    ISBN-10: 0-520-24590-3 (cloth : alk. paper)
    ISBN-13: 978-0-520-24646-1 (pbk. : alk. paper),
    ISBN-10: 0-520-24646-2 (pbk. : alk. paper)
    1. Women—Employment—United States—History—20th
century.   2. Women—United States—Economic conditions.
3. Women—United States—Social conditions.   4. Work and
family—United States.   I. Title.

HD6095.T49   2006
331.40973'09045—dc22   2005031019

Manufactured in the United States of America

14   13   12   11   10   09   08   07   06
11   10   9   8   7   6   5   4   3   2   1

To my mother,
Mary Burnham MacCracken,
with thanks

CONTENTS

FIGURES

TABLES

ACKNOWLEDGMENTS

Writing a book is like running a very long race. One of the major tasks is to keep going until the end. Much support from others sustained me during this endeavor, cheering me on. I am fortunate to have friends with both keen analytic minds and kind hearts. Their ability to think in large theoretical terms was invaluable, as was their ongoing enthusiasm for this project. In particular I would like to thank Lyn Spillman, whose superb intellectual strengths, repeated assertion of the value of larger conceptual projects, and gracious encouragement were invaluable. I also thank Hilarie Lieb, for long walks and talks in which to think through the details of this project. Always supportive as a friend and colleague, she generously offered her perspective and skills as an economist and was crucial to this project's success. I thank as well Orville Lee, for his ability to develop the logic of an argument and for his appreciation of grand theory and both the strengths and vulnerabilities of his friends; and Russ Faeges and Marc Steinberg for again affirming the value of theory and for supportive comments.

The Department of Sociology at Northwestern University is a place of great minds and collegial spirit that is keeping alive the grander traditions in sociology, a sociology still committed to big ideas. I am grateful to everyone in the department for providing a supportive institutional and intellectual environment in which I could write this book. Special thanks go to Carol Heimer, for ensuring that I had a room of my own and £500 or so, and for warmly believing in the value of this work. A similar thanks to Wendy Espeland, who kept encouraging me as I labored through the difficult last stretch. I also thank in particular Paula England, for her constant willingness to talk about sex, pregnancy, and shotgun weddings and for her generous spirit; Mary Patillo and Ann Orloff; and, in the Department of Psychology, Alice Eagly, for kindly reading chapters. You have all done your best; any failures are my own.

I also thank Mike Hout, who got me excited about statistics; Erik Wright, for providing a space in which my thoughts could develop; Vicki Bonnell, Mary Ryan, and Kristin Luker, for encouraging me to take on this large endeavor; and Ann Swidler and Jane Mansbridge, for later support when needed. Thanks as well to my first professors at the Jackson School of International Studies at the University of Washington—Bruce Cumings, Dan Chirot, Joel Migdal, and Liz Perry—who may be surprised to see the use to which I put their teachings.

A grant from the American Association of University Women provided support in more than financial terms, as it also validated research on women's lives. I am grateful to the National Science Foundation for a grant funding my initial analyses of women's poverty. I also thank the Helen Whiteley Center at the University of Washington, and the Friday Harbor Marine Lab of which it is a part, for providing a lovely place in which to write parts of this book.

This book could not have been written without an enormous amount of earlier work done by a wide range of scholars, as the lengthy endnotes make clear. Key to its research were the Integrated Public Use Microdata Series from the U.S. census, admirably standardized by Steve Ruggles, Matthew Sobek, Trent Alexander, Catherine A. Fitch, Ronald Goeken, Patricia Kelly Hall, Miriam King, and Chad Ronnander at the Population Center at the University of Minnesota. I am grateful to Ann Janda for directing me toward these and other archival data.

I would also like to thank my family in all its extended forms. Each of you helped in your own way. Much appreciation also goes to all my friends of many years, some of whom I have lost touch with while this book consumed my attention. You know who you are, and I still appreciate you. This is especially true of Ellie Dorsey, who lived her short life to the fullest and whose cheerful kindness, keen intelligence, and love for both her family and her work remain an inspiration.

During one stretch in writing this book I ran with the Concord Runners, a group that has been together more than twenty-five years. Early Saturday mornings we would run six miles and then all eat breakfast in the basement of a town building. As we passed the halfway point of our run and turned for home, the others would take off, leaving me further and further behind. Exhausted, wanting to walk but having miles to go, I would plod on, chanting "Just keep going, just keep going," envisioning the good friends and food waiting up ahead. For all of those in academia struggling to move forward in difficult times, I encourage you also to keep going. Better times may lie ahead.

American homes changed dramatically over the second half of the twentieth century. Wives and mothers entered the labor force in great numbers; the laws and customs that once framed marriage and parenthood came apart; and government aid to single mothers all but disappeared. Pregnancy, child care, and even the most intimate sexual acts became topics of public debate.

The end result, as we begin a new century, is that the lives of women and those closest to them have been turned inside out. Many mothers and children as well as men now spend most of their waking hours outside their own homes, and wages, not marriage, provide women's main source of support. Breast pumps are carried in briefcases; conception may take place in clinics. Family life is carefully fitted in at the edges of the day or week. These changes have been major and traumatic ones. We are still struggling to adjust to them, without fully grasping what has happened to our lives or the consequences of these events for our children.

The shape of the American economy has changed as well. Office buildings and shopping malls have replaced factories and farms; faxes and e-mails have taken the place of letters. There is much talk of the "new economy" that has emerged, symbolized by computers, cell phones, and the Internet. Yet technological advances, unimaginable in earlier times, have been joined with unanticipated hardships, at work as well as at home. Despite all the new inventions, time seems to have grown increasingly scarce, and jobs more intense and demanding, yet less secure, than in the past.

Women born in the first decades after World War II have traced out their lives across this stretch of years. Looking back, it is clear they undertook a great journey, one leading them not just out into the terrain of paid work but also far from the old domestic realm of their mothers, in its different shapes and forms. A world has been lost as well as gained. Each wave of women coming after them has sought a better balance of home and work. Yet members of each group, from those in their 50s to those just entering adulthood, are still struggling to fit the pieces of their lives together. Whether lawyers or secretaries, married or single, women talk of being overburdened by the demands of work at home and for pay. Many do sink, despite their efforts, into poverty.

As women struggle to carry out their labors of love in the face of waning private and public assistance for such tasks, we have to ask ourselves how we came to such a place. What happened to the older world where most women focused on care of their families and homes, and were supported in these tasks? Why is it so hard for women to realize the new American dream of both meaningful work and satisfying personal lives?

The Hidden Half of Women's Story

Many excellent studies have examined one or another of the cultural, social, and political upheavals in women's lives in the decades after World War II, from the battles over abortion or the Equal Rights Amendment in the 1970s and 1980s to the difficulties facing working mothers at the start of the twenty-first century.[1] However, most social scientists have analyzed these issues separately. Yet these are not isolated problems but intertwined pieces of a larger process of historic change that has not yet been fully grasped.

In this book, I provide a new understanding of the underlying causes of the events dramatically transforming women's lives, and the very nature of gender itself, in the last decades of the twentieth century. I explain both how and why women's relationships to marriage, motherhood, and the labor force have altered profoundly over these years and the consequences of these shifts for the new economy of today.

Rather than focusing as many others have on the loss of the male breadwinner wage, I argue that behind the traumatic events of recent decades lies a fundamental transformation of women's own work, resulting from a decisive encounter between the domestic realm and a maturing market. A lessening of household chores by an expanding post–World War II economy also offering new opportunities led several different groups to challenge and dismantle the old rules not only holding women in the home but also committing men, employers, and the state to some support for such labor. The transformation of women's household tasks and labor into work done for pay then played a key role in the rise of a new cycle of economic growth and prosperity in the United States, creating great gains in free time and income. Yet women and their families have realized few of these gains, and they have done so unequally.

I develop this argument through a detailed examination of the experiences of African American women and white women, especially between 1960 and 2000. Careful comparison of these two sharply contrasting situations is one of the most effective ways to unearth the deeper causes of the past and present difficulties in women's lives. I also set these women's experiences in the context of a larger process of social change. By stepping back to this larger view, we are able to see connections between events not evident with too close a focus.

Such an analysis reveals a hidden side to the story of women's lives that has not yet been told. We cannot fully understand the dramatic alterations in gender relations, or in the worlds of home and work, without it. Only when we lift the domestic realm clearly into view can we see what once held this realm together, even in the face of great poverty, and why it has now come apart. Many of the problems that confronted women over the second half of the twentieth century, from the rise of single mothers among the poor to the recent time crunch faced by many families, are tied to the failure to consider this half of their story. This oversight has also limited efforts to explain why such difficulties arose.

In tracing what has been hidden in the women's story, I challenge several accepted beliefs, including some held by feminists. This account shows that women's movement into the labor force will not in itself bring equality. It also sees many of the recent problems confronting women as stemming not from the persistence of men's control but rather from the collapse of the arrangement on which men's power was based, as interest in supporting women's domestic labor lessened. Finally, it makes clear that a focus on the market alone, or any one group of women or men, cannot explain recent alterations in gender relations and family structures. However, while looking closely at differences by race and class, this book also uncovers important similarities in the events transforming women's lives, suggesting a path as well toward a common resolution of the problems they now face.

The Changing Shape of Families

While scholars have analyzed women's entrance into the labor force in detail, changes in family structure have been harder to explain. For many decades now, arguments have raged over whether such changes are caused by failures in individual behaviors or in the structure of the economy itself. Some emphasize the disappearance of an old set of family values that once stabilized home life. They point to a loss of discipline, particularly among the poor, or to the rise of individualism, especially in women intent on their careers.[2]

Others argue that shifts in the market economy underlie the new patterns in marriage and parenthood that have emerged. Women's increased employment is often seen as fueling the rise in divorce or challenges to the old domestic role. Some have stressed instead the changing circumstances of men's work, arguing that the disappearance of well-paid manufacturing jobs lies behind lower rates of marriage. Analysts also often point to men's declining wages to explain the end of the family centered on the male breadwinner and married women's movement into the labor force. However, women's turn to paid work began well before men's employment difficulties, and marriage rates, though falling more among the poor and unemployed, have declined across the economic spectrum.[3]

All these approaches, whether emphasizing changes in people's beliefs or in the labor force itself, are marred by a similar flaw, a failure to fully grasp the relationship between developments in both private and public realms. The links between changing economic, cultural, and legal conditions and new forms of family life are still poorly understood. To perceive these connections, we need to consider more than how behaviors or the wage economy have changed. We also need a clear sense of how women's work in the home—not only the tasks themselves but also the framework of support for such labor—has altered. This requires a look not just at the domestic realm but also at its relationship to the market, and how this relationship has been transformed over time.

Women and the "New Economy"

There has been much talk recently of the "new economy" that has emerged from the difficulties of the 1970s and 1980s. A reorganization of production, joined with new technology, appears to have resulted in strong gains. Returns to capital have increased by more than 40 percent since the early 1970s, and national income per person has risen more than one-third over its level thirty years ago.[4] Though it has faltered somewhat in the first years of the twenty-first century, an economy based on a distinctly different foundation than in the past appears to be firmly in place.

A commonly noted feature of this economy is the unequal distribution of its rewards. Employers' strategies to cut costs have resulted in a loss of job security and many benefits, the closing of paths for advancement, and the proliferation of low-wage dead-end jobs. Several analysts have spelled out clearly how these problems stem from the breakdown of the old compact that shaped relations between employers and workers in the first decades after World War II. They make an effective argument for the need to create new rules to improve the conditions of employment today.[5]

However, the prosperity of the first post–World War II decades was also based in part on women's household labor and on a set of rules that supported such work. The old rules shaping the domestic realm, as well as those of the workplace, have collapsed. The conditions of women's work in the home have also grown increasingly insecure. Marriages are easily dissolved, and the arrangements that once committed employers and the state as well as fathers to some support for family maintenance have vanished.

It is widely acknowledged that women's entry into the labor force in large numbers was one of the central ways the economy changed over the latter half of the twentieth century. Changes within the home during this period were equally dramatic. However, analyses of these two areas have not yet been effectively joined, despite growing recognition of the need for such a synthesis.[6]

One area of analysis forging links between these two areas is that of care work. This book adds an important dimension to such discussion by grounding moral debates in the actual, changing conditions of women's lives, revealing how and why tasks of caregiving and support for such tasks altered in the late twentieth century and who has benefited from such changes. The movement of much of women's work outside the home, for example, has played a major role in recent economic growth. But because this contribution is largely unrecognized, the market has taken too much and given too little back, in terms of time and support, to women and their families.[7]

Righting this situation, however, requires another type of synthesis as well. Issues of economic inequality have long dominated discussions of social justice. More recently, though, many scholars and political activists have argued that viewing some groups only in negative terms or not at all is a graver injustice, blocking their claims for basic human rights. A full understanding of the problems facing women today requires that we think about both areas. As the philosopher Nancy Fraser argues, we must consider "the ways in which economic disadvantage and cultural disrespect are . . . entwined with and support each other."[8] To claim more of the gains that women have played a key role in creating for home and family and to ensure their more equal distribution, we must recognize the rights of all women to such resources. We also must make visible an area of life long denied recognition, revealing the contributions made both by the domestic realm and by its transformation.

Gender and Theories of Social Change

In considering the interaction between women's lives and a still-unfolding process of economic and political development, this study sets issues of gender in the context of the grand questions that first gave rise to sociological theory. The central focus of these early theorists was the impact of an emerging market economy on the established social order. Women, however, were absent from such discussion, as their lives were thought to be determined by nature rather than society.[9]

A key contribution of feminist theory was the uncovering of the social forces holding women in the home, thereby exposing men's control of women's work and sexuality. Pioneering feminist scholars strove not only to explain the underlying causes of women's inequality but also to assess the effect of a developing market economy on women's status.[10] Their attempts to conceptualize the interactions between gender and ongoing commercial and industrial growth soon ran into difficulties, however. In part, they were hampered by trying to fit women's experiences into a template based on men's lives.

A large body of scholarship has analyzed the interactions between an expanding market and older ways of work. The early classics of historical comparative sociology focused on men's varying paths from fields to factories and the impact of those paths on state formations.[11] However, these old classics were framed too narrowly. Only when we broaden their explanations beyond an agenda and set of categories based on one group of men, and the heavy-handed role often given to capitalism in some accounts, can we gain a clear understanding of the profound changes now taking place among women themselves. Thus, in dialogue with these older accounts of social change, this book develops a new explanation of women's own varying routes from an older form of work into the wage labor force, based on the experiences of African American and white women, especially in recent decades.

In doing so, this analysis also builds on earlier examinations of the relationship between women's work and a developing market economy. In the first decades after World War II a pathbreaking generation of scholars took on dauntingly large projects, exploring changes in women's lives and work in the United States and in other countries over three centuries or more. The large historical studies of Alice Kessler-Harris and Jacqueline Jones, for example, tracing the shifting nature of the work done by women within as well as outside the home since colonial times, have laid the groundwork for understanding the changing relationship between these two realms. Jeanne Boydston and others, detailing the organization of women's domestic labor under men's control and the continued importance of such work during the first stages of market development, have expanded those foundations.[12] The central focus of these inquiries, however, was the period before World War II. A few scholars, such as Heidi Hartmann and Kessler-Harris, have perceptively analyzed the dramatic alterations in gender relations that began to unfold after the war.[13] However, the explosive events of subsequent decades have not been fully explored. Yet the immense changes in women's lives and the American economy that took place in the second half of the twentieth century and are continuing to unfold at a rapid pace clearly merit careful analysis.

In part, further efforts at broad explanations were fractured by a growing recognition that women's experiences differ significantly by race, ethnicity, and class. Greater attention to the past and present situations of women of color has increased our understanding of the varied ways in which home and market may be connected. For example, by showing how African American and other families have been shaped by the pressures of economic survival and discrimination, scholars such as Evelyn Nakano Glenn and Bonnie Thornton Dill have established the importance of looking at the domestic realm, and its relationship to the larger economy, rather than at the labor force alone. They have also stressed the changing nature of this relationship and how it has varied by race and ethnicity. As Glenn has put it, "reproductive labor has divided along racial as well as gender lines, and the specific characteristics have . . . changed over time as capitalism has been reorganized."[14] Their studies remain highly relevant, revealing, for example, the ways that the market can devour time needed for family life.

A growing number of analysts are also assessing how different groups of women of color are faring in the wage economy, documenting the persistence of inequality despite some gains in education, occupational status, and earnings. However, as several scholars have noted, the end result has been a rather fragmented approach to issues of racial and ethnic difference. What is needed now, they stress, is a clearer grasp of the larger processes lying behind the variations in women's experience.[15]

To create such an analytic framework, we need first to take on again the larger questions once asked of women's lives, reframed to consider differences by race and class. Second, rather than assuming the persistence of old inequalities, we need to think about ways in which the abandonment of established systems of control may have contributed to today's problems. While emphasis on women's role as mothers, for example, once blocked their opportunities outside the home, the withdrawal of support for women's domestic labor in recent years is creating new hardships. Further, the breakdown of such support—however minimal it was—has had far more negative consequences for black women than for white non-Hispanic women. Thus, this study seeks to explain the great changes taking place in women's lives and American homes, and how they are shaping the new economic and social order of today. In doing so, it reveals the outcome of a long interaction between gender, race, and the market.

A Comparative Analysis

In the largest sense, what is needed is comparative analysis of the ways in which gender has interacted with varying processes of industrialization among all racial and ethnic groups of women, both within and outside the United States. Such analysis would consider women's different paths from household to wage labor, the alliances influencing such transitions, the new state formations they are resulting in, and how such transitions are shaped by and help shape the global political economy. Here I contribute to this project by focusing on the experiences of white women and African American women in the United States, especially during the last decades of the twentieth century.[16]

My intention thus is to provide not a detailed, continuous history spanning all racial and ethnic groups but a new analytic framework that can make sense of the recent traumatic changes in women's lives. In order to effectively explain current differences between women, we must first clearly understand the larger forces underlying such variations. A close comparison of two different groups enables us to see some important similarities in their experiences and their deeper causes.[17]

In brief, this book uncovers the larger dynamics shaping the lives of women today by comparing how African American and white women interacted with a developing market economy at selected key moments. These two groups were, respectively, the largest racial minority and majority in the United States over the past two centuries. Also, recent advances in data analysis provide access to detailed information about both groups over the past 150 years, allowing consideration of how two different relationships between home and market have unfolded over time.

While issues of class have blurred the lines of this distinction by race, creating variations within each group, the experience of African American women has been markedly different from that of white women. Thus race provides the central comparative dimension, though this study also examines how recent changes in the domestic realm have played out differently by education, or class, within each group of women. A close look at the experiences of African American and white women makes possible a clearer understanding of how and why women's relationships to the home have altered profoundly in recent years, and the connections between such alterations and the changing shape of the market economy. Such comparison provides a rough theoretical map that can then be used to explore other women's experiences.[18]

This is an interdisciplinary study, drawing together research from history, economics, political science, sociology, and government documents, and original analysis of census data, primarily from the Integrated Public Use Microdata

Series. These recently standardized samples of decennial census data enable us to carefully assess women's relationships to home and work in the first decades of the twentieth century as well as today. The large number of cases that they provide also enables us to consider differences among African American women by education, marital status, and cohort, for example, rather than relying on general comparisons with white women, as in the past. By looking closely at such data, we can see previously indiscernible variations in women's changing relationships to marriage, motherhood, and the labor force among African American and white women at different educational levels over several decades. Such analysis gives empirical detail to the larger story, enabling us to compare the experiences of, for example, college-educated women and high school dropouts over time, revealing similarities as well as differences in their experiences by race.[19]

As we follow the rapid changes in women's lives over the second half of the twentieth century, a sense of how such shifts have affected successive generations or, more precisely, cohorts of women is useful. This study looks at groups familiar to the American public: the parents of the baby boomers, who raised their families in the 1950s, and the baby boomers themselves, that large cohort born between the late 1940s and the early 1960s, who rebelled against the traditional domestic role and entered the labor force in large numbers. The smaller "bust" cohort, perhaps better known as Generation X, and the children of the baby boomers themselves, carry this account into the present. This study traces the breakdown of marriages, struggles with poverty, and acquisition of elite professions or poorly paid service jobs over successive cohorts of African American and white women as paid employment replaced marriage as their central means of support.

Gender, Race, and the Market

To knit the details of women's lives into a coherent analytic framework requires, finally, a new way of thinking about gender itself and its interactions with a developing market economy. That the social construction of differences between women and men shapes a wide range of human experience is now widely recognized. But the nature of what many have come to call this "structure" of gender is still poorly formulated and lacks a dynamic of change.[20] Though women's lives have altered dramatically, our understanding of gender has not kept pace. Feminist theorists themselves recognize that theoretical developments in discussions of gender have stalled. The grand analyses that began to appear in the 1970s, as Fraser observes, "soon reached an impasse: having begun by supposing the fundamental distinctness of capitalism and patriarchy, class and gender, it was never clear how to put them together again."[21]

In this book, I provide a means of joining these areas. I do so first by grounding gender in women's work, which long centered on a set of domestic and reproductive tasks organized under men's control and support. I then argue that the relationship between this gender division of labor and a developing market economy has been a dynamically changing one, in which new possibilities have been shaped by competing sets of interests.[22]

In the United States, this relationship has had three major moments. First, in the nineteenth and early twentieth centuries, the gender division of labor was sustained in early encounters with the emerging commercial and industrial economy. Initially, the market brought women not new opportunities but rather threats, as it did little to reduce the domestic chores crucial to family survival while raising new demands for labor. Like many groups before them, women sought to fend off such demands, with varying degrees of success, resulting in two divergent relationships between home and market. Over the first half of the twentieth century, though a growing industrial economy lessened some household chores while offering new possibilities, these gains were less than commonly thought and were largely contained within the old frameworks of women's domestic economy, though they raised increasing tensions.

In the years after World War II, however, a second dramatic encounter with the market brought radical changes. Many analysts have focused on the shift from a manufacturing- to service-based economy in the years after World War II and its negative consequences for men. I look at another aspect of the market's growth—its movement outward into older arrangements of work, not just overseas but deep in the heart of American homes.

The decline of traditional manufacturing industries and the loss of the male breadwinner wage have dominated our understanding of the post–World War II period. I argue instead that changes in women's own work within the home in the first decades after World War II underlay the profound alterations in family structures, sexual relations, and gender roles over the second half of the twentieth century. As a rapidly expanding economy sharply reduced women's domestic chores while creating new options at home and at work, the old gender division of labor felt increasingly constraining to many groups, who challenged and then undid many of its social and legal framings. The changes in divorce law, the sexual revolution, and the demise of AFDC (Aid to Families with Dependent Children) were all part of this dismantling. How and why this framework of support came apart in varying ways for both African American and white women and the intersection of this process with periods of economic expansion and decline in the decades after World War II are central concerns of the first part of this book.

However, this is not just a story of destruction and collapse. Out of the pieces of women's old ways of life and work a new social and economic order has been built. The transformation of women's tasks and labor into work done for pay has fueled much of the rise of the new economy of the twenty-first century, contributing to a dramatic growth in profits and national income overall. However, women and their families have realized few of these gains, which have instead been divided mainly along the old lines of power. While employers and the state played key roles in taking apart the old rules that obligated them to provide some support for family care, they have thus far largely avoided new commitments to these tasks. Instead, many mothers are badly overworked while others are falling back on vestiges of the old gender division of labor to accomplish their domestic tasks. As a result, this century—like the last one—begins with time and space for home and family treated not as rights equally available to all but rather as privileges enjoyed by some at the expense of others. Once this process has been clearly grasped, we can more deeply understand the problems now facing families of all backgrounds and can better fashion the social policies that can most effectively ease their burdens.

.   .   .

These points are developed in greater detail in the chapters that follow. If we are to make sense of how women's work and family life altered radically in the late twentieth century, we first need a new understanding of gender and of economic development, and the ways in which these two areas interact. These issues are the focus of chapter 2. Anchoring gender in women's work, this chapter directs attention beyond a set of domestic tasks themselves to how such work was organized and supported, and how such support may have changed over time. It also shows that behind the familiar story of men's rapid movement off the land and into work for wages lay a far more gradual process of change, as many old ways of life and labor remained essential to survival and were initially reinforced. Only when most such work had shifted to the market did these old forms of labor finally collapse.

This new framing of gender and economic development is then used to provide a fresh view of women's differing relationships to home and work in the nineteenth- and early-twentieth-century United States. Providing clear evidence that women continued to be responsible for a sizable number of domestic chores through the early twentieth century, this chapter shows how the central issue for women was thus how to defend space for these domestic tasks against new claims on their time, and the severe costs when such efforts failed. While white women largely succeeded in such efforts, the experience of African American women shows, in cruel form, an alternative relationship between home and market. Overall, however, whether through public policies or private strategies, the gender division of labor was sustained in different ways through the first half of the twentieth century, though in a form imposing great burdens on African American women.

However, these early resolutions were not final ones. In the years after World War II, further encounters with a maturing industrial economy led not to reinforcement of the framework supporting women's household work but instead to its collapse among both African American and white families, though in somewhat different ways. Chapter 3 looks at the first moment in this process, showing how an initial period of postwar expansion lessened the need for women's domestic labor while opening new possibilities for several groups. Not only many women but also many men, employers, state officials, and even rebellious adolescents found the old cultural and legal practices framing women's domestic realm restrictive and began to question and ultimately overturn many of these old codes. The institution of no-fault divorce, the rising acceptance of cohabitation, the legalization of abortion, and the disappearance of shot-gun weddings enabled women as well as men to avoid bad marriages and pursue better options in the wage economy. But these changes also removed the old arrangements obligating fathers, business, and the state to provide some support for tasks of family care while constructing little in their place.

Chapter 4 then examines how the economic difficulties of the 1970s and early 1980s placed great pressures on the already weakened framework of support for women's household work, hastening its demise. Rather than causing the breakdown of the male breadwinner family, the decline of the traditional manufacturing sector and the stagnation of men's wages simply accelerated a process that was well under way. Financial pressures forced many men to accept their wives' employment, for example, pushing another wave of women into the labor force and increasing frictions within the home. Resistance to the loss of the traditional division of labor between the sexes also led to an uneasy coalition of white housewives, working-class men, employers, and right-wing politicians. However, this was a contradictory alliance that, while voicing vehement support for the male breadwinner family, in fact furthered its collapse, through abandonment of the family wage and espousal of cutbacks in government aid. These steps had particularly harsh consequences for less-educated women and for black women generally.

At the same time, however, new forms of home and work were emerging, though the foundations for such family life were denied to many, especially those at the bottom of the economic ladder. This chapter ends by showing how the old gender division of labor, in its different forms, broke down differently for black and white women by education (or class). While giving women greater control over motherhood and marriage, for example, such breakdown left them with little support for the tasks of family maintenance, creating a crisis for those still defined primarily in terms of the domestic role.

Chapter 5 provides a new explanation of the rise in female-headed families among the poor. The economic hardship faced by single mothers is generally seen as changing little over time, stemming simply from the loss of marriage and burdens of single parenthood. This study instead views the "feminization of poverty" as a dynamic process, placing it in the context of women's historic transition from household to paid work. Close examination of women's poverty from such a perspective reveals heretofore unseen changes in the causes and composition of such hardship over time. It shows how marriage as a means of resolving such poverty is a solution better suited to the 1950s than today. This examination also reveals the steps that women themselves took to cope with the difficulties they faced and how a changing market economy aided or hindered their efforts. In so doing, the analysis traces the formation of a female underclass, caused not just by men's employment difficulties but by women's own changing relationships to work at home and for pay.

Chapter 6 then looks at the social and economic order that has been built out of the pieces of women's old ways of life and work. It begins by demonstrating the role played by the commercialization of women's domestic chores and labor in the rise of the new economy of the twenty-first century. Women's massive entrance into paid employment, while bringing women themselves new earnings, also resulted in new profits for their employers and great gains for the economy overall. Behind such contributions lay a pivotal shift in women's lives, as the breakdown of their age-old arrangements of life and work at first enabled and then increasingly forced them to depend on wages as their central means of support. This chapter documents the historic change in the source of women's livelihood, comparing the reliance of African American and white women on income from men or on their own wages in 1960 and today. It then assesses the outcomes of such a shift for women of different backgrounds, asking to what extent those at different levels of education of either race are succeeding in "having it all."

Chapter 7 examines the crisis created by the transformation of women's work, providing a deeper understanding of why women are having such difficulty combining work and family. It looks closely at mothers, asking first if they are really working harder now than in the 1960s—and if so, why, given that the market's takeover of many domestic tasks has created a new pool of free time as well as income. It also examines what the turn to paid employment has meant for black and white mothers of different educational backgrounds, comparing their earnings, hours of work, and overall family income in 1970 and 2000. It shows that few of the gains from the transformation of women's tasks and labor have gone to women and their families. Also, while support for women's household work has broken down among both African American and white women, it has done so unevenly. Though some mothers have sufficient time for the domestic realm, others are badly overworked. Thus, though women's turn to work for wages, like men's earlier move off the land, has given them new legitimation and leverage to realize their own interests, increasing disparities among women themselves threaten such efforts.

Chapter 8 summarizes changes that have unfolded in women's lives and work and the consequences of these changes for the new social and economic order of today. It also sketches some of the implications of such analysis for our understanding of the difficulties faced by other groups of women in the United States and abroad, and for our understanding of the process of social change itself.

The picture that emerges from this analysis is a troubling one. Women have made great gains, especially over the last half of the twentieth century. Many of the old rules and customs that constrained their lives have been overturned. They have much greater economic resources and political power than in the past, and far more opportunities to pursue meaningful work. These gains are in large part the result of women's own efforts, through both organized political action and courageous private decisions. Yet, in different ways for those of different backgrounds, this turn from home to market was also a difficult one, filled with unexpected twists and turns, especially for those with the fewest resources. Though women are often blamed for these hardships or for the crises faced by families today, other groups also played a key role in taking apart the old arrangements for tasks of family care, stepping free from many obligations in the process. They, not women, have been the main beneficiaries of the new time and wealth gained in the latest encounter between home and market. In the absence of new policy, two different relationships between home, work, and state now appear to be emerging, much as happened in the early twentieth century, giving new form to the inequalities of gender, race, and class.

Thus, when we lift the hidden half of women's story into view, we see a radical transformation of women's work in the home, which in turn has dramatically altered the shape of American families and of the market economy itself. Beneath the economic and political turmoil of the late twentieth century, a change of profound proportions was unfolding, as women turned from household work—supported, however minimally, within marriage—to wages as the primary source of their livelihood. By the century's end, women had crossed an immense historical divide, with great consequences both for their own lives and for American society as a whole. We must grasp the immensity of their journey, for it opens new political as well as economic opportunities for women and their families.

SUPPORT FOR WOMEN'S DOMESTIC ECONOMY IN THE NINETEENTH AND EARLY TWENTIETH CENTURIES

To fully grasp the striking changes that took place in women's lives and the American economy in the last half of the twentieth century, we need to step back a bit from the present. In order to see the underlying connections between these events, and their deeper causes, we need a larger perspective. To understand why support for women's work in the home has come apart in recent years, for example, we must first gain a clear sense of what once held support for such work together.

In the early United States, both white and African American women were responsible for an arduous set of domestic tasks essential to the survival of their families. Women butchered hogs and hung them to bleed, cooked over wood fires, and hauled water in and out of their homes as part of their daily chores. The growth of a market economy brought changes to such work, but initially these involved mainly new demands for labor rather than much reduction of household tasks. African American women were subjected to cruel burdens under slavery; the daughters of northern farmers filled the early textile mills. Yet at the end of the nineteenth century, though African American women were much more likely to work outside the home, most black women as well as white women gave priority to their domestic chores. Miners and factory workers staged fierce demonstrations for wages that could support their wives' household work, and in rural as well as urban areas, men married, even if very poor.

In the second half of the twentieth century, both African American and white wives turned in large numbers to work for pay. Though the early advocates of women's rights had decided not to tackle "the differences in the male and female contributions to take care of themselves," in the years after World War II women fiercely challenged this division of labor and the Supreme Court found in their favor.[1] Though some men resisted their wives' employment, no great demonstrations by male workers for a new family wage took place. Instead, by the 1980s male college students scoffed at the idea of supporting a full-time housewife, and marriage rates had plummeted among both rich and poor. Why did men once fight for wages generous enough to support women's work in the home, but now no longer do so? Why did women once embrace their domestic role and later challenge it?

To answer these questions, we need to broaden our understanding of the nature both of the relationship between the sexes and of economic development itself. Thus, I begin this chapter by looking at these two areas from a new angle, focusing on the interactions between gender and a developing market society and examining how and why such interactions changed over time. I then use this analytic framework to provide a fresh perspective on the experiences of white and African American women in the nineteenth and early twentieth centuries in the United States, thereby setting the stage for a deeper understanding of the dramatic changes that would follow.

Women's Household Work and the Rise of the Market

The Gender Division of Labor

At the heart of gender, stretching back to earliest times, lies a separation of tasks by sex, commonly referred to as the *gender division of labor*. However, this arrangement has involved more than men and women's performance of different chores. We must also consider how this division of work was organized and sustained. While both men and women engaged in productive tasks, men controlled this arrangement and the land and homes in which women worked. Though women's work was crucial to their families, their access to much of what they needed for survival lay in men's hands. Thus, in essence, women worked for men, who supported and benefited from such domestic labor. Marriage was the primary institution formalizing this arrangement, giving men legal and economic authority over women. In the nineteenth-century United States, for example, husbands were expected to support their wives in exchange for their performance of domestic chores, a bargain reinforced by many cultural and political codes and practices.[2]

This gender division of labor has been central to agricultural life in almost all regions of the world.[3] Today, this term (or the *sexual division of labor*) commonly refers to women's continued responsibility for domestic chores and child care, and men's focus on paid work and avoidance of domestic tasks despite their wives' employment. The key issue, however, is whether the means of organizing and supporting the tasks of family maintenance have altered. Do men still continue to support such work through marriage? Do cultural and legal institutions still reinforce women's performance of domestic tasks? The difficulties faced by growing numbers of women as they juggle work at home and for pay, often entirely on their own, make clear how little support remains. Thus, we must ask how and why this age-old arrangement of labor has broken down. Answering this question requires a closer look at the interaction between gender and a growing commercial and industrial economy in the United States.

The Industrial Revolution

Most accounts of the Industrial Revolution, focusing on the lives of white men in Europe and the United States, have stressed the rapid and decisive remaking of an earlier way of life. A central theme in this story is that men, no longer able to support themselves on their land or through craft work, were forced to sell their labor to survive. Recent historical research, however, has shown that this turn to wages was a much more gradual event than first realized.[4] Moreover, in its narrow focus on one group of men, this approach has obscured and distorted the experience of other groups. Though some men's lives were indeed turned upside down, many of the old ways of life persisted. As one theorist has put it, "industrialization . . . bites unevenly into the established social and economic structures," dramatically altering some areas of work while leaving others largely untouched.[5] A closer look at this uneven process helps us understand women's experiences in the United States, and differences in these experiences by race, over the past two centuries.

A clear grasp of the interaction between the market and women's work also requires another shift of focus, from Europe to other areas of the world claimed as colonies. The intrusion of new commercial relations only rarely resulted in a sudden and complete destruction of the old social fabric. Rather, the growing group of merchants usually drew on and reinforced many of the existing arrangements of work; only gradually did the market come to dominate. Even in the United States, as one historian notes, "the early bourgeoisie did not emerge as a bull in a china shop, smashing all in its path: it treaded very softly indeed."[6]

However, as the market economy grew, it took over an increasing number of tasks, undermining many of the old ways of producing goods and services. This led, in the end, to the collapse of the earlier forms of labor, creating a pool of potential workers for hire. Two well-known examples of this process are the dispossession of tenant farmers by landowners who saw greater profits in grazing sheep and the disappearance of many artisans' guilds as factory production undercut their craft work. Some have stressed the role of capitalism in determining these interactions. In actuality, however, these were more open struggles, shaped by a series of negotiations and alliances, as some resisted the market while others welcomed its embrace.[7]

When we look at the relationship between a growing commercial and industrial economy and the gender division of labor, or African American and white women's work within the home, we can see a similar pattern of change over time. In the nineteenth- and early-twentieth-century United States, both African American and white women's engagement in household work was first, in different ways, reinforced in their encounters with the market. But over the first half of the twentieth century, both women's domestic tasks and the customs and laws shaping such tasks were gradually eroded. In the decades after World War II, as a rapidly expanding market took over many household chores, the old arrangements for their accomplishment came to feel unnecessarily confining, not only to many women but also to those supporting their labor. This brought struggles to undo the framings of the gender division of labor, allowing and then increasingly requiring women to rely on wage work.

Thus, the dramatic changes in gender roles in the years after World War II cannot be attributed simply to the decline of traditional manufacturing jobs, men's shifting economic fortunes, or even new options for women in the wage economy. Rather, we must look at alterations in women's domestic realm itself. To prepare for that investigation, we need a fuller understanding of women's initial confrontations with an emerging market economy in the early United States.

This understanding requires a further shift of focus, a reversal of the emphasis of many early studies, from women's work for pay to their work within the home. As other scholars have noted, such a shift exposes the space accorded most white women but commonly denied to women of color for care of their families.[8] However, it also reveals important though previously overlooked similarities between the market's encounters with earlier arrangements of work and women's domestic realm.

Such encounters typically led to fierce struggles. At their heart lay efforts by the market to impose new demands on people still very much engaged in meeting their own needs for food and shelter. Such demands were resisted with varying degrees of success. Some groups were able to fend off the encroachments of the new economy at first, holding it at a distance. Others, as studies of Indonesia and Africa have shown, were held in their old ways of work while also forced to take on the production of goods for sale. They then faced serious problems, as they had little time to grow their own food or carry out other tasks still crucial to their survival. They managed only through intense effort. Yet such extreme effort brought them not increased gain but deeper poverty, ever-greater exhaustion, and even death.[9]

Such comparison provides a deeper understanding of women's diverging experiences in the early United States. Like others successful in resisting the intrusions of the market, white women in the United States in the nineteenth century were able to hold the demands of the new economy at bay, preserving space for their domestic tasks. In contrast, a second set of burdensome chores was imposed on African American women, bringing the "intense exploitation and prolonged pauperization" that is the consequence of such doubled labor.[10] Their central struggle then became how to carve out space for the domestic tasks still necessary to sustain their families. They managed through strategies seen elsewhere: intertwining the required tasks, drawing on a wide network of kin, and pushing themselves to their limits. Thus, the experience of African American women provides a look at an alternative relationship between the gender division of labor and a developing market, and the consequences when the demands of the new economy could not be held off.

By looking more closely at African American and white women's experiences in the early United States, we can better grasp this process. We can also better understand how and why the gender division of labor was sustained in differing ways at the turn of the last century, only to collapse fifty years later.

Initial Encounters with the Market

In the eighteenth and early nineteenth centuries, both white and African American women carried out a clearly defined set of tasks involving the production of food, clothing, and other items for use within their homes. Such work was crucial to their own and their families' survival. However, in this period, the demands of the market were reshaping household production. "In this respect," historians have noted, "the slave plantations of the Old South and elsewhere had much in common with the households and farms of the northern North American colonies and states."[11] For women, the growing market did little to reduce their domestic chores, while raising threats to their ability to accomplish such tasks, with differing outcomes.

White Women

In northern farms and towns, households were organized around a sharp division of tasks by gender. In rural areas, women tended gardens and poultry, prepared meals, made and mended clothes, hauled water, stoked fires, and gave birth to, in 1800, an average of seven infants, raising roughly five children to adulthood. While some of these tasks were done outside the walls of the house, and some women helped in the fields or sold their surplus eggs or butter, women's primary work centered on production for their own households.[12]

Men had clear need of, as well as control over, women's domestic labor. Wives were recognized as a source of wealth in the household economy. Single men went to some effort to find women to live and work on their farms, recruiting their sisters if they could not obtain wives. Children were also an important source of labor, and women's work in giving birth to, feeding, clothing, and raising their offspring was great.[13]

As the commercial economy developed, many women's interactions with the market initially intensified, as they sold an increasing amount of the products of their gardens, chickens, and cows. Still, men remained in charge of overall farm or craft production for exchange, even when areas once considered women's province became the family's main source of income. By the end of the 1840s, when most household economies were oriented toward the market, men were devoting their energies mainly to producing goods for sale, while women remained primarily engaged in meeting household needs. Some young women entered the early textile mills, providing a much-needed supply of inexpensive labor, as men generally preferred farming their own land to working for others. Only a handful of all women were mill workers, however, and most worked little more than four or five years before leaving to marry and focus once again on domestic tasks.[14]

The handling of women's dairy work exemplifies both how women were held in household work and how space for their domestic tasks was preserved in their initial encounter with the market. As commercial and urban development increased, women on many farms at first were pulled into greater production for sale. As demand for their goods grew, many farmwives put more time into making butter and cheese, hiring dairy maids as assistants. But as dairy production became the farm's main source of income, the male head of the family took control of this work. Such a move lessened the workload of women burdened with household chores but also kept them from economic gains of their own. This outcome, the historian Marjorie Cohen notes, resulted from "male control of capital and the primary responsibility of women to maintain the family unit," or the gender division of labor within the home.[15] Men also took steps to retain control in craft work, relegating women to menial tasks in shoemaking, for example.[16]

Thus, the market did not simply transform men's tasks first, freeing husbands from the home before their wives. Rather, men kept control of any work that had the potential to make money, while women were steered toward housework. In this way, the existing division of labor between the sexes was sustained in early encounters with the developing commercial economy.

However, women's persistence in the home did not mean an end to their work, as the doctrine of separate spheres evolving in the early nineteenth century implied, except among a small elite married to wealthy merchants and southern landowners. The view that women were left only with "reproductive" tasks when men's work moved outside the home reflected a devaluation of women's domestic labor as a market economy, focused on work for pay, grew dominant. In actuality, while women gave less assistance to men's tasks, they still faced a strenuous set of chores that, while differing across the emerging classes, filled their waking hours and were very necessary to survival. "Families were still . . . critically dependent on a certain level of subsistence production in the home," Cohen states, "because alternative sources for the goods and services supplied by females in the home were not available."[17] Young men were still advised to marry if they wanted to do well.

Even women in the growing towns and cities were still burdened by many household chores. Most women faced long days of strenuous labor, hauling water and coal or wood for their stoves and shopping daily for food. Even women in the emerging middle classes spent hours each day making and mending clothes as well as cooking, baking, doing laundry with hired help, and cleaning the house. "[I am] too busy to live," a lawyer's wife in one northeastern city wrote to her sister in 1845, as so consumed by household tasks and the "filling up" and other care of her six children.[18]

Despite their long hours of work, the great majority of women saw their interests as lying within rather than outside the framework of their domestic economy. The other avenues of support offered to women by the market were few and easily blocked. Even those women organizing for greater rights decided not to challenge the division of labor between the sexes. Instead, though they called for political equality with men, they took steps to limit the market's claims on women's time.[19]

In short, the domestic tasks done by women still needed doing. Until those tasks could be accomplished in some other way, gathering supporters, the existing configuration of interests worked to perpetuate the gender division of labor, thereby reducing the possibilities of its transformation in the process.

African American Women

African American women, unlike most white women, were not spared the demands of the market. Slavery crudely and brutally imposed a second set of tasks on them. More than 90 percent of African American women on plantations in the mid–nineteenth century worked eleven to thirteen hours a day in the fields for most of the year.[20] At the same time, they continued to carry out essential tasks for their own families. Accounts by ex-slaves make clear that women retained primary responsibility for child care and domestic chores. They prepared meals, sewed and washed their families' clothes, cleaned their households, and tended their children. Such domestic tasks were not done by men, who strenuously avoided tasks considered women's work, such as laundry or the care of infants. When assigned such chores as punishment by slaveholders, most endured the lash rather than comply. Women were also punished in similar fashion. One former slave, describing the capture of a young woman who had run away, remembered: "When they got her back they made her wear men's pants for one year."[21] Thus a strong sense of gender roles prevailed. African American men were denied direct support of their wives' household work, though it was primarily their labor in the fields that created their owners' fortunes. However, several historians provide evidence that black men still had authority within their own homes.[22]

African American men had need of women's household work. On Saturday nights, according to one observer, the roads were full of men traveling to see their wives on other plantations with bags of dirty laundry on their backs. As one ex-slave testified to Congress, "The colored men in taking wives always do so in reference to the service the women will render."[23] Though plantation owners also relied on African American women's domestic labor, they were far more concerned with the production of their crops and gave African American women little time to care for their husbands and children, with grave consequences.[24]

Slavery has commonly been seen as dealing a heavy blow to the two-parent family. Even those scholars who argue that most children lived with their fathers and mothers document the separation of many husbands and wives.[25] However, the African American family faced destruction in a more direct and devastating sense, as the demands of slavery made it very difficult for women to carry out the domestic tasks crucial to survival.

African American women succeeded in accomplishing their household chores through strategies like those used in other places when the market imposed new demands on an older economy. Like peasants in Indonesia forced to grow sugarcane for the Dutch as well as rice for themselves, black women interwove their different tasks, relied on a web of relatives for help, and worked extremely long hours. Many women took their infants to the field each day, nursing them while hoeing. Older women provided child care for those who worked in the fields, and a number of other domestic tasks were carried out collectively. Women also pushed themselves to the limits of endurance. Children remembered mothers and grandmothers sewing their clothes late into the evening. "Work, work, work . . . I been so exhausted working. . . . I worked till I thought another lick would kill me," one old woman told interviewers from the Federal Writers' Project in 1937. Plantation owners also ordered a brutal communal handling of meal preparation and other chores, which serves as a reminder that the collectivization of domestic tasks is not in itself freeing.[26]

Like other groups forced to take on new burdens while still engaged in other tasks, their long hours of work did not bring black women themselves increased wealth, but only greater hardship. Despite their efforts, their domestic realm suffered. Lack of time to grow gardens, prepare meals, or tend to children resulted in much sickness among young and old, and the heavy workload resulted in many miscarriages, and early deaths among children and mothers themselves. "My last old marster would make me leave my child before day to go to the cane-field; and he would not allow me to come back till ten o'clock in the morning to nurse," remembered one ex-slave from Louisiana. "I could hear my poor child crying long before I got to it. And la, me! my poor child would be so hungry when I'd get to it!" Asked how her children had fared when she was forced to spend long such hours in the field, this mother answered bluntly: "They all died . . . they died for want of attention. I used to leave them alone half of the time."[27]

That the black family persisted at all is testimony to the efforts of African American women. Second, slavery was followed by a form of work that drew on and thus reinforced the gender division of labor, that of sharecropping.

The First Encounter with Industrial Capitalism

In the second half of the nineteenth century, an industrial economy was built on the foundation laid by a growing market. Only about 5 percent of the population worked in manufacturing in the United States in 1850. In the following decades factories grew rapidly, powered by the increasing numbers of people pushed off the land at home and, to a greater extent, abroad.[28]

This early moment of industrialization also did little to reduce women's domestic chores. Though the early textile mills took the arduous task of making cloth out of the home, few further inroads were made into women's household tasks. Instead, initial emphasis was on creating an industrial base, through the construction of transportation networks, and factories that could turn out the powerful new machinery. However, the rise of industrial capitalism raised a second, more intense challenge to women's persistence in household work, in the form of wage work.

Employers at first made heavy use of female workers. Cities in the Northeast and Midwest were referred to as "hives of female and child labor." Because most women had access to some income from men in exchange for their domestic labor, employers could escape paying the full cost of their upkeep. One employer explained that his rule was "never to hire a woman who must depend entirely upon my support."[29] Low wages, however, not only consigned many women to miserable poverty but also once again left them little time to carry out their own household tasks. This led to a renegotiation of the relationship between the gender division of labor and the market. Once again the outcomes of these negotiations differed by race.[30]

White Women

Men's efforts to exclude women from better-paying factory jobs and the emerging professions due to fears of competition have been well documented. However, there was another important side to this struggle. Women's domestic work was still much needed at the end of the nineteenth century. In rural areas, household chores remained arduous. A farmer's wife in North Carolina, for example, estimated she carried close to a dozen buckets of water to her house and back outside again each day, as well as emptying chamber pots. Women in the growing towns fared little better. No homes in a typical Midwest town had running water in 1885; five years later, a water tap in the front yard was considered a grand thing.[31]

Some large houses with piped water and gas lighting were built in the growing urban areas, but these new services were priced beyond the reach of most. In 1912, only 16 percent of households had electricity. Even in the largest cities, most families were still using outhouses. Women continued to collect coal or wood for cookstoves and to lug water from city faucets, and making meals remained time-consuming. While basic provisions could be purchased, women still shopped every day for food, plucked and cleaned poultry, and made most baked goods from scratch.[32]

Though the new machines of the Industrial Revolution did little at first to reduce women's household work, unequal distribution of the profits from such production brought differences in the burdens of housework. Growing numbers of women were able to hire help, while others took in boarders, laundry, or sewing as household chores began to be converted to work for wages, much as had occurred in agriculture. Still, even middle-class women had much to do preparing meals, sewing clothes, and cleaning their homes. "I . . . am to[o] tired to talk with [my children] much of the time," one such mother confessed.[33]

Husbands, government officials, and female reformers recognized the importance of women's household work. "Those men in the iron mines in Missouri need women to do the cooking and washing," one woman summoned to join her husband was told. Unmarried workers sharing living quarters often pooled their wages to keep one woman at home. Male workers repeatedly demanded a "family wage" that could support their wives' domestic labor, and most working-class women preferred marriage and its duties over poorly paying factory jobs.[34] Middle-class women and their husbands also took steps to ensure that women had sufficient time for care of their homes. Though individual women, in their choices, often implicitly acknowledged the connection between the performance of household tasks under men's control and support and exclusion from economic and political power, only a small and unpopular minority raised this issue openly. Most women sought instead to preserve, defend, and, among the more progressive, reform their domestic economy.[35]

Thus, at the start of the twentieth century, women's organizations made up of white middle-class housewives sought to shore up the domestic realm against the threats posed by the developing industrial order. Some lobbied for pensions for single mothers; others worked to improve the conditions of women's work in the home. Educated women living among the poor deplored the hardships faced by employed mothers. Condemning the "wretched delusion that a woman can both support and nurture her children," Jane Addams raged: "How stupid it is to permit the mothers of young children to spend themselves in the coarser work of the world!" Rather than free women from household tasks, these reformers fought to curtail employers' access to women's labor.[36]

Employers themselves fiercely resisted such restrictions, even though it was women's persistence in household work that made possible their low wages and provided new generations of workers. However, the Supreme Court, declaring the need to protect women "from the greed as well as the passion of men," ruled in favor of limiting women's hours and regulating their conditions of work.[37]

Thus, in the initial encounter between an emerging industrial economy and the gender division of labor, women's engagement in household tasks was sustained for some families through such measures as the family wage, protective labor legislation, and the creation of small pensions for single mothers. At the same time, as some women fought to pursue the "careers open to talent" becoming available to their brothers, and others were driven to work for wages to ensure the survival of their families, women's relegation to home and hearth grew increasingly vulnerable to attack.[38]

Yet, much as men had often resisted the loss of control over their own land or craft work and the new demands on their labor, so most women strove to defend their old way of life. In the early stages of market development, women fought to hold the demands of this new economy at bay and to shape the terms on which they would enter its terrain. The most privileged among them envisioned retaining control of the domestic realm while elevating it to greater power within the new economic order, not recognizing the contradictions in such an attempt. These efforts, however, were undertaken by white women for themselves alone.

African American Women

As the United States underwent rapid industrialization and urbanization after the Civil War, most of the African American population remained concentrated in the rural South. For black women, emancipation initially meant freedom from the additional work forcibly imposed on them by slavery, allowing them to focus on the care of their own families. Blocked from owning land, many African American men leased plots on which to grow cotton or tobacco. Women's domestic labor in bearing and raising children, making clothes, and growing and preparing food was essential to these undertakings. "A wife and children were assets in sharecropping," one scholar notes.[39] This arrangement between southern landowners and black men thus built upon and shored up the gender division of labor within the household.

However, African American families were soon caught in a financial vise by southern landlords, who sold them seed and bought their crops, forcing an increase in production, which drew black women back into farmwork. Their husbands directed such labors, though, and kept control of any income that resulted. Once, women's work in the fields threatened their ability to accomplish domestic tasks. And again they drew on the help of kin, worked long hours, and did multiple tasks at once, as one oft-quoted description from the 1890s illustrates. "It was not an unusual thing," notes this observer, "to meet a woman coming from the fields where she had been hoeing cotton . . . briskly knitting as she strode along . . . [often with] a baby strapped to her back."[40]

In towns and cities, some African American men gained access to skilled work; but they were soon driven out of the better-paying occupations, forcing many of their wives to seek jobs. Some worked as teachers or seamstresses, but most could find only low-paid work in domestic service, earning far less than their husbands. Despite such employment, black communities made concerted efforts to sustain women's engagement in household tasks and men's authority in the home. Women were urged from pulpits and from the editorial pages of African American newspapers to obey their husbands.[41]

Black women themselves took pride in caring for their homes and families, an interest reflected in the multitude of women's clubs that sprang up in the late nineteenth century. Though the National Association of Colored Women, formed from these clubs in 1896, firmly asserted women's equality with men, it did not challenge their domestic and maternal role but sought instead to improve conditions of work in the home. Many clubs put much effort into showing women "the best way to sweep, to dust, to cook and to wash." Women's organizations associated with the black Baptist church instructed poor African American women in child care and household tasks, as white reformers did among immigrants.[42]

However, black women's organizations also strove to improve rather than limit women's conditions of employment and to devise ways to ease the integration of work at home and for pay. The NACW called for higher wages for female workers, fought for married women's right to teach, and sought to provide job training and day care centers. This relationship between home and market was not pursued by most women, however, causing hardships for some.[43]

The first wave of industrialization had even less impact on African American women's household chores than those of white women. Even professional women found that the demands of their domestic role made working outside the home difficult. "When there are two babies and a husband and a house to look after, it keeps one busy," noted one harried teacher. Many gave up their jobs when they married; others collapsed from the strain of working at home, for pay, and for the good of the community.[44]

The majority of African Americans in urban areas lived in crowded tenements, and women devoted countless hours to collecting fuel, water, and food every day, cleaning dark rooms, and making meals and clothing with limited resources. Here as on the farm, working outside the home left little time for arduous household tasks, forcing a resort to private strategies as in the past. However, wage work raised a greater threat than sharecropping, in part as it could not be interwoven with women's care of their own families. Thus, black women took in sewing, laundry, or boarders when possible and drew on help from other female kin or neighbors if they could.[45]

Once again, this doubled workload took a harsh toll. At the start of the twentieth century, one-third of black children died before the age of 10, and their mothers often perished "before the youngest left home." The mortality rates of women in childbirth and their infants were approximately twice those of whites.[46] Such statistics have been attributed to poverty, poor diets, crowded and dirty living quarters, and disease. While these factors played a role, the central issue is that black women did not have sufficient time to do what was necessary to keep their families alive. The squalid living conditions, low fertility, and high death rates of African American women and their children are evidence that their own domestic economy was near collapse.

Urbanization and an Expanding Industrial Economy

By 1920, about half of all Americans no longer lived in rural areas. In this decade, the move to cities and towns and the continued growth of the industrial economy did result in some reduction of domestic tasks. Early studies of women's time doing housework revealed savings of nine to eleven hours a week on chores related to meal preparation, in large part because few urban housewives were tending cows and chickens or growing vegetables. While farm families still produced approximately two-thirds of the food they ate, urban families purchased all but 2 percent of their food.[47] The industrial economy had begun to take on the production of consumer goods and services. Some of women's household work shifted to factories, and other tasks were mechanized by new inventions, such as vacuum cleaners and washing machines. Gas, electricity, running water, and sewage collection became more widely available in urban areas.[48]

Yet the standard view of the 1920s as the key moment when the developing industrial economy penetrated the home overemphasizes the actual change in women's lives. Although new services and appliances made a dramatic impression, they were not available to all. Early researchers into housework were misled in part by Siegfried Gideion's *Mechanization Takes Command*, the classic account of changes in household technology, which erroneously equated the entry of new appliances into most households with the year of their patenting. Others failed to recognize how existing arrangements of labor at home and in the larger economy shaped both inventions and the time they freed.[49]

A more realistic view is offered by Robert and Helen Lynd's study of Muncie, Indiana. In 1925 they found that one-half of dwelling units had no furnaces and one-fourth lacked water. While almost every home had electricity and an electric iron, few had a refrigerator or an early washing machine. Domestic tasks remained a substantial burden even for middle-class wives. Though many women said they spent less time on household chores than their mothers had done, the Lynds observed that for the typical housewife, "each day [was] a nip-and-tuck race to accomplish the absolute essentials between morning and bedtime."[50] A pocket of time did open up for a small segment of wives, who set aside the afternoon for children's school activities or civic works before resuming chores in the evening. However, these women represented less than 10 percent of Muncie's female population. Moreover, their free time was channeled within the traditional framings of the gender division of labor, into activities that complemented rather than challenged their domestic role.[51]

The majority of American families, whether white or nonwhite, were not middle class, however. In cities as well as towns, most endured rudimentary living conditions. At the decade's end, most urban families still relied on blocks of ice for refrigeration, making shopping an almost daily chore, and few had central heating. Even women in more modern homes faced a multitude of household tasks, including sewing, ironing, and care of their children. "My work is never done," lamented one urban housewife in 1926. "I am tired enough to drop when night comes and in the morning look with dread upon the day ahead of me."[52] Furthermore, one-quarter of the population still lived in rural areas, with limited access to basic utilities and services. In these homes, domestic chores remained so arduous that government pamphlets for farmwives bore titles like "Saving Strength."[53]

Thus, although the potential of technology to lessen the housewife's load was clearly great, it was applied, as Heidi Hartmann has argued, within the existing framings of the home and larger economy. In addition, most families lacked access to the new appliances and services. During this period, the industrial economy had only begun to reshape the home.[54]

African American Women

African American women in the 1920s were even less likely than white women to enjoy a lessening of domestic chores. Only a handful of African American homes in the coal-mining towns of West Virginia, for example, had indoor plumbing of any sort. There, women still gardened, canned, raised pigs and chickens, and made almost all their families' clothing.[55] Life in urban areas, to which African Americans began migrating in large numbers after World War I, was not much easier. Though a small elite in Harlem or on Chicago's South Side resided in elegant homes with steam heat and other modern conveniences, most lived in poor neighborhoods, many of which still lacked running water or electricity. A door-to-door survey of housing in five West Virginia cities in the mid-1930s, for example, found that two-fifths of African American households in one city had no electricity and more than one-third had only minimal plumbing. Also, few black families could afford the new appliances. Thus, urban life brought little reduction in burdensome household chores. As late as the 1940s, poor African American families in Washington, D.C., had no indoor plumbing, used kerosene lamps for lighting, and did their laundry in washtubs.[56]

As in earlier decades, their engagement in work for pay severely hampered women's ability to carry out domestic tasks.[57] However, we need to look more closely at the nature of African American women's employment in the first half of the twentieth century if we are to understand the traumatic changes that were to come later. Studies emphasizing how black families differed from white families have distorted the realities of black women's experiences. Black women's higher rates of employment, for example, have encouraged the view that almost all African American wives always worked for wages, and commonly provided the bulk of the family income as well. This view is based primarily on anecdotal evidence, in which the situation of the very poorest African Americans was taken as the norm. "In the southern cities and towns," one classic study of black urban life in the early 1900s states, for example, "the masses of Negro men . . . look to their women as the ultimate source of support."[58]

In actuality, close reexamination of the data reveals that most black wives did not work for pay in the first decades of the twentieth century. Instead they focused mainly on domestic tasks for their own families, supported, however minimally, by their husbands' wages. Moreover, almost all of those who were employed still depended heavily on their husbands' earnings. African American men played an important role in enabling their wives to care for the family and maintain the household.

Though the 1910 census is often seen as overcounting women's employment by a large margin, it provides a way to look closely at the actual circumstances of black women. In other decades, women's work taking in boarders or laundry or their unpaid labor on the family farm was often ignored. Census takers in 1910, though, were firmly instructed to count women's work in such tasks as well as for wages, resulting in far better estimates of women's work for pay. In that year, 68.3 percent of black women between the ages of 22 and 54 were married and living with their husbands. One-third of these wives were reported as earning wages. In 1910 this number included "unpaid family workers . . . who regularly assist[ed] the family head in running a family business or farm, but who receive[d] no direct monetary compensation." Another 8.6 percent stated they were working "on their own account," most frequently taking in laundry. Overall, about two-fifths of black wives were engaged in work for pay in some way.[59]

Thus, even when types of work overlooked in other decades were included, the majority of black wives were not employed. To be sure, some of women's paid work undoubtedly remained uncounted, but clearly, many African American women were able to focus primarily on caring for their own families. This was true both in rural areas and in cities. On farms, where approximately two-fifths of married black women in their prime adult years still lived, less than half of black wives stated they were engaged in more than household chores. In urban areas, 27.8 percent of black wives worked for wages. Another 18.5 percent worked "on their own account"—most did laundry, some were cooks, and a small number were seamstresses. All in all, less than half were working for pay.

Moreover, almost every one of the husbands of these women was employed. Even in urban areas, less than 5 percent of these husbands were unable to find work, and two-thirds held blue-collar jobs in brick and tobacco factories, in sawmills, on railroads, and the like.[60] Further, although black men earned far less than white men, they were much better paid than their wives. For example, a study of unskilled workers in Chicago in the mid-1920s found that 47 percent of black wives were employed, a figure in agreement with that of the 1910 census. Most were private domestic workers or did laundry. However, such work was usually intermittent, and the vast majority of these women made less than $600 per year. On average, black male workers earned more than twice that amount. In one typical couple in the study, the husband made $1,032 per year. Though his wife did domestic work "to supplement" his earnings, her wages raised the total family income only marginally, to $1,208.[61]

We therefore find that, though many African American women engaged in low-paid work at the margins of the industrial economy, unlike many men who entered the paid workforce, they did not become wholly reliant on wages. Instead, they were long involved in two forms of work. Most black women gave their primary attention to domestic tasks for their own families, and family income came largely from their husbands' earnings. Thus, while black women received much less support for their work in the home than did most white women, black families also sustained their own form of the gender division of labor as the industrial system developed.

Private Domestic Workers and the Persistence of the Gender Division of Labor

In urban areas, white and black women's differing relationships with a developing industrial economy converged in an arrangement that prolonged the gender division of labor, much as slavery had slowed the transformation of the southern economy.[62]

Market takeover of women's household work involved more than factory production of household goods or the invention of new appliances. As had happened earlier in agriculture, women's domestic tasks were also increasingly turned into work done for wages, as a growing middle class hired domestic workers or, in a form of "putting-out work" like that preceding factory labor, sent out their laundry to be done.

By 1920, African American women made up more than two-fifths of domestic workers, as an increasing number of white women found jobs in factories, stores, and offices, while war stemmed the flow of labor from overseas. In the following years, restrictions on immigration made black women a key source of domestic labor. While the use of paid domestic workers decreased in the early twentieth century, it was still seen as a common way to cope with the more difficult household chores. The U.S. Bureau of Labor included the cost of "Help—one day a week (or laundry)" in the minimum budget for a working-class family in 1920. Two-thirds of middle-class wives in the Lynds' study hired outside help for one or more days a week. In the early 1930s, one-third to four-fifths of lower-middle-class families paid for laundry or help with other household chores.[63]

About half of the African American women working in private domestic service were married. Once again, they faced the difficulties caused by the addition of a second set of tasks to an already heavy workload. One domestic worker wrote in despair, "[We] don't have time to work for ourselves or even to cook a decent meal of food at home for our husband," a complaint repeated in many letters to the Department of Labor in the 1930s.[64]

We have seen how black women managed through strategies used by other groups forced to work for little pay while continuing in tasks of subsistence. Such comparison is illuminating in another way here. It is very difficult to keep workers in very low wage jobs when better-paying work exists. Often emphasis on supposedly "natural" attributes, as well as blatant racial discrimination, has been used to tighten the hold on such workers.[65] Such strategies also played an important role in the case of domestic workers in the United States. White housewives commonly stressed the strong maternal feelings of the women they employed, conveniently ignoring these women's own families, while racial discrimination blocked domestics' access to better jobs. While white women did not necessarily work deliberately to create a captive supply of labor, they benefited from its existence and resisted its alteration. "In general," one scholar notes, "housewives [tried] to pay as little as possible," and they generally fought efforts to improve the conditions of domestic work.[66]

Moreover, white women's own confinement within the gender division of labor encouraged racism, as they lacked the resources to carry out or profit from the transformation of domestic work into employment paying higher wages. Instead, during this period women's household work took on an intermediate form, as white, middle-class housewives exploited the labor of African American women in a semi-wage relationship sustained in part by the ideological mechanisms of gender and race and in part by a pause in the growth of the larger industrial economy.

This arrangement was costly in several ways. First, the use of "hired help" contributed to the persistence of the gender division of labor, as it lessened pressures to alter this old form of work. Without the help of low-paid labor, as Phyllis Palmer notes, middle-class women might have turned to paid work to buy more appliances or begun earlier to challenge their relegation to household tasks. Second, domestic workers, unable to move into better jobs, were excluded from the gains won by most workers in the 1930s, such as the regulation of hours and wages, the right to Social Security, and unemployment insurance. Further, their separation from much of the working class lessened demands by organized workers for policies better integrating women's work at home and for pay.[67]

.   .   .

In sum, the emerging commercial and industrial economy in the United States presented serious threats to the gender division of labor, or women's domestic economy, in its different forms. Most damaging was its attempt to place new demands on women, thereby hampering their ability to accomplish tasks still essential to the survival of their families. The fundamental issue was thus not whether women could escape from the domestic role, but whether such new claims on their time could be resisted.

These initial encounters between home and market took divergent paths for African American and white women. While white women's efforts to keep the demands of the new economy at a distance were largely successful, African American women were forced to take on another heavy load of work. However, while over two-fifths of black married women worked for pay in the first half of the twentieth century, this did not represent the loss of all support for their own domestic chores and reliance solely on their own wages, but a stalled straddling of two forms of production raising its own set of problems.

The main threat in this situation was that the demands of the new economy left little time for tasks necessary to life. As elsewhere when the market added new demands to earlier arrangements of labor, African American women coped by combining their two sets of chores, using the help of young and old family members and working to the point of exhaustion. Rather than leading to greater wealth, however, their efforts resulted in overwork and the increasing impoverishment common to such situations.

The situation of black women illustrates, in extreme form, the difficulties facing all employed women. Women's continued performance of domestic tasks in their own homes allowed employers to escape paying the full cost of their upkeep, while subjecting these women to long hours of work. In other words, women's work for their own families subsidized their labor at low cost in the larger economy. Further, the use of African American women as private domestic workers illustrates how two forms of discrimination—one based on race and one on gender—intersected to hold black women in very low-paid work. The availability of such extremely cheap labor enabled women's domestic economy, much like the southern cotton economy, to persist despite its inefficiencies.[68]

In short, whether through public policies or private strategies, the gender division of labor was sustained in different forms through the first half of the twentieth century, in the face of challenges by a developing market. Several different moments of negotiation and reinforcement can be seen in the United States: in the early 1800s, when women were shielded from increased production for the market or exposed to its demands under slavery; in the late nineteenth century, when women's growing engagement in work for wages generated a new set of tensions; and in the early twentieth century, when, despite some reduction of household chores, women's acceptance of their homemaking role was maintained in part by the relegation of African American women to low-paid domestic work.

Yet the new arrangements that kept women in household work were themselves unstable and riddled with contradictions. As increasing numbers of young women moved to the city to work for wages or pursue an education, as private domestic workers demanded better working conditions, and as the market lessened men's dependence on women's household labor, new nodes of tension were created, which would eventually lead to the breakdown of the frameworks supporting women's work in the home.[69]

A severe contraction of the industrial economy around the world and the vying for leadership of that economy resulting in World War II postponed the moment of confrontation with women's household work in the United States until the latter half of the twentieth century. Production of consumer goods stalled in the 1930s, slowing penetration of industrial technology into the household. Also, few could afford such goods; 41 percent of the population had only subsistence-level incomes in 1934. The process of urbanization also slowed. The share of the population living in the countryside with limited access to basic utilities barely altered over the decade; 23.2 percent of Americans still resided on farms in 1940.[70]

At the same time, demand for women's paid labor was sharply curtailed during the Depression. Because of the high levels of male unemployment, businesses commonly followed such practices as the "marriage bar," refusing to hire married women. Labor force participation of African American and white married women alike dropped sharply over the decade, and most women engaged in household work within their own homes. While industrial production expanded during World War II, the focus was on weaponry rather than consumer goods. An increased demand for labor did pull married women into the labor force; but such employment ended for most women with the war, though it laid the groundwork for future changes.[71]

In sum, developments in the first half of the twentieth century merely eroded the frameworks sustaining women's work in the home. Not until the decades after World War II did the radical breakdown of this old arrangement of labor, in its divergent forms, take place.

In the years following World War II, after a brief period when the male bread-winner family flourished, divorce spiraled upward, women and children filled the ranks of the poor, and fierce struggles raged over men's and women's proper roles. Many of these events have been analyzed in detail. The real question, however, is why such a cluster of traumatic changes erupted in these years. We cannot answer this question by looking at the labor force alone, or analyzing each event in isolation. Instead, we need to widen our perspective to consider the larger processes behind these issues. To do so, we must again examine women's domestic realm and its changing relationship to a maturing market.

The discussion in the preceding chapter of the gradual erosion of household work done by women in the nineteenth and early twentieth centuries by a developing industrial economy sets the stage for an understanding of the events after World War II. The changes of these years were not simply cultural, the result of less restrictive attitudes toward sex and marriage. Rather, both African American and white women faced a full-scale breakdown of the economic, political, and cultural framework of support for their work in the home as the old forms of the gender division of labor came apart in differing ways along the fissures of race and class.

There were two main moments in this process. In the years just after World War II, as an expanding economy lessened domestic chores while opening new possibilities, the laws and customs framing women's household work began to feel restrictive to many—to women seeing opportunities outside the home, to men expected to provide lifelong support for their wives' household work, to employers eager to have greater access to women's labor, and to government officials increasingly reluctant to support women's work in the home. This led to a series of steps that took apart some of those older framings. The changes in divorce law, feminists' rejection of marriage and early motherhood, and the decline of the male breadwinner ethic were all part of such dismantling.

The economic difficulties of the 1970s and 1980s then placed great pressures on the weakened framework of support for women's household work, hastening its collapse while provoking fierce opposition from those who saw their interests as best met within this old arrangement and fought to preserve it. Yet, in sharp contrast to the start of the twentieth century, such opponents found themselves increasingly in the minority, no longer able to shore up their old way of life. Instead, their actions simply furthered the breakdown of support for women's domestic labor, especially among the poor, while blocking the construction of new ways to provide for tasks of family maintenance.

Changes in family structure are often attributed to men's difficulties in finding work or to a lack of discipline or proper morals among the lower classes. However, a striking feature of the first decades after World War II is that shifts in marriage and in women's relationship to home and work took place all across the economic spectrum, and before men's earnings showed any decline. Thus, it is important to recognize that good times as well as bad brought alterations in the old gender division of labor.

In this chapter I look at the first moment in this process, in which a period of postwar prosperity, fed in large part by the market takeover of women's household work, offered new opportunities to those with the resources to explore such options. Others resisted these developments, fearing the hardships they would bring. Indeed, even for those eager to move beyond old restrictions, the dismantling of women's domestic economy brought unexpected difficulties and outcomes. This process did not occur smoothly, but in a disjointed, often contradictory fashion, with much shortsightedness and narrowness of grasp among progressive as well as conservative factions, and women as well as men.

The resulting chaos gives new relevance to an earlier assessment of the Industrial Revolution by the historian Eric Hobsbawm. It wrought, he stresses, "*a fundamental social change. It transformed the lives of men beyond recognition. Or, to be more exact, in its initial stages, it destroyed their old ways of being and left them free to discover or make for themselves new ones, if they could and knew how. But it rarely told them how to set about it.*"[1]

Women's "Employment Revolution"

In the first decades after World War II, women surged into the labor force at unprecedented rates. Married women dominated this move. "Before 1950," the economist Claudia Goldin notes, "the increase in married women's labor force participation was slow and evolutionary, but after 1950 the process quite simply explodes." Further, she observes, this dramatic turn to paid work was strikingly similar among African American and white women. Although about one-third of black wives were already in the labor force in 1950, their numbers would more than double over the next thirty years.[2]

"Housewives with little prior experience," primarily older women whose families needed income, led this turn to work for wages.[3] In the following decades they were joined by young mothers, who combined work for pay with their work at home at ever earlier stages in their children's lives. By 1980 most wives as well as single women were in the labor force, and many were working full-time. An "employment revolution," analysts concluded, was taking place in women's lives.[4]

As this term suggests, however, women were not simply entering the workforce. Rather, behind this move lay a less obvious event, the collapse of their older realm of work. This collapse preceded and contributed to women's embrace of paid employment. To fully understand the problems that have accompanied this move, we need to bring this hidden side of women's lives and work into view. Simply put, there was a push as well as a pull to women's turn to the labor force. While new employment opportunities drew women into paid work, the dismantling of support for their older form of work also increasingly encouraged such a turn.[5] Why, when an expanding market reached once again for new workers, was there less interest or success in defending women against its demands, in contrast to earlier moments?

To clearly grasp the relationship between the post–World War II economy and women's domestic realm, we must challenge two long-dominant assumptions: first, that industrialization did not lessen household chores, and second, that the key moment an expanding industrial economy entered American homes was in the 1920s. In the 1950s and 1960s, some economists and sociologists predicted that ongoing industrialization would bring about changes in women's household work, with important consequences for family life. Technology was commonly expected to make inroads into women's domestic tasks, much as it had lessened manual labor in other areas. Such reductions in housework, some sociologists argued further, would be accompanied by a sharp rise not only in women's participation in the labor force but also in the divorce rate.[6]

A number of feminist scholars countered that more than technological developments were needed to free women from their domestic role. Pointing to the 1920s as the time when many new appliances and services came into widespread use, they observed that married women's work at home had changed little in this decade, or seemingly even after World War II. This led some to conclude that industrialization would never lessen domestic chores or bring challenges to the arrangements holding women in household tasks. Rather, the rigid framing of the gender division of labor would persist, ensuring that technological advances would lead only to "more work for mother" in the home.[7]

Industrialization and Women's Household Work

When we reexamine the evidence, we find that only after World War II did the industrial economy have a substantial impact on women's household work, as factory production of goods increased, the basic appliances invented earlier became widely available, and many domestic tasks were converted to work done for wages. It was in the early 1950s, not the 1920s, that household appliances entered most American homes, as an industrial economy whose growth had been spurred by the manufacture of weapons machinery turned to the full-scale production of consumer goods. A closer look at conditions in earlier decades makes this clear.

"As one lifts off the roofs of Middletown's homes," Robert and Helen Lynd noted in 1935 of a community seen as representative of American life, "one looks down upon a ragged array of physical facilities for meeting such basic human needs as keeping clean, sanitation, cooking, keeping warm, and securing artificial light." Fifty-five percent of all families in Middletown, or Muncie, Indiana, were still heating by stove, 37 percent had no bathtubs, and only 20 percent had refrigerators. The poorer half of the community fared far worse; fewer than 20 percent had hot and cold running water, less than 5 percent had refrigerators, and most used outdoor privies and cooked on old-fashioned stoves fueled by wood or coal.[8]

Little had altered by the end of the war. As Andrew Cherlin points out: "Fifty years later we tend to forget how much lower the average standard of living was in the mid-1940's: one-third of all homes did not have running water . . . [and] two-fifths did not have flush toilets."[9]

In the 1950s, however, the number of basic household appliances and access to utilities climbed sharply. By the early 1960s, well over 90 percent of all U.S. households had hot and cold running water, refrigerators, and gas or electric stoves, and half had automatic washing machines, which were too expensive for common use immediately after the war. Even poor households had access to stoves and refrigerators, which were provided in most rental units, while washing machines increasingly became available in the basements of apartment buildings or in nearby laundromats.[10]

Thus, unlike in earlier decades, when possession of such appliances and services had differed sharply by class, now mass production of these goods, extension of utility services throughout the country, and rising postwar incomes meant that relief from the burdens of domestic work became more uniform. The 1950s "represented for millions a great leap forward into the middle-class."[11] For many African Americans, for example, movement northward to urban areas and blue-collar jobs brought greater access to household appliances and utilities. By 1961, the economist Walt Rostow notes, "durable consumers' goods . . . lacked the momentum to qualify as leading sectors," as most demand for such items had been met. Increases in the sale of such appliances in the following decades were small by comparison.[12]

The acquisition of consumer durables was joined with an intense focus on domestic life and high levels of childbearing, which also had been interrupted by the Depression and war, among both African American and white women. However, technological advances also made a mother's physical presence less essential to her child's survival than in the past. Bottle-feeding, for example, which once resulted in much infant mortality due to gastroenteritis, was rendered safe by pasteurization and sterilization, and the practice became widespread. Technological advances also altered the reproductive side of women's labor. While access to birth control was mainly limited to the middle class in the 1920s, in the 1950's the diaphragm came into widespread use by married women of all backgrounds. Early marriage and childbirth, together with effective control of reproduction, meant that most women had completed caring for young children by their mid-30s.[13]

Time Use Studies

Recent studies of women's household work have recognized the later timing of the industrial economy's movement into the home. Some have continued to argue, however, that this process did not reduce women's domestic chores in the first decades after World War II. Discussions in the 1980s frequently drew on time use studies as evidence that women spent as many hours in domestic tasks in the 1960s and 1970s as they did in the 1920s. Once again, however, close reexamination of the evidence reveals a different pattern.

The work cited most often in these discussions was Joann Vanek's analysis of time spent on housework. Vanek compared a series of studies of household time use carried out between the 1920s and 1960s. She did indeed find that non-employed married women spent 55 hours a week on housework in 1965, compared with 52 hours in 1924. However, by 1965 time spent in the more demanding tasks of meal preparation had dropped from 17 to 11 hours per week, care of clothing and linens had decreased by 3 hours, other tasks such as care of fires for cooking and heating had been eliminated or vastly simplified, and the physical labor expended in such chores had been greatly reduced. Added to an earlier reduction of 9 to 11 hours of poultry, dairy, and garden work with women's move off the farm, the result was a significant reduction of more than 20 hours in time spent on the more necessary and strenuous domestic tasks. "As increasing proportions of married women entered the labor force and families moved from the farm to the city," Vanek states, "housework decreased for all but one subset, nonemployed women."[14]

Her findings are supported by the comments of women themselves in these decades. Exulting over "all the amazing and wonderful mechanical equipment that has . . . lightened woman's load," one study of housework in the 1950s concluded: "For women who work . . . [t]here can be no question that doing the laundry, cooking, washing dishes and cleaning are easier to accomplish with mechanical equipment, large and small." The author also noted dismissively: "There are, however, many sociologists who think that all these machines have simply complicated the running of homes."[15]

Indeed, a number of scholars have argued that the old household tasks were simply replaced by a new set of demanding chores, such as shopping, again citing Vanek's study. Vanek herself, however, stressed that new demands alone—primarily shopping and the travel associated with it—did not explain the large number of hours still spent on housework. Instead, nonemployed women chose to improve their care of their homes and families, devoting 10 additional hours a week to "teaching, counseling, amusing and entertaining" their children, for example, and 2 hours per week to care of plants and pets. More important, Vanek found that employed wives spent only half as much time as nonemployed wives on housework, despite little increase in help from their husbands or reduction in the time they gave to their children.[16]

A second study also found that wives' employment was the major factor affecting time in housework, though once again husbands' contributions were minimal. Both groups of women performed a similar set of chores, but employed wives spent at least 2 hours less per day on such tasks, making simpler meals and spending less time on the care of their homes, clothing, and, in this analysis, children.[17] Yet another study later revealed a more dramatic decline in housework between 1965 and 1975, especially among women under 30. As earlier, employed women spent little over half as many hours on housework as those not in the labor force; and once again, such reductions were not due to increased help from men. Rather, time was saved mainly by technological advances in routine cleaning, household maintenance, and shopping.[18]

We thus find that all women in the first decades after World War II enjoyed substantial savings in the time spent on essential chores of household maintenance and food preparation. Also, as employed women demonstrated, thanks to the new appliances and services, the hours required for domestic chores could be even more sharply reduced if desired. As Vanek concludes, "The time that working women spend in household work probably approximates the irreducible amount of time necessary to keep a household. The additional time spent in homemaking by nonemployed women represents 'just' keeping busy."[19]

That most women in the 1950s and early 1960s put the time they gained into further housework, improving the care of their families and homes, highlights once again a key aspect of women's household work. Such work involved not only a set of chores but also a way of organizing and supporting the performance of these tasks, through the gender division of labor, in which women were expected to focus on domestic concerns under their husbands' control and support. Marriage was the central institution stabilizing this arrangement, reinforced by many laws and cultural practices.

Some analysts in the 1960s tried to find a direct relationship between technological advances and women's turn to the labor force, counting the number of appliances in homes, for example, and comparing them with wives' hours of paid work.[20] However, developments in the 1950s merely created potential for women's turn from domestic tasks within marriage to work for wages as their central means of support. Any real transformation of women's lives required alteration of the structures framing their work within the home as well.

The Dismantling of Support
for Women's Household Work

As time use studies illustrate, technological change alone did not end support for women's household work. Rather, such change opened up a potential that could be used in different ways. While some women drew satisfaction from taking better care of their homes, some husbands did not want or could not afford to support their wives in such work and other women saw more appealing or important ways to use their time. For such men and women, the old framework that served to hold women in household work began to feel constraining, as it no longer served an obvious need and kept them from realizing new opportunities.

It is important to recognize that women were not alone in seeking to change the framings of the gender division of labor. Though many men initially expressed strong opposition to women's equality, some had an interest in altering the old structure of marriage, which required them to support one woman in household work for her entire life. The state also displayed increasing ambivalence about supporting such work, while employers in expanding sectors of the economy, looking for new workers, began to drop practices that blocked the hiring of married women.

Many of those who took steps to end legal or cultural practices they found restrictive did not foresee the full consequences of their actions. Rather, they were often simply trying to remodel the old domestic realm—to add, so to speak, more doors and larger windows, widening women's access to the labor force or removing some inequities within marriage. In the end, however, so much of the framework supporting women's work in the home was weakened or demolished that at last the whole structure collapsed completely. The troubled U.S. economy of the 1970s and 1980s delivered the final blow.

By examining more closely the steps taken by these different groups, we can gain insight into how and why the old framings of support for domestic labor came apart for both African American and white women. Only when we grasp the multifaceted nature of this process can we understand why it had such negative consequences for many women.

Women's Steps from Household to Paid Work and Challenges to the Gender Division of Labor

Looking first at women themselves, we see that many wives were drawn into the labor force in the decades after World War II as the need for their full-time household labor decreased and opportunities in the workplace grew. Though working outside the home was initially seen as a way to improve the family economy, it also increasingly raised challenges to the old domestic role.

The first wave of married women workers entering the labor force in the 1950s were not intending such a confrontation. Many were older women from lower-middle-class households who had fewer domestic demands because their children had grown up. They were not seeking work outside the home because of dissatisfaction with housework or their traditional role. Rather, these women turned to the labor force, concluded one detailed study in the 1950s, "not to pursue a career . . . but to supplement the family income."[21]

Many, however, came to find combining work at home and for pay was stressful, especially if their husbands disapproved of their employment. They handled their conflicting demands, though, not by protesting their domestic duties but by subordinating paid work to family needs, through taking jobs closer to home, for example. Even professional women in this decade resolved such tensions by reducing their involvement in paid work. They wrote of changing or curtailing their career plans, first as young women, anticipating marriage and families, and later in the face of their husbands' career requirements and the demands of motherhood. An attitude of compromise predominated. "I have been able to manage successfully," one woman engaged in biological research reported, "only by recognizing that I could not expect to work anywhere near my full potential."[22]

African American women were among this early wave of entrants. The 1950s and 1960s were decades of great movement into the labor force for black married women. While the majority of white wives delayed working until their children were grown, many black women entering the workforce in the first years after World War II were young mothers in their 20s and early 30s, who combined child rearing with paid employment. By 1960, African American wives between the ages of 25 and 34 were more than one and a half times more likely to be working than white wives of the same age. In taking on paid work, African American wives were also seeking to improve conditions within their homes rather than challenge traditional arrangements.[23]

Employment in professional and other white-collar occupations rose among African American women in the 1950s, even as it decreased among white women. Three-fourths of black wives under 55 with college degrees were in the labor force in 1960, and a small group of black female lawyers and doctors emerged. This early group of professionals sought to combine career and family, while continuing to accept primary responsibility for household tasks. However, they came to find their dual roles exhausting and to express resentment toward their husbands' expectation of their domestic labor. "I am a little fed up," protested one black female professional in the 1950s, "with the notion that woman is the homemaker and man is the breadwinner."[24]

These strains were felt throughout African American families. By 1970, well over half of black married women in their prime adult years were in the labor force, and two-thirds of these wives were working full-time. At that time, care of home and children was still seen as women's responsibility, husbands showed little inclination to help, and no policies were yet in place to help women manage both sets of tasks. However, though black wives still earned much less than their spouses in 1970, their wages had risen rapidly over the previous decade and their jobs, while low paying, often had the higher status of white-collar work.[25] Researchers found that black couples were more open than white couples to the idea of married women's employment and their contribution to family decisions. However, black wives' actual work for wages brought increased tensions and fights, often becoming the central source of family conflict.[26]

In the late 1960s, white married women in their mid-30s began to join African American women of their age in the labor force. Middle-class wives with college degrees turned most rapidly to paid work, driven less by a need for family income than a sense, once their children were grown, that there was not enough to do at home. "I [had thought] . . . that being some man's wife and some child's mother would occupy my mind and my hands for the rest of my life," the sociologist Lillian Rubin wrote of her own experience as a 38-year-old housewife in 1962. "[Instead] I awoke each day wondering how to fill the time."[27]

By the 1960s, child care had become the central activity to fill the gap left by the reduction of other tasks. Thus, as their children grew, many mothers found themselves with free time they could use in returning to school or taking up "second careers." Younger women, however, increasingly sought work outside the home while still caring for small children, a choice that intensified the conflict between wage-earning and domestic roles. "Looking at the intricacies of shadow and light around me," wrote one photographer of her early struggles, "I experienced a strong pull away from my house and children. . . . I bought photographic books, but had little time to read them. I prowled the house in the middle of the night, desperate for a few extra hours."[28]

African American women were less concerned with escaping from the domestic role than with finding ways to join family and paid work more effectively. Alice Walker, for example, unlike white women writers her age, strongly asserted her ability to combine writing with raising a child. At the same time, though, she argued firmly for "one child only" despite her mother's urgings that she have many more. A growing number of black college graduates began to postpone marriage and motherhood into their late 20s and early 30s, adopting early the strategy that many women would later embrace.[29]

As the early baby boomers, born in the first ten years after World War II, reached adulthood and entered the labor force in large numbers, women's dissatisfaction with their domestic role heightened. Paid employment climbed steeply among young black married women with high school degrees or some college education, increasing their frustration with the chores awaiting them at home.[30] Among college graduates of both races, the proportion seeking degrees in the traditionally male professions of law and medicine began to rise. For these young women, the solution to the conflict between paid work and the domestic role seemed clear: to avoid marriage and children, at least in the first decades of adulthood. "Market work," one study observed of this new generation, "[has become] a socially acceptable alternative to domesticity in providing women with a means of identity."[31]

Steps Taken by Organized Women's Movements

The frustrations felt by individual women were given focus in organized women's movements. In the first decades after World War II, the leading women's organizations had concentrated on improving women's position in the labor force. The National Council of Negro Women had sought to improve employment opportunities for black women since its founding in 1935.[32] The National Organization for Women, formed in 1966 and made up mainly of white women, believed that equality between the sexes would come with women's access to good jobs. While no longer working to protect women's domestic realm, as white women's organizations had done at the turn of the century, NOW did not actively challenge the division of labor between the sexes or recognize its role in women's absence from the labor force.[33]

The members of both the NCNW and NOW were primarily professional and middle-class women. The head of the NCNW, Dorothy Height, though remaining unmarried herself, supported the traditional division of gender roles, seeing men as the primary breadwinners and women as responsible for domestic tasks. NOW's first members had resolved the conflicts between household and paid work through strategies of compromise and privilege—postponing full careers until their children were grown, hiring domestic help, or working extremely long hours.[34]

Another group of women, less visible and mostly working class, voiced their interests through unions. Knowing full well the difficulties of combining work at home and for pay, they pressed for policies such as paid maternity leave that would make their dual lives easier. Their efforts laid the groundwork for later gains. However, these "labor feminists," as the historian Dorothy Sue Cobble calls them, also did not question women's continued responsibility for household tasks.[35]

That questioning erupted instead among a younger and more radical generation, whose members came to recognize the constraints inherent in the gender division of labor and to rebel against its framings. The upsurge in radical feminist organizations in the late 1960s has often been attributed to women's greater resources, as they gained college educations and paid employment in increasing numbers. However, such dissatisfaction at a time when women's situation was growing rapidly better is puzzling, as one scholar notes.[36]

We can only understand the widespread protest voiced by women in these years by recognizing the dramatic changes also taking place at this time within the home. As the importance of women's domestic role dwindled sharply, the cultural and legal framings surrounding it came to seem clear barriers to the realization of larger personal and social goals. One founder of the Black Women's Liberation Committee described the conflict she felt in the 1960s: "My mind is expanding and becoming very intellectually active, and on the home front, I'm being told to put myself into this little box. . . . And the contradiction becomes just too big."[37]

All around the country, small groups of women began speaking of their dissatisfactions, uncovering the role played by the gender division of labor in their subordination. "The marriage contract . . . legalizes . . . the bondage of women," one such group declared in a leaflet handed out on the steps of a New York City courthouse, "both their internal (reproductive) and external (domestic labor) functions."[38] A central goal of these younger feminists was greater control over reproduction. They worked hard to win women's right to birth control and abortion. Their efforts brought great gains, freeing women from many of the old restrictions that confined them primarily to marriage and motherhood.[39] In the end, though, this freedom was for most temporary. Their demands resulted more in the postponement of domestic responsibilities rather than in the construction of an alternative means of handling such tasks. Divisions among feminist organizations also limited the vision of the dominant groups, resulting in insufficient attention to issues of class and race.

The costs of such limited vision would become apparent in subsequent years as increasing numbers of women struggled to combine work at home and for pay, or to raise children without the help of a spouse. However, the hardships accompanying the dismantling of women's domestic economy were also caused in large part by the way this process was shaped by other interests.

Husbands, Employers, and the State

Men's Growing Dissatisfaction and the Changing Basis of Marriage

Women were not the only group that found the framings of the old gender division of labor restrictive. A growing number of men also grew increasingly critical of the traditional framing of the relationship between the sexes. While dissatisfaction with marriage rose among both sexes from the late 1950s to the early 1970s, men's frustration grew most rapidly. For many, lifelong support of women's domestic labor had begun to feel like a poor bargain. Marriage had become disadvantageous to men, one speaker complained at a conference in 1964, "restricting them sexually and entailing burdensome financial responsibilities."[40]

Barbara Ehrenreich has traced the breakdown of the ideology surrounding traditional marriage among men. "The collapse of the breadwinner ethic had begun well before the revival of feminism," she argues, "and stemmed from dissatisfactions every bit as deep." In her account, a "professional-managerial class" took the lead in challenging the old breadwinner role. Marriage rates for both white and African American men did drop sharply over the 1970s among college graduates, though they fell among men with less education as well. Discontent with men's traditional responsibilities in the home was widespread. By the mid-1970s, 60 percent of men saw marriage as restrictive. Those viewing the institution in almost entirely negative terms had increased by one-third since the mid-1950s.[41]

Redbook magazine, interviewing a group of bachelors in their late 20s and early 30s in 1968, found that most had devised ways to cope with household chores. "I find I just have to own an awful lot of underwear and shirts," said one man living on his own. In general, these men saw a wife as bringing only increased demands. "It's easy enough to get a girl," explained another bachelor. "The only reason to get married is if you want to have kids."[42]

It was not simply that women's household labor no longer seemed worth its cost. Rather, behind such complaints a fundamental shift in the nature of marriage was taking place. Many analysts have noted the declining economic necessity of marriage in the years after World War II, commonly stressing women's entrance into the labor force. However, it was not only women's greater opportunity to support themselves through wages but also men's reduced need for women's domestic chores that underlay such a shift.[43]

Further, the key issue was not that men and women lost interest in marrying as the value of each other's work shrank. Rather, the lessened economic necessity of marriage opened a new possibility, that of developing emotional intimacy in relationships. This view of marriage, which appeared in discussions of middle-class families in the 1920s, became common in assessments of relationships in the 1960s. Young men and women, as well as family therapists, came to see the primary goal of such unions as the meeting of emotional and sexual needs. By the mid-1960s, "love" had become one of the most important issues for male college students in choosing a wife, while their preference for a woman who was a "good cook and housekeeper" dropped precipitously over the following years.[44]

Social commentators predicted that unions based on emotional gratification would be more fragile than those grounded in each spouse's need for the other's labor. Indeed, in the early 1960s the divorce rate began to rise rapidly, doubling between 1964 and 1975. Divorce and separation shot up among all educational levels and ages, marking a dramatic break with marriage as traditionally conceived. Divorce manuals, once rare, proliferated, and they increasingly viewed the termination of an unsatisfying marriage not as a sign of failure but as a necessary, if painful, step toward emotional development.[45] Challenges to the division of labor in which marriage was rooted also raised stresses in and of themselves, as both men and women chafed at traditional gender roles. Some men rebelled against the part of provider; some women found men's assumption of authority in the home increasingly unacceptable. A strikingly high percentage of women who attended graduate school in the 1950s and early 1960s divorced.[46]

Over the ensuing decades, marriage grew still more vulnerable. As the cultural and legal frameworks that shored up this institution were dismantled, couples were left with little support as economic pressures mounted.

Changes in Divorce Law

Support for women's work within the home did not break down simply because individuals came to view relationships or gender roles differently. Rather, the laws and customs that had formalized support for women's work in the home were also altered. The central such institution was marriage, and the new emphasis on its role in ensuring emotional and sexual satisfaction led to far-reaching changes in the law that, less obviously, radically weakened support for women's domestic labor.

In the early 1960s, marriage was still defined as a lifelong relationship in which the husband was expected to provide financially for his spouse in exchange for her domestic services. Divorce was strongly discouraged, and it did not end a man's economic obligations toward his ex-wife. Support for women's household work within marriage thus had strong legal backing. However, as divorce rates climbed, the old laws framing marriage seemed cumbersome and outmoded, and lawyers pushed for reforms. In 1970, no-fault divorce was instituted in California, and most other states soon enacted similar legislation.[47]

Much has been made of this change in divorce law and the economic difficulties faced by women after their marriages ended. What has not yet been clearly seen is that this reform also removed the central legal buttress of the old gender division of labor. Stressing the "ability of the supported spouse to engage in gainful employment," state legislatures and the courts stipulated women should rely not on their ex-husbands for support but instead on their own wages.[48] With half of marriages in the 1970s expected to end in divorce, legal support for women's performance of domestic tasks was thus dismantled at its core. These changes spelled the end not of marriage or women's performance of domestic tasks, but of marriage as the means of support for such work.

This "silent revolution" did not result from organized efforts by feminists pursuing equality. "Not only did few women play a substantial role in the formulation of early no-fault proposals," observes Herbert Jacob, a legal analyst, "but no evidence exists of feminist prodding."[49] During the initial legal reforms in the mid-1960s, the feminist movement was just emerging and was focused on discrimination in the workforce rather than on revisions in family law. Further, though some women envisioned more equitable ways to structure marriage, the specific form given the new divorce laws represented the interests of those in power, not of women. The California state legislature, for example, rejected recommendations that some women receive long-term support from their ex-husbands or more than half the marital property and included measures asserting men's authority over the family. Thus, as Jacob concludes, "the new law was not in any way a feminist product."[50]

At first, feminist organizations showed little awareness of the importance of such changes. Radical feminists, while critical of the traditional structure of marriage, advocated its complete abolition rather than reform. Liberal feminists sought greater rights for women in the wage economy, emphasizing equality without recognizing the costs entailed for many women in the dismantling of their old arrangement of labor. The liberalization of divorce law did make it easier for women as well as men to escape bad relationships. However, the ways in which this law was framed, the many difficulties still faced by women in the labor force, and the domestic responsibilities that they still were expected to bear brought great economic hardship to women whose marriages ended. As these costs became apparent, feminists made concerted efforts to raise awareness of them and blunt their impact.[51] Yet society in general continued to overlook the importance of the domestic tasks still done by women and thus failed to recognize that a new legal and institutional framework had to be constructed that would commit employers and the state, as well as men themselves, to support such work.

The Sexual Revolution and Changes in Family Law

Another set of sanctions, embedded in culture as well as law, had long worked to keep childbearing and child rearing within the framework of marriage and men's support. However, perhaps no group felt the restrictiveness of the old framings of women's domestic labor more intensely than adolescents. Strong religious and moral codes had long limited sexual intimacy, especially for women, to marriage and the tasks of reproduction. By the 1920s, the pleasures of sex for women as well as men were being acknowledged, and the percentage of couples engaging in intercourse prior to marriage rose steadily in this and the following decade. Yet women's fears of becoming pregnant or losing social status remained strong. In the 1950s being perceived as a "nice girl" was still important to both white and African American adolescents, and unwed mothers faced severe social ostracism.[52]

Changes were in the offing, however. "As family life ceases to be a means of economic production," one sociologist had warned in the 1920s, "marriage [will become for many] . . . an obligation they have to accept in order to enjoy the physical pleasures of sex." By the early 1960s, even nice girls were rebelling against such obligations. Both *Newsweek* and *Time* ran stories of college co-eds and career girls "going all the way" with their boyfriends.[53] Lillian Rubin found that 80 percent of the working-class couples she interviewed had had sex before marriage, as teenagers in the early 1960s. Only 36 percent of these wives said their husband was their first and only sexual partner. Among Americans as a whole, the percentage of couples engaging in sex prior to marriage rose rapidly over the decade.[54]

Rejection of the old rules prohibiting sex before marriage was encouraged in part by technological advances. By the end of the 1960s, the birth-control pill and intrauterine device offered young women the option of having sexual intercourse with little risk of pregnancy. However, this option was unequally enjoyed. "In high school maybe we didn't use contraceptives fifty per cent of the time," explained one young woman. "I was ridden with guilt and secrecy, plus it was hard to get contraceptives." She noted that college brought a more "matter of fact" handling of sex and birth control.[55]

Further, this potential, much like the option of leaving an unsatisfactory marriage, was largely shaped to men's advantage. The writer Marge Piercy, at first greeting the new freedoms for women with enthusiasm, soon came to the same conclusion that Simone de Beauvoir had reached in Paris two decades earlier: men's greater economic and political resources gave them greater power in emotional relationships as well. The consequences went beyond whose heart was broken. Access to effective contraception and abortion did give some women more control over motherhood. At the same time, though, such access also lessened pressures on men to marry women they impregnated.[56]

At first, as the strictures against sex before marriage began to give way, many of the old cultural practices framing women's domestic role still held. In the early 1960s, as growing numbers of adolescents engaged in premarital sex, the share of births conceived outside of marriage also rose sharply. Initially, this brought a rise in weddings as well, and most of these expectant mothers became wives before their children were born. Young men as well as women saw marriage as inevitable in the face of pregnancy. "I was too young, I was too irresponsible; I didn't want to settle down," one husband admitted, "[but] I knew I'd have to marry her."[57]

Within a few years, however, this custom was also breaking down. By the end of the 1970s, less than one-third of young mothers who had conceived out of wedlock had married by the time their infants were born. Some found their boyfriends retreating; others were glad to be able to avoid what they viewed as a bad marriage, yet keep their babies rather than put them up for adoption as many unwed mothers had done in earlier decades.[58] They were setting out on a difficult path, however, with little support for their efforts.

·   ·   ·

These cultural shifts, like the rise in divorce, were accompanied by a series of legal decisions that formally removed a set of rules shaping women's performance of domestic tasks. Family law, usually handled quietly in the lower courts, was catapulted into prominence as it became the central arena in which the traditional framings of marriage and motherhood were challenged and over-turned. In the 1950s, the legal code still strongly defined marriage, and thus implicitly men's support of women's domestic labor, as the context within which children were to be born and raised. Laws restricting access to contraception and prohibiting abortion tied women's sexuality tightly to marriage, and there was little legal recognition of the relationship between parents and children born out of wedlock. In the mid-1960s and early 1970s, much of this old legal framework was taken apart.[59]

The alterations in reproductive law—again, like the changes in divorce—initially took place without great furor as a few professionals attempted to revise rules that were proving cumbersome in changing circumstances. Though married couples had gained increasing access to birth control from the 1920s on, that of unmarried individuals, particularly minors, was restricted. Up until the late 1960s, for example, doctors throughout the country were legally prevented from prescribing contraceptives to unmarried women under the age of 21 without parental consent. In the early 1970s, when almost all states lowered the age of legal adulthood to 18, young women gained the right to purchase birth control on their own, and family planning services became available on many college campuses.[60]

Legal constraints against abortion had been tightened in the late nineteenth century, in part because of fears that women might refuse their childbearing role if given the choice. In the mid–twentieth century, state laws were an inconsistent patchwork, but most prohibited abortion. In the late 1960s, growing numbers of women did indeed seek dangerous and illegal terminations of unwanted pregnancies, leading women's organizations and medical practitioners to press for reform. The result was the landmark *Roe v. Wade* decision in 1973, in which the Supreme Court legalized abortion, subject to state regulation only after the first trimester of pregnancy. The larger implications of this decision were not initially recognized by these justices, all of whom supported the traditional structure of the family.[61]

The laws restricting motherhood to marriage were revised around the same time. Before the late 1960s, unwed mothers were harshly punished, and they and unwed fathers had few rights over their children born outside of marriage, in part because the absence of such rights was believed to discourage illegitimacy. By the early 1970s, however, unwed mothers could no longer be expelled from school, and some legal recognition was accorded the relationship between unmarried parents and their offspring. Children could no longer be denied their deceased father's government benefits simply because he had not married their mother, for example, and unwed mothers won the right to make decisions about their children's medical treatment and to sue in the case of wrongful death.[62]

The Removal of Barriers to Women's Employment

Another set of reforms and legal rulings had indirect though significant effects on the framework supporting women's household work. Legislation limiting women's paid employment had been passed near the beginning of the twentieth century to defend space for women's domestic labor against the intrusions of an emerging industrial economy. Many of these regulations now appeared to be unduly restrictive to employers and the courts, as well as to women themselves.

As the economy expanded rapidly after World War II, a complex system to distribute and maintain goods, finance production, and provide social services took shape. A growing share of private and public incomes was spent on health, education, and recreation, and such growth generated a strong demand for new workers. Married women were the key group that still remained largely outside the wage economy. Practices designed to reinforce the gender division of labor now blocked employers' access to such labor, and thus were rapidly abandoned.

The "marriage bar," for example—the widespread practice of denying jobs to married women—had served to keep many wives in the domestic role. Several surveys found that in the 1920s more than half of schools and offices deliberately engaged in this practice, which the shortage of jobs in the Depression only made more common. In the 1950s, however, employers found it in their best interest to drop this barrier. They also sharply altered their views of married women. Once dismissed as unreliable, the mature wife and mother was now described in highly positive terms as a dependable and "ideal employee" providing "service . . . of great value." Approximately 20 million new jobs were created in the first two decades after the war, and married women provided the majority of these new workers.[63]

The idea that women doing the same work as men were entitled to the same pay also gained wider support, leading to passage of the Equal Pay Act by Congress in 1963. In explaining the measure's importance, Arthur Fleming, who had served as Dwight D. Eisenhower's secretary of health, education, and welfare, stressed the importance of women workers as "resources that will be desperately needed in the years to come." Wages in general rose strongly for female workers in the 1950s and 1960s. For women and their families, such gains increased the cost of keeping a wife at home.[64]

Moreover, the series of laws enacted in the late nineteenth and early twentieth centuries to protect the domestic realm from the demands of the market came to be widely recognized in the 1960s as serving primarily to bar women from better-paying positions and to undercut their job security and opportunities for advancement. Title VII, the amendment to the 1964 Civil Rights Act that prohibited discrimination based on sex, was initially met with derision on the floor of Congress and in the media. Yet it soon became the standard against which the old legal framings of women's domestic economy were measured and found wanting. After its passage, a number of states repealed laws limiting the jobs women could hold or hours they could work.[65]

The nation's courts played a central role in this change, overturning statutes that had been justified in terms of the importance of women's domestic tasks. At the start of the century, judges had restricted employers' access to women's labor; now, once again pressured by organized women's groups, they reversed their stance. From 1970 on, as one attempt after another to exclude women from certain jobs was ruled unlawful, protective labor legislation crumbled on the grounds that it was discriminatory. As Justice William Joseph Brennan put it, laws based on "outdated misconceptions concerning the role of females in the home" were now seen to "put women . . . in a cage" and so could no longer be accepted.[66]

The most visible symbol of women's domestic role was pregnancy. In the 1960s, a number of laws and practices still defined childbearing as an activity to be carried out and supported within the home, or the old gender division of labor. Many teachers, for example, were still legally required to leave their jobs when pregnant, and in some cases they were forced to remain at home for at least three months after giving birth, during which time they were expected to be supported by their husbands' earnings. In 1974, in *Cleveland Board of Education v. La Fleur*, the Supreme Court decided in favor of expectant mothers' right to continue to work and collect pay. This decision strengthened women's position in the workforce, as pregnancy was often used as an excuse to deny them jobs, promotion, and seniority.[67] At the same time, however, it weakened the perception that marriage and men's income should support women's reproductive role.

Thus, efforts to realize a number of new possibilities—to increase women's participation in the labor force, or to form more emotionally and sexually satisfying relationships—led to a remaking of legal and cultural structures in ways that took apart the frameworks that had supported women's domestic labor. As Jo Freeman notes, "Until 1971 the judicial approach to women was that their rights, responsibilities, opportunities, and obligations were essentially determined by their position in the family. Women were viewed first and foremost as wives and mothers. . . . [By 1990] most of such laws [had] been found unconstitutional."[68]

In sum, as the courts ordered women to turn to wages rather than their ex-husbands for support, as abortion was legalized, and as the laws confining sex and childbirth to marriage were overturned, the legal shell that gave form to the old domestic economy crumbled. While many women welcomed such a change, others found it thrust upon them.

ECONOMIC DIFFICULTIES
AND A CONTRADICTORY ALLIANCE

The first decades after World War II were a time of growing prosperity, open-ing new possibilities at home as well as at work. To many, the existing gender division of labor seemed to create barriers to the exploration of such potential.

Not all women and men were drawn to these new opportunities, however. Some resisted changes to their old way of life. For a sizable segment of women, for example, paid work held little appeal, while many husbands staunchly re-sisted their wives' employment. However, the slowdown in the U.S. economy in the mid-1970s and early 1980s placed growing pressures on the framework of support for women's household work, already greatly weakened by the chal-lenges and alterations of the preceding years. These pressures and the political reaction accompanying them furthered the breakdown of such support. Some women were pushed out of the home and into the labor force against their wishes; some men were forced to relinquish the breadwinner role as their wages declined or their jobs disappeared altogether. African American families, despite their historical lack of access to the family wage, were disproportion-ately hurt by these changes and the responses they provoked.

Families and Work in the 1970s

In the mid-1970s, opposition to the dismantling of the framework of support for women's work within the home began to mount as such changes acceler-ated and affected a growing number of lives. Much of this opposition consisted of women pulled into political action for the first time as they mobilized in defense of their domestic realm. Their protests gained strength, however, only as the breakdown of support for women's work in the home intersected with another shift in the U.S. economy: the decline of the old manufacturing industries that had carried the country to prosperity after the war. These two events overlapped, neither determining the other but each significantly affecting the major social and economic change that was taking place. Though many analysts have stressed the collapse of the accord between employers and workers in the 1970s and 1980s, the gender division of labor had begun to break down well before the faltering of factory production, and its continuing disintegration played a key role in the economic and political turmoil of these years.

Threats to their old way of life, at home as well as at work, generated fierce opposition on several fronts, among some housewives, workers, employers, and politicians, bringing these groups together in protest. Yet there were serious contradictions in this alliance, as each group rejected key pieces of the framework supporting women's household work at the same time as vehemently supporting it. Business and government abandoned the family wage; the New Right and workers themselves attacked state support for women's domestic role in the form of aid to single mothers. Thus, it was not economic pressures alone but a series of political actions as well that further undercut support for women's work in the home.

A century earlier, when an emerging industrial economy had posed threats to the gender division of labor, widespread resistance had led to its reinforcement in different ways. In the years after World War II, in contrast, resistance, though intense, only slowed and distorted the breakdown of women's domestic economy, rather than reversing such collapse. While this breakdown extended across differences of race and class, its consequences were far harsher for those at the bottom of the economic spectrum. Poor women, thrown out of marriage and then off welfare, faced the greatest hardship. As Eric Hobsbawm has observed of an earlier moment in such economic development, "The successful middle class and those who aspired to emulate them were satisfied. Not so the laboring poor . . . whose traditional world and way of life the Industrial Revolution destroyed, without automatically substituting anything else."[1]

Women's Opposition to Change

In the 1970s, some women fiercely resisted the loss of their old way of life and means of support. White women's lives changed more dramatically in this decade than in any other after World War II. They turned to paid work most rapidly in these years, their divorce rate soared, and rates of motherhood as well as marriage declined sharply among young women. Accompanied by new legislation that gave women greater access to the labor force while also weakening support for their domestic role, these changes provoked sharp responses.

College-educated white women were much more likely than other women to be working for pay in the late 1960s. The youngest graduates in particular surged into the labor force after obtaining their degrees and showed little inclination to return home. This move into work for wages was joined with an increasing avoidance of marriage. By 1970, barely half of recent college graduates were married; many would remain single well into adulthood. Their rejection of motherhood was even more dramatic. Almost half of college graduates nearing 30 were still childless; less than 15 percent of those in their early 20s were mothers. Instead, almost two-thirds of college graduates in their prime adult years were employed. Paid work appeared to be replacing home and family in these women's lives.[2]

But college graduates, though rapidly growing in number, were still only a small segment of all women. The lives of most white women continued to be dominated by the domestic realm. Few white wives had shown a desire to work outside the home in the first years after World War II. They spoke of enjoying housework and their days, noted one observer, had a "relaxed rhythm." As the 1970s opened, most wives who had not attended college, especially those with children to care for, still gave home and family their full attention. The majority expressed continued satisfaction with their household chores and the control they had over these tasks, despite their husbands' overall authority.[3]

The youngest white high school graduates continued to marry at much the same rate as those before them and, unlike college women, quickly became mothers. In 1970, the great majority of high school graduates were married and caring for children by their late 20s, and only one-third of these wives were employed. Those who had not finished high school, still close to one-third of white women in their prime adult years, were even more likely to persist in the domestic role. Home rather than paid work remained the central focus of these women's lives.[4]

Yet this was a period of wrenching change for white women who had not attended college. Increasing numbers were being drawn into the labor force. The most rapid rise was among married mothers, especially those with young children. Though a segment of white wives had worked when needed in earlier decades, few had done so while raising a family.

Further, this turn to paid employment was joined with growing insecurity at home. While college graduates were postponing marriage, a growing number of less-educated women were facing the more traumatic process of divorce. Though some welcomed the chance to escape a bad marriage, in these years the costs of doing so were very steep. It was far easier for their husbands to take this step. A study in one state found that approximately two-thirds of requests for divorce in the early 1970s were filed by men.[5] Even older women found their marriages crumbling. The number of female-headed families rose sharply among high school–educated women in the early 1970s, as did their presence among the poor.[6] Though feminist organizations largely ignored the harsh consequences of divorce until the end of the decade, the prospect of such hardship sent waves of fear through those still dependent on housework for their livelihood. For many of these women, the domain of home and motherhood seemed to be falling apart, spurring some to action.

.   .   .

Government actions sparked such protest, as Congress approved the Equal Rights Amendment in 1972, sending it on to the states for ratification, and the Supreme Court legalized abortion the following year. In the ensuing months, bitter battles erupted over both issues. At the heart of such battles stood women themselves, confronting each other across a chasm separating their old and new worlds of work. While feminists were attempting to escape confinement to marriage and motherhood, other women felt their interests were better met within the old domestic realm and fought to prevent its alteration. Their political positions were shaped largely by how they defined their main arena of work. "An important determinant of women's attitudes toward feminism," a summary of attitudinal surveys concluded, was "whether they perceive[d] that over the life span their work . . . [was] located primarily in the sphere of paid labor or primarily in the institution of the family."[7]

This divide was clear among women actively engaged in the struggle over the ERA and abortion. Though opposition to abortion began among the Catholic Church and other established conservative groups, ordinary housewives fed the larger surge of protest. Thus in California in the early 1980s, and in North Dakota as well, "mothering and the domestic domain" were the determining characteristics of women working against abortion, while pro-choice women had turned away from traditional household roles.[8]

Battles over the Equal Rights Amendment revealed a similar division. "The women against the ERA were overwhelmingly housewives," a study of ERA activists in North Carolina reported. "Almost all the pro-ERA women worked outside the home, and more than half had professional occupations."[9] Again and again, in interviews or in the literature they prepared, women opposing abortion or the ERA expressed concerns that these measures would weaken the framework of support for their domestic labors. They saw such dismantling as playing into men's interests and voiced fears that husbands would abandon their wives and children. "[Women are] scared to death of what's happening to them," one ERA opponent confessed.[10]

To comprehend the intensity of these women's resistance, we need a clearer understanding of the full scope of the changes unfolding in their lives. Men's difficulties in the 1970s and 1980s as high-paying factory jobs disappeared have received much attention. Women, however, were undergoing a far more traumatic event in these years, a historic move from household to paid work as their central means of support. Many earlier groups of men, confronted with the loss of their land, had fought hard to retain their holdings. They saw working for wages as far less preferable than tilling their own fields, and gave up their old way of life only under great pressure. Similarly, many women in the post–World War II United States found the domestic role more appealing than the jobs available to them in the labor force and also held tightly to their established way of life. They were driven to work for wages only by the collapse of support for their work within the home.

Their fierce defense of family and motherhood stemmed from a deeper sense of violation as well. Behind the breakdown of support for women's household work lay the penetration of the wage economy far into the home. As its critics have pointed out, the market has little interest in meeting people's needs beyond the minimum necessary to sustain its daily source of labor. Many housewives and mothers sensed the destructive side of its expansion. For these women, abortion symbolized this disregard for human life, giving vehemence to their opposition.

Thus, the negative side of the encounter between home and market in the years after World War II was first voiced primarily by those with much to lose in this collision, who recognized the need to preserve space in which human desires could be realized from the demands of the larger economy. For these women and their supporters, however, the only way to effectively defend that space was to preserve traditional hierarchies.

While many women mobilized to defend challenges to their traditional way of life, their resistance gained real clout only through alliances with other groups. As was true of efforts to dismantle the traditional framings of support for tasks of family maintenance, the fight to preserve these old arrangements involved more than women alone. Full grasp of the opposition to changes in women's work in the home thus requires an understanding of alterations in the market economy as well.

Economic Difficulties and the Further Breakdown of the Gender Division of Labor

The breakdown of the gender division of labor intersected with an important sectoral shift in the post–World War II economy. The economic difficulties of the 1970s and 1980s, and the resultant rupturing of past agreements between employers and workers, are now a familiar story. A number of analysts have dissected the decline of the traditional manufacturing sector and its costs for male workers.[11] Gender, however, is largely absent from these accounts. Yet it was not only the post–World War II accord between capital and labor that was collapsing in these decades, but an economic arrangement of far longer duration, that of men's support for women's work in the home.

Many now see the breakdown of the gender division of labor as simply one consequence of the decline of traditional manufacturing jobs, a casualty of the disappearance of the male breadwinner wage. However, this alone is not a sufficient explanation. As previous chapters have shown, the framework of support for women's work within the home had begun to come apart well before the economic problems of the 1970s and later years, and its continuing disintegration played a key role in the political turmoil of these decades.

The loss of blue-collar jobs dealt a further, but not primary, blow to support for women's domestic labor. Instead, we see the intersection of two important independent events: the fading of an aging sector within the industrial economy *and* the breakdown of women's older arrangement of work, still largely outside the market. Though these two realms had become entwined to some extent, both were failing in their own ways as they were confronted with more efficient production abroad or outside the home.

There has been much debate about whether women themselves, an expanding religious right, or an increasingly conservative working class was the main force behind the rise of reactionary protest of the 1970s and 1980s.[12] In actuality, all these groups faced threats to their old ways of life. Their shared loss was that of the traditional organization of tasks of family maintenance, or the gender division of labor. Opposition to that loss thus brought these different groups together. This was a conflicted alliance, however, full of contradictions and betrayals, which led in the end to further dismantling of support for women's work in the home, especially among the working class and poor.

Working-Class and Poor Families

In the early 1970s, the expansive growth that had made the United States the undisputed leader of the world economy since the 1940s stalled. Inflation climbed, men's wages stopped rising, and investment in production slowed. The factory jobs offering good pay to men with high school educations rapidly disappeared. Pennsylvania and New York lost approximately one-quarter of their manufacturing jobs between 1970 and 1974; Michigan and Illinois fared little better. By 1975, the American economy was in serious trouble.[13]

This economic decline threatened many workers with the loss not only of high-paying jobs but also of their wives' domestic labor. For many men, retention of their wives in household work was tied to the rise of the manufacturing sector, which had carried the United States to great economic and political power. Employers and workers in these industries had reached an agreement that ensured a stable workforce while also benefiting organized labor. One central gain had been the family wage, which enabled a segment of male workers to support their wives' work in the home. The decline of the old "smokestack industries" meant the end of this arrangement.[14]

In the early 1970s, most white men still opposed their wives' engagement in paid work. Though women's full-time work in the home was no longer essential to their daily survival, its ending stripped one more right from the working class. Like the ownership of a house and small piece of land, a man's command over his wife's labor provided "an important protection against the exposure of total hire . . . [and] an area of control of one's own . . . [u]nder the long pressures of a dominating wage economy."[15] However, economic pressures in the 1970s forced an increasing number of men to accept their wives' employment. Labor force participation climbed sharply among young married women with high school degrees, and full-time employment rose even among those caring for young children. This effort to shore up the family economy had only partial success, however, as it introduced further tensions into the home. Divorce continued to become increasingly common among young as well as older high school–educated white women throughout the 1970s.

African American families, despite their historical lack of access to the family wage, were on the whole more severely hurt than white families by the decline of traditional manufacturing industries and their shift from the central cities. However, it is important to note first that a growing segment of black women and men had gained college educations in the early 1970s and, aided by legislation prohibiting discrimination, attained better jobs and wages.[16] By 1970, 13.3 percent of African American women between the ages of 22 and 55 had attended college; the share of those completing a full four years had almost doubled by the end of the decade. Young black female college graduates, like their white peers, delayed marriage and sharply curtailed their involvement in motherhood, both postponing childbirth and bearing far fewer children than had the generation before them. They were much less likely to be mothers by their late 20s than black women with a high school education or less.

However, most black married women, unlike white wives, had already turned strongly toward work for wages, almost doubling their presence in the labor force over the previous three decades. By the early 1970s, 60 percent of African American wives who had completed high school were working or looking for jobs. Thus, rather than fighting to stay at home, most black wives saw the survival of their families as depending on their as well as their husbands' earning good wages, and they strongly supported women's right to better-paying jobs.[17]

The decline of the traditional manufacturing sector subjected these families to severe pressures, however. Unemployment soared among black men, and even those with full-time jobs faced shrinking wages.[18] Black wives with high school degrees or some college education continued to enter the labor force in large numbers over the 1970s. But in a growing number of families, such employment, joined with men's increasing difficulties, caused conflicts and raised challenges to the gender division of labor. Rates of divorce and separation rose strongly among high school–educated African American women in the 1970s, becoming much more common than for college graduates, joined with an even sharper rise in those who had never married.[19]

As manufacturing jobs disappeared in the Northeast and Midwest, and families headed by women climbed most sharply in these areas, men's employment difficulties seemed to many scholars to explain the decline in marriage. However, we must then ask, as several analysts have done, why poverty broke apart so many more families in the years after World War II than previously.[20] In the nineteenth and early twentieth centuries, African American men faced greater economic hardship, but the vast majority still married. Further, as a number of scholars have pointed out, in the post–World War II years marriage rates fell among the rich as well as the poor, and in times both of prosperity and decline. Close analysis has confirmed that men's employment problems could explain only part of the drop in those rates.[21]

In order to fully understand such breakdown, we need to look at changes in women's work as well as men's loss of jobs in steel and auto factories. Women's increased employment did give a growing number the option of leaving difficult or abusive men or, as scholars such as William Julius Wilson have stressed, those with poor employment prospects.[22] However, we must also consider how alterations in women's work in the home, not just in the labor force, affected working-class men's attitudes toward marriage. In the nineteenth and early twentieth centuries, as detailed in chapter 2, women performed a large number of domestic tasks essential to the survival of their families. The necessity of women's household labor made marriage not only desirable but crucial in times of economic hardship. Given the rudimentary conditions of early urban life, women's work in the home remained important through the first half of the twentieth century.

However, while women's household labor was once essential to men's work in fields or factories, the takeover of many domestic tasks by an expanding industrial economy in the first decades after World War II lessened men's desire to bind women tightly to such work through marriage. A wife became an economic burden rather than an asset, unless she too entered the labor force. Second, as children lost importance as workers, they both reduced the value of women's reproductive labor and increased the costs of marriage.[23] Thus, men had less interest in taking on the long-term support of a wife. For those with little income, marriage became a luxury few could afford.

Moreover, poor men also questioned the financial and sexual constraints of marriage. They talked readily, for example, of the pleasures of sleeping with many women. Though some sociologists saw such talk as the men's attempt to disguise their failure as breadwinners, middle-class men in these years were also voicing a preference for wider sexual gratification over marriage. Dissatisfaction with the domestic role, voiced by middle-class women of both races, was also expressed by even the poorest young women. As one young black girl explained, her friends disliked marriage because it meant "you do what he say, stay in the house, cook."[24]

The decline of traditional manufacturing sectors thus did not cause but rather accelerated the breakdown of marriage in the 1970s and 1980s among the poor and unemployed. As the economic basis of marriage became less important for men as well as women, and many of its cultural and legal framings were taken apart, financial difficulties that had created strains in earlier decades now ended marriages altogether or prevented them from taking place, especially among those with the fewest prospects for success in the wage economy.

The Poorest Women

The strains within many African American families were heightened as increasing numbers of women as well as their partners had difficulty obtaining work. Analyses of employment problems in the 1970s and 1980s have focused primarily on men. Young African American men with low levels of education were indeed hit especially hard, suffering much higher rates of unemployment than their white counterparts.[25] However, unemployment also rose substantially in the 1970s among all black women except college graduates. The youngest women in particular could not find jobs.

African American women who failed to complete high school faced the greatest problems. This group shrank substantially over the decade, falling from well over half to about one-third of African American women by 1980. But those still without high school diplomas lagged far behind other women, especially in terms of paid employment. They turned to the labor force more slowly and increasingly had trouble securing jobs. Over the 1970s, unemployment climbed well into the double digits for young black female high school dropouts.

These difficulties were joined with growing problems at home, as divorce and separation began to accelerate for black women with a high school education or less. Further, marriage began to disappear entirely among the youngest, a decade or more before dropping sharply among their white counterparts. The share of black high school dropouts still single in their early 20s almost doubled over the decade.

By the end of the 1970s, black women who had not finished high school were as likely to be on their own as those with college educations. However, their turn from marriage had taken a very different form. These young women leaving high school were not delaying marriage until established in the labor force, but losing it altogether. Few of those who had not married by age 25 would ever have husbands, in sharp contrast to college women.[26] Those who did marry fared little better, as most of these early unions broke apart. Yet this loss of marriage was not accompanied by a similar delay of motherhood. These young women still held tightly to the domestic role, though support for such work was collapsing around them.

White women with little education were experiencing similar changes, though their full impact was delayed until the 1980s. In the 1970s, white women who did not finish high school also began to fall markedly behind other women, failing to keep up with their rapid movement into the labor force. Like their black counterparts, white high school dropouts both turned more slowly to the labor force than other women of their race and had increasing difficulty finding jobs; their unemployment rates were one and a half times higher than the previous decade.[27]

While the labor force was growing inhospitable, support for women's work in the home also showed signs of coming apart. Unlike more-educated women, most white women quitting high school continued to marry young and take on the traditional domestic role. An increasing proportion, though, soon found themselves divorced or separated. Among the youngest, formal unions were becoming increasingly rare. But the postponement of motherhood failed to keep pace with the loss of marriage. By the end of the 1970s, 77 percent of white high school dropouts in their early 20s were mothers, compared to only 6 percent of white college graduates.

A Contradictory Alliance

Despite wide-scale changes in household and paid work, the media and politicians continued to define family breakdown as a racial issue, confined primarily to African Americans and caused by a set of behavioral rather than economic problems. Such a definition served to reassure white workers that their own status as breadwinners could be preserved. Rather than uniting to demand wages adequate to support every family, workers responded in ways that split along the lines of race and gender. Conservatives appealed to the white working class by depicting marital breakdown as a problem among the poor that was aggravated by government transfer programs and proclaiming their desire to preserve the traditional family structure. As a result, many white male workers formed alliances not with African American men, or with the growing numbers of women workers of either race, but with employers and the New Right.

The economic difficulties of the 1970s badly hurt employers as well as the working class. Profits slowed in the late 1960s and early 1970s, and then became losses. The United States' share of the world's gross national product dropped from 40 percent in 1950 to 27 percent in 1973.[28]

Business owners also mobilized in response to threats to their well-being, turning toward right-wing politicians who rejected government interference with the market and pouring money into conservative think tanks. Not only in the declining traditional manufacturing industries but also in new sectors emerging in the West and South, areas that had long fed raw materials to northern factories, employers pursued a conservative course. This regional economic growth, tied to oil, agribusiness, and increasingly computer electronics, encouraged a crude libertarianism that supported men's power in the family. Traditional manufacturers also favored the family structure that had long accompanied their production.[29]

.   .   .

For many, the traditional division of labor between the sexes, long preceding the rise of industrial development in the United States, had a deep legitimacy. The loss of this old way of life thus seemed an unsettling violation of the natural order at a fundamental level, calling forth a response in moral and religious terms.

Right-wing politics took on a new shape in the early 1970s. Long opposed to government interference with the market, its focus shifted to a defense of traditional gender roles, as a new generation of conservatives both voiced their fears over the costs entailed in the loss of this old arrangement and saw a way to broaden their political base. Male leaders warned that the breakdown of the gender division of labor would seriously undermine men's power over women at home and in society as a whole. For female leaders, playing a visible part in conservative politics for the first time, support for women's work in the home lay at the center of their concerns.[30] The New Right also saw endorsement of the traditional family structure as a way to gain allies. It devised strategies to reach the white male working class by defending men's power in the home in the early 1970s. It also wrested leadership of the fight against abortion from the

Catholic Church in order to reach housewives seeking to protect their domestic realm.[31]

Threats to the established order between the sexes fed the growth of religious fundamentalism and drew its leaders into politics. Jerry Falwell, for example, the leader of the Moral Majority, which he founded in 1979, stated clearly that concerns over abortion and homosexuality had driven him to political action. The religious fundamentalist movement increasingly dominated conservative protest and gained a strong voice in the Republican Party, which also came to see defense of men's and women's traditional roles as an effective means of attracting a large group of voters.[32]

Many businesses, seeking to recoup losses or consolidate new gains, also shifted support to the Republican Party. Employers and politicians joined in appealing to workers and their wives by promising to preserve the traditional family structure and bring a return to past prosperity. Yet these business owners were at the same time abandoning the very arrangements with labor that had made the male breadwinner family possible.

In the first decades after World War II, employers had accepted unions, high wages, and the welfare state as the price of ensuring a stable workforce and a market for their goods. But as their profits fell, manufacturing firms could no longer afford such arrangements; and emerging industries, such as electronics firms in Silicon Valley seeking cheap labor, found them unnecessarily costly and constraining. Business leaders responded to the economic crisis unfolding in the 1970s by lowering wages, breaking unions, and attacking government support for the poor.[33]

Thus, in the late 1970s, an increasingly religious New Right, employers, white male workers, and housewives came together to voice support for the gender division of labor. However, their alliance contained sharp contradictions, as each group rejected part of the very arrangement it sought to retain. Employers and conservative politicians loudly championed the male breadwinner family even as they simultaneously denied men the means to support their loved ones. Working-class men and their wives wanted a family wage but expressed increasing hostility toward government support for women's work within the home. Thus, these groups were trying to hold onto the gender division of labor while at the same time rejecting the private and state supports necessary to sustain it. In the end, they succeeded not in restoring this old arrangement but in stripping it more completely from the working class and poor.

Initially, this loose coalition appeared to win some gains for traditional family values. Opposition to abortion carried many conservatives into office in the late 1970s. In 1977 they succeeded in passing the Hyde Amendment, which restricted the use of public funds for abortion, and they proposed a "family protection act" that offered support for traditional gender roles.[34] However, behind the championing of the traditional family, employers continued to pursue a strategy of low wages and hostility toward unions, and well-paying manufacturing jobs continued to disappear. The costs for workers were high. Individual income fell more in 1980 than at any point since the Great Depression. Again, African Americans suffered the most. The unemployment rate of black men was almost two and a half times that of white men.[35]

Still, rather than coming together to fight such losses, the working class remained divided by race, class, and gender. Well-paid workers and their wives were openly hostile to the poor, defining them as primarily black and female and blaming their hardships on a lack of personal effort. The conservative alliance of business and right-wing politicians also encouraged divisions among workers by launching intentionally racist campaigns.[36]

Throughout the 1970s, blue-collar workers in the Northeast and Midwest abandoned their traditional loyalty to the Democrats. Younger workers and those with few skills or protections against layoffs and wage cuts saw the capital–labor accord championed by the Democratic Party as having failed them. As wages fell and inflation rose, only government spending on social programs seemed to persist, generating heightened opposition to support for single mothers. While the poor, unemployed, African Americans and other minorities, and a growing number of working women voted Democratic in 1980, white male workers and their employers turned sharply to the Republicans, electing Ronald Reagan to the presidency.[37]

Families and Work in the 1980s

In the 1980s, the gender division of labor broke down more completely, as heightened economic difficulties placed further pressures upon this old arrangement. Political actions also hastened this breakdown and increased the hardships faced by many workers. The central casualties were the family wage and Aid to Families with Dependent Children, which were fatally weakened. Both had been key elements of the old framing of women's household work, committing business and the state to some support for tasks of family maintenance. Organized opposition to the dismantling of support for women's household work had faded. Instead growing numbers of wives and mothers began working for wages. A few, however, finding the market economy inhospitable, clung to their old way of life as it came apart around them.

Economic Difficulties and Political Reaction

The U.S. economy fell into a deep recession in the early 1980s. The Reagan administration responded by cutting business taxes and increasing defense spending. The growing national deficit raised interest rates and the cost of American goods, furthering the flight of manufacturing overseas. The government also supported the use of low-cost labor, failing to increase the minimum wage to keep pace with inflation and encouraging nonunion production. Economic conditions worsened for all but college-educated workers in the 1980s. As high-paying manufacturing jobs disappeared and the real value of the minimum wage shrank, hourly earnings fell for those who had not gone beyond high school.

Workers responded not by trying to restore the gender division of labor, through demands for a new family wage, for example, but by abandoning it. Men's economic difficulties were largely met by a further turn to paid work by their spouses or an avoidance of marriage altogether. Wives entered the labor force in ever greater numbers. By the early 1980s, more than half of white married mothers with high school educations were employed, compared to little more than one-third of such mothers in 1970.[38] These women were both taking jobs when their children were younger and putting in more hours in an effort to help meet their families' financial needs.

For some in the white working class, this strategy succeeded, but it also continued to introduce new tensions. Marriages broke down more rapidly in the 1980s than in any other decade for white high school–educated women. While established marriages continued to come apart, a growing number of young couples simply no longer formalized their relationships.

White women who had not finished high school, in the past the first to become brides, increasingly found themselves without husbands. The share who had never married rose by more than half over the decade. Divorce and separation also climbed sharply. The collapse of marriage seen in the 1970s among less-educated African American women was now taking place among white women as well.

For their part, African American families were under even greater pressures in the 1980s than in the 1970s. In the early years of the decade, the percentage drop in their median income was almost three times greater than that for white families. While the great majority of African American wives who had completed high school were already in the labor force by the mid-1980s, still more turned to paid work and others spent longer hours at their jobs to make up for their husbands' lost earnings.[39]

Again, changes at home accompanied these shifts. Divorce rates continued to rise among older black women, while the turn from marriage among younger high school graduates persisted. Among those with little education, marriage rates fell steeply. Only one-third of black women who had not finished high school were married by mid-decade, about half as many as in 1960.[40]

A Changing Economy

Thus, as the old rules and reasons holding couples together ended, and women turned increasingly to paid work, marriages became more vulnerable to economic and emotional pressures. At the same time, however, as the traditional forms of family life were coming apart, both the home and the economy were being rebuilt on new foundations.

Organized labor, though, was mainly looking backward, and did not see the new potential that was emerging or how to shape it to the advantage of a working class also taking on new form. Because they had not reached out to a broader range of workers in the preceding decades, unions were unable to win political and economic measures that would help the working class as a whole. By the 1980s, even pro-labor analysts were observing that most unions had become "dominated by a conservative white male gerontocracy that deeply opposes any mobilization that threatens their own power." By the mid-1980s, only 15.6 percent of workers with jobs in the private sector were in unions.[41] Scholars sympathetic to workers' difficulties, while skillfully dissecting the problems caused by de-industrialization and the limits of government strategies, also looked back to the old manufacturing jobs and the compact between business and labor that had enabled men to support their wives' work in the home.

However, as in earlier moments, the American economy was yet again undergoing a major sectoral shift. The industrial economy of the United States did not emerge full-blown but developed through several cycles of technological advance and decline, each of which laid the basis for further growth. The first wave of industrialization in the nineteenth century, based on textile production, soon faltered. Railroad construction then carried the country into a new period of prosperity, while also creating the transportation network necessary to distribute goods for sale. Overconstruction of railroad lines led to a deep recession at the end of the nineteenth century, ended in turn by new advances involving electricity and chemicals.[42]

In brief, in each cycle the leading sector ran into difficulties as its markets became saturated, its aging companies failed to reinvest their profits productively, and newer industrializing countries began to carry out such production at lower cost. At each point of crisis, prosperity was renewed by expanding into new geographical regions and sources of labor, inventing new technologies, and enacting social policies that placed more money in workers' hands. Failure to take such steps often resulted in long-term stagnation, as happened in the late nineteenth century when England, investing in defense rather than new scientific research, fell behind the United States and Germany.

The most severe economic downturn of the twentieth century, the Great Depression, was finally ended in the United States in part by a new cycle of development, led by the manufacture of automobiles, stoves, and refrigerators and the redistribution of wealth through the family wage, the policies of the New Deal, and women's increasing turn to paid work. These measures carried the American economy to world dominance after World War II. By the 1970s, however, the old manufacturing industries and the social arrangements accompanying them had reached their limits.[43] Instead, the greatest potential for growth lay in the emerging service sector. Yet many analyses saw the service sector as the cause of America's economic problems, rather than the solution.

Indeed, in the 1980s tax cuts on business profits and other elements of Reagan's supply-side program did encourage unproductive speculation in real estate and stocks. However, most analysts sympathetic to labor failed to see the larger, potentially progressive nature of the economic changes taking place. In part, gender bias blinded their vision. Workers in fast-food restaurants or health care centers were rarely viewed as engaged in productive labor that might achieve higher output or win higher wages, for much the same reason that the domestic tasks on which these businesses were built had earlier been dismissed. For many analysts, "real work" was tied to images of blue-collar workers and heavy machinery.[44] Organized labor and its supporters were therefore slow to recognize the emergence of a new working class or ally with it to claim a greater share of the gains arising from the transformation of women's domestic realm.

New Forms of Family Life

During the United States' new moment of economic growth a different type of family structure appeared, one no longer based on the old gender division of labor. By the early 1980s, opposition to the dismantling of the traditional relationship between the sexes had ebbed. Despite voicing its objections ever more loudly, the New Right had failed to restore the traditional framework of the family. Both the Supreme Court and the Senate rejected efforts to restrict women's reproductive rights, and three-fourths of those newly elected to Congress in 1982 supported abortion.[45] Instead, social acceptance of changes in gender roles increased. By the mid-1980s, less than half of Americans felt that women should focus on the home and men on success in the larger economy, and less than one-fifth felt that women should not work for pay. The social policies proposed to Congress shifted markedly, from attempts to return women to the home to provisions for domestic tasks shaped around their engagement in paid work.[46]

This shift in attitudes reflected the changing shape of the workforce. Behind the story of economic decline of the previous decade lay another one of progress, as some children from working-class as well as middle-class backgrounds gained college educations and began providing skilled labor for the upper tier of the emerging service sector. This growing group of professionals and managers, many of whom had rebelled in their youth against the restrictive framings of sex and marriage, displayed a greater acceptance of women's new role than did earlier generations.[47]

Opposition to gender issues also lessened as an increasing share of male workers had spouses who were also employed. By the early 1980s, most white wives and mothers had joined African American women in paid work. A new basis for home life was appearing, in which marriage was delayed until women as well as men were established in the wage economy. Later and more stable marriages became a pattern among college graduates of both races, though the marriages of those with less education continued to break down at high rates.[48]

Thus, this was a confusing time, in which the old arrangements that had supported women's work in the home were coming apart, while new forms of family life were only beginning to emerge. Developments in both directions often appeared similar on the surface. The sharp drop in marriage rates, for example, reflected two diverging paths. Many young women were postponing marriage until their positions in the workforce were secure. Others, in contrast, found that men were increasingly unable or reluctant to take on the burdens of a wife or child.[49]

Men's difficulties in finding good jobs were the focus of much discussion. Many could no longer earn wages sufficient to support a wife and children. High school–educated black men able to find jobs tended to work as poorly paid salesmen, construction workers, and janitors rather than in good union jobs. Few men without high school diplomas made enough money to keep a family out of poverty.[50]

However, women with little education also faced growing difficulties in the labor force, limiting their ability to contribute to family income. One-fifth of white high school dropouts in their early 20s and a far greater share of young African American women with little education seeking work were unable to find jobs.

Thus, while the old codes framing support for women's domestic tasks were disappearing, many were being denied access to the new foundations for family life, based on the earnings of both spouses. Women—especially those who failed to complete high school—were put in a very precarious position. By the mid-1980s, African American and white women without high school degrees had few prospects in the wage economy, while marriage was disappearing far more rapidly than their ties to the maternal role. Their access to secure control over their fertility also remained limited. Though most women who quit high school bore fewer children than had earlier cohorts, they continued to become mothers at an early age. More than three-fourths of black and white high school dropouts in their early 20s were caring for children. As they lost the protection of marriage, these young mothers became very vulnerable, especially since the state was withdrawing its support for household work as well.

Attacks on Aid to Families with Dependent Children

As the economic, legal, and cultural framings of women's work in the home came apart, state help for women's domestic tasks, in the form of Aid to Families with Dependent Children (AFDC), appeared increasingly anachronistic. Though often blamed for the breakdown of the traditional family, aid to single mothers was first proposed in the early twentieth century by middle-class housewives seeking to defend the domestic realm against the emerging industrial order, and was endorsed by a large segment of society. "Mothers' Aid is a wage paid to a mother to bring up her children," the state legislature of Pennsylvania had declared upon adopting such a program.[51]

But as early as the 1930s, support for women's household work had waned. The Committee on Economic Security only reluctantly included grants for single-parent families in the Social Security Act of 1935, renaming the policy Aid to Dependent Children and denying benefits to mothers themselves, who were seen as doing little in the home. "The very phrases 'mothers' aid' and 'mothers' pensions' place an emphasis equivalent to misconstruction of the intention of these laws," declared this committee. "These are not primarily aids to mothers but defense measures for children."[52]

The target of repeated reform efforts from the 1960s on, the program faced growing criticism and opposition in the 1970s. The cause of complaint was not government support itself, as new aid to the disabled and elderly poor was created in these years, and Social Security benefits were expanded with little protest. Nor was the issue simply women's turn to paid work, as dissatisfaction with aid to single mothers surfaced before most women, especially those with young children, were in the labor force. Though some analysts have pointed to the increasing share of African American women among AFDC recipients in the years after World War II, racism alone can not explain the growing rejection of welfare.[53] The real explanation is more complex, requiring once again a look at the domestic realm itself. Changing views toward women's work in the home intersected with issues of race to heighten hostility toward AFDC.

In the post–World War II period, the belief that women's household work deserved government support had largely vanished. Liberal policy makers in the 1960s War on Poverty viewed women on AFDC in sympathetic but negative terms, seeing them as "unemployable dependents." Reformers seeking aid for poor single mothers stressed their lack of education or their inability to hold down a job rather than the importance of their work in the home, though the majority of women on AFDC were caring for small children. Racism accelerated this devaluation of women's domestic tasks, as once again the work done by black women in tending to their own families was denied recognition.[54]

The souring of the economy in the mid-1970s heightened antagonism toward AFDC, as many saw government spending on women's domestic role as an unproductive use of the country's resources, especially when increasing numbers of men were no longer able to support their own wives' work in the home. Married women in families living just above the poverty level were the most likely to be employed, and the difficulties of their dual role often led them to resent women on welfare.[55]

Yet, like many housewives, many women on welfare resisted a turn to wage work. They too continued to value motherhood and the domestic role, though support for such work was rapidly vanishing. Moreover, because most women on welfare had no more than a high school education, they were likely to find only poorly paying jobs with no benefits. Though AFDC payments dropped in value in the late 1970s and early 1980s due to inflation, so did the minimum wage. Many studies have confirmed what these women had already figured out themselves, that it cost more to work than to stay on welfare.[56]

However, as growing numbers of women took jobs, those left behind became an increasingly isolated minority who were often attacked by the government and the press. In the 1980s, a conservative administration launched a full-scale assault on AFDC. Reagan circumvented the courts and many members of Congress that had balked at ending payments to single mothers in the absence of any alternative aid, using block grants to give states the power to dismantle much of the old entitlement. States were first urged and then required to institute "workfare" programs to force recipients toward the labor force. Some also tried to limit motherhood directly, capping payments to recipients who bore additional children or even encouraging once again their sterilization.[57] These steps took away one of the last pieces of support for the gender division of labor, leaving women little refuge from the demands of the market.

Women's Lives in the Late 1980s

By the late 1980s, the Democrats had regained the support of much of the working class and many employers, and an expanding group of professionals and technicians was embracing liberal social values.[58] The right wing, dominated now by religious fundamentalists, found itself alone in opposition to changes in the traditional family. Thus, a conservative alliance had not managed to halt the disintegration of the gender division of labor. Instead, it had furthered the old arrangement's demise by failing to protect the family wage and severely undercutting AFDC. At the start of the twentieth century, white middle-class women and their allies had been effective in fighting off the market's reach into the home. At the century's close, however, those defending the domestic realm had become a diminishing minority, unable to prevent such an intrusion. Both inside and outside marriage, financial, legal, and cultural support for women's household work was further reduced in the 1980s by economic pressures and by political actions, directed now primarily at those with the fewest resources to protect themselves against such attacks.

As the decade drew to an end, only remnants of the traditional manufacturing sector and the male breadwinner family remained. Most women now worked outside the home, and many spent long hours in such employment. In essence, women were turning from marriage to the labor force as their primary means of support.[59] However, they were doing so in strikingly different ways, resulting in a range of relationships to home and paid employment.

College Graduates

By the end of the 1980s, 55 percent of white women and 44 percent of African American women in their prime adult years had attended college, and approximately one-third of black women and one-half of white women in this group had completed four or more years.[60]

College graduates trying to combine paid employment with the domestic role in the 1960s and 1970s had had a difficult time. Many African American and white graduates born during World War II or the following decade had divorced. Now in their late 30s through early 50s, few had been able to combine high-paying jobs with motherhood. However, they had managed to make strong inroads into the professions.

The next cohorts of female graduates eased the strain of working both at home and for pay by increasingly waiting to take on the domestic role until they were established in their careers. Less than one-quarter of those in their early 20s were married in 1990, and far fewer were mothers. These steps appeared to create a new way to sustain family life, as the delay of marriage reduced divorce rates among younger women and resulted in more stable unions. Though marriage rates of less-educated women of both races continued to fall steadily in the 1980s, they showed signs of leveling off among both black and white college graduates.

By 1990, the vast majority of women who completed college, whether mothers or not, were in the labor force, and more than three-quarters were working full-time (see figure 1). These women had largely curtailed their domestic role to fit the demands of the labor force. Though pursuing careers while raising a family had proved unexpectedly difficult, well-educated women had made a highly effective turn to the wage economy. The majority found professional or

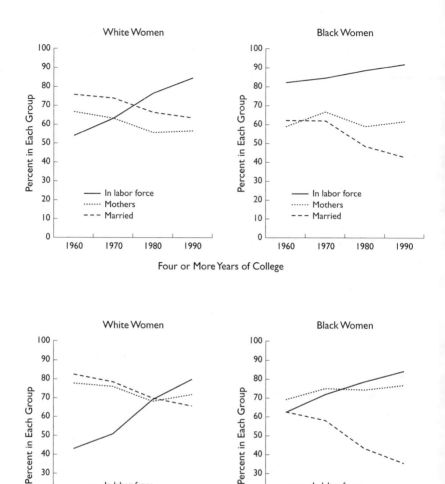

FIGURE I.

Labor force participation, motherhood, and marriage among college-educated women, by race, 1960–90. From author's calculations based on unpublished 1960–90 IPUMS data. *Mothers* are women ages 22–54 who have had one or more children.

managerial positions in the top tier of the expanding service sector in the 1980s, though African American college graduates were less likely to be in elite professions and had lower earnings than white graduates. The costs to their home life had also been far greater.[61]

High School Graduates

Women who were not college graduates also experienced dramatic changes. In 1960, African American as well as white women who had not graduated from college still gave the domestic role their primary attention. Over the ensuing decades, however, their lives altered greatly, as they turned strongly to the labor force and lost much of their support from men for their work in the home (see figures 1 and 2).[62] A look at those completing high school illustrates this change. By 1990, 38 percent of African American women and 35 percent of white women in their prime adult years had finished high school but not gone on to college. These women were both being pulled into paid work by expanding opportunities and being pushed into it as men's employment difficulties grew.

Black women completing high school had entered the labor force in large numbers in the 1960s and 1970s. Most ended up in clerical and sales work or in low-paying service occupations. Most had also found husbands and started families by their early 20s, and thus worked both at home and for pay throughout their first decades of adulthood. The majority of these early marriages fell apart, however, joined over the 1970s and 1980s with the increasing disappearance of formal unions among younger women. By 1990, most black women with four years of high school were putting in long hours at their jobs; a large percentage were also raising their children alone (see figure 2).

A similar pattern unfolded among white women who had completed high school, though it began to take shape more than a decade later. Despite some initial resistance, white wives with four years of high school had entered the labor force in large numbers in the 1970s and 1980s. Like their black counterparts, they worked as secretaries and salesclerks or, though to a lesser extent, in low-paying service occupations. They too took on more hours as their husbands' earnings fell. In the early 1970s, young white women who had finished high school had become wives and mothers much as those in earlier cohorts had done, though they had their children a bit later and fewer of them. However, many of these marriages soon ended in divorce. In the 1980s, the youngest among this group began marrying at lower rates, while divorce and separation persisted. Marriages ended or were avoided in part because a growing number of these women were refusing to stay with men who treated them badly. However, many then had to take on the difficult task of single parenthood, with little help for their efforts.

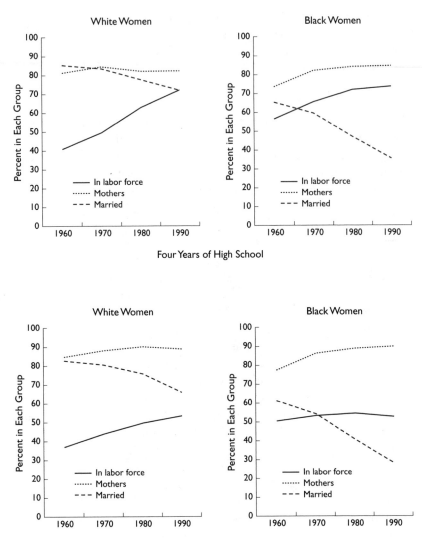

FIGURE 2.
Labor force participation, motherhood, and marriage among
high school–educated women, by race, 1960–90. From author's
calculations based on unpublished 1960–90 IPUMS data. *Mothers*
are women ages 22–54 who have had one or more children.

Thus, women of both races who finished high school but did not go on to college saw dwindling support for their work at home, which remained a central part of their self-definition. Rather than favoring paid employment over domesticity, African American and white women who completed high school straddled the two worlds, strongly pulled by the demands of each.

High School Dropouts

Black and white women who failed to finish high school found themselves in increasingly difficult straits, far behind other women. This group had grown dramatically smaller over the past two decades. By 1990, less than 10 percent of white women and 18 percent of African American women in their prime adult years had not completed high school.[63]

The turn to wage work had stalled badly for this group. In the thirty years since 1960, the labor force participation of white high school dropouts increased only half as much as for other white women (see figure 2). In the 1980s, unemployment rose among white dropouts, especially the youngest. Those who found jobs worked mainly in low-paid service occupations whose wages dropped over the decade. "I don't know one of my friends that has ever got a good job," observed one such single mother.[64] Personal relationships also fared badly among this group, which had held staunchly to traditional roles in the early 1970s, only to have their home lives shatter in the following years. By 1990, one-third of white high school dropouts, like college graduates, were not living with spouses. However, in sharp contrast to more-educated women, most dropouts on their own were divorced or, increasingly, never-married mothers.[65]

For the least-educated African American women, the 1980s were a disaster. Though still seeking employment, these women were less likely to secure jobs than their counterparts in 1960. The youngest women fared worst. By the decade's end, almost half of black female dropouts in their early 20s could not find work. As the market economy grew increasingly inhospitable, marriage rates fell even more precipitously than in the previous decade. Less than one-fifth of black high school dropouts under 35 were married.

African American women who had not completed high school were much less likely than white women with little education to find the jobs they sought or to gain support for their domestic roles through marriage. However, for both, the turn from marriage had taken a very different form than for more-educated women. Rather than postponing the start of their families until they secured good jobs, those quitting high school were struggling to hold on to the domestic role in the face of increasing odds. White dropouts still followed a pattern of early marriage followed by high divorce rates, though the practice of marriage was rapidly disappearing among the youngest. By 1990, most African

American high school dropouts in their late 20s were still single. Unlike most black college graduates, however, few would later wed.[66]

For African American and white women with little education, support for their domestic role was vanishing far more rapidly than their investment in this traditional path toward adulthood while they faced obstacles in gaining access to paid employment. Unlike more-educated women who were achieving careers, little lay ahead for these women. As at earlier points in history, once again an expanding market economy had "created . . . unusually acute social problems . . . for the emerging, exploited working class, a mass of people whom at this stage it was better at uprooting than at finding work."[67]

The growing difficulties faced by less-educated women over the second half of the twentieth century reveal the dark side of the encounter between home and market, a side few had anticipated. "Think what would happen to you if you suddenly had no husband and no savings," Johnnie Tillmon, a black single mother and a welfare rights activist, urged members of the National Organization for Women in the late 1960s. Her audience, though sympathetic, did not see poverty as a women's issue. A few years later, almost half of poor families in the United States were headed by women. Soon after, *the feminization of poverty* had become a common term.[1]

Over the following years, a multitude of studies established the role played by marital breakdown and the burdens of single parenthood in women's poverty, and marked similarities in the causes of economic hardship among both white and black women.[2] The dismantling of support for women's work in the home had clearly left many mothers with no effective way of providing for themselves or their children. However, in focusing on the loss of a husband, analysts failed see the larger nature of such poverty. Such focus obscured the steps single mothers took themselves to deal with such a loss, and the ways in which a changing market economy aided and impeded such efforts. It also encouraged the idea that the best solution to women's poverty was to strengthen the bonds of marriage, using the old gender division of labor to once again secure support for caregiving and other household tasks.

Explanations of women's poverty that repeatedly emphasize marital disruption or the burdens of single parenthood are vulnerable to a criticism made decades ago of discussions of the poor in general. Pointing to the "failure to see poverty in dynamic, or longitudinal terms," one historian stressed instead the difficulties that arise when people move from an older way of life into the wage labor force.[3] Indeed, the hardships faced by many men as they were pushed off the land and into work for wages are a well-known story, part of any history of working-class formation.

In this chapter, I set women's rising presence among the poor in the decades after World War II in a similar context. Rather than the result of simply "a time of transition" between husbands, it is here seen as tied to a far larger and more historic journey, that of women's turn from marriage to work for wages as their central means of support. By looking closely at women's poverty from this perspective, we can see important and hitherto unseen changes over time in how such poverty is caused and who it affects, as women turned to the labor force and reassessed their relationship to the domestic role, and as the shape of the market economy also altered. We also clearly see the importance of employment, as well as the presence or absence of a spouse, for women's economic well-being.[4]

The pattern that emerges, however, is not one of constant progress. While uncovering the gains made by a growing number of single mothers, such analysis also traces the formation of a female underclass, stemming not simply from men's loss of jobs but also from women's own shifting relationships to work at home and for pay. It also makes clear that marriage, though once the key to economic security for many women, was a solution better suited to the 1950s than to later decades. By examining the poverty faced by poor single mothers over the last decades of the twentieth century, we can gain a more detailed understanding of these changes.

Poverty in the 1960s

Poor Single Mothers in 1960

At the beginning of the period under consideration, poor women—here defined as women with an income at or below 125 percent of the government-defined poverty level—raising children on their own were much like other women (see figure 3). Though the great majority of poor African American and white unmarried mothers had not gone beyond high school, the same was true of most other women. Poor single mothers also held jobs fairly similar to those of other women. They were employed mainly as secretaries or salesclerks, if white, and in service work, primarily in private homes, if black. They were also caring for a similar number of children as other mothers who were of the same race.[5]

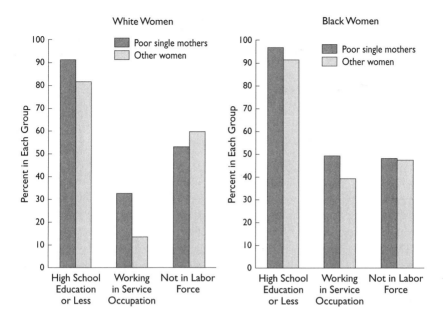

White Women   Black Women

FIGURE 3.
Poor single mothers compared to other women, by race, 1960.
From author's calculations based on unpublished 1960 IPUMS
data. *Mothers* are women ages 22–54 with at least one child
under 18 in the household.

The main difference was that poor single mothers had lost their husbands,
often with little warning, and with them all or a substantial portion of their traditional means of support. They were thus more likely to be working for wages
than other mothers, and to be putting in longer hours than other mothers who
were employed.[6]

In the first years after World War II, women were caught short by the breakdown in support for their caregiving and other household tasks. Forced to provide for their families on their own, the majority of white single mothers and
almost all black single mothers lived in poverty. Even women who had attended
college found it very difficult to raise children by themselves. Fully one-quarter
of both white and black unmarried mothers with college degrees were poor in
1960. Most women had not anticipated the loss of their old way of life and
work, and they were unprepared to earn their living outside the home. One
white single mother, after listing all the unexpected challenges she'd faced since
her divorce in the early 1950s, concluded, "The way might have been easier if
I had known what to expect."[7]

Society as a whole was unaware of this crisis beginning to unfold in women's lives. When two sociologists, Richard Cloward and Frances Fox Piven, ventured into Harlem in the mid-1960s to tell men of new employment programs that were part of the Johnson administration's War on Poverty, they found door after door opened by a poor black woman with a child at her side. The predicament of these mothers had been largely ignored by policy makers. Most faced options so limited that no amount of preparation on their part could have helped. Those employed were trapped in low-paid jobs that made it almost impossible to meet their families' needs.[8]

In general, employment was no guarantee against impoverishment. Because of their limited experience and opportunities in the wage economy, most women found a husband a more effective means of escaping economic hardship than a job. Figure 4 illustrates this point, showing how marriage and employment affected the likelihood of poverty for women in 1960. We can see that marriage reduced the chances of poverty by about 14 points more than did paid employment for the typical single mother of either race. But while either a husband or a job substantially improved the lot of a white unmarried mother, neither did much to lessen a black single mother's likelihood of being poor.[9]

Changes in Poverty over the 1960s

Over the 1960s, the fortunes of wives, and those of women overall, improved. At the same time, however, the number of marriages breaking apart or failing to form began to grow, leading to a rise in single motherhood among both black and white women.

The loss of a husband sharply reversed some women's improving fortunes. Black married women with high school degrees, for example, saw a dramatic rise in their standard of living during these years, which abruptly disappeared if their marriages ended. Women of both races who had started their families in the late 1940s and early 1950s were especially hard-hit by divorce. For white women in particular, intense focus on domesticity had left them with many children to care for and little training for or access to skilled jobs. Even most college graduates reported that they had considered a career far less important than the role of wife and mother when making their life plans.[10] Early studies of poor single mothers stressed the difficulties faced by "displaced homemakers," as these women came to be called. "For women who wed when young and have never held a job," a 1967 feature story in *Newsweek* observed, "divorce can be traumatic."[11]

More than one-fifth of white and black single mothers had little experience in the labor force; most of these women were "keeping house." Efforts at employment were also hampered by the absence of child care or other provisions

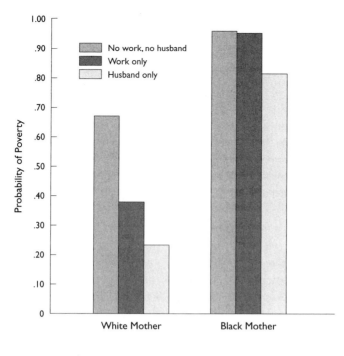

FIGURE 4.
Effect of marriage and work on probability of poverty for a typical mother, by race, 1960. From author's calculations based on unpublished 1960 IPUMS data. For details, see note 9.

for domestic tasks. In 1966, the Department of Labor reported that 40 percent of women not in the labor force but desiring employment gave "family responsibilities" or lack of "child care" as the reason. "A mother, particularly one without a husband," one study of poor women in the early 1960s concluded, "finds it very difficult to earn money outside the home."[12]

Such difficulties were heightened by discrimination by race as well as sex. The central problem for African American single mothers was less a lack of work experience than their confinement in poorly paying jobs, especially private domestic work, where median earnings were only one-third those of sales workers. Most older black single mothers in the early 1960s had spent long years in the labor force but seen little growth in their wages over time. "[My] marriage didn't work out," said one such woman, born in 1920, who had worked cleaning homes all her life. "But I still was stuck with a couple of children after the divorce. And I went on . . . work[ing] and working and working."[13]

Despite such obstacles, over the 1960s poverty dropped substantially for single mothers of both races, primarily as they made great gains in the wage economy. By the end of the decade, well over half of employed white and black single mothers were working full-time, many of them all year long. Both black and white single mothers had also completed on average one more year of school, thereby improving their returns from paid work.[14]

The reasons for the decrease in poverty differed somewhat by race, however. The share of white single mothers in poverty fell over these years primarily because they had turned strongly toward paid employment. This was especially true of younger women, most of whom continued to find work mainly as secretaries and salesclerks. As the head of one personnel agency handling college graduates reported, "My first question to every girl is, 'How fast can you type?' "[15] Though segregation in such work meant low earnings, the growing number of these jobs increasingly enabled white mothers to avoid severe economic hardship when on their own.

Poverty also dropped sharply for African American single mothers. However, this drop was due less to a turn to the labor force than to gains within it. Over the 1960s, an increasing number of black unmarried mothers found positions in offices, stores, and factories, often on a full-time basis, while employment in private domestic work fell steeply. One result was higher wages. Growing numbers of young black women set their sights on getting an education and a good job, and succeeded. One woman, forced to drop out of high school in the late 1960s when she became pregnant, recalled her determination to get her degree after having her baby: "I went back to school and I finished because I felt that was important to do," she explained. "[I]f you had a high school education that was very good back then. You could get a job."[16]

An expanding economy helped women cope with the loss of marriage, creating an abundance of jobs in schools and hospitals, as well as in sales and clerical work. For black women, movement outside the South also improved access to such jobs. Men's rising wages also helped somewhat, as single mothers living with their fathers or other male relatives benefited from an increase in family income. In many ways, young unmarried mothers in the late 1960s faced greater difficulties than had those a decade earlier. Fewer were widows, with claims on their former husbands' incomes, and many sought to set up their own households rather than live with relatives despite the greater cost of doing so. Yet overall, young single mothers of both races were more successful at avoiding poverty than those before them, mainly because of their success in the wage economy. White single mothers in particular were much more likely to combine care of children with work outside the home than in the past, and those outside jobs were likely to be better paying, especially for single black mothers.[17]

Between 1960 and 1970, poverty had dropped by 15 percentage points among both black and white single mothers. However, even the best-educated women were still badly hurt by the loss of a spouse. Among those who had attended college, more than four times as many African American single mothers, and almost seven times as many white single mothers, were as poor as those with husbands. Further, black women raising children on their own were still much more likely than white single mothers to be struggling to make ends meet. They had on average about one year less education than white single mothers, were often caring for an additional child, and were less likely to be widowed or divorced. More important, they had greater difficulty securing employment, especially of a full-time nature, and were in worse occupations, with a segment still trapped in private domestic service.

Poverty in the 1970s

In the 1970s, the breakdown of marriage accelerated among both white and black women, resulting in a further rise in single motherhood. Poverty is commonly seen as altering little for unmarried mothers in this decade, in contrast to the gains of previous years. In actuality, however, beneath the surface important changes were unfolding in different directions.[18]

Single Mothers Ages 25 and Older

As figure 5 makes clear, poverty continued to fall for single mothers 25 years of age and older, especially for those who were African American. This drop was caused in large part by continued gains in education. The 1970s saw a sharp rise in the proportion of single mothers of both races who had completed high school; an increasing share had also gone on to college. In addition, single mothers had fewer children to care for, as the high fertility rates of the baby boom years diminished. By the end of the 1970s, half of white single mothers had only one child under 18 at home, and most black single mothers were caring for one or two children rather than three or more.

White single mothers, especially those with college educations, increasingly turned to work for pay even when their children were little. A "survival manual" for divorced and separated women published in 1972 gave simple instructions on how to apply for a job. Those who had gone beyond high school found lower-level white-collar jobs; some landed professional or managerial positions, though they still faced many barriers. A career counselor offering advice to one divorced mother saw her as well qualified to move into a better-paying job. However, he warned, "you're in a conservative bank that's still, in my opinion, pretty tight about advancing women."[19] Those with less education

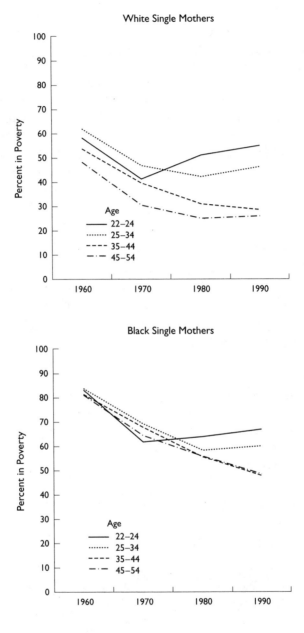

FIGURE 5.
Single mothers in poverty, by age and race, 1960–90.
From author's calculations based on unpublished
1960–90 IPUMS data.

had even fewer options and worked primarily in service occupations or, if lacking a high school diploma, in factories.

As in the previous decade, gains within the labor force rather than a further turn to paid work helped a growing share of African American single mothers avoid poverty. *Essence* magazine carried stories of one single mother who put herself through law school by starting her own business and of another who became an electrician. More-educated black single mothers secured professional, managerial, or sales positions, as well as jobs in factories and offices. "The promise of a fatter paycheck," reported *Ebony* magazine in 1977, "lure[s] many women out of clerical jobs into manual labor, sales or professional fields."[20] Even those who had not completed high school no longer worked in private domestic service.

There was still little recognition of the difficulties facing single mothers. An article by Diana Pearce, in which she coined the term "feminization of poverty," initially met with little interest. Finally published in 1978, its points would soon be taken up by many others: the inadequacy of child support awards and the failure to enforce even those relatively meager orders, the lack of child care, poor wages. Despite such hardships, growing numbers of women were managing to stay out of poverty through their own efforts, aided by some policies that chipped away at constraints to their employment.

Less-Educated and Young Single Mothers

The gains among single mothers who were employed were offset by others' growing difficulties in the wage economy and at home. An increasing number of African American single mothers of all educational groups, especially those who had once held blue-collar jobs, could not find work. Reliance on government aid rose, particularly among the least educated. For black single mothers, the way in which marriage ended or failed to occur mattered less than their own prospects for employment.[21] White single mothers, especially those with only a high school education or less, also turned to government aid in substantial numbers. However, their poverty rate rose due not only to lack of employment but also to the continued crumbling of their domestic realm. By the end of the decade, a growing share of these mothers were never married rather than widowed.[22]

Signs of trouble were most evident among the youngest of both races. Over the 1970s, the poverty rate rose steeply for white and black single mothers in their early 20s at almost every level of education.[23] These young mothers were having increasing trouble finding jobs, especially better-paying factory jobs. By 1980, two-fifths of black single mothers in their early 20s who sought paid work were unsuccessful, and unemployment climbed among young white single mothers as well.[24]

Problems in the labor force were joined with worsening circumstances at home. Never-married motherhood increased substantially among the youngest white and black women, many of whom chose to live on their own in poverty rather than with their parents. In the absence of any other policy providing support for tasks of family care, participation in welfare by the youngest mothers of both races—especially those who had never married—also rose sharply.

In many respects, these young women were caught between two worlds. The old codes that had protected them from unmarried motherhood were being rejected, but no rules safeguarding their interests were yet in place. While older women were actively framing the terms on which they would sleep with men and were protecting themselves from pregnancy, young girls faced relentless pressure and temptation to have sex, with little aid in navigating this terrain. The percentage of teens engaging in sexual intercourse before marriage climbed steeply over the 1970s, especially among white girls, but access to birth control failed to keep pace.[25] The vast majority of pregnancies among unmarried teenagers were not desired. However, the uneven breakdown of traditional moral codes left young women with little ability to refuse sex, prevent pregnancy, or achieve marriage, while they still took the maternal role seriously.

Though paths leading to paid employment were few and hard to find, motherhood had long represented the traditional female route to adulthood. Asked why they wanted to have a baby at an early age, poor black teens a decade earlier had responded with such answers as "So it can give me some responsibility of my own." The sociologist Joyce Ladner, noting that these girls "accepted and believed in the same symbols and criteria for achieving womanhood as their older sisters, aunts, mothers and grandmothers," had warned that it would be a long time before the maternal role lost its primacy.[26]

In the late 1970s, this role still had attractions for many young women of both races. Echoing the words of girls before her, one young expectant mother told an interviewer from *Parent Magazine*, "He or she . . . is my responsibility and I'm not going to shirk it." What did change abruptly over the decade was that far fewer pregnancies led to marriage.[27] While these young women could now avoid tying themselves to young men who were also struggling to survive, as single mothers they were taking on a heavy burden.

The main picture is that of a cohort of less-educated women setting out into a world where men could not be counted on, good jobs were becoming scarce, and hostility toward young single mothers was growing. Their lives would be plagued by these difficulties through the next decade as well.

Poverty in the 1980s

In the 1980s, unmarried mothers appeared to make little headway in avoiding economic hardship. In actuality, poverty continued to rise among some groups while falling among others, as patterns appearing in the 1970s grew stronger. Overall, by the end of the decade both white and black single mothers had completed more years of school, spent more hours in paid work, and had fewer children to care for than, on average, single mothers before them. However, behind this picture of apparent progress lay two divergent trends. As figure 6 shows, poverty rose steeply among less-educated single mothers of both races, especially white high school dropouts, while decreasing for college graduates. While all less-educated women and men did poorly in these years, women raising children on their own fared worst.[28]

Less-Educated Single Mothers

A deteriorating economy dealt a sharp blow to less-educated black and white single mothers in the 1980s. Though most single mothers had now completed high school, employment options for those not going on to college were growing worse. "The fact is," one such mother noted flatly, "the jobs just aren't out there."[29] Less-educated single mothers increasingly found work in poorly paying service and sales jobs rather than blue-collar, technical, or clerical positions. The prospects for the youngest looked particularly bleak. Though the loss of highly paid manufacturing jobs created hardships for many men, especially young black men with little education, young black women were also hurt when such jobs disappeared. The employment of black female high school dropouts in their early 20s in factory work dropped by more than 50 percent over the 1980s. These young women instead took work as low-paid cashiers, maids, and hospital workers.[30]

Employment in service occupations climbed among older unmarried mothers as well. Older white single mothers who had not completed high school, for example, also found work as health care attendants, cleaning women, and waitresses. African American single mothers were even more likely to be trapped in such jobs. By 1990, almost two-fifths of employed black single mothers who had not gone on to college worked in service occupations. Overall, service workers had the highest rate of poverty, lowest hourly wages, and fewest hours and weeks of employment of any workers.[31]

Further, finding work of any kind at all was becoming increasingly difficult, especially for those under 35. By the end of the decade, almost 40 percent of black single mothers in their early 20s with a high school education or less were unemployed. Even young single mothers with some college had a hard time in

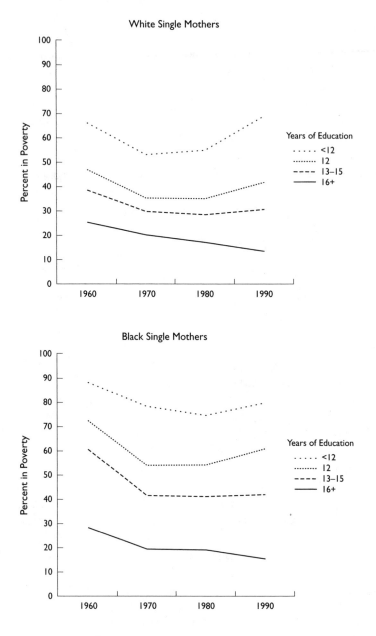

FIGURE 6.
Single mothers in poverty, by education and race, 1960–90. From author's calculations based on unpublished 1960–90 IPUMS data.

the 1980s; an increasing share ended up in low-paid service occupations if they could obtain work at all.[32] The central issue, though, was that real wages fell for less-educated single mothers wherever they managed to obtain employment. Whether working in factories, offices, or grocery stores, these women found their earnings shrinking as inflation rose.

Though all women without college educations had difficulty in the 1980s, single mothers faced the greatest hardships. Among black women, for example, unmarried mothers were more than one and a half times as likely to be poor as unmarried women without children, mainly because they had the worst jobs and worked fewer hours. Further, while a job at a fast-food restaurant or grocery store might keep a woman on her own out of poverty, it rarely sufficed when she had dependents. The difficulty of supporting a family on such low pay was a common theme in studies of welfare mothers in this period, who were being forced into jobs or job training as a condition of receiving assistance. "Every one of [my friends] has gotten jobs like at fast food places," one such welfare recipient observed in the late 1980s, "and can't make it, and then they get back on Public Aid again."[33]

As opportunities in the wage economy worsened, conditions at home also continued to deteriorate. Support for the domestic realm, all but gone among less-educated black women, was unraveling rapidly for white women with a high school education or less. Those entering their late 20s and early 30s continued to grapple with the difficulties of never-married motherhood, while a much greater share of young women in the cohort after them were having children on their own.

The poverty facing less-educated women of both races took on a new form as the cultural framings of marriage became undone and increasing numbers of couples lived together without marrying. A growing number of poor single mothers lived with male partners. While some of these men were poor themselves, others were quite well-off, allowing a small percentage of single mothers to live in what we might call debatable poverty. A woman's access to her partner's income was uncertain, however. While marriage still imposed some obligations on men toward their wives and children, and some possibility of support even if the relationship ended, cohabitation offered far fewer protections.[34]

Among white women, problems at home and in the labor force were accompanied by a continued rise in reliance on government aid among the least educated. Well over two-fifths of white high school dropouts under 35 were on welfare by the end of the decade. Among black women, the share of less-educated single mothers on government aid did not climb over the 1980s, though the rate remained at a higher level than among white single mothers.

The shrinking value of AFDC payments meant increased hardship for those forced to rely on such support.

Thus, despite finishing high school and often going to college, having fewer children, and persisting in the labor force, both black and white less-educated single mothers lost ground in the 1980s. While a growing share of young mothers were never married rather than divorced or widowed, the central issue was the decreasing value of their wages (and less so, AFDC) as the policies pursued by employers and the government in the 1980s exacted a harsh cost.

In general, for women moving through their first decades of adulthood, the 1980s were difficult years in which to establish any foundation to build a life, unless they were equipped with a college degree. By the end of this decade, poverty among less-educated single mothers had climbed above the levels of two decades earlier, especially among white women, in part because young single mothers in this group were having a very hard time. Their situation would have been even worse had many not taken shelter in their parents' homes. The share of white single mothers heading households dropped back almost to the level seen in 1960, and it fell somewhat for black women as well.[35]

College Graduates

College graduates of both races had a markedly different experience than less-educated women. Over the past two decades they had entered paid employment in large numbers and were aided by the persistence of good job opportunities. In the 1980s, poverty continued to drop among unmarried mothers with four years or more of college. In part, this group was growing older, with many now in their late 30s and early 40s. The main issue, though, was that most of these mothers were now full-time year-round workers, and more were in professional and managerial positions. Such gains offset the hardships caused by the ongoing breakdown of marriage.

Their ability to support themselves on their own earnings also brought a new twist to single motherhood, as some college graduates actively chose to have children on their own. Though the fictional pregnancy of Murphy Brown, a reporter on a television sitcom, dominated discussions of this phenomenon, it also involved real women. Organizations with names like Single Mothers by Choice sprang up in Chicago and other metropolitan areas; even the staid *Ladies' Home Journal* ran a story of a woman deciding to become pregnant and have a child by herself. However, only a tiny fraction of women were pursuing this course. On the whole, unmarried college graduates escaped poverty by increasingly avoiding single motherhood altogether.[36]

Over the 1970s and 1980s, a growing number of college graduates had postponed the domestic role in favor of careers. Now many of these women were entering late and more stable marriages. As already noted, less-educated women still took on motherhood at an early age and then found themselves caring for children alone, either because their marriages had fallen apart or, as was becoming more common, because they never married. As a result, less-educated women were increasingly overrepresented among single mothers, especially those in poverty.[37]

Thus, in the 1980s we see the culmination of patterns that began unfolding over earlier years. College graduates, though initially poorly prepared for the loss of their husbands' incomes, learned fairly quickly to rely on their own wages instead, helped by their increased access to good positions in the market economy. Poverty fell substantially for this group of both black and white single mothers between 1960 and 1990, and much of the drop took place after 1970, especially among white women. Moreover, a growing share of young college graduates avoided single motherhood altogether, postponing both marriage and children.

However, among less-educated women, marriage had decreased more rapidly than motherhood, especially among those failing to finish high school, while good jobs became harder to find, and wages and government aid shrank. These women were caught between the continuing collapse of their old means of support and worsening prospects in the wage economy.

Poverty by Cohort

Another way to get a sense of these changes is to consider them in terms of cohorts, so that we can see how successive waves of women coped with their changing economic landscape. Most mothers of the early baby boomers, women who began their families in the first decade after World War II, found themselves in dire straits if they lost their husbands, for they often had many children, little work experience, and access only to poorly paying jobs.

In the next two cohorts, the war generation and the early baby boomers, poverty dropped sharply among both black and white single mothers in part because of their gains in education and their decreased fertility. Most important, though, was their changing relationship to the wage economy. White single mothers turned strongly to paid employment; black single mothers made gains by shifting out of private domestic service into clerical and sales jobs and working longer hours. Their efforts were aided by legislation banning discrimination by sex and race. The result was that the early baby boomers fared markedly better than their mothers' generation when raising children on their own, despite the rise in rates of divorce and never-married motherhood.[38]

Yet the great gains in dealing with marital breakdown did not continue over what are often called the *late baby boom* and the *bust* cohorts. Single mothers coming of age in 1980 actually did worse than those before them. Poverty rates climbed among both races for all but those with college degrees. Progress stalled for single mothers entering adulthood in the 1980s partly because the sharp rise in education and employment seen in the two previous cohorts leveled off, as did the decrease in fertility.

Further, marriage rates dropped substantially for these women in their early 20s. But while college graduates also delayed having children, never-married motherhood soared among less-educated white women and continued to rise among black women, though less rapidly than earlier.[39] But changes in the wage economy played a greater role in the rise in poverty, especially for black single mothers. Young single mothers in the 1980s really felt the loss of good jobs. A growing number could not find any work, and fewer of the jobs they did get were blue-collar or clerical positions. Instead, a growing segment could find only low-paid service occupations. Most crucially, real wages fell for those without four years of college, wherever they were able to obtain employment.

Thus, women in these two later cohorts entered adulthood in very difficult circumstances, especially if they did not go on to college. Support from marriage and from the government was diminishing, while they as well as their partners found fewer opportunities in the wage economy. By 1990, both black and white young women with high school educations or less were more likely not only to be single mothers but also to be raising their children in poverty than they were twenty years earlier.

Women's Poverty, 1960–1990

In sum, as support for women's old ways of life and work fell away, women were turning in large numbers to the wage economy and making solid gains within it. Their employment helped a growing number of unmarried mothers avoid poverty when on their own, especially in the 1960s and 1970s. But worsening job options, particularly in the 1980s, joined with few new supports for tasks of family care, stalled their progress, trapping many less-educated women in lives of hardship.

The Changing Causes of Poverty

Women's entrance into and gains within the market economy not only helped a growing share of single mothers avoid poverty but also altered the causes of and solutions to such hardship. Whereas in 1960 the presence or absence of a husband had the greatest impact on women's economic circumstances, this was

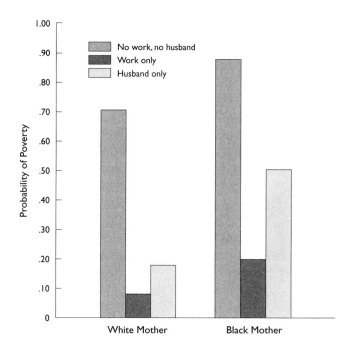

FIGURE 7.
Effect of marriage and work on probability of poverty for a typical mother, by race, 1990. From author's calculations based on
unpublished 1990 IPUMS data. For details, see note 40.

no longer true thirty years later. Instead, as women looked increasingly to their
own wages to meet their needs and got better jobs or worked longer hours, the
role of paid employment came to play a greater role in keeping women out of
poverty, far more so than marriage. This was true even for those caring for children on their own.

Figure 7 illustrates these changes among both black and white unmarried
mothers. By 1990, employment reduced poverty by more than 60 percentage
points for the typical white and black unmarried mother, and markedly more
so than a spouse. A husband was no longer the most effective way for mothers
to avoid economic hardship, in part because less-educated men themselves were
facing difficulties in the changing economy. For black mothers in particular,
marriage had become a second-rate strategy for escaping poverty.[40]

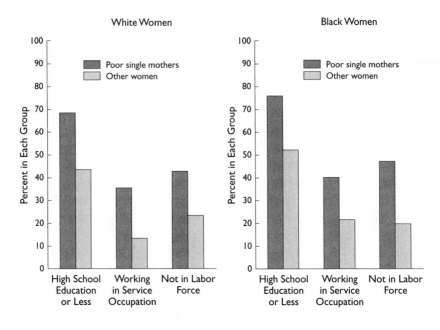

FIGURE 8.
Poor single mothers compared to other women, by race, 1990.
From author's calculations based on unpublished 1990 IPUMS
data.

The Changing Characteristics of Poor Single Mothers

More than the causes of poverty had changed. While poor unmarried mothers
were once fairly similar to other women, this was no longer true by 1990. Figure 8 illustrates the growing share of poor single mothers with little schooling,
in service occupations, or with no employment at all, compared to other
women. In 1960 there had been little difference in education between single
mothers and other women, for example (see figure 3). Thirty years later, the
great majority of both poor white and black single mothers still had not gone
beyond high school, but more than half of other white women and more than
two-fifths of other African American women had attended college. Also, poor
unmarried mothers now held worse jobs than other women. In 1960, poor
black single mothers were not much more likely than other black women to
work in service occupations; by 1990, they were more than one and a half times
as likely to do so. Poor white single mothers were also increasingly overrepresented in these low-paying jobs.[41]

The most important difference, however, was that single mothers had fallen

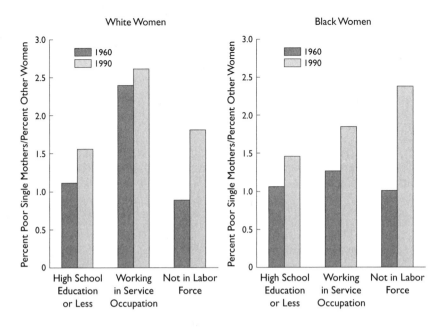

FIGURE 9.
Ratios comparing poor single mothers to other women, by race,
1960 and 1990. From author's calculations based on unpublished 1990 IPUMS data.

far behind the rest of the population in participation in the labor force. In 1960, as figure 9 makes clear, they were as likely (if black) or only slightly less likely (if white) to be employed. By 1990, however, they lagged well behind other women in this area. The central change was that while once a far smaller share of married women with children had worked for pay than women without husbands, over the previous thirty years they had first caught up with single mothers and then passed them by. In sum, as women spent more years in school, turned further to the labor force, and gained access to better occupations, poor single mothers were increasingly those who were not able to take these steps.

While these changes in the nature of poverty occurred among both black and white women, one essential aspect of such hardship remained the same. In 1990, as in 1960, the poverty rate of black single mothers was one and a half times that of white single mothers. Black single mothers were less likely to be college graduates, to have only one child, or to be divorced rather than never-married. Just as important, however, they had greater difficulty securing full-time jobs or any work at all; their unemployment rate was twice that of white single mothers. Also, fewer were employed in professional, managerial, or technical positions than white single mothers with similar levels of education. Thus, black women remained overrepresented among poor unmarried mothers.

·   ·   ·

Thus, over the last decades of the twentieth century, we see the growth of a female underclass, for reasons of women's own. The disappearance of good jobs for men was only one piece of this story.[42] The central event was the collapse, in the first decades after World War II, of the frameworks supporting women's work in the home, which threw many mothers into poverty.

Nevertheless, an increasing number of women who found themselves without husbands were able to negotiate an effective turn to the wage economy and to find better positions within it, thereby managing to keep their children out of poverty or to avoid the trap of single motherhood altogether. Such gains, however, were stalled by deteriorating employment opportunities for those with less education, many of whom remained strongly tied to the domestic role.

The picture of women's economic hardship presented here is more dynamic than that given in earlier accounts, showing its ties to the shifting circumstances of women's own work. Marriage, or its absence, did not remain the central determinant of the economic well-being of successive waves of women. Instead, their situation changed markedly, as increasing numbers of women adjusted to the new primary source of their support—their own wages. Even more might have done so had better jobs or provisions of support for tasks of family care been available.

Some might argue from this analysis that women could, if they simply applied themselves, follow earlier groups up the economic ladder. But more important are its implications for a new moment of policy formation. Women's turn to paid work did not simply help them avoid poverty. It also played an important role in the exceptionally long stretch of prosperity enjoyed over the last years of the twentieth century, in part as the breakdown of support for women's work in the home created a pool of labor that helped make possible the rapid growth of a "new economy" in the 1990s. The next chapter looks at the consequences of women's turn to the market, and the commercialization of many household tasks, both for society as a whole and for women themselves.

In 1960 most women, both white and African American, were married. Though a growing number also worked for pay, the days of most still revolved mainly around care of their immediate families, as they made breakfast, readied their children for school, cleaned their homes, ran a load or two of laundry, and shopped for the evening meal. Woven into these daily tasks were those of lending support to an extended network of kin, as toddlers became teenagers, husbands strayed or proved difficult, and parents grew frail.[1]

Today most women as well as men rush out the door each morning, many dropping their children at day care centers on their way to work. Some start their days removing a brain tumor or assessing the progress of twenty or more expectant mothers. Others prepare meals for an entire high school or office building. No longer tending only to their own aging parents, women are also seeking the underlying causes of senility or caring for scores of elderly patients.

Out of the ashes of the dying manufacturing sector and women's domestic realm, whose declines dominated the 1970s and early 1980s, a new economic and social order has emerged, ushering in a long wave of prosperity that has lasted through the beginning of the twenty-first century. While analysts of this "new economy" have focused on computers and other high-tech inventions, there is an unseen side to such development. This latest moment of growth has been driven in large part by the transformation of women's work in the home into work done for pay.

This transformation has had enormous consequences, not only for women and their families but also for the American economy. For women themselves, the very core of their lives has altered as they have turned in large part from domestic tasks performed within marriage to work for wages as their central means of support. In itself, this is a historic event, one of the major occurrences of the late twentieth century. However, the takeover of women's old domestic realm has also played an important but as yet little-noted part in recent economic growth.

Earlier chapters have shown how the absorption of much of women's household work by an expanding market in the first decades after World War II led to the dismantling of the old framework that had supported such labor, a change that created many unanticipated hardships for women. The loss of much or all of their traditional livelihood threatened many women with poverty until they could gain secure access to paid employment. However, the breakdown of women's old domestic economy was not simply negative. Its collapse has created a large pool of potential workers enabling the rapid growth of both the upper and lower tiers of the service sector. The conversion of tasks once done in the home into market activities has also spawned many new businesses.

This transformation has had benefits for women as well as Wall Street, as seen in the increase in women's earnings and their access to occupations once reserved for men. However, it has also given rise to new problems. Most significantly, while the market takeover of women's household work has generated an abundance of wealth and time, few of the gains in productivity and profits have come to women or their families.

Before exploring these problems further, we need to look more closely at the changes that have taken place. In this chapter I lay out clearly the ties between recent developments in the American economy and the transformation of women's domestic realm and examine their consequences, both for the world of work and for women themselves.

Women's Work and the Growth
of the American Economy

In the last quarter of the twentieth century, the U.S. economy changed dramatically as expansion of the service sector, which had been strong since World War II, accelerated further. By the end of the 1990s, only 15 percent of jobs were in manufacturing. More than 80 percent of workers were located in the service sector, which continues to generate most new employment.[2]

This shift was initially deplored and blamed for the drop in productivity that plagued the U.S. economy in the 1970s and 1980s. Traditionally the service sector has been seen as the area that, in contrast to the production of real goods, handled the shipping and sales of such products and maintained or serviced existing goods, firms, and workers themselves. In the eyes of many, the growing service sector thus appeared to be a parasite that threatened to devour the productive core of the American economy. The expansion of the financial, insurance, and real estate sectors and the replacement of high-wage manufacturing jobs with poorly paid service occupations contributed to such negative assessments.[3] Yet rather than crippling American productivity, the service sector has been the site of much recent growth, both through research that has led to revolutionary inventions and through the creation of many jobs.

The rise of this new sector helped lift the United States out of a recession tied to the decline of traditional manufacturing. With its growth, the economy was expanding into new areas that could generate great profits. It grew in part through technological advances in computers and communications. However, it also grew by reaching further outward, into regions not yet fully under its domain. Many analysts have noted the movement of the U.S. economy westward and overseas, where the development of new geographical regions brought financial gains.[4]

However, the market was also expanding into another less-noticed area, turning the bulk of tasks still done in the home into work done for pay and women themselves into wage workers. This change also created new profits, as household chores became services for sale and as women, freed from long hours of domestic drudgery, put their energies into more productive labor. A closer look at this process reveals the key role played by the transformation of women's tasks and labor in the rise of the new economy of the late twentieth century.

· · ·

While many recognize that the service sector has been the source of technological breakthroughs and the bulk of new jobs, attention has focused on changes in business services. Advances in computer software and telecommunications, which have revolutionized the handling of information, have indeed brought gains in productivity. Life without the Internet, e-mail, faxes, and cell phones now seems unimaginable. But advances in other areas have also been central to recent growth. As one economist observes, "The computer . . . is the basis for many new goods and services. . . . [However], perhaps the most dramatic examples of the creation of new services 'wants' have been in the health and medical services industry."[5]

Many of the developments at the forefront of medical research involve tasks that were long an intimate part of women's domestic role. Conception, pregnancy, and even the cloning of human tissue have become the focus of lucrative ventures. Biogenetics is frequently touted as the wave of the future.

The conversion of women's domestic tasks into work done for pay has also been the area of greatest job growth over the past thirty years. Economists have commonly referred to the service occupations dealing with food preparation, home cleaning, and routine health and personal care as *women's work* because they involve tasks that were long part of women's daily household routine. Some economists are now stressing that another, much larger segment of the service industries—health, education, and social services—also involves the public provision of work once carried out in the home, namely, the caregiving traditionally done by women. The economists Nancy Folbre and Julie Nelson note: "While some of women's tasks were largely instrumental—cleaning and cooking, for example—[w]omen were [also] in charge of children, the elderly and the ill."[6] They provided the emotional and physical labor that helped the young learn the skills necessary for adult life, aided the sick in regaining their strength, and eased the decline of those at life's end.

There is growing recognition of the economic contribution made by women's unpaid work in the home. The failure to count women's domestic labor for their own families as work by census takers and in national income accounts has contributed to a chronic devaluation of their labor. Further, women's work, especially that of caregiving, is also undervalued when done in the market. Though the benefits of such care extend far beyond its immediate recipients, those performing such tasks are poorly paid for their efforts.[7]

This chapter draws attention to another important, but little-noted, piece of this process, that of the gains created by the transformation of women's household work, not only through technological advances but also through the conversion of such tasks into work done for pay. Failure to see this contribution has also played a key role in the unequal distribution of its rewards.

Market provision of work traditionally done by women in the home, in the form of "professional care services" and tasks of cleaning, food preparation, and routine care, has dominated recent economic growth. Between 1970 and 2000, employment in these areas of women's work, more largely conceived, rose steeply and steadily, outstripping all other job growth (see figure 10). Almost two-fifths of the increase in jobs since 1970 was due to market takeover of household and caregiving tasks. Such takeover has markedly changed the face of the American economy. By the mid-1990s, more workers were employed in providing food, lodging, and health services than in all of manufacturing.[8]

Though business services also grew rapidly over this period, they make up a

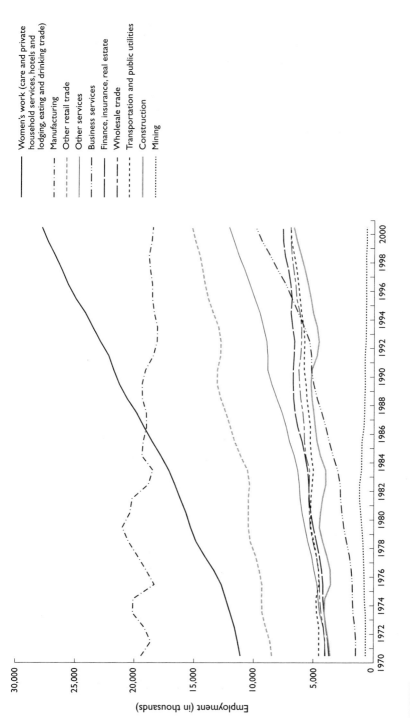

FIGURE 10.

Employment growth (in 1000s) in the private sector, by industry, 1970–2000. From author's compilation of successive years of data from Bureau of Economic Analysis, National Income and Product Accounts tables.

much smaller segment of the economy, employing approximately half as many people as the areas of women's work. Further, though computer-related work rose sharply in the 1990s, much of the growth in business services was in the area of temporary help, as using "just-in-time labor" became a common strategy. Many agencies were supplying maids, cooks, and other food service workers for offices and institutions. Thus, even in the last decade of the twentieth century, the area of women's work continued to dominate growth. "Huge gains [arose] from serving people," the Department of Labor concluded after examining employment trends in the 1990s.[9]

Household Tasks and the Market

Behind the job growth in the U.S. economy lay the rapid conversion of many of women's remaining household tasks into work done for pay. In the 1950s and early 1960s, much of family life centered around the breakfast and dinner table. The kitchen was women's primary domain and meal preparation was one of the most time-consuming of domestic chores. Though the hamburger had been invented by the early twentieth century, most Americans still ate at home. "[In] the 1950s and 1960s," the co-founder of Burger King recalls, "the fast food business and chain restaurant operations were still virtually unknown. . . . [We] were pioneering a new, relatively untried and untested concept in food service."[10]

The number of meals purchased outside the home grew rapidly in the late 1960s, as fast-food outlets—led by the golden arches of McDonald's—appeared in ever more towns across America; chains aimed at a more upscale market followed. One key to their success was the conversion of meal preparation into a factory-like production process that carefully standardized all steps, from the making of french fries to the grilling of burgers and even exchanges with the public, to ensure that "buying a hamburger at one store differ[ed] little from buying it at another."[11]

By the 1990s, spending on food prepared away from home had doubled compared to the early 1960s. Employment in eating and drinking places had grown twice as fast as the rest of retail trade, and food service sales had reached more than $250 billion, far beyond any of the early founders' wildest dreams. The chains that survived, many of which had begun as small roadside stands or restaurants, had either been taken over by big companies like General Foods or had grown to resemble them.[12] In recent years, grocery stores have also taken on the tasks of meal preparation. New chains offering expansive selections of ready-to-eat meals are driving older supermarkets out of business. Cooks have joined butchers behind the counters, preparing a vast array of freshly made dinners each day for immediate consumption or for quick reheating at home.[13]

The market's provision of the basics of home life has reached into people's nights as well as their days. The transiency once characteristic of traveling salesmen is now a regular feature of family life, as many workers routinely spend parts of each month or even each week out of town. These travelers must purchase not just meals away from home but places to sleep, spurring employment growth in hotels and other lodgings.[14]

.   .   .

Household cleaning has also been transformed by the market. The conversion of women's domestic tasks into work done for pay began with the hiring of domestic servants to help with household chores, much as field hands were used in agricultural tasks. In the late nineteenth and early twentieth centuries, many housewives themselves commonly employed a single long-term worker, often on a full-time basis. By the 1950s, a number of small family enterprises were offering cleaning services. In the following decades, large companies took over these small firms or drove them out of business. Cleaning companies nearly tripled in size over the 1980s, and in the following years expanded across the nation through franchises. By the mid-1990s, the largest companies were taking in almost $2 billion a year. Today agencies with names such as "Dial-A-Maid" and "Minit-Maid" employ crews of workers that sweep rapidly through a series of houses each morning, and still more in the afternoon. "Trained teams clean your home in one hour," one such company now boasts.[15]

The area of greatest expansion, however, has been health care. For centuries, women have nursed ailing family members and tended to the needs of aging parents. Though medicine largely became the province of highly trained specialists using sophisticated technology, day-to-day care of the sick remained one of women's central domestic tasks. Over the past three decades such routine care has increasingly shifted to paid workers. Jobs in health care have grown at six times the rate of manufacturing positions—indeed, more rapidly than any area except computer work.[16]

At the dynamic core of this growth is the market takeover of the simplest level of tending to the sick, through provision of care in the home. In 1985, a survey by the National Association for Home Care found that "only 38% of the population could name a home health care service."[17] Since then, home health care has expanded faster than any other industry. Central to such expansion was the creation of a new occupation, that of "home health aide," which quickly became one of the areas of greatest and fastest job growth. These aides now make up the bulk of workers tending to the needs of the sick in their homes, outnumbering doctors, nurses, or physical therapists. Moving from one household to another, they help their patients bathe and eat, make patients' beds, and see that they take their medications. The aides' duties, as outlined in official job descriptions, involve services "traditionally . . . provided by family members in the home"[18]—that is, the work once done by wives and mothers.

More dramatic still is the conversion of yet another layer of routine physical care into work for wages, as daily care of small children and aging family members also shifts to the market. In the last years of the twentieth century, commercial provision of such care exploded, outstripping most other areas of employment.[19] Though the numbers of the elderly have grown, their use of paid caregivers has risen far faster. Almost one-fourth of old people need help with such basic tasks as getting dressed or eating. Providing such aid has traditionally been part of women's domestic role. However, with the appearance of another new and swiftly growing occupation, that of "home care aide," such chores are also being converted into work done for pay. These aides give assistance at its most rudimentary level, stripped of any medical component. As the Department of Labor explains, "personal and home care aides provide mainly housekeeping and routine personal care services. They clean clients' houses, do laundry, . . . shop for food, and cook."[20] Residential centers for the elderly that offer meals, household cleaning, and assistance with daily tasks have also proliferated.

Care of young children is also moving rapidly into the marketplace, making up one of the largest areas of job growth in the past decade. By 2000, well over 1 million people, a number surpassing all those employed in secondary school education, were being paid to care for infants and toddlers. More than half of American preschoolers now spend much of their day outside their own homes, tended by paid workers.[21] Routine care of the sick, elderly, and young has led overall job growth in recent years, and such jobs are expected to keep growing more than twice as fast as the economy as a whole in years to come.[22]

In short, the dramatic expansion of the service economy has been driven in large part by the conversion of chores long done by women in the home into work for wages. Overall, about one-quarter of employment in the service-producing sector involves tasks that were once a central part of women's household work.[23] The commercialization of women's domestic realm will continue to provide the bulk of new employment over the first decades of the twenty-first century.

The Growth of the Gross Domestic Product

The move into the market of work once done by women in the home not only has dominated job growth but also has made up an increasing share of the nation's gross domestic output, contributing to the prosperity seen at the twentieth century's close. Total output in the United States grew from approximately

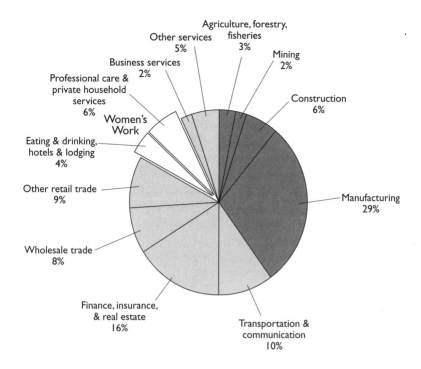

FIGURE 11.
Women's work as share of private-sector GDP, in current dollars, 1970. From author's calculations based on Bureau of Economic Analysis, Annual Industry Accounts Data, Gross Domestic Product by Industry, 1970. For a definition of women's work, see page 102.

$1,000 billion in 1970 to more than $9,000 billion by 2000. Controlling for inflation, this is an increase of over $5,000 billion.[24]

Industries providing care, hotel and lodging, and eating and drinking services have played an increasingly important role in this growth. Their contribution to private-sector GDP alone has grown by 50 percent since 1970, while that of manufacturing has shrunk by more than one-third (see figures 11 and 12). Altogether, the areas of women's work now make up 15 percent of the nation's private-sector output, over twice as much as that of business services. They are also one of the largest contributors to the overall gross domestic product.[25]

The practice of not counting women's unpaid work in the home leads to an overestimate of the gains from the movement of such work into the market, in terms of the growth of the GDP.[26] But even when the value of household chores

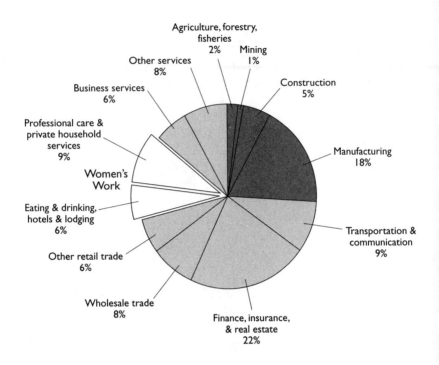

FIGURE 12.
Women's work as share of private-sector GDP, in current dollars, 2000. From author's calculations based on Bureau of Economic Analysis, Annual Industry Accounts Data, Gross Domestic Product by Industry, 2000. For a definition of women's work, see page 102.

is taken into account, the transformation of these tasks and labor into work for pay has brought real and substantial increases in productivity and income for employers and for the nation as a whole. Also, given that women's housework is still excluded from national accounting systems, to count it only when assessing the value of women's work in the market unfairly lowers such estimates. Clearly, whether we look at the growth of jobs or at contributions to the nation's gross domestic output, the market takeover of tasks once done by women in the home has been crucial to the recent growth of the American economy.

The Importance of Women's Paid Labor

Women as a Key Source of New Workers

Women have been and will continue to be a central source of labor fueling economic expansion. They have filled over 60 percent of the more than 65 million jobs created since the mid-1960s and are expected to make up two-thirds of new workers in coming years.[27]

Though they have long predominated in low-paid service and clerical jobs, women are now also providing an important and growing share of highly skilled workers. More than half the growth in jobs in the 1980s and 1990s was in professional, managerial, and technical positions, as the upper tier of the service sector expanded rapidly, and women supplied the majority of these new workers.[28] Over the last two decades of the twentieth century, the proportion of women working in such upper-tier jobs increased dramatically, growing by more than half for white and black women in their prime adult years.[29]

Women were able to provide such skilled labor because many born after World War II had put their time freed from household work into increased education and training. In 1960, less than 7 percent of all women had completed college, but over the next three decades the numbers of college graduates soared among both white and African American women. The early baby boomers, adamant in their desire to pursue careers, made good on their intentions. The share of women earning professional degrees rose sharply in the 1970s and continued to climb in the following decades. By 2000 more than 40 percent of medical, law, and doctoral degrees had gone to women.[30]

These educational gains have translated into professional achievements. Women now make up more than half of professional workers and close to one-third of mathematicians and computer scientists. They are working at the forefront of developments in health care, providing more than two-fifths of medical scientists and four-fifths of health technicians.[31] Applying their intelligence in such areas as molecular biology, neurophysiology, and biogenetics, women are seeking the causes of cancer, AIDS, Alzheimer's, and other diseases. Some are inventing new technologies and developing computer software, such as a program enabling doctors to use ultrasound rather than invasive surgery to assess patients' hearts. Others are using their advanced training in math and science to guide satellites around the earth or to stretch the very boundaries of knowledge, giving us a new understanding of the evolution of life itself. A desire to help society spurs the efforts of many. "The ability to restore vision is the ultimate reward," explains one eye surgeon who, having vowed as a teenager to improve medical care for African Americans, invented a new way to remove cataracts. "It is a really great joy . . . [when] the patient can see again."[32]

Thus, women have provided an important share of the skilled workers carrying the American economy forward, and women of color as well as white women have made significant contributions. Approximately three-fourths of African American and white female college graduates hold jobs in the upper tier of the service sector. Though their presence in elite professions remains small, the proportion of black women employed as physicians, lawyers, and engineers almost tripled between 1980 and 2000. Though black women still tend to be in the lower-paying professions and are poorly rewarded compared to those working in the corporate sector, their pursuit of advanced training has been essential to recent growth, especially in the area of health care. As the neurosurgeon Frances Conley has recently stressed, "If every female nurse, technician, and hospital housekeeper in this country were to go on strike, modern medicine in the United States would come to an abrupt halt."[33] Black women have played a key role in meeting the increased demand for nurses over the past two decades, and their labor is crucial if the sick are to receive care.

More new workers will be needed in professional and technical occupations than any other area in coming decades. Government analysts stress that women with college educations are essential if the United States is "to meet the growing need for doctors[,] . . . computer technicians and systems analysts, and the continued large demand for engineers and scientists." Many economists concur. "The need for scientific brainpower will only increase as we proceed into an information age," warns one study. "Add to that the demands of global competition and it's clear that . . . the cost of excluding any group has become too high."[34] Thus, women's labor has played a key role in recent advances in research, technological development, and productivity, and it will be increasingly central to such growth.

Half of all women, however, are still in low-wage service jobs or in sales and clerical work. Long dominating these occupations, women have been instrumental in the rapid expansion of the low-wage lower tier of the service sector, providing the bulk of workers in both the fastest and largest areas of such low-wage growth. Nine-tenths or more of child care workers, private household cleaners, and nursing aides and orderlies are women.[35]

Despite fears of a shortage of health care workers in the early 1990s, much of the growing demand for paid caregivers was met over this decade. Many employers in this field recognize that their businesses have been built on the growth of a "pool of women . . . who depend upon their daily wages for survival."[36] Behind the availability of these women's labor lie stories of the loss of traditional support. Most come from failed marriages or are never-married mothers. Some have been denied government aid as their children have grown up and as eligibility restrictions have tightened. The new workers filling low-paid service jobs in the 1990s were almost entirely unmarried mothers with a high school education or less, whose turn to the workforce was accompanied by a drop in the share on welfare.

Government agencies steer women on welfare toward job training in the care of children and the sick or work in fast-food restaurants. Analysts tracking the employment outcomes of former welfare recipients in Wisconsin over the 1990s found that some businesses, especially health care facilities and temporary agencies supplying maids and food service workers, drew heavily on women moving off government aid, hiring more than a hundred former recipients apiece. Most women leaving welfare initially took jobs, these analysts note, at "the bottom of the ladder" in hospitals and other low-paid service or sales occupations. Though some moved on to better jobs as they gained experience, at the end of the decade most were still caring for the sick, cleaning homes and offices, or selling food, drinks, and other goods. Ex–welfare recipients commonly ended up in such low-paid jobs in other parts of the country as well.[37]

In sum, as many women lost the support of marriage and as Aid to Families with Dependent Children was replaced with temporary assistance, a large pool of potential workers was created. The availability of such labor has made possible the swift growth of the bottom tier of the service sector.

Women with little education make up the majority of such workers. Both black and white high school dropouts provide much more than their share of low-paid health care workers and cashiers, for example. However, black women, like other women of color, are far more likely to hold service jobs than white women with similar educations. Though their employment in private household work has dropped sharply, black women are overrepresented among teaching assistants in preschools, maids in hotels, cleaners in office buildings, and cooks and cashiers in fast-food outlets, and they make up one-quarter of those in poorly paid health service occupations. Black women with little education have been a key source of such labor. The share of black high school dropouts employed as health aides almost doubled over the 1990s, for example. They have also provided a steady supply of food counter, kitchen, and child care workers.[38]

While poorly rewarded for their efforts, these women provide much-needed services that are of great value to society. "The better I take care of my patient," one health aide points out, "the longer she's going to live."[39] These low-paid workers have also helped businesses and government cut costs, especially in the area of health care. Their labor has fed the rapid expansion of home health chains and fast-food outlets, generating sizable profits for their employers. All these low-paying occupations—home health aide, home care aide, child care worker, nursing aide, and teaching aide—are expected to undergo substantial growth in the coming years, and women, especially less-educated women and women of color, will continue to be the central source of labor enabling such expansion.

In sum, at the lower end of the occupational spectrum, as well as at the higher, women have provided the majority of new workers. It is the availability of their labor that has fueled the rapid expansion of both tiers of the service sector and of the economy as a whole over recent decades.

Economic Gains from Women's Employment

Women's turn to paid employment, as well as the market takeover of household tasks, has created tremendous new profits for business and a great increase in national income overall. Though the service sector has often been criticized for its low productivity, such analysis overlooks an important side of economic development. The typical focus on output and other measures of performance in the market alone fails to take into account a key source of economic growth: the market's move into a new area previously outside its domain. Economists have long recognized that the development of new regions and the conversion of nonwage workers into wage workers can create great profits, leading corporations to set up factories overseas. To understand the gains of the past forty years, we must realize that a similar lucrative process was happening within the United States itself, in the very center of American homes. As the market reached into kitchens and bedrooms, turning many household tasks into work for pay, and as women themselves applied labor freed from domestic chores in research labs, hospitals, factories, and fast-food restaurants, productivity rose greatly and a large new pool of income was created.

Between the early 1970s and the end of the 1990s, business profits grew significantly, increasing by roughly half. Some of this profit was won at workers' expense, as employers pocketed a greater share of their firms' gains. However, much of it is explained by women's turn from household to paid labor. As David Ellwood puts it, "More women were working and earning more dollars. Capital earned its usual profit on those women. . . . Thus, profits went up."[40] In other words, each woman entering the labor force or working longer hours created gains for her employer as well for herself.

Women's increased involvement in paid work also had benefits for the nation as a whole. We can gain an estimate of such benefits by assessing women's contribution to the growth of gross domestic output in the private sector. Between 1970 and 2000, private-sector GDP rose by an average of 3.6 percent per year, almost tripling in size to $7,176.1 billion.[41]

Economists see such growth as caused primarily by increased input from three areas: workers, capital, and a mix of technological improvements and other factors. Between 1970 and 1999, the rise in workers' hours and their skills made up 38 percent of the growth in output in the private sector. At least 44 percent of that growth, in turn, is clearly attributable to women's increased employment and skills.[42]

Further, this estimate understates women's contribution for several reasons. For one, economists rely on wages to determine worker productivity, and there is much evidence that discrimination has made women's wages lower than they should be. If women were paid more fairly for their work, assessment of their contribution to the growth of the economy would be quite a bit larger. If we adjust women's share of wages to correct for the undervaluing of their productivity, we find that women's turn to paid work since 1970 was responsible for more than one-fifth of the growth of the GDP in the private sector.[43] Thus women's turn from household to paid work over the last thirty years of the twentieth century made up at least one-sixth, and perhaps more than one-fifth, of the rise of the private sector's GDP during that period—a gain of well over $700 billion.[44]

Women have also played a key role in the sharp rise in prosperity seen in the late 1990s. By the second half of the decade, GDP was growing more rapidly than it had in the previous twenty years, in large part because new computer and telecommunications technology made manufacturing more efficient. Indeed, gains from information technology appear to explain at least one-third of the growth in the GDP in the late 1990s.[45] However, economists also point to a continued increase in labor that was both more skilled and less costly. Women have continued to be a major source both of skilled workers and of low-paid temporary workers used to staff offices or perform janitorial services.

Further, economists also assess growth in the GDP by looking at expenditures on final good and services. Here, too, factors tied to the transformation of women's household work played an important role in economic growth and prosperity as the 1990s drew to a close. Advances in computer and communications technology created an array of popular new products for sale. However, economists also point to the appearance of many new services and a rise in consumer spending tied to increased personal income. Most of the new services that appeared were based on the conversion of women's domestic tasks into work done for pay. Also, much of the rise in personal income occurred among women themselves, suggesting that to a large extent women's spending drove the economy forward.[46]

Thus, overall, both market takeover of tasks once done in the home and the transformation of women's labor into work done for pay have played key roles in the recent growth of the American economy over the last third of the twentieth century. However, the magnitude of this event has not yet been adequately recognized, nor have women received their fair share of the gains they have been instrumental in creating.

The Consequences for Women's Own Lives

Many social commentators have noted the great changes that have taken place in the U.S. economy over the past few decades. However, they have emphasized new technology that makes possible communication at the speed of light or the rapid processing of huge piles of information, arguing that such advances make this "postindustrial" period markedly different from the country's previous two centuries of development. In actuality, such developments represent a new sectoral moment within a still-evolving market economy.

Though the products and services for sale may now deal with information, the creation of life itself, or the provision of meals and elder care, such activities still take place within the framework of market capitalism—that is, private production and work for wages. Bill Gates is the latest in a long line of entrepreneurs, such as Andrew Carnegie and John D. Rockefeller, who have amassed great wealth as the head of a new leading sector. It is not the old economic system's end but its further expansion that is driving current changes.

The strong sense of epochal change felt by many is not due to a radical break in the process of commercial and industrial growth that has transformed American life over the previous two centuries. Rather, what has changed dramatically is the age-old division of labor between the sexes. The breakdown of this old arrangement—in which women focused on domestic chores, supported, for most, within marriage, and still met many of their families' needs in this way—has sent shock waves through American society. While this shift has been traumatic, the movement of household tasks and of women themselves out into the market has produced great gains for business and the nation as a whole. What, however, has it meant for women themselves, and how have its consequences among them differed by class and race?

Women's Turn from Marriage to the Market

Even a quick glance reveals obvious changes in women's lives. Marriage rates have decreased dramatically, and motherhood has altered markedly as well. Almost twice as many women in their early 40s are childless today as in the mid-1970s, and far more of those with children are coping with parenthood on their own.[47]

At the same time, women's labor force participation has grown enormously. More than 70 percent of women in their prime adult years are now employed, and most mothers return to work before their child is 1 year old. All in all, today's young women will spend more years of their life in the workforce than in marriage, and more hours of their day at a job than in unpaid labors of love for their families.[48]

However, behind this shift in where women spend their time lies a more historic event, a profound alteration in the key source of women's livelihood. In 1960, most women's days not only centered around care of home and family, but the performance of such domestic tasks was also still the main way almost half of African American women and two-thirds of white women still earned their living. By the end of the century, this situation had changed dramatically. In a few short decades, the gender division of labor, or men's support for the domestic tasks done by women, had all but disappeared, and women had turned instead to wages to meet their basic needs.

A large body of scholarly literature has analyzed men's movement off the land and into work for wages. However, there is still little understanding of the full nature of the momentous shift that has taken place in women's lives. For men, the turn to wages brought new freedom and gains in political as well as economic resources. It raised frightening new specters as well—of inadequate pay, insufficient work, and the difficulties of accomplishing many tasks previously carried out in the home. Many of these specters are now haunting women's lives.

Before looking at these issues more closely, it is first useful to gain a clear understanding of women's recent turn from marriage to the market for support, and the varying outcomes of this event by class and race.

Women's Reliance on Their Own Earnings

In 1960, the majority of both white and African American women were married, and they focused primarily on performing domestic tasks for their own families. However, the crucial question is what role marriage, or men's income, played in women's actual support. In other words, how much of each woman's income came from her own earnings and how much from her husband, other men, or other sources? And how have these sources of support changed over the last half of the twentieth century?

We can get an answer to this question by looking closely at the different components of income in women's households. If we make the (generous) assumption that husbands' and wives' income is divided equally between spouses, we can then determine how much of a woman's share of household income came from her husband, if she had one, and how much from her own earnings or other sources. We can also estimate how much of her support may have come from other men or women in the household. Finally, by comparing the role played by each source of income in 1960 and 2000, we can see how these sources have altered over time.[49]

Figure 13 summarizes married women's economic dependence in 1960. On average, almost three-fourths of white married women's support came from

1960

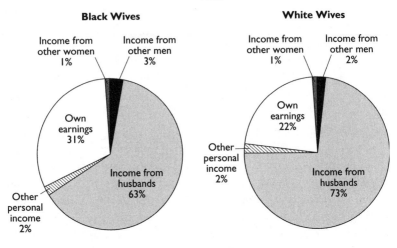

Black Wives

Income from other women 1%

Income from other men 3%

Own earnings 31%

Income from husbands 63%

Other personal income 2%

White Wives

Income from other women 1%

Income from other men 2%

Own earnings 22%

Other personal income 2%

Income from husbands 73%

2000

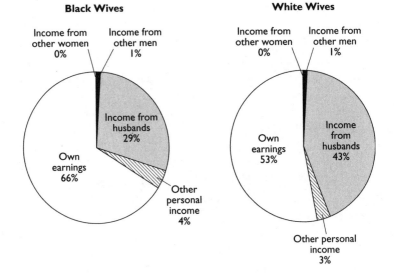

Black Wives

Income from other women 0%

Income from other men 1%

Income from husbands 29%

Own earnings 66%

Other personal income 4%

White Wives

Income from other women 0%

Income from other men 1%

Income from husbands 43%

Own earnings 53%

Other personal income 3%

FIGURE 13.
Married women's sources of support, by race, 1960 and 2000.
From author's calculations based on unpublished 1960 and
2000 IPUMS data. For details, see note 49.

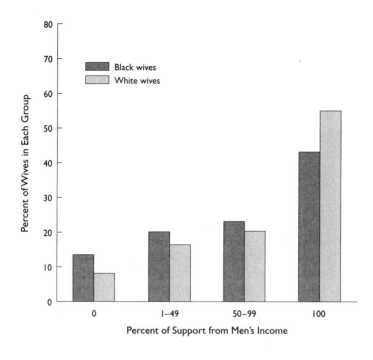

FIGURE 14.
Married women's reliance on men's income, by race, 1960.
From author's calculations based on unpublished 1960 IPUMS
data.

their spouses. Almost two-thirds of black wives' support also came from their
husbands. However, this situation altered markedly over the last decades of the
twentieth century. By 2000, personal earnings were playing a major role for
married women of both races, as figure 13 shows. Two-thirds of black wives'
support and more than half of white wives' support came from their own
wages and salaries. The share of support from husbands (and other men in the
household) had dropped by more than 30 points for both black and white
wives.

Looking more closely, we can divide wives into groups, from those completely dependent on their husbands to those relying solely on their own income. Figure 14 shows what percentage of married women relied heavily on
their husbands or their own earnings for their livelihood in 1960. We find that
well over half of white wives and more than two-fifths of black wives depended entirely on income from their husbands, making no financial contribution themselves. Approximately one-fifth of white and black wives drew the

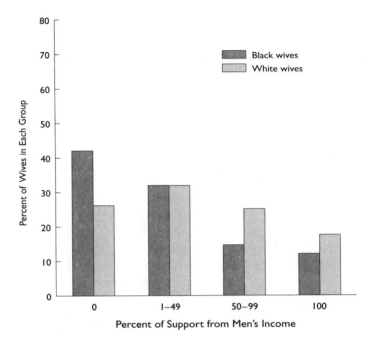

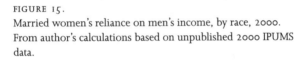

FIGURE 15.
Married women's reliance on men's income, by race, 2000.
From author's calculations based on unpublished 2000 IPUMS
data.

majority of their support from their spouses. Wives' earnings were the main
source of income for only one-fourth of white couples and one-third of black
couples.

In 2000, however, far fewer married women were counting on their husbands as the sole or even main breadwinner (see figure 15). Instead, well over
half of white wives and almost three-fourths of black wives were relying primarily on their own earnings. Less than one-fifth of white wives and just over
one-tenth of black wives still depended almost entirely on their husband's income for support.[50] Thus a historic shift took place over the last half of the
twentieth century, as women turned from marriage to their own wages for support.

It is informative to look as well at what this shift in their sources of support
has meant for all women (see figure 16). Unmarried women, of course, depended more on their own earnings than married women. But in 1960, barely
half of single mothers' support came from their own wages, because a sizable

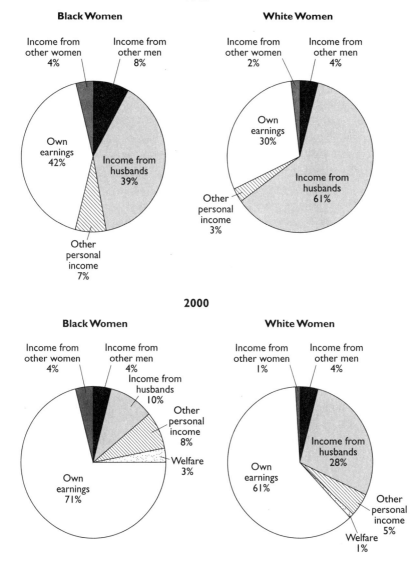

FIGURE 16.
All women's sources of support, by race, 1960 and 2000. From author's calculations based on unpublished 1960 and 2000 IPUMS data. For details see note 49.

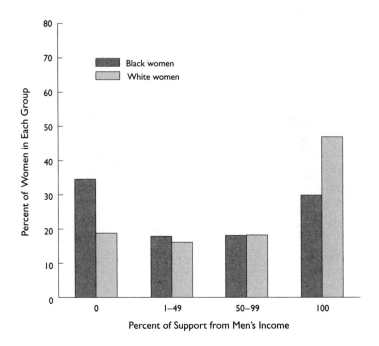

FIGURE 17.
All women's reliance on men's income, by race, 1960. From author's calculations based on unpublished 1960 IPUMS data.

segment of both black and white unmarried mothers lived with their parents or other relatives. In such cases, their father's income, or that of their brothers, uncles, or other male relatives, played a significant role in their lives. Thus overall in 1960, even when we look at both married and unmarried women, on average less than one-third of white women's support and only about two-fifths of black women's support came from their own earnings.

This situation has also changed dramatically in a few short decades. As one might expect, unmarried women, even those caring for children, now depend almost entirely on their own wages. When combined with married women's increasing reliance on their own earnings, the result is a marked drop in women's economic dependence on men. As figure 16 shows, in 2000 the majority of both black and white women's support came from their own wages.

Dividing all women into groups based on the role men's income played in their lives, we can see that for the majority of white women and almost half of black women in 1960, men's income made up half or more of their support (see figure 17). However, by 2000, less than one-third of white women and a

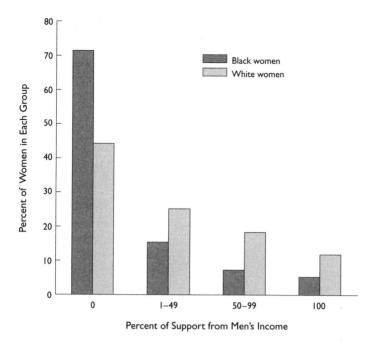

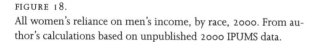

FIGURE 18.
All women's reliance on men's income, by race, 2000. From author's calculations based on unpublished 2000 IPUMS data.

little more than one-tenth of black women drew half or more of their support from the performance of domestic tasks, whether that support was provided by men or by the state (see figure 18). Alimony and child support are included in "other income"; see figure 27 in chapter 7 for details.

In sum, women's situation today contrasts starkly with that of the years immediately after World War II. Women's own earnings, rather than marriage and with it access to men's income, now provide the central source of support for most African American and white women.

Two factors were most important in this shift in the source of women's livelihood. For both white and black women, their strong turn to paid employment, together with access to better jobs, explains most of their lessened reliance on men's income. However, for black women a decrease in marriage played almost as great a role, and accounted for about 15 percent of the drop for white women. The impact of these changes was offset slightly by an overall increase in men's earnings since 1960, despite the later stagnation of their wages.[51] Clearly, though, the decline in marriage rates and women's turn to paid employment have profoundly changed not only the location of women's central work but also the main source of their livelihood.

Women's Wages and Women's Needs

The calculations and illustrations above give a sense of how much of women's overall support comes from their own earnings. However, we might also ask to what extent women's wages meet their basic needs or provide a minimal level of subsistence. Though men's income may still play a large role in some women's support, it may not play a necessary one for many. Conversely, while some women rely almost entirely on their own wages, these may not keep them out of poverty. The poverty threshold, while far below what is needed for a reasonable quality of life, can serve as a contemporary definition of subsistence.

In 2000, about two-thirds of both white and black women ages 22–54 had annual earnings above the amount needed to keep a single individual out of poverty. Thus, it could be argued that their wages met their basic needs. Most black and white women made enough to meet the needs of two children as well. In contrast, in 1960 only one-quarter or so of either white or black women earned enough to meet their basic needs, and substantially fewer could also meet the needs of two or more children.[52] Thus in a remarkable change from their situation forty years earlier, the great majority of both African American and white women in their prime adult years were both relying on their own earnings and meeting their basic needs through these wages rather than the performance of domestic tasks within marriage.

More broadly, these figures provide clear evidence of the breakdown of the old gender division of labor. Whereas formerly both white women and women of color had depended primarily on men's income and marriage to survive, this situation has radically altered. Men—as husbands, fathers, or lovers—now play a minor role in women's economic well-being. This gain in economic autonomy has enormous consequences, a central one being the possibility of ending gender inequality. Yet rather than winning real freedom, women have traded one master for another. They now find themselves at the mercies of the market and the demands of their employers. Their greatest problem is that the wages on which most women depend for their support are inadequate in many ways, especially for women raising children on their own.[53] We can gain a clearer sense of why women have lost out at this historic moment by examining how the turn from marriage to the market has played out among women of different educational and racial backgrounds.

Women's New Relationships to Home and Market

In 1960, the vast majority of women of both races had not gone beyond high school, most quitting before their senior year. Most white and black women were married. Only one-third of white wives and two-fifths of black wives in their prime adult years were employed. White women worked mainly as secretaries or salesclerks; most black women were still largely in service occupations, though many no longer worked in private homes. Factory work was the second most common job for women of either race. Income from husbands, and to a lesser extent from fathers or other male relatives, made up the largest portion of women's support, but a sizable segment of them—one-fifth of all white women and almost three-fifths of all black women—lived in poverty nonetheless.

Today most women, both black and white, have attended college and only a small fraction have not finished high school. Women's participation in the labor force has skyrocketed, especially among wives and mothers, and women have made great inroads into prestigious occupations as well. Behind such progress, however, lies a second story. The gender division of labor, which shaped women's lives for centuries and was sustained in different ways in earlier encounters with an expanding market, has fundamentally broken down. Thus, women have not simply taken on work for pay. They have also lost much or all of their support for the work they do in the home.

Earlier chapters have traced how this old framework of support came apart, how the turn to work for wages unfolded for different groups of women, and how employers and the American economy as a whole benefited. The question considered here is what the outcomes of this historic journey have been for women themselves. In particular, how are different groups of women now faring in their efforts to handle work at home and for pay?[54]

In the 1990s, the dramatic alterations in work and marriage seen in the previous decades slowed almost to a halt. As the twenty-first century begins, women seem to be settling into their new ways of life, though in differing ways. However, the arrangements that are appearing are not particularly satisfying for women of any background.

The breakdown of the old frameworks that kept women in the home has opened new worlds to women, and new aspirations. A common definition of the good life today is the dream of having it all, or both a career and a family. Underlying this dream are two basic desires—for access to work that, if perhaps not interesting or highly paid, at least covers the bills and for satisfying personal relationships that most still envision as culminating in motherhood. While a growing number of highly educated women have entered the professions and the great majority of those with a high school education or less have become mothers, very few women manage to achieve both parts of this dream. Success in accomplishing these goals has differed sharply by education as well as race.

College Graduates

Over the second half of the twentieth century, one real gain that gave women the resources to realize better lives has been that of education. The share of both African American and white women completing four or more years of college has more than quadrupled since 1960. By 2000, 30.5 percent of white women and 17.0 percent of black women in their prime adult years had achieved such education. These college graduates had very different lives than their counterparts in the 1960s. In the ensuing years, white graduates had entered the labor force in large numbers; black graduates raised their high level of employment even further. This strong involvement in paid work was accompanied by a sharp retreat from the domestic role, both motherhood and marriage. Increasing numbers of college graduates delayed becoming wives or having children until well into their 30s or later.

Today, these women have more or less completed the transition from work in the home to work for wages. The great majority of their support comes from their own earnings, and almost all make enough to meet the needs of two children as well. Thus, they have achieved a high degree of economic autonomy, which is satisfying in itself. "I like being in charge, paying my own bills, being responsible for my own livelihood," explains one such woman.[55]

Many, though still on average earning less than men in the same positions, have interesting and relatively well-paid careers. More than three-fifths of employed female college graduates of both races work in professional or managerial positions. Others are in jobs requiring technical training. Thus, many are doing work that they find highly gratifying. "We have exciting intellectual discussions and generate new ideas," one scientist says of her collaboration with two other women to stem the progress of Alzheimer's disease. The early thrill of discovering botany remains vivid for a professor at Howard University. "People do this for a living, and they get paid and this is fun, exciting and interesting," she had marveled as a young woman. "I could travel . . . I could go to tropical places."[56]

These women have secured a place in the labor force. They have done so in large part by subordinating the domestic role to the demands of the market. Both white and African American college graduates are now far more likely to be working for pay than to be married or caring for children, especially in their first decades of adulthood.[57] In the years of greatest turmoil, it seemed that highly educated women might forgo families altogether, but recently the trends of earlier decades have come to a halt and even reversed slightly. Employment

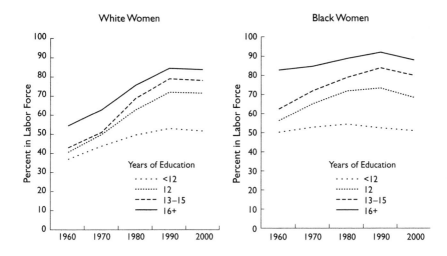

FIGURE 19.
Trends in labor force participation, by race, 1960–2000. From
author's calculations based on unpublished 1960–2000 IPUMS
data.

rates have ceased climbing, and marriage rates have stopped plummeting (see figures 19 and 20). Also a few more of the youngest college graduates of both races are becoming mothers. Having established themselves in the labor force, women college graduates appear to be constructing a new form of home life on this foundation. Successful employment has become an asset for women as well as men, and they are usually postponing marriage and motherhood until their careers are established. Because of these delays, the frequency of divorce has decreased. College graduates, especially African American women, are among the most likely to be married (see figure 20).[58]

But rather than managing to neatly sequence career and family, many college graduates are unable to find a balance between the two realms of work. In 2000 one-third of both black and white women graduates in their late 30s and early 40s with advanced training were childless. While some relish the chance to focus fully on their work, others feel that career pressures forced them to sacrifice motherhood.[59]

Those choosing to embrace only the domestic role also pay a price. "Good mothering isn't considered successful or sufficient," laments one college graduate. "One must have a MotherPlus Plan—maybe have the MotherPlus law career or be a MotherPlus novelist." Another, who gave up her job to care for her infant, notes sadly, "Without work I lacked an identity, a community, a purpose."[60]

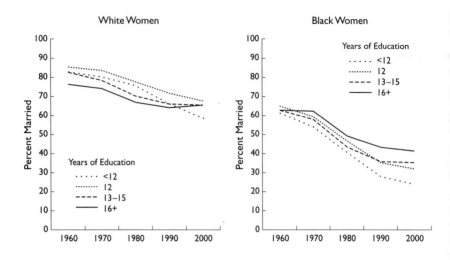

FIGURE 20.

Trends in marriage, by race, 1960–2000. From author's calculations based on unpublished 1960–2000 IPUMS data.

Yet those who pursue both careers and motherhood are very overworked, because the elite professions now require "supernormal drive and ambition."[61] Part-time lawyers at top legal firms are expected to work more than forty hours a week; assistant professors today must publish more than twice as much as their predecessors. Such pressures take their toll. "Over and over again I was told," reports one academic who interviewed female scientists, "that today many young women and an increasing number of young men are unwilling to take on the frenetic lifestyle they see among scientists at elite institutions or that they simply lack the stamina to do so."[62]

High School Graduates and Those with Some College Education

Most women, however, are not college graduates. About two-thirds of white and black women have completed high school but not four years of college. These women, like those with college degrees, have undergone profound shifts since 1960, undertaking paid work in even greater numbers and experiencing a greater fall in marriage rates (see figures 19 and 20).

In the 1990s, changes slowed among this group of women as well. Paid work became a customary part of life and the drop in marriage eased, especially among African American women, perhaps because their employment opportunities increased. However, the lives these women were settling into were full of tensions. Unlike college graduates, this group of women has held strongly to the domestic role upon entering the labor force. Most studies focus on highly educated professionals desperate for more time for their families or on welfare mothers struggling to meet their children's needs, but it is the women in between who end up juggling work at home and for pay over the first decades of adulthood. They are also the most likely to be doing so on their own.

These women face conflicting pressures, both internal and external, from the worlds of work and home. In adolescence, their talk of future plans, notes one observer, is a "cascade of contradictions." Those who wish to attend college often encounter strong objections from their families and boyfriends. Pregnancy often tips the balance, keeping them at home.[63]

About one-third of white and black women now go to college but do not complete a full four years. Many of these women zigzag between meaningful work and mothering, both in their dreams for the future and in their daily lives. Often unwilling to postpone motherhood, some devise tightly plotted schedules, then exhaust themselves rushing from home to class, perhaps even to work, and home again. "I am going after my goal," reports one full-time student and mother of two, "but I am beginning to wonder . . . can this be done?"[64] Too often, the answer is no. In their struggle to combine responsibilities at school and at home, the domestic role frequently triumphs. The clear value of raising children wins out over the long training required for many careers. One obvious consequence of that choice is a decreased likelihood of finding interesting or well-paid jobs.

Yet these women have also achieved a basic turn to the market. More than half their support comes from their own earnings. For most, work for wages meets their own basic needs, and half can meet the needs of two children as well.[65] However, their autonomy is of a very limited form. The most common occupations for women who have completed high school but not four years of college are clerical and sales work. In the 1990s, both black and white women in this group found jobs primarily as low-level office managers, as secretaries, or on the bottom rungs of health care. Much of this work offers little satisfaction. "It's a job," notes one nurses' aide. "But there's nothing to look forward to. You come to work. It's a heavy workload and you try to get through."[66]

Work in such jobs from early adulthood is commonly combined with many responsibilities at home. Though they become mothers a bit later and have fewer children than in the past, these women remain strongly invested in the domestic role early in life. More than 50 percent of those with no education past high school, black and white alike, and almost as many of those with only a year or two of college, are mothers by their early 20s. Thus, almost half of

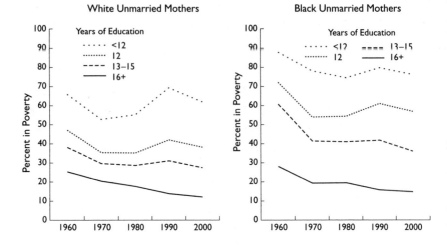

FIGURE 21.

Trends in poverty among unmarried mothers, by education and race, 1960–2000. From author's calculations based on unpublished 1960–2000 IPUMS data. *Mothers* are women ages 22–54 with at least one child under 18 in the household. *Poverty* is defined as income at or below 125 percent of the government-established poverty threshold.

these women spend the first stretch of adulthood coping with heavy demands at home and at work. Their efforts have far fewer payoffs than those of more-educated women.

In addition, these women more often watch their marriages crumble or take on motherhood in relationships that are never formalized. They are far more likely than college graduates of their own race to be working and raising children on their own. Though they have gained the option of avoiding or ending a bad marriage, in practice that freedom is sharply limited. Husbands' income is more important to less-educated women of both races, and thus its loss is a heavy blow. Further, the difficulties of single parenthood often force them to cut their hours of work, often bringing severe financial hardships. Though, as figure 21 shows, poverty rates dropped sharply for single mothers of both races over the 1990s, one-third of white single mothers and almost half of black single mothers who have completed high school but not four years of college are still poor.

Thus the move into the market economy has been hard for these women. Rather than giving up the domestic role, they have combined it from an early age with work for wages, while traditional support for their caregiving and other household tasks has dropped away.

High School Dropouts

In 1960, 44.7 percent of white women and 71.8 percent of black women had not finished high school. By the end of the century, this group had shrunk dramatically: only 5.7 percent of white women and 11.7 percent of black women in their prime adult years had less than twelve years of education. Over the period from 1960 to 2000, these women experienced the greatest fall in marriage rates while making the fewest gains in the labor force (see figures 19 and 20). In the 1990s, when transformations at home and work slowed for most women, this group continued to experience rapid changes.[67]

In the 1990s, employment rose sharply among young unmarried mothers of both races, many of whom left welfare for work.[68] Less than half of white and black high school dropouts are employed, however. Though more jobs became available over the decade, the youngest still had difficulty finding work. Black high school dropouts had an especially hard time, facing an unemployment rate over twice that of white dropouts.

Marriage also continued to become more rare for these women. Though its decline slowed for both races, high school dropouts fell even further behind other women over the 1990s, confirming their status as the least likely to be married (see figure 20).[69] Though far fewer of the youngest black women on their own became mothers, most white and black high school dropouts still have children while quite young, and the gap between them and other women in this respect has grown wider. Though the share of black teens becoming pregnant fell over the late 1990s, almost two-thirds of both white and black high school dropouts in their early 20s are mothers.

These women still value the maternal role highly, despite the dreams of some to have careers. "No kids for me, no marriage, just well-paying jobs," one such young woman had vowed. On finding herself pregnant, however, she was hit with an "unstoppable desire to have a baby." Seventy-five percent of high school girls from disadvantaged backgrounds in one study stated firmly that they would not have an abortion if they were to become pregnant; all said they would never give a child up for adoption.[70] Thus, most become mothers at an early age. Like other women, they also struggle to manage work and family, but their efforts bring few gains.[71]

Both white and black dropouts most commonly work in low-paying service occupations. Since 1960, the share of white dropouts in such jobs has almost doubled. While black women who have not completed high school have shifted out of private domestic work, almost half are still employed in service jobs. Tracy Chapman's song of a young woman whose dream of a better life ends at a checkout counter in a grocery store captures the fate of many dropouts. In the 1990s, both white and black women who had not completed

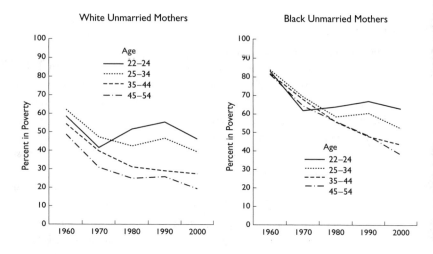

FIGURE 22.
Trends in poverty among unmarried mothers, by age and race,
1960–2000. From author's calculations based on unpublished
1960–2000 IPUMS data. *Mothers* are women ages 22–54 with at
least one child under 18 in the household. *Poverty* is defined as
income at or below 125 percent of the government-established
poverty threshold.

high school found work primarily as low-paid cashiers, often in fast-food outlets or grocery stores, as care workers, or as maids.[72] Such work is notorious for
its poor pay, low hours, lack of benefits, and on-call nature. Some of these
women hold more than thirty different jobs in a year. The conditions of work
are difficult and demeaning. "Sometimes it gets too much for you," confesses
one home care worker.[73]

The stories told by women with little education are less of combining work
at home and for pay than of alternating between these two worlds. Although
those raising children alone are often blamed for turning to welfare, their access to government aid has enabled their employers to pay very low wages without benefits. When crisis hits, most often in the form of sickness, these women
are forced back onto state support. Despite a drop in the poverty rate, especially
among the youngest white mothers (see figure 22) and those with little education, most single mothers who have not finished high school live in poverty.[74]
Even among those employed full-time, over two-fifths of white single mothers
and almost two-thirds of black single mothers are poor.

These women have little hope of realizing their dreams. In recent years, the
precariousness of their situation has generated much anxiety. "Panic seemed to
set in . . . with talk of welfare cutoffs," notes one longtime observer.[75] They are

caught between the proverbial rock and a hard place, facing a difficult new world of work while the domestic role no longer offers any security.

Differences by Race

Despite strong similarities in how the turn from household to paid work has played out among white and African American women with similar levels of education, there are also important differences by race. Both in the market economy and at home, black women face more difficult circumstances. Some of these are fairly well known. Black women work longer hours than white women and experience unemployment rates almost three times as high. They are less likely to be in professional or managerial positions, and almost twice as likely as white women to be in poorly paid service occupations.[76] These poorer outcomes are not explained simply by lower educational attainment. Among both college graduates and high school dropouts, African American women hold less-desirable occupations and have more difficulty securing work than white women. Overall, the turn to the wage economy has brought black women fewer gains.[77]

In the domestic realm, as well, black women have fared worse than white women at each educational level. While marriage rates have dropped for women of both races, black women are half as likely to be living with spouses. Two-thirds of white high school graduates are married, for example, compared to less than one-third of black high school graduates. One result is that a much greater proportion of black women are caring for children on their own. Though single motherhood has risen rapidly for white women, black women are still more than three times as likely to be raising children by themselves. They are also far more likely to be living in poverty while doing so.[78]

Thus the breakdown of women's domestic economy and women's turn to work for wages have had different effects on women according to their educational level and their race. We are seeing a two-pronged process of adjustment and collapse, as women continue to be pushed as well as pulled out of the home. While some women are adapting to the new location of their support, subordinating their domestic role to the demands of the wage economy, others are straddling both worlds with difficulty. A diminishing few still cling to their old way of life while it collapses around them.

.   .   .

Overall, support for women's domestic realm has come apart in a much more brutal way, with far harsher consequences, for some women. In general, the negative impact of this historic turn has been much greater for less-educated women, and for black women as a whole.

These harsher consequences are most evident in women's struggle to combine work at home and for pay. The breakdown of support for women's domestic realm does not mean that such tasks themselves, or women's desires to engage in them, have completely disappeared. Further, though most women now rely primarily on their own earnings, neither their wages nor existing policies are adequate to meet their needs, especially for those raising families. In the next chapter, I look more closely at what the turn from marriage to the market for support has meant for mothers in particular, thereby exposing the underlying causes of the difficulties they now face.

In the early 1960s, women's complaints centered on being trapped in the home, with little to do but endlessly clean a set of spotless rooms. Today their conversations revolve around the problem of overwork and whether anything can be done about it. "I am so stressed and tired," confesses one working mother. "I work all week to work all weekend cleaning, doing laundry and paperwork so that I can go back and work all week. . . . Lately I feel like I could just sit and cry. . . . Does anyone else feel like this? Or has anyone figured out how to cope with it?"[1]

The transformation of women's work has created great material gains for the United States as a whole and helped lay the foundation for the new economy of the twenty-first century. Yet while these changes have meant increased earnings for most women, and greater access to careers for many, they have also brought real problems. The issue dominating both public and private discussions today is how hard it is for women to combine home and work. This problem is felt most acutely by mothers, especially those with small children. Many work long hours at jobs that leave scant time for domestic tasks while often paying wages too low to meet their families' needs. Single mothers, juggling paid work and parenting with little help from the men in their lives, the state, or employers, are caught in a particularly difficult situation. However, many married women with children are also overwhelmed by the demands of work at home and for pay, while women without families find they have little time to form them. Whatever their class or marital status, a common thread runs through the hardships that women face today: the lack of new supports for the domestic tasks they still do within the home and the lack of time for a life outside paid work.

Descriptions of women's difficulties in balancing work and home now abound, accompanied by many proposals for easing the tensions between the two worlds. What is missing is a larger grasp of the underlying causes of such strains. Far more is involved than men's falling wages or the increase in women's employment. To gain a real understanding of the problems currently confronting mothers, we must look once again at the hidden half of this story. As we have seen in earlier chapters, preceding and contributing to women's turn to paid work lay the breakdown of their old domestic economy, or the gender division of labor, in its different forms.

The dismantling of this old arrangement opened new opportunities for women in the workforce and gave employers greater access to their labor, creating a new bounty of time and wealth. At the same time, however, it also undid the old agreements that had once committed not only fathers but also employers and the state to some provision for the care of children and other chores essential to daily life.

By the mid-1990s, the key supports for women's household work—marriage as a lifelong institution, the family wage, and government assistance in the form of Aid to Families with Dependent Children (AFDC)—were gone. Little has replaced them: a mere three months of unpaid family leave, a few small tax credits, a scattering of benefits among employers, and child care programs that often cost more than college tuition.

Many analysts of today's economy stress the breaking of the old agreement between labor and capital, which ensured workers some share of the United States' prosperity following World War II. They emphasize the need to re-create such a compact in a new form. However, an important part of that old arrangement involved support for tasks of family maintenance. Thus, provisions for such tasks must be a key piece of any new social compact between workers, employers, and the state.

This is not just a moral plea. Rather, the dismantling of women's domestic economy and the shift of many household tasks and women's own labor to the market have played an important role in recent economic growth. They have also created new potentials for the home, for market takeover of household tasks has lessened the time required to meet our basic needs. However, few of these gains have come to women and their families.

This chapter begins with a close look at mothers, because their lives most vividly reveal the incompleteness of the new world we have built. I look first at how the demands of the domestic role have altered, asking whether mothers are really working harder now than in the 1960s, and if so, why, given recent savings in time at home and in the market. To answer such questions we must ask further ones. Who has benefited from the new potential created by market takeover of women's tasks and labor? How can women themselves enjoy a greater share of these gains?

These questions, in turn, lead us into the realm of social policy. In essence, the crisis now confronting women is similar to that faced earlier by many men as they moved from fields to factories. Women's turn from marriage to wages for support has opened a new moment of negotiation over the relationship between home, work, and state.

Further, while this turn has created unexpected problems, it has also given women greater leverage for their demands. Why, then, are we settling into arrangements of home and work that are furthering inequalities of gender and race, while widening those of class? By carefully examining differences as well as similarities among mothers today, we can begin to answer these questions.

Are Mothers Really Worse Off Than in the 1960s?

Today most mothers, whether high school dropouts or college graduates, work for wages, and approximately half of those employed are working full-time and year-round.[2] A phenomenal change has taken place in the space of a few years, and women and their families are still reeling from its impact.

Women across the occupational spectrum are feeling pressured. A study of recent graduates from Stanford University, one of the most elite educational institutions in the country, reveals that family obligations are still derailing women's efforts to enter the professions. A survey of lawyers reports that almost three-fourths of women completing law school experience conflicts between home and work. Such conflicts are felt even by childless women, and by two-thirds of male law graduates as well.[3]

It is not only women pursuing high-pressured careers who are feeling overburdened. Complaints are heard across the country, from office workers to nurses' aides, whether they are caring for infants or teenagers. "I'm back at work and feeling like I'll never get eight hours of sleep," sighs one new mother. "The laundry will never be done and you can just forget about eating another hot meal." "I come home at night and the second shift starts and I feel so depressed and exhausted when I go to bed," says another. "I think I should just quit, but financially it will be a struggle."[4]

Young women's accounts of becoming mothers in the late 1990s, while infused with a determined optimism, continue to reflect many strains. A few fathers are staying home with the babies, a few mothers are carrying breast pumps to work, but overall the struggles are strikingly familiar. An intense conflict between work and the maternal role persists, resulting in exhaustion, confusion, and a scaling back of career aspirations.[5] It seems that the majority of women are being shortchanged in terms of support for their domestic tasks. But are women caring for children really worse off than in the 1960s? To answer the question, we must look more closely at the radically altered structure of mothers' support and their overall hours of work.

Support for Mothers' Work

Assessments of mothers' lives typically focus on what chores they do compared to their husbands. However, a crucial issue is how such domestic tasks are supported. Who pays for the time women spend preparing meals or caring for children?

In the late nineteenth and early twentieth centuries, marriage was the key mechanism of support, as husbands were expected to meet many of their wives' material needs in exchange for their domestic labor. Men's income played an important role for black mothers as well as white mothers. In 1910, for example, though approximately two-fifths of African American mothers worked outside the home, almost all gave priority to domestic tasks within their own families while their husbands brought in the bulk of the household's cash. Though receiving far less income from men than most white women, almost all black mothers had access to at least some support for their domestic labors.[6]

Even in 1960, mothers of both races still relied primarily on their husbands' earnings. As figure 23 illustrates, half of black mothers' support and three-quarters of white mothers' support came from their spouses. However, the source of their central support has changed even more dramatically for mothers than for other women. By 2000, the role played by men's income had plummeted by almost 40 percentage points for both black and white mothers. As the figure depicts, only two-fifths of white mothers' support and less than one-fifth of black mothers' support was coming from men.[7]

Some of this decreased reliance on men's income, especially for African American mothers, is explained by the shrinking share of women who were married. Overall, the rise of single parenthood explains about one-fifth of the drop for black mothers and close to one-tenth of the drop for white mothers. The changing circumstances of unmarried mothers have also contributed to the loss of men's support. Only half as many single mothers of either race were living with their fathers or other male relatives in 2000 as were in 1960. The primary cause, however, is the growth in mothers' own earnings as they entered the labor force in great numbers and increased their hours of paid work in the years after World War II.[8]

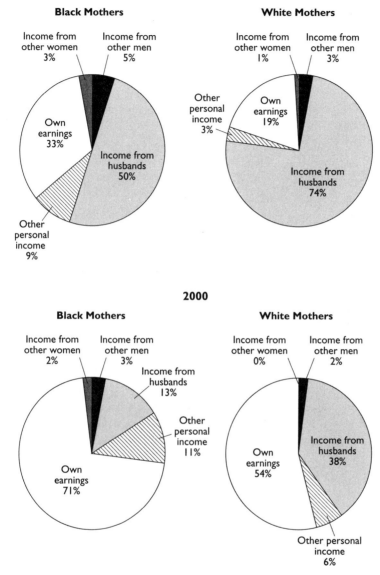

FIGURE 23.

Sources of mothers' support, by race, 1960 and 2000. From author's calculations based on unpublished 1960 and 2000 IPUMS data. *Mothers* are women ages 22–54 with at least one child under 18 in the household. For details, see chapter 6, note 49.

Thus, over the last few decades of the twentieth century, a major shift took place in the framing of motherhood. While white mothers were once almost entirely dependent on men's income and black mothers partially so, this arrangement has altered markedly for both groups of women. Today most black mothers receive almost no support for their domestic labors, and most white mothers receive only partial support for their work in the home. What has this change meant for mothers' daily lives?

Hours of Work at Home and for Pay

There has been much discussion recently of how Americans are increasingly overworked. However, it is often not realized that most of those working longer hours are women, especially those caring for children. By the end of the twentieth century, mothers in their prime adult years were putting in about twice as much time at paid work as in 1970.[9]

Focus on wage work alone paints too harsh a picture, for time spent on housework has decreased since the 1950s. Still, two large and growing segments of mothers—those working full-time, especially when caring for small children, and those juggling work at home and for pay on their own—are facing great hardships. The growth of these two groups is largely responsible for the sharp shift in mothers' sources of support, and they are the most likely to complain of extreme overwork.

Close examination confirms these mothers are indeed working exceptionally long hours. Married women employed full-time and caring for preschoolers are spending a ghastly eighty hours per week in work at home and for pay. Because most still give birth to two children, they face years of unrelenting pressure. Even when their children enter school, these mothers are still putting in much longer hours than women without children or than most men, including their husbands.[10]

Mothers in another growing group are coping with domestic tasks and paid work almost entirely on their own. Over two-thirds of black and white single mothers with children under 18 are full-time year-round workers. If they spent as much time on domestic tasks as the adults in two-parent families, they would be working more than a hundred hours per week! Their dual demands take a heavy toll. "I get home from work and I am so exhausted," sighs one such weary mother. "I am a single parent and I feel I have no time with my kids. I get home, cook, clean, bathe the kids, help with homework and then it's time to go to bed."[11]

A third less-noted group of women, those working full-time while caring for aging parents or other relatives, are also experiencing time strains. More than three-fifths of women between the ages of 35 and 54, the group most likely to take on such care, are full-time year-round workers; many still have teenagers at home. Thus, a large segment of women face a second time crunch as they reach middle age, perhaps just when they were expecting some relief from their responsibilities at home.

Women's turn to full-time employment obviously has added enormously to the burdens of those caring for families. A comparison between working mothers today and homemakers in the 1960s clearly illustrates this point. The typical mother today combines domestic chores with full-time year-round employment. In doing so, she faces an overall workload of about seventy-three hours per week. This is over seventeen hours more each week than the typical mother in 1965, who focused solely on home and children. Thus, the typical mother today is working 30 percent harder than her counterpart forty years ago. The relaxed rhythm once common to housewives' days has disappeared. This speedup has taken place even though fathers are helping much more with domestic tasks today than in earlier years.[12]

Long hours and inadequate pay are not women's only problems. Mothers must also cope with family responsibilities when at their jobs. They often describe the added stress when a child or aging parent falls sick, or when any piece of an elaborate set of caregiving arrangements breaks down.

Many analysts have noted that the first decades after World War II were golden years for America's workforce. However, in some ways these years were also golden ones for many mothers. Despite the inequities of gender, most mothers had sufficient time and support for their household chores and caregiving tasks. A full turn to paid work has clearly placed a heavy burden on women caring for children and aging parents, especially on those women who are single parents. Further, the burden is being borne by an ever greater proportion of mothers, as increasing numbers work full-time or handle child rearing and work for pay on their own.

New Time for Home and Family

The irony of the long hours of labor and great stress now faced by many mothers is that behind such overwork lies a new gift of time. A substantial number of hours that women once devoted to household tasks has been freed up. The typical mother today spends almost twenty hours less per week on housework than the average homemaker in the 1960s.[13] This drop is primarily due to a further influx of household appliances, such as dishwashers and microwaves, and the increasing availability of domestic goods and services for pay. Also, gains from earlier decades have been translated into greater efficiency rather than ever higher standards. Thus, market takeover of women's household work has created real benefits for the home as well as for the larger economy. Yet where has this time gone?

One segment of mothers, those giving their full attention to homemaking, does have more leisure. Also, more of women's domestic energies are now devoted to their children rather than to cooking and cleaning. However, the great bulk of this freed time, and more, has gone to paid work. The share of mothers working full-time has more than doubled since 1970.[14] For a growing number of families, home life is being devoured by market demands.

Market takeover of tasks once done in the home does not have to consign women and their families to lesser lives. Rather, it has opened up a new potential, if we can only claim it. Many women, overwhelmed by demands at home and on the job, resent the suggestion that their domestic tasks may have been reduced. Yet the real injustice is that the hours freed from many household chores and more productive use of women's labor have gone not to mothers but to the new economy of the twenty-first century, which has taken too much of women's time while paying too little for it.[15] A society that once recognized the importance of home and family, and set aside space for this realm, now no longer does so.

A Classic Welfare State Problem

A Female Working Class

When we set the problems faced by women in the context of the historic transition they are undergoing, it becomes clear that women's current crisis is similar to that confronted by men entering the workforce in the late nineteenth and early twentieth centuries. These men also struggled to find ways to continue to care for their families and to support themselves in sickness and old age. They too worked long hours and found their wages far from adequate to meet the full cost of their needs.[16]

While men's turn to work for wages brought new gains in productivity and wealth, few of these gains went initially to workers and their families, creating instead great fortunes for their employers. Further, men's shift to wage work undid many of the old provisions for care. Such tasks did not disappear. Rather, they could no longer be provided for within the old arrangements of labor. Farmers, for example, expected their land to yield sufficient produce to see their families through bleak winters and times of infirmity and to allow their wives to focus on domestic chores as well. As early theorists of the welfare state noted, men's move off the land broke down such arrangements, requiring "a partial shift of traditional family functions . . . to the state, school and industry."[17]

Such a shift was not an inevitable outgrowth of these changes, however.

Rather, struggles took place in the late nineteenth and early twentieth centuries in the United States to direct more of the new wealth produced by workers to their own families and to create social policies that could replace the old systems of care, reshaped around men's involvement in the labor force. These efforts, while less successful than those in other industrialized countries and restricted primarily to white men, did result in programs to handle periods of unemployment, poor health, and old age; a "family wage" for some men; and other legislation providing some support for women's domestic role.[18]

Efforts to extend programs devised for male workers in the early-twentieth-century United States to meet the needs of women workers have not worked very well, however. The awkward handling of pregnancy as a medical "disability" is one example of the limitations of this strategy. Difficulties in fitting women's needs into policies designed for a previously male working class have brought about a resurgence of the idea that women are biologically different from men and thus require special treatment. Yet there is a long history of the costs of such an approach, which has resulted in unequal status and opportunities for women. The way forward lies in looking not at men's and women's physical attributes but at their work, and how encounters with the market have altered women's work as well as men's.

Some scholars have argued that a focus on workers and employers in discussions of welfare state formation has excluded women and the issues central to their lives. They have directed attention instead toward the domestic realm, examining how policy has shaped this area and gender inequality itself.[19] This focus has brought an important new dimension into discussions of the welfare state, uncovering as well the key role played by women themselves in policy construction a century ago and revealing variations in such policy formation and their consequences. But attention to the home has also led to calls for a return to programs shaped around women's domestic role, as in the early twentieth century. Such proposals fail to grasp the dynamic changes that have taken place in women's work in the home.

The main problem is not that looking at class formation has left women out of analyses of social policy. Rather, this process has been viewed too narrowly. Focus on the experience of white male workers has obscured the full scope of the move women have undergone and its role in the crisis of care that has resulted.

Women's turn to work for wages in the years after World War II, like that of many men before them, has also resulted in a great gain in productivity, little of which has come to women themselves. Further, women's move from home to market has also broken down yet another layer of old arrangements for care. However, important tasks essential to human life, from cooking meals to caring for children and aging parents, remain and still fall primarily on women's shoulders. With motherhood, women confront the core of their current dilemma. The old supports for their domestic tasks have been taken apart, but no new framework has been constructed in their place, forcing most mothers to scramble for solutions.

Women's need for, and right to a new set of, social policies thus rests not on some essential difference from men but on their movement out of another old form of labor, which has left its own set of tasks unmet. Like men's move off the land, this historic turn from household to paid work is also opening struggles to give women a greater share of the wealth they are creating and to create new provisions for the tasks of care that remain. It is also providing women with new resources to make such demands.

Single Mothers and Social Policy

The form that new policy should take has been much debated, even among scholars and activists who strongly support women's interests. Some fear that single mothers in particular will be left with little time to tend to their own families. Entangled in such concerns are several different issues, giving them a compelling resonance. Laying these issues out clearly can help us see the full scope of women's policy needs, for, more than most women, single mothers have been thrown almost totally upon the market for support. Thus their situation reveals the dangers of such reliance.[20]

First, that single mothers find it almost impossible to juggle the demands of both home and work highlights the need for new arrangements for the care of children and other dependents. It also makes clear the importance of ensuring sufficient time as well as material support for tasks of family maintenance.

However, a second fear runs through concerns over single mothers: that reliance on wages alone may expose them to harsh poverty. Because they generally have less education and greater family responsibilities than other women, single mothers often have trouble securing jobs that pay wages high enough to meet their families' needs or that offer coverage during periods of poor health or economic downturn.[21] This problem, too, was earlier faced by groups of men when they were stripped of all support but their own earnings. As they struggled to survive on wages alone, they learned that they needed both protection against market failure and new arrangements for providing care.

The plight of single mothers thus captures women's vulnerabilities as a new group of workers entering the wage economy, as well as the difficulties they face as primary caregivers. These two sets of problems illustrate all women's needs for new policies, not only to address tasks of family maintenance but also to buffer reliance on an unreliable market.

Finally, the wrenching changes now confronting many single mothers point to a deeper cost as well. As several scholar-activists concerned about caregiving note, work done for wages is indeed more alienated than that of tending to one's own family. With women's full turn to the labor force, yet another segment of life and time for human needs and desires will be engulfed by an expanding economy, unless we find new ways to reclaim such space.

The Struggle over the New Potential

No simple logic of development will determine the shape new programs may take or ensure their creation. Instead, their formation raises a fundamental question of social policy, that of who is to pay for such programs. The issue is not how to come up with new funds. Rather, it is how the income generated by the transformation of women's tasks and labor is to be distributed. Men, employers, and the state once had certain obligations—in the form of marriage, the family wage, and AFDC, for example—to provide some support for tasks of family maintenance. As earlier chapters have shown, each of these groups helped take apart the old arrangements that formerly framed women's work in the home. In doing so, each stepped free of those old commitments. Thus far they have also avoided taking on much in the way of new obligations toward the caregiving and household tasks that remain.

More progress has occurred within the home than outside it. Fathers once spent little over an hour and a half in all unpaid work per day, and much of this time went to traditionally male tasks like yard work. Since the mid-1960s, however, married fathers' time in unpaid work has doubled. More important, the bulk of it is now spent on housework and child care. Fathers' time making meals, cleaning, and caring for children has increased fourfold, for example. Those with very young children now put eighteen hours a week into housework and child care if their wives are employed. Nonetheless, their wives, even if working full-time, continue to do about one and a half times as much housework as their husbands. In addition, the gains in men's time spent on domestic tasks have been offset by the growth of single motherhood, which has left many women bearing those tasks alone.

Yet no area of new policy has grown more rapidly than that of strengthening child support payments by absent parents. From the mid-1970s on, the federal government has taken several steps to enforce payment of child support by noncustodial fathers. Still, enforcement remains patchy, and when fathers have little or no work, unfeasible. Moreover, some policy analysts have warned that such legislation, joined with the reduction of aid to single mothers, "may be seen as an attempt to privatize the cost of children and to shift some of the burden from the state."[22] In brief, this approach still leaves the burden of domestic support in families' hands.

Far fewer policies have been set up to secure new commitments to the home from the state or employers. Indeed, the state is doing less than before to assist families with the household and caregiving tasks essential to daily life. By replacing AFDC with an emphasis on "personal responsibility," or work and marriage, the federal government has renounced its obligation to support tasks of family care. The central thrust of government policy is that mothers should rely on their own earnings or, preferably, those of a husband. Though the government provides temporary aid to very poor families, gives a small tax credit to parents with limited earnings, and mandates that businesses over a certain size offer a few months of unpaid family leave, these are meager gestures. Wages in and of themselves are expected to meet family needs.[23]

Though wages alone can never replace the substantial framework that once supported women's household work, they are particularly poorly suited to do so at present, as employers have also withdrawn support for family maintenance. The social contract won by male workers in the first half of the twentieth century committed employers to paying some of the costs of household and domestic tasks, primarily through the family wage and a package of health care and retirement benefits. The abandonment of this contract has released employers from many of their old obligations.

Business has made great gains over the past thirty-five years. The economy has grown substantially since the mid-1970s. Though women's earnings have also risen, a disproportionate share of the income generated by such growth has gone to employers and the upper tier of managers. By the mid-1990s, capital's overall share of national income was, as David Ellwood observes, "very near a fifty-year high."[24] Salaries for those at the top of the corporate ladder grew even more dramatically. The economists Lawrence Mishel, Jared Bernstein, and Heather Boushey note, "As wages fell for the typical worker, executive pay soared. . . . In 1965 CEOs made 26 times more than the typical worker; this ratio had risen to 72-to-1 by 1989."[25]

In the late 1990s, these trends accelerated. Though wages rose as productivity increased, a growing portion of the gains from economic growth went to profits at the expense of labor. Corporate salaries also skyrocketed. By the end of the decade, chief executive officers made 310 times more than the typical worker, who earned less, when earnings were adjusted for inflation, than in 1979. Overall, between 1970 and 2000, the share of income going to the top 5 percent of families grew by more than one-third, far surpassing that received by the lower two-fifths of American families.[26]

This income could be used instead to fund new ways to carry out domestic and caregiving tasks rather than increasing profits or enhancing the wealth of the top layer of corporate executives. As one poorly paid single mother struggling to care for her children observes, "Don't tell me there's not enough money because I am not a fool. . . . There's money around, lots of it. We just got to decide who we are going to spend it on."[27]

Paid Leave for Every Family

There is an important side to employers' gains at the expense of workers that has not yet been clearly seen. Women have made up the majority of new workers over the past three decades. Though the gender gap in earnings has narrowed since the 1960s, women's hourly wages are still approximately three-fourths those of men's.[28] One result is that employers have also benefited from hiring a growing share of female workers and paying them lower wages than male workers typically receive.

Some economists, looking closely at both firms and their workers, have recently found that the greatest portion of this wage gap is due to differences in hourly pay between men and women holding very similar jobs. In other words, businesses are indeed realizing savings by employing female rather than male workers, because they can pay women less to perform the same tasks.[29]

To understand how large a pool of potential funds for families this withheld pay represents, consider what it would mean to pay women at the same rate as men in similar jobs. Close analysis of firms and their workers shows that, after controlling for differences in education and experience, approximately half the difference in men's and women's wages is due to within-job discrimination.[30] The typical full-time woman worker between the ages of 22 and 54 now works 2,080 hours per year at an hourly wage of $12.50. If her wages were raised to what they would be in the absence of within-job discrimination, she would receive about $3,255 more per year.[31] Alternatively, she could work almost six weeks less per year, while taking home the same amount of pay. This extra income could fund nearly one and a half months of paid annual family leave.

Thus, a look at the difference in wages paid women and men doing almost identical jobs dramatically illustrates the gains to employers. Further, a number of analysts have long noted that the pay for jobs filled primarily by women is substantially lower than that earned by workers doing tasks of comparable value in male-dominated jobs.[32] These lower wages also represent savings for employers at the expense of women. Close analysis of firms and workers finds that about 30 percent of the gender wage gap is due to occupational sex segregation. Correcting for such discrimination would raise the typical woman worker's wage by about another $1 per hour. She would then take home a total of $5,200 extra in pay, or work more than two months less per year while receiving her original pay. Employers have also saved money by paying lower wages to women of color than to white women in similar jobs, and less to male workers of color than to their white counterparts. Returning these amounts to workers in the form of fair earnings would result in even greater gains for families of color.

The goal, of course, is both to raise the wages of all women and to provide paid family leave for all workers, both male and female. However, these examples provide some sense of the funds that have gone to employers rather than to families.

More Work, Little Gain

A look at trends in income among mothers over the last three decades of the twentieth century provides a further sense of how women and their families have been shortchanged. Several analysts have shown that hours of paid work greatly increased for families over those thirty years, with little gain in income, especially among the less educated. Because this rise in paid employment took place almost entirely among women, especially those raising children, it is both useful and important to tell this story from their perspective and to look as well at how such trends may differ among black and white mothers.[33]

At first glance, married mothers, both black and white, seem to be faring much better in 2000 than in 1970. As tables 1 and 2 show, they saw real growth in their earnings and personal income. Further, family income rose for all but high school dropouts. However, these gains are less than they initially appear and were realized unequally. Increases in both family income and personal earnings differ markedly among mothers with different levels of education. Patterns are very similar by race.

Family income actually fell among white high school dropouts, rose by less than 15 percent for most other mothers of both races, and grew more than 30 percent among black and white college graduates (see tables 1 and 2 and figure 24). Further, most of the increase in family income came from wives' earnings—especially during the 1970s and 1980s, when the wages of many men were stagnant or fell. Among the less educated, wives' earnings fully or partially offset losses in husbands' income. Thus, women's turn to paid work helped families stay afloat during a time of transition to the new service and high-tech economy.[34]

However, these limited gains were accompanied by a great increase in married women's employment. Black mothers put in one and a half times as many hours of paid work in 2000 as in 1970, while hours of paid work more than

TABLE 1   Income and Work of Married White Mothers, 1970 and 2000
(mean income in 1999 dollars)

	1970	2000	Absolute Change	Percentage Change
Four or more years of college				
Total earnings	$11,209	$29,148	$17,939	160
Total personal income	$12,682	$31,076	$18,394	145
Other family income	$71,311	$82,624	$11,313	16
Total family income	$83,993	$113,700	$29,707	35
Mothers' mean annual hours of paid work	471	1,277	806	171
Mean number of children	2.2	1.9	−0.3	−14
Some college				
Total earnings	$6,458	$17,385	$10,927	169
Total personal income	$7,132	$18,476	$11,344	159
Other family income	$61,045	$56,559	−$4,486	−7
Total family income	$68,177	$75,035	$6,858	10
Mothers' mean annual hours of paid work	428	1,249	821	192
Mean number of children	2.3	1.9	−0.3	−15
Four years of high school				
Total earnings	$6,172	$13,137	$6,965	113
Total personal income	$6,418	$13,949	$7,531	117
Other family income	$49,976	$46,223	−$3,753	−8
Total family income	$56,394	$60,172	$3,778	7
Mothers' mean annual hours of paid work	471	1,160	689	146
Mean number of children	2.3	1.9	−0.4	−18
Less than four years of high school				
Total earnings	$5,215	$7,628	$2,413	46
Total personal income	$5,510	$8,475	$2,964	54
Other family income	$41,336	$34,534	−$6,802	−17
Total family income	$46,846	$43,009	−$3,838	−8
Mothers' mean annual hours of paid work	446	819	372	83
Mean number of children	2.5	2.1	−0.4	−16

SOURCE: Author's calculations based on unpublished 1970 and 2000 IPUMS data.

NOTE: *Mothers* are women ages 22–54 with at least one child under 18 in the household; zero incomes and hours of work are included; hours of work for 1970 are estimates. Some numbers do not add up precisely due to rounding.

TABLE 2 Income and Work of Married Black Mothers, 1970 and 2000
(mean income in 1999 dollars)

	1970	2000	Absolute Change	Percentage Change
Four or more years of college				
Total earnings	$25,612	$35,563	$9,951	39
Total personal income	$26,078	$36,669	$10,591	41
Other family income	$42,248	$52,488	$10,240	24
Total family income	$68,326	$89,157	$20,831	31
Mothers' mean annual hours of paid work	1,105	1,699	595	54
Mean number of children	2.0	1.8	−0.2	−9
Some college				
Total earnings	$13,629	$20,918	$7,288	54
Total personal income	$13,895	$21,827	$7,933	57
Other family income	$38,885	$38,576	−$308	−1
Total family income	$52,780	$60,403	$7,625	14
Mothers' mean annual hours of paid work	977	1,534	557	57
Mean number of children	2.4	2.0	−0.3	−14
Four years of high school				
Total earnings	$9,669	$15,310	$5,641	58
Total personal income	$9,954	$16,186	$6,232	63
Other family income	$33,050	$32,689	−$361	−1
Total family income	$43,004	$48,875	$5,871	14
Mothers' mean annual hours of paid work	790	1,329	538	68
Mean number of children	2.7	2.1	−0.6	−21
Less than four years of high school				
Total earnings	$5,650	$9,342	$3,692	65
Total personal income	$6,110	$10,726	$4,615	76
Other family income	$27,296	$27,784	$488	2
Total family income	$33,406	$38,510	$5,103	15
Mothers' mean annual hours of paid work	598	948	351	59
Mean number of children	3.5	2.4	−1.1	−32

SOURCE: Author's calculations based on unpublished 1970 and 2000 IPUMS data.

NOTE: Mothers are women ages 22–54 with at least one child under 18 in the household; zero incomes and hours of work are included; hours of work for 1970 are estimates. Some numbers do not add up precisely due to rounding.

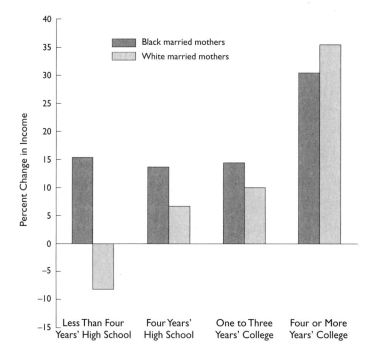

FIGURE 24.
Change in total family income among married mothers, by education and race, 1970–2000. From author's calculations based on unpublished 1970 and 2000 IPUMS data.

doubled among white mothers. We must remember that women had once spent some of that time cleaning their homes and washing their family's clothes. Household appliances and the market takeover of domestic chores enabled mothers to cut their hours of housework almost in half. This savings is not captured when we look only at changes in hours of paid employment. Taking it into account, we find that each hour of paid work actually represents, on average, an increase of about thirty minutes in the overall workload borne by mothers.[35]

Still, this increase is substantial. If we look at the amount these mothers would have earned without working longer hours, the earnings of both black and white women drop to about half that of their reported income. Among both races, the rise in family income of those without college degrees would shrink to little over 5 percent; the losses to high school dropouts would be even greater. In other words, in trading housework for paid work these mothers won almost no gains for their families. The rise in family income results mainly from a lengthening of their workday. Alternatively, if mothers were actually paid for their increased hours of work, families would have a sizable extra chunk of income. Instead, married mothers are putting in longer hours without sufficient rewards for their increased labor.

.   .   .

Unmarried mothers also reaped few rewards from their turn to the market, as tables 3 and 4 illustrate. While annual hours of paid work rose significantly among high school dropouts as well as college graduates of both races from 1970 to 2000, single mothers ended up with little more cash in their hands. Among each educational group, hours of paid work rose more than personal income or even these women's own earnings. Overall family income actually fell for most (see figure 25). This is mainly because gains in earnings by single mothers were largely undercut by a large drop in income from public assistance in the 1990s.[36] In general, these trends among single mothers were also quite similar by race. However, white single mothers benefited somewhat more from earnings by other family members in the 1990s, primarily because those in the less-educated group were more likely to live with their fathers, whose income rose more in the 1990s than that of black fathers.

In addition, the lack of gain from single mothers' turn to paid employment becomes even more obvious when these women's total hours of paid and unpaid work are considered. Almost half the growth in single mothers' earnings was due to an increase in their overall hours of labor. When adjusted for such overwork, losses grow larger. Even college graduates of both races saw little increase in family income. In other words, single mothers won no financial gain for their families in putting time once spent with children into paid work; even as they lengthened their workday, they fell further behind.[37]

Thus, though women's turn to the market, and the reduction of household work contributing to that turn, did bring some benefits to women and their families, these gains were unequally distributed and smaller than they initially appear. To a significant extent, they are explained by mothers' working more hours each day. Single mothers in particular won little from their turn to paid employment. Though the transformation of women's work has created a new abundance of time and wealth, women and their families have received little of either.

TABLE 3 Income and Work of Unmarried White Mothers, 1970 and 2000
(mean income in 1999 dollars)

	1970	2000	Absolute Change	Percentage Change
Four or more years of college				
Total earnings	$28,096	$37,713	$9,617	34
Welfare	$215	$45	−$170	−79
Total personal income	$35,922	$45,056	$9,134	25
Other family income	$8,474	$6,148	−$2,326	−27
Total family income	$44,396	$51,204	$6,808	15
Mothers' mean annual hours of paid work	1,177	1,793	616	52
Mean number of children	2.0	1.6	−0.5	−23
Some college				
Total earnings	$17,965	$21,636	$3,670	20
Welfare	$497	$206	−$291	−59
Total personal income	$24,482	$25,602	$1,120	5
Other family income	$9,984	$7,749	−$2,235	−22
Total family income	$34,466	$33,351	−$1,115	−3
Mothers' mean annual hours of paid work	1,157	1,648	492	43
Mean number of children	2.0	1.6	−0.4	−18
Four years of high school				
Total earnings	$15,432	$16,301	$869	6
Welfare	$851	$320	−$531	−62
Total personal income	$20,039	$19,410	−$629	−3
Other family income	$9,966	$9,050	−$917	−9
Total family income	$30,005	$28,460	−$1,546	−5
Mothers' mean annual hours of paid work	1,165	1,481	316	27
Mean number of children	2.1	1.7	−0.4	−19
Less than four years of high school				
Total earnings	$10,027	$9,857	−$171	−2
Welfare	$1,683	$680	−$1,003	−60
Total personal income	$14,936	$12,932	−$2,003	−13
Other family income	$8,754	$7,867	−$887	−10
Total family income	$23,690	$20,799	−$2,890	−12
Mother's mean annual hours of paid work	821	1,022	201	25
Mean number of children	2.4	1.9	−0.4	−18

SOURCE: Author's calculations based on unpublished 1970 and 2000 IPUMS data.

NOTE: Mothers are women ages 22–54 with at least one child under 18 in the household; zero incomes and hours of work are included; hours of work for 1970 are estimates. Some numbers do not add up precisely because of rounding.

TABLE 4 Income and Work of Unmarried Black Mothers, 1970 and 2000
(mean income in 1999 dollars)

	1970	2000	Absolute Change	Percentage Change
Four or more years of college				
Total earnings	$29,316	$33,051	$3,736	13
Welfare	$127	$118	−$9	−7
Total personal income	$30,773	$35,558	$4,785	16
Other family income	$9,565	$9,220	−$345	−4
Total family income	$40,338	$44,778	$4,440	11
Mothers' mean annual hours of paid work	1,355	1,778	431	24
Mean number of children	1.9	1.6	−0.3	−0.17
Some college				
Total earnings	$15,844	$19,974	$4,130	26
Welfare	$1,303	$337	−$965	−74
Total personal income	$18,461	$22,022	$3,561	19
Other family income	$9,927	$7,834	−$2,093	−21
Total family income	$28,388	$29,856	$1,468	5
Mothers' mean annual hours of paid work	1,158	1,566	408	35
Mean number of children	2.4	1.9	−0.5	−20
Four years of high school				
Total earnings	$11,843	$13,689	$1,846	16
Welfare	$2,131	$573	−$1,557	−73
Total personal income	$15,136	$15,763	$627	4
Other family income	$8,981	$6,784	−$2,197	−25
Total family income	$24,117	$22,547	−$1,570	−7
Mothers' mean annual hours of paid work	985	1,258	273	28
Mean number of children	2.7	2.1	−0.6	−22
Less than four years of high school				
Total earnings	$6,285	$8,003	$1,718	27
Welfare	$3,361	$1,007	−$2,354	−70
Total personal income	$10,907	$10,831	−$76	−1
Other family income	$6,177	$5,756	−$421	−7
Total family income	$17,084	$16,587	−$497	−3
Mothers' mean annual hours of paid work	618	813	196	32
Mean number of children	3.4	2.5	−0.9	−26

SOURCE: Author's calculations based on unpublished 1970 and 2000 IPUMS data.

NOTE: *Mothers* are women ages 22–54 with at least one child under 18 in the household; zero incomes and hours of work are included; hours of work for 1970 are estimates. Some numbers do not add up precisely because of rounding.

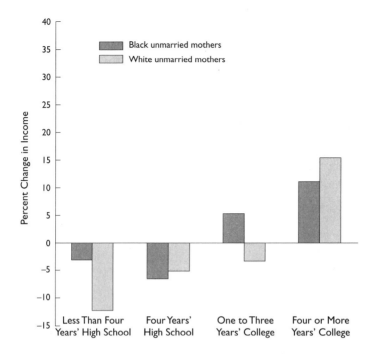

FIGURE 25.
Change in total family income among unmarried mothers, by education and race, 1970–2000. From author's calculations based on unpublished 1970 and 2000 IPUMS data.

Divisions among Women

New Resources for Social Policy

Thus far, the new gains in time and wealth have been distributed mainly along the old lines of power. However, women's historic turn to wages as their central means of support is also giving them greater ability to make demands on men, employers, and the state.

As increasing numbers of women rely on their own earnings, they are coming to perceive their interests as wage workers more clearly. Women's full move into the labor force has also given them greater economic and political resources, and women workers are becoming more organized. While manufacturing unions have faltered, union membership is growing rapidly among the service and clerical sectors, where women hold most of the jobs. In the past, unions have helped women workers voice demands for policies easing their domestic responsibilities, such as paid maternity leaves. Most recently, unions have succeeded in winning paid family leave at the state level, auguring well for future gains through this route.[38]

Further, the long-expected gender gap in voting has finally appeared.[39] Women workers now make up a larger portion of the Democratic constituency than they did thirty years ago, and their numbers give greater weight to their issues. Also, women's organizations have created a broad institutional framework. Though they originally focused mainly on improving women's access to good jobs, they may now be able to help gain new structural support for domestic tasks.

The changing base of women's support has also opened possibilities for new alliances. Most male workers now have wives in the labor force and therefore see policies that ease the difficulties of combining home and work as being in their own interest. Employers, for their part, would realize gains from shifting the costs of such policies to the state.

In sum, much like men's move off the land, women's turn from household to paid work is giving them a stronger base from which to claim entitlement to new policies to aid families in domestic and caregiving tasks. However, divisions among women themselves may fracture their efforts to realize such demands.

Inequalities in the Home

In the absence of effective social policies for family care, women have been thrown back on their own resources, widening the differences among them. Many analysts have stressed the inequalities among women in the labor force, arguing that highly paid women will meet their needs for domestic care privately, through the market. However, once again focus on the labor force alone has obscured another more important and pervasive inequality, that of differences among women in time for the home. Women workers in well-paid managerial and professional positions often do have access to family-friendly policies and are able to hire others to carry out domestic tasks.[40]

However, many women also benefit far more from a less-acknowledged strategy, a retreat from paid work that is bitterly envied by others. "Since when is being a working mother a choice?" asks one such overburdened woman. "I would have loved to have had the privilege of staying home to raise my children. Getting them out of bed at 5:30 am to get them fed, dressed and driven to daycare before I went on to work was never a picnic. . . . I have always HAD to work full-time."[41]

TABLE 5 Mean Labor Force Attachment of Mothers, by Education and Race, 2000

(percent)

Years of education	White Mothers				
	<12	12	13–15	16+	Total
Work					
Full-time, full-year	24.8	39.4	42.7	37.8	39.3
Full-time, part-year	16.4	13.2	12.5	17.5	14.4
Part-time, part- or full-year	18.7	22.6	25.7	26.0	24.5
Nonworker	40.1	24.8	19.1	18.7	21.8
Total	100.0	100.0	100.0	100.0	100.0

Years of education	Black Mothers				
	<12	12	13–15	16+	Total
Work					
Full-time, full-year	23.7	41.8	52.2	59.2	46.2
Full-time, part-year	20.9	21.5	22.3	22.7	21.9
Part-time, part- or full-year	15.9	13.8	13.3	10.3	13.3
Nonworker	39.5	22.9	12.2	7.8	18.6
Total	100.0	100.0	100.0	100.0	100.0

SOURCE: Author's calculations based on unpublished 2000 IPUMS data.

NOTE: *Mothers are women ages 22–54 with at least one child under 18 in the household.*

Withdrawal from the Labor Force

While most women are now in the labor force, this great shift toward paid work conceals another pattern. Most also withdraw from paid employment to a great extent while raising their children. As table 5 shows, less than half of either white or black mothers with children under 18 are full-time, year-round workers. Most work only part-time, part-year, or not at all.[42] Two-thirds of mothers caring for preschoolers have also withdrawn partially or completely from paid labor. Mothers working part-time have not dramatically increased their overall hours of labor beyond those of housewives in the 1960s. Instead, time use studies show, they are partly filling time that used to be spent on household tasks with paid employment. Full-time homemakers who focus solely on their family's care actually have more leisure than they did in the past, as the market has lessened many domestic chores.

Despite its appeal, this retreat from the labor force has obvious costs. Many analysts have pointed out that women working part-time have lower earnings and less job security or upward mobility than those working full-time. This

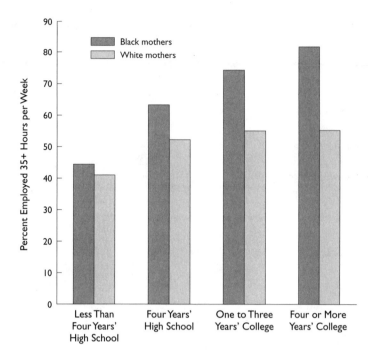

FIGURE 26.
Mothers employed 35+ hours per week, by education and race,
2000. From author's calculations based on unpublished 2000
IPUMS data.

arrangement also sustains gender inequality, giving men more power both in the workplace and at home.[43] However, there is another important inequity in this arrangement. The option of relying on a remnant of the gender division of labor for some space in which to carry out domestic tasks is not open to all mothers. As earlier chapters have shown, white and black women of the same level of education display roughly similar rates of involvement in motherhood and the labor force. However, when we consider women's access to support for their maternal role, another pattern stands out.

There are strong differences by race in time spent in homemaking. A much smaller share of African American mothers, whether married or on their own, cut back their hours of paid work when raising their families. Over two-thirds of black mothers with children under 18 work thirty-five or more hours a week, compared to little more than half of white mothers (see figure 26).[44] This disparity is most striking among women with college educations. White graduates are three times as likely to stay home as black college graduates when caring for children, and they are much less likely to work full-time when employed (see figure 26). At every level, down to high school dropouts, white mothers are able to devote more of their energies to the domestic realm than their black counterparts are. Though black women have long accorded greater value than white women to combining careers and family, economic pressures also clearly play an important role.

Support for Domestic Tasks

Women's ability to withdraw from the labor force when raising children is tied primarily to their husbands' income. Though homemaking as a lifelong occupation has all but disappeared, mothers now commonly rely partly on their own wages and partly on those of their husbands during the years of child raising. Their partial withdrawal from the workforce is the primary way in which women and their families are coping with the difficulties of combining home and work.[45]

However, access to such support differs greatly by race, as a detailed look at the sources of mothers' support illustrated in figure 27 makes clear. Overall, income from men plays more than twice as great a role for white mothers as for black mothers. Less than one-fifth of black mothers' support comes from men, and only a fraction from welfare. Instead, African American mothers rely overwhelmingly on their own earnings. White mothers also have more money to draw on than black mothers, enjoying access to more income from other family members (see tables 1–4). A similar disparity by race exists among women caring for young children.[46]

Behind these inequities by race lies a second crucial difference between mothers, that of whether a husband is present or not. Single mothers of both races have almost no support for their domestic labors, relying only minimally on either men or the state. Further, their total family income is about half that of married mothers of their own race (see tables 1–4). Black mothers not only are far more likely to be raising children on their own than white mothers but also do so under more difficult circumstances. The small amount of support that black single mothers receive for their domestic labors is more likely to come from the government. Also, at each educational level, they are more likely to be in poverty than white single mothers. They are also more likely to lose custody of their children. As the legal scholar Dorothy Roberts notes, "Black children make up nearly half of the foster care population, though they constitute less than one-fifth of the nation's children."[47]

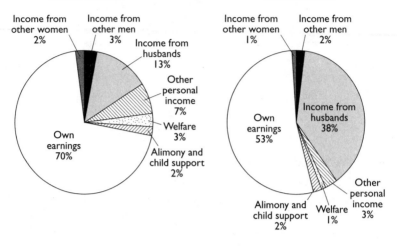

FIGURE 27.
Detailed sources of mothers' support, by race, 2000. From author's calculations based on unpublished March 2001 CPS data. For details, see chapter 6, note 49.

The painful reality revealed by these statistics is that while a substantial segment of women still receive some support for their household work, enabling them to limit their involvement in the labor force and focus on the domestic realm when its demands are greatest, many women do not. Thus withdrawing from paid work as the central strategy for handling work at home and for pay leaves almost half of mothers with little support for their domestic role. Instead, most are quite overworked.

This strategy also denies the chance of a family to other women, who may find they cannot take time off from their jobs without great costs or who may have children that are taken from them as the stress of raising them without help becomes too great. The absence of other options also pushes many women in a conservative direction, as the stress of juggling domestic chores and work encourages a turn back toward the old division of labor between the sexes. In recent years, the number of women giving up careers to care for their children has risen; even young women themselves receiving top-level college educations are making such plans.[48]

Finally, sharp disparity in provision for domestic tasks may cause divisions between women, preventing them from working together to realize policy shaped in their common interests. Indeed, as at the start of the previous century, a two-tiered relationship between home and market is emerging, giving some women space for their domestic tasks while leaving others to fend for themselves.

Inequalities in Women's Relationship to the Home

Thus, as the above examination of the situation of mothers today makes clear, women have been badly shortchanged in their turn from household to paid work, and some more so than others. Mothers as well as other women have turned strongly to the labor force. Most, in sharp contrast to forty years ago, now rely mainly on their own earnings rather than men's income for support. This change has imposed heavy demands on a growing number of mothers, while limiting the possibility of family life for others.

Women employed full-time or juggling work at home and for pay on their own are severely overworked during their years of raising children. The typical mother today is working far longer hours each week than in the 1960s. Such overwork is at first glance puzzling, because household tasks, and market production of a given set of goods as well, now require far less time than they did in the first decades after World War II. Further, the movement of these tasks and women's labor out into the market has created a new pool of income. As we have seen, however, the increase in time and wealth made possible by the transformation of women's domestic labor has not been equally enjoyed. Men, employers, and the state have pocketed much of this gain, in part by escaping their old obligations to provide some support for tasks of family care. Employers, for example, have realized profits by paying women workers less than men doing the same jobs. More-equal pay could give the typical woman worker or her partner one and a half months or more of paid family leave.

Women's turn to wages has given them new resources to claim more of the gains they have played a key role in creating. However, in the absence of alternatives, many women are falling back on a remnant of the old division of labor between the sexes. But this solution not only furthers gender inequality, it also gives some mothers some support from men for their domestic tasks while leaving others with none at all. This may fracture efforts for new collective provisions for family care.

In sum, the old arrangements between home and market have broken down dramatically over the past forty years. Reliance on their own wages has risen markedly for both white and black women, and most of the cultural and legal codes framing women's work in the home have come apart as well. However, the dismantling of the old gender division of labor, in its different forms, has given women fewer gains than initially appear. Once all the work they still do in the home is brought into the picture, it is clear women have received an inadequate share of the rewards from the transformation of their tasks and labor.

Further, while the old gender division of labor was radically altered over the second half of the twentieth century, it has not completely vanished. Instead, each of the old resolutions between home and work has been reduced by a fairly similar amount among white and black women.

The end result is that differences by race in women's relationship to the domestic realm have not disappeared along with the traditional framings of gender. Rather, the old double burden long associated with black women has taken on another shape. Once, most white women were able to focus solely on home and family while many black women had to supplement income from their husbands with their own work for pay. Today, though most white women are now only partially supported by their spouses' earnings, two-thirds of black women receive no financial help at all from men. Thus, a sharp divide by race in women's relationship to the domestic realm remains. Black women are almost three times as likely to be managing single parenthood and paid employment, for example. They are also far more likely to be raising their children in poverty despite such efforts.[49]

These differences by race have been joined by growing inequality by education, or class, in women's relationship to the home as well as to the labor force. Over the past forty years, rates of marriage have dropped and single motherhood risen far more rapidly among less-educated women than among those completing college. Among both black and white women, for example, high school graduates are now twice as likely as those with college degrees to be raising children on their own.

Unless reshaped by social policy, the result re-creates a divergence similar to that seen at the turn of the last century. A segment of predominantly white middle-class women is managing to secure some space for their household work. Another group, however, one in which African American and other women of color are overrepresented, is being left with no support for their domestic chores and must work long hours to accomplish both sets of tasks. Still others are denied families altogether. In short, this latest encounter between home and market appears to be resulting once again in differing resolutions, which are furthering the inequalities of gender and race while widening those of class.

New Possibilities for Social Policy

The divisive resolutions of women's involvements with family and paid work are not inevitable. Rather, as at the start of the 1900s, we have come to a moment in which the relationship between home, market, and state is being reshaped. We can look forward or backward for solutions to women's problems.

Several centuries ago, when a wave of poor, displaced farmers appeared across the English countryside, some argued for a return to the hierarchies of the past. Others recognized that economic and legal changes had undercut the old way of life so thoroughly that it could not be restored and that to do so would undercut England's rise to world power. Instead, they sought new policies suited to the emerging commercial economy.[50]

Today in the United States, the desire for more time for home and family has encouraged a look back toward the policies of the early twentieth century, which provided some protection for women's maternal role. But those policies were just one component of a large and complex framework of support built around the old gender division of labor. We cannot put this old arrangement of work, or the cultural practices and legal rulings that helped sustain it, back together again. Earlier chapters have traced out the reasons for its demise, as a reduced need for women's full-time work in the home and more productive use of their labor in the wage economy opened new possibilities in both private and public realms.

Just as the breakdown of the old arrangements between home and market was not slow and gradual but a dramatic rupturing after the buildup of long tensions, so there are moments in which new approaches suddenly crystallize. Certain strategies win out over others, made concrete through new government legislation, for example, or through pacts between workers and employers. We are at such a point. Women still have the potential to shape the outcome, if they can recognize their common interests.

The number of books and articles presenting detailed proposals for resolving the conflict between home and work is already large and rapidly growing.[51] Here I briefly outline approaches that might best ensure more space and time for the home in ways more equal across gender, class, and race, from the perspective of the historic transformation of women's work.

There is much room for progress. At present, the U.S. government provides little beyond a small set of tax-based credits; temporary aid to poor, primarily single female, parents; and three months of unpaid leave to those caring for new infants or ailing family members. As one scholar notes, "This country's puny social programs and abysmal support for families are a glaring exception among Western democracies."[52] The extraordinary changes in women's relationship to home and work require a revolution in social policy as well. We cannot construct viable new supports for the home within the old policy framework, which was designed in response to men's move off the land and women's persistence in the home. Instead, we need new ways of thinking about and funding tasks of family care, and new ways of committing employers and the state, as well as husbands and fathers, to their provision.

A New Pool of Funds for Caregiving

We have seen a vast increase in national income over the past thirty years. A disproportionate share of this increase has gone to employers and the top third of male workers.[53] These funds could be used instead for new supports for family care. Most advanced industrialized countries include provisions for family maintenance in their system of social insurance, paid for by a mix of contributions from employers, employees, and the government. The United States is alone in not legislating paid maternity leave and provides far less in the way of family maintenance. Only one-half of 1 percent of its gross domestic product goes to cash benefits to families, less than one-third as much, on average, as in European countries.[54]

Thus, rather than dismantling the supports that remain, we need to widen their scope. Restoring taxes on corporations and the wealthiest families to the levels of thirty-five years ago would help preserve existing payments to the elderly. We could create as well a new national fund for family maintenance, to which employers as well as workers would contribute. This could be used to pay for universal child support, other caregiving allotments, and family leave. These funds could be supplemented by private pensionlike plans funded by monthly deductions from workers that are matched by their employers, thereby creating a further source of income on which families could draw when caregiving demands become high.[55]

A Shorter Workweek and Higher Wages

We also need to reduce the amount of time claimed by paid work. Here, workers' organizations at both the top and bottom of the occupational spectrum, as well as women's organizations, can play a key role in demanding limits on hours of work, fair overtime compensation when those limits are exceeded, and wages sufficient to support a family. Such organizations can also work to heighten job security and improve the access of all to training and employment opportunities.[56] The professional associations that gave doctors, lawyers, and professors power must be remade in stronger yet more equitable form, essentially as unions. One task is to reshape the standard career track. A secure midrange path in the professions, for example, rather than the existing system of intense pressure resulting in an all-or-nothing payoff, in which some make partner or get tenure and others lose their jobs, would ease conflicts between work and family.

Unions can also play an important role in raising wages for less-educated workers and women, especially women of color. Female-dominated and caregiving occupations have disproportionately low wages. Raising women's wages to equal those of men doing similar jobs would not only provide families with more money (or, alternatively, time) but also encourage a more equal division of labor both at home and in the workplace. Unions are crucial players in the fight to win higher pay in such jobs, both directly through negotiations with employers and indirectly by pressuring legislators to raise the minimum wage. They can also push to improve benefits and basic conditions in low-wage jobs.[57] Such conditions discourage or destroy marriages. Raising the minimum wage, the central cause of wage inequality among women, may put out of business certain employers that are dependent on very cheap labor. However, such companies feed off and sustain inequality and slow the development of new technology and of more effective social policy.

More Time for the Home

The primary goal in setting limits on hours of paid employment and raising wages is to create more time for the home. The current patterns, of one full-time and one part-time worker, or two full-time workers, should be replaced by three-quarter-time work from each individual, or a thirty-hour week. Between tending to children and aging relatives, most individuals spend their prime years of adulthood involved in caregiving tasks of some kind. We need to claim and defend space for such care against the demands of employers and build the time it requires into our overall concept of work, with provisions to expand it further when such burdens are heaviest.[58] A key step is to broaden the concept of family leave, to include pregnancy, for example, and to insist on the right to pay during such leave, whether the recipient is currently employed or not. Universal child support would also help families safely cut back on their paid employment when they find the demands of care particularly high.[59]

A New Definition of Adulthood

The creation of new social policy requires more than the championing of specific programs, however broad in scope. We also need a new definition of citizenship, one that recognizes the right of every adult to be involved in work at home and for pay, and thus the right of each person both to a good job and to time for caregiving and a life outside of work. This new definition requires reframing men's and women's concepts of adulthood.

Of particular importance, as our examination of women's differing paths from household to paid work has shown, are policies that shift young women from an early and primary identification with the maternal role toward preparation for both paid work and parenthood. Giving them control over childbearing through access to reliable birth control is one way of doing this, but access to good education and good jobs is even more important.[60] High-quality public education for all would give young women, and young men, many more options in life, preparing them for jobs that make both individual autonomy and marriage possible. It would also reduce inequalities in women's, and men's, relationships to home and family.

At the same time, we need to take steps that encourage men to take on greater responsibility for and pride in caregiving and other domestic chores, and that promote the idea of marriage as an equal partnership. While their time spent on household tasks and child care has increased markedly in recent decades, men still do far less than women in the home. Restructuring work and family roles to encourage them to spend much more time in caregiving when their children are little would ease women's domestic burdens and set good patterns for the future.[61] But urging men to assume an equal share of household labor and women to contribute outside the home as well as within it, though important, is not enough. We cannot leave the burdens of domestic care in the hands of families alone.

Collective Provision of Caregiving

Caregiving must also be provided collectively—for example, through expanded high-quality public child care, early childhood education, after-school programs, elder care and assisted living facilities, and universal health care. The low returns that women have received for their increased hours of paid work are further undercut by their need to pay for domestic tasks once done in the home. Child care, for example, now consumes almost one-tenth of a typical family's income.[62] Government subsidies of such collective provisions for care would also create a large number of fairly well-paid jobs, held by trained workers whose much-needed assistance would aid families caring for dependents, from newborns to aging relatives. Finally, every family needs and deserves a place to live. Affordable housing is a basic necessity.

Greater Equality of Family Income

New social policies, such as public child care and paid family leave, together with higher wages for the lower segment of workers, would reduce the demand for and the supply of market-based solutions. Inequality of family income both enables some women to stay at home while others work long hours and creates a situation in which some have the money to hire help while others must accept their low terms. Giving a greater share of corporate profits to workers, especially female workers, rather than top executives and creating a more equitable tax structure are two approaches that we might take to lessen inequality among families.

Help for Single Mothers

The group most vulnerable at this moment are women who have lost all support for their domestic tasks while still facing a heavy workload at home, as they struggle to raise their children by themselves. Government aid to poor single mothers has been one of the few programs providing both some cushion in times of economic difficulty and some support for caregiving. However, the best way to meet these needs is not to conflate them or focus on one group alone but to translate them into a set of basic rights for all women and men—rights to time for caregiving tasks, to decent jobs, and to protection against downturns in the market. All the policies suggested above, from equal access to high-quality education and good jobs to paid family leave, would greatly improve the situation of single mothers. Higher wages and universal child support allotments, for example, would make it easier for these women to work part-time. Collective services like child care not only are essential to their employment but would also shift some of the weight of caregiving off their shoulders.[63]

A New Concept of Rights

For these policies to be adopted and succeed, our concept of rights must be transformed as well. The liberal tradition dominant in the United States frames rights as an assertion against control by the state rather than as claims to its support. Such rights are also limited insofar as they are conceived in individual terms. Yet the right to life and the pursuit of happiness claimed in the Declaration of Independence assumed women's labor in caregiving tasks and the context of a family in which to thrive. Individual freedom from domination is still crucial to the struggle for gender and racial equality. However, to fully realize that freedom we must conceive of rights—and with them, obligations—not as individuals but as deeply interconnected equals.[64]

At present, women's relationships to home and work are being framed primarily by other interests. To see such arrangements as final resolutions is prematurely negative.[65] The dismantling of obsolete policies shaping the relationship between the domestic realm and an old industrial order, while fraught with danger, has also opened space for new rules to be devised.

The first decades after World War II are now often referred to as great years for labor, when a compact between workers, employers, and the state bore fruit. Yet this was also a time of great inequalities of gender and race. Women's turn from household to paid work may make it possible to lessen such inequalities. It also offers the chance to create a new paradigm of citizenship shaped to fit the needs not just of male workers but rather of all adults, acknowledging their right to provisions for care as well as to decent jobs. The key is to widen our vision to include both private and public realms. Women are now realizing that the world they have lost, while rife with inequities, offered some space for care and love. If this loss is honored, and if the economic and political realities of its demise are understood, then women, and men, may recognize their common interest in demanding new supports for the home as well as paid work, in a form that will reduce rather than heighten existing inequalities.

Women's lives have altered profoundly over the past forty years. The baby boomers have followed very different paths than their mothers; their own daughters are now setting off further into the future. The forms of family, work, and community that these young women will build in the new terrain claimed by those who preceded them remain to be seen.

It has been hard to grasp the full scope of these changes. It is clear that women, particularly wives and mothers, have taken a great step into the labor force. But behind this move lies another little-noticed story, that of the breakdown of women's age-old arrangements of life and labor, and of their transformation into work done for pay.

The worlds of home and motherhood as we have known them have all but disappeared. Only remnants of these old ways of life remain. Women no longer work primarily in the home, supported by their husbands, but for employers, and their own wages now provide the bulk of their support. The American economy has changed as well. Many of women's old domestic tasks, from the preparation of meals to the creation of life itself, are now generating vast profits. Women's turn to work for pay has also led to great gains for the market economy. However, only makeshift arrangements for care have replaced those of the past, leaving most women scrambling to find time for those they love.

Most of us are pulled, in one way or another, by images of the world we have lost. However, it does not make sense to retrace the steps of the long and difficult journeys women have undertaken, looking for the homes they have left.

Rather, we need to keep going forward, toward new dreams of what family life might be, freed from endless rounds of drudgery. The vision of female reformers at the start of the twentieth century, that of lifting the domestic realm to a position of respect and power in the new economic and social order, offers one path to the future. Their vision was premature, as the realm they championed was based on an unequal and increasingly outmoded form of labor that had to be taken apart before it could be rebuilt in new form. However, today the means exist to create time and space for life outside the demands of the market in more humane and equal form. Understanding the immense alterations in the relationship between home and market that have occurred in recent decades is a first step in this process.

The Changing Nature of Home and Work

This book has addressed the dramatic changes that took place in women's lives over the second half of the twentieth century, and the shifts in the market economy that accompanied them. Numerous studies have analyzed one or another of these events, from the rise of female-headed families among the poor to the hardships faced by mothers working at home and for pay today. Others have traced the development of a world of work marked by growing inequality and job insecurity. These are not separate issues, however, but deeply related parts of a larger process of change that has long eluded analysts.

This book has provided an understanding of how these profound alterations in both private and public realms fit together, and the deeper causes underlying and joining them. In doing so it has uncovered a story which has not yet been clearly told, that of the historic transformation of women's work within the home, which preceded and underlay their turn to work for wages. Such changes have also played a key role in the rise of the new economy in the United States in the late twentieth century, but one that has not yet been adequately recognized or rewarded.

Telling this story first required grounding gender in the actual conditions of women's lives and work, which long centered on their performance of domestic and reproductive tasks under men's control and support. The second step was to see the relationship between this gender division of labor and a developing market economy as a dynamically changing one, in which this old arrangement of labor was first sustained, then eroded, and finally, in the years after World War II, radically broken down. These interactions between home and market were shaped by different groups seeking to realize the potential created by the transformation of women's tasks and labor into work for pay. Close examination of the experiences of African American and white women in the nineteenth- and twentieth-century United States, with focus on the period from 1960 to 2000, provided the details from which this account emerged.

However, the full story of women's lives could be seen only by breaking free from established explanations of social and economic change—both the grand theories that gave rise to the discipline of sociology and the accounts of men's moves from fields to factories built upon these theoretical foundations. These accounts, focusing on men's experiences in the nineteenth century, assumed too rapid and complete a process of social change, ignoring women's persistence in a heavy set of household chores and the importance of their labor. Further, they failed to see that such work might one day also be taken over by the market, dismissing it as "natural" in form. Clear grasp of the changes in women's lives also required several further shifts of focus, not only from men but also from the market economy alone, and from emphasis on differences between women to recognition of deep similarities among them.

These shifts of focus raised the domestic realm, that area of seemingly trivial and mundane household chores, fully into light. They forced consideration not only of a set of tasks essential to survival but also of the way such work was organized, through a large number of cultural and legal codes and customs that held women in the home and committed men, employers, and the state to some support for such labor. Only when this "domestic economy," in its differing forms, was lifted clearly into view could we see how and why support for this realm changed over time, and how such changes varied by race and class.

Too often, women's experiences have been distorted by forcing them into a timeline and set of concepts based on men's past. Clear perception of the gender division of labor, or women's domestic economy, and its own interactions with an expanding market, allows instead consideration of parallels with and differences from men's experiences. The social turmoil, economic hardship, and struggles over welfare state formation accompanying men's move off the land to work for wages has generated a vast literature. This book has placed battles over the domestic realm, the rise of female-headed families among the poor, and recent furor over social policy in the context of a similar historic move on the part of women. It has also drawn attention to less familiar moments, such as the market's imposition of new demands on groups still engaged in older forms of work, or the abandonment of a system of labor when it no longer seemed useful.

Many scholars of gender have turned to culture or politics as existing economic explanations failed to make sense of the dramatic alterations of women's lives. Full understanding of such alterations and their consequences, however, required bringing the economy back in, remade in women's own language. To see the missing half of women's story, we had to look at changes in women's work within the home, not simply outside it. More important, we had to look at how different groups have shaped and benefited from the dramatic changes in women's lives, and how their actions affected the legal and cultural structures framing support for caregiving and other domestic tasks, both in the first years after World War II and today.

That the market is embedded in society is now a popular concept in academia. However, how the market becomes so embedded is also an important issue. Often its incursions are resisted, for while they bring gains to some, they mean only the loss of an older way of life or increased burdens for others. The distribution of those gains is another great source of conflict. Over the past forty years, women's lives and American homes have been a key site of such battles.

Three Encounters between Home and Market

The comparative approach of this book has highlighted three main moments of negotiation between home and market in the United States. First, in early America, production within the family was organized through a division of labor by gender, with both African American and white women carrying out a large number of burdensome domestic chores under men's control. The emerging market did little to reduce such tasks, which remained essential in both rural and urban areas through the nineteenth and early twentieth centuries, but instead made new demands on women's labor.

Like many groups before them, women sought to resist such demands. Most white women were able to secure space for their domestic tasks through the mid–twentieth century, in part through public policies, such as the family wage, protective labor legislation, and "mothers' pensions." African American women, in contrast, were forced to take on another set of chores, leaving them little time for tasks crucial to family survival. As elsewhere when the market imposed new burdens upon an earlier form of work, they managed by intertwining the two sets of chores, drawing on an extended network of kin, and pushing themselves to the limit. Such efforts, though, brought not greater wealth but only exhaustion, poverty, and early death.

For women of both races, however, the cultural, legal, and economic steps that reinforced their persistence in household work achieved only a fragile balance, full of tensions and contradictions. As new goods and services appeared, and as increasing numbers of women worked for wages or sought greater rights outside the home, these tensions grew. The full impact of a developing industrial economy on women's household work was delayed several decades, however, by the use of African American women as low-paid domestic workers, and by the Great Depression and World War II.

In the latter half of the twentieth century, a second collision between the home and a maturing market reduced each of the old arrangements framing women's work in the home to a shell of its former self. This process was furthered by periods of economic expansion and decline. As a booming post–World War II economy lessened women's domestic tasks while also opening new possibilities, the laws and customs that held women in the home and committed others to the support of their labor came to seem restrictive to many. This led different groups of men, employers, and government officials, as well as women themselves, to challenge and undo many of the cultural and legal framings of women's domestic economy, though others fought furiously to preserve their old ways of life. Economic difficulties in the 1970s and 1980s brought a contradictory alliance that, while championing the male breadwinner family, allowed employers and the state to abandon support for women's work in the home, forcing increasing numbers of men to do so as well.

The changes in divorce law, the alterations in family structure, and the debates over social policy that caused much furor in the decades after World War II were all part of this dismantling of the old gender division of labor. The withdrawal of their old means of support also threw many women into new or deeper poverty until they could secure access to decent jobs. Though an increasing number of women came to avoid such hardship by turning to the labor force and making gains within it, others held to their domestic role despite the disappearance of support for such work, in part because their options in the wage economy worsened. The result was the creation of an underclass among women themselves.

However, this was not just a story of loss and devastation, or one affecting women's lives alone. Rather, the pieces of women's old domestic economy have furnished much of the raw material for constructing a new and more prosperous social order. Market provision of tasks once done only by women in the home, from the preparation of meals to care of the young, has dominated job growth over the last third of the twentieth century, and women themselves have been the primary source of new labor. The use of their skills, whether in advanced research or routine tasks of care, contributed almost $1 trillion to the gross domestic product over this period.

Such changes have also had major consequences for women themselves. In 1960, most white women and almost half of black women still depended primarily on their husbands' earnings. Today, less than one-third of white women and barely over one-tenth of black women rely mainly on men's income for support. Instead, the livelihood of the great majority rests primarily on their own earnings.

This turn from marriage to the market has played out differently among college graduates and high school dropouts, and has varied by race as well. But on the whole, though the transformation of women's tasks and labor has created a new pool of time and money, few of these gains have come to women and their families. The costs of this outcome are most evident among women caring for children and other dependents. A growing segment of mothers, those employed full-time and single mothers coping with work at home and for pay, are gravely overworked. They are working longer hours than most mothers in the 1960s, or even the first decades of the twentieth century, despite the sharp reduction of their domestic tasks by an expanding market. Further, though spending many more hours in paid employment than thirty years ago, most have seen little rise in family income.

Instead, the potential created by market takeover of women's household work has gone primarily to other groups. Employers have benefited, for example, from the use of women as workers, paying them lower wages to do the same work as men. If these savings went instead to women, they would have more money or time for themselves or their families. The state, in emphasizing marriage and women's work for wages, has also renounced almost all obligation to help families survive.

The problems facing women today are much like those confronting earlier groups of men when they moved off the land. They too found their wages insufficient, and old arrangements of care no longer viable. However, their turn to work for wages brought struggles forcing their employers and the state to take on a greater share of the costs of family maintenance. Similarly, women's turn from household to wage labor has also given them new resources to demand more of the wealth they are producing, and new commitments from men, employers, and the state to the tasks of care that remain.

However, while the old gender division of labor that once supported women's work in the home has broken down, it has done so unevenly. Most women still have some time for domestic tasks, especially when their children are very young, because they are able to draw partly on their husbands' income, and so can retreat from paid work partly or altogether. However, an increasing number of women must rely solely on their own earnings and efforts. Such inequity may fracture attempts to frame a new relationship between home, market, and state that reflects the interests of all women.

In sum, comparison of the experiences of African American and white women shows that this latest encounter with the market is once again playing out on two different tracks, with far more negative consequences for some women than others. These differences arise not simply because some have more limited opportunities than others in the wage economy. Perhaps more crucially, support for women's work in the home has also come apart in different ways, creating new disadvantages as well as gains in doing so. In general, the turn from marriage to the market has been more abrupt, the loss of support from men and the state more complete, and the consequences of that loss much harsher for less-educated women, and for black women overall. As a result, some women are far more heavily burdened with domestic tasks than are others, preventing them from succeeding in the wage economy and creating a legacy of inequality that will stretch far into the future.

Broader Implications for Women

This book has stressed the importance of looking at women's work in the home as well as at the wage economy and of seeing the relationship between these two areas as a dynamically changing one. In doing so, it provides an analytic framework that can help us better understand the past and present hardships facing other groups of women, both in the United States and abroad, and the differences in their experiences.

Women in Industrialized Countries

A sea change in the relationship between home and work similar to that seen in the United States took place in many other industrialized countries over the last decades of the twentieth century. Married women's labor force participation increased dramatically in Europe over these years, and many policy arrangements framed around the old gender division of labor were dismantled. By the 1970s in Sweden, as one scholar observes, "the basis for women's social entitlements was transformed from that of dependent wife to worker."[1] In France in the 1970s and 1980s, policy supporting women's work in the home suffered attacks similar to those seen in the United States, and in Britain as well the male breadwinner model altered significantly. Once-socialist countries have also removed many of their mechanisms that had provided for tasks of family maintenance.

To date, cross-national comparisons have focused primarily on shifts in social policy and their impact on gender inequality. While such studies also provide useful assessments of variations in the drop in marriage rates or in the rise of female-headed families, we also need to understand how these events are connected if we are to comprehend their deeper causes. We therefore must look at economic as well as political changes, particularly the interactions between women's work in the home and a growing market economy both at the start of the twentieth century and today. A wide range of scholars, whether focusing on policy elites or on class struggle, have acknowledged the dynamics of industrialization underlying and giving rise to the formation of welfare states. However, we have lacked a clear understanding of how those dynamics have played out in women's lives. This book provides an understanding of their impact among two different groups of women in the United States.

The interactions between home and market have no predictable or inevitable pattern, however. Rather, the task is to widen our understanding of how these encounters are unfolding in other countries, including those now setting out on their own paths to development. We need to look at women's varying routes from household to wage labor, the role played by the transformation of their domestic realm into work for pay, the relations of power influencing the distribution of gains from this transformation, and how such encounters between the realms of home and market are shaped by and are shaping a new economic and political world order.

The United States represents one extreme in this encounter, exceptional not only in the weakness of its welfare state but also in the ability of most American women to stave off the market's initial demands for their labor until it had assumed and thereby substantially reduced many of their household chores. While this same pattern has been seen in a few other areas, most notably Great Britain, it is unusual and requires further study. The explanation may lie in the leading role played by private rather than state-led development in these countries. The emergence of a large group of prosperous employers not only enabled many men to keep their spouses at home but also gave their wives and daughters great resources, in the form of education, money, and political networks, that could be wielded in defense of the domestic realm. Further comparative research can help us better understand the factors shaping women's relationships to work at home and for pay.[2]

Though the United States lies at one end of a range of variations, this book points to several issues that are important to examine elsewhere. Most comparative analyses of gender have looked primarily at the experience of the majority of women in the countries under consideration. Taking into account African American women as well as white women in the United States brings new insights into relationships between gender, market, and the state. It highlights the extreme inequality that can result when the market is only weakly regulated, and in the interests of one group of women alone. While some women in the United States were able to preserve their domestic realm, others were denied the time and resources necessary to care for their families. In addition, great disparities in income, justified through discrimination by race and class, enabled some women to hire others, prolonging the existence of the gender division of labor itself.

An examination of the experiences of women of both races not only shows how the relationship between the gender division of labor and the market can unfold in different ways but also throws into stark relief aspects of that unfolding that might otherwise not be so noticeable, such as the extent to which support for women's household work may collapse as the market takes over many domestic chores and men, employers, and the state lose interest in paying for such labor. The dramatic rise of female-headed families and their overrepresentation among the poor also make clear the hardship that the collapse of such support often brings to women, in the absence of new ways to provide for domestic tasks.

Tracing the dynamic relationship between home and market in the United States through the start of the twenty-first century also adds an important dimension to women's demands for new social policy. A growing number of scholars have drawn attention to the value of caregiving and the importance of supporting it. By closely examining women's work in the home, we can uncover the gains in time and money created by the conversion of these tasks and women's own labor into work for pay. Such an analysis grounds moral pleas that more national income go to child care or paid family leave, for example, in real material conditions. It reveals a pool of income that women could claim and use to fund new provisions for domestic tasks in ways that are more equal across gender, class, and race.

Women in the United States

Once we recognize the dynamic relationship unfolding between the gender division of labor and a maturing market, we can better understand the hardships faced by Latina, Asian American, Native American, and other groups of women within the United States. It is particularly important to consider Latina women, now the largest minority in the United States.

On the whole, Latina women are still more tied to the domestic realm than are African American or white non-Hispanic women. A greater share of Latina women overall, and less-educated Latina women in particular, are married than African American and white non-Hispanic women; a smaller share of Latina mothers are employed; and their reliance on men's income is greater. At the same time, however, Latina women are now experiencing the fastest rise in single motherhood and the highest rate of poverty among women heading families. These growing problems are clear evidence that the gender division of labor, or men's support for women's household work, is breaking down among this group as well. This breakdown is causing great hardship, because many of these women work for very low wages. Latina women have largely replaced African American women in private domestic work and also provide much of the labor for other low-paid service jobs. Their contribution to the ranks of private household workers tripled over the last two decades of the twentieth century.[3]

A full assessment of the experience of Latina women would be a complex project, requiring a separate volume. Adding to such complexity is the large number of groups encompassed by the term. To further complicate the issue, there are important differences within each group of Latina women. For example, Puerto Rican women with college educations are faring better than black college graduates in many ways. They are more likely to work in professional or managerial positions, for example. But among women with little education, Puerto Rican women hold worse jobs on average than black women, and they are much more likely to face poverty if they become single mothers.[4]

Behind such differences lies the crucial role played by immigration. New arrivals to the mainland United States confront many difficulties, from language barriers to a lack of legal rights. However, immigration also often brings, or results from, a sharp collision between home and market. Many women are making an abrupt move from a poor agricultural setting to an economy in which men's need for a wife's household labor has been sharply reduced, and government and employer support for such work is minimal. Indeed, immigrants are among the least likely to secure jobs paying a family wage. Under these adverse conditions, many marriages end or fail to take place. Further, immigration in and of itself often breaks apart families. The result is that yet another group of women are being subjected to poverty and the struggle to survive on their own wages alone. To understand these issues more deeply, we must widen the scope of comparative analysis.

Women in Newly Industrializing Countries

Cross-national comparisons have focused on highly industrialized countries. However, we must consider as well how women's work is being transformed in other countries now struggling to industrialize and in the global economy as a whole. Such an analysis can enlarge our understanding of the various ways the gender division of labor and a growing market economy may interact. It also makes clear the importance of paying attention to real material conditions and issues of economic inequality as well as issues of cultural representation.[5]

A growing number of studies are exposing the use of women as a cheap source of labor by corporations setting up factories overseas.[6] It is crucial to uncover the inhumane conditions of such work. However, behind such abuse lies a still larger process of exploitation that is brought to light when women's work in the home in these countries is taken into account as well. Their domestic labor makes possible the low wages of all workers and imposes a heavy double burden on female workers caring for children or other family members. The encounters between the gender division of labor and an emerging market in the nineteenth-century United States (described in chapter 2) have relevance here, as they demonstrate the costs to human life when the market succeeds in imposing new demands on women still engaged in domestic tasks essential to family survival.

Other lessons can be drawn from that early encounter in the United States as well. The growing demand for goods traditionally produced by women, such as handicrafts made by peasant women in China or Central America, has led some to argue that increasing involvement with the market will itself bring women economic independence. But that is not what happened in the nineteenth-century United States. Instead, men took control of women's dairy production when it became the central source of family income, steering their wives once again toward household tasks.

The key is to look at the gender division of labor, as well as the market and state policies, and to see the relationship between them as a historically dynamic one. From such a perspective, we see more clearly how old arrangements for family care are breaking down around the world, at different moments in the process of industrialization and in different ways than in the United States. We can also better appreciate the multifaceted nature of this breakdown and its consequences.

A brief look at the experiences of women in the People's Republic of China illustrates the markedly different ways interactions between home and economic and political development can occur. It shows, for example, that the state, not only through social policies but also in the role of employer, can also make claims on women and pursue its interests at their expense.

A new demand for labor was successfully imposed on Chinese women early in the process of industrialization, long before their household tasks were significantly reduced. Though the Maoist regime drew women into the workforce in the 1950s and 1960s, praising them for "holding up half the sky" and pledging to fund collective domestic services in exchange, the state fell far short of meeting the need for such services. Instead, almost all the gains from women's work outside the home went to building more factories rather than providing for family care.[7]

The price paid by women was vividly described by successive generations of Chinese women writers over the following decades. A story by Shen Rong, for example, herself made ill by overwork in the 1960s, describes an eye surgeon who suffered a serious heart attack when quite young, brought on by pressures at the hospital and at home. Though Shen Rong blamed herself for failing to carry out her dual roles, worrying she had been "a bad wife and mother,"[8] women coming after her grew increasingly critical of the burdens placed on them. The conflicts between paid work and domestic demands have brought growing protests against the inequities of the gender division of labor, culminating in its rejection altogether. Stunned by motherhood and the tasks expected of her sex alone, for example, Li Xiaojiang, a pioneering scholar of women's studies, has recently condemned the "more than forty years of mental and physical exhaustion caused by the extraordinary stress of the double role."[9]

Further, the old arrangements for family care are clearly breaking down in China, as increasing numbers of fathers and the state itself escape such obligations. In the absence of new policy, such breakdown is imposing great hardships on women. *The Ark*, a novella by Zhang Jie published in the early 1980s, foresaw their problems, describing the difficulties faced by three women in their 40s living on their own.[10]

Since then, the numbers of single mothers have grown rapidly, and the problems they face are now much discussed in China. "Single Chinese Mothers Beset with Troubles" announced a 2004 headline in the *China Daily*, a national newspaper. A survey by a Chinese trade union found that many single mothers faced a sharp drop in income after divorce, and had difficulty getting jobs, in part because of the time they had given to domestic tasks. Almost one-third were responsible for aging parents as well.[11]

In the cities educated young women are recognizing the costs imposed by the domestic role and giving primacy to their careers. However, they are also beginning to assert their rights to love and children. Well aware that they contribute significantly to the country as productive workers, they are demanding greater support for tasks of family care. At present, Li Xiaojiang notes, given the burdens they shoulder both in and outside the home, women in China "are required, in fact, to shoulder the whole sky."[12]

The lack of new policies committing employers, fathers, and government to provide support for tasks of family care is forcing women to resort to private strategies. In Hong Kong, for example, mothers are driven to accept low-paid factory work as way to gain the flexibility they need to take their children to school or care for them when they become sick.[13]

In other regions of the world, from Latin America to Africa, women are struggling with similar problems. Thus, whether we look at countries that industrialized a century or so ago, or at those now undertaking such development, or at different groups of women within a given country, we can see dramatically changing relationships between gender, market, and state, and similarities as well as differences in their unfolding. We see the creation of a "double burden" when private or public employers gain access to women's labor while arduous domestic chores persist, but we also see the dismantling of old supports for women's household work, bringing hardships as well as new opportunities. We see the contributions made by women's work in the home but also by the transformation of these tasks and women's own labor into work for pay, generating profits that could be used to provide for family care. Finally, as women rely increasingly on their own wages for support, we see their growing defense of their own interests against those of other groups, yet also inequities between women themselves, which may thwart such efforts.

Women and the Global Economy

In considering the situation of women throughout the world, we must also step back to look at the relationship between home and market in the global economy as a whole. Inequities between women in the handling of domestic tasks are more extreme when viewed on this scale. There is growing attention, for example, to the use of women from low-income countries as poorly paid domestic labor in richer countries, such as the United States, Taiwan, and Canada.[14]

Difficulties of industrializing in the current global order and the policies of international lending institutions have created hardships in many countries. The lack of jobs and the burdens of the gender division of labor in their own countries, and demand for service workers in postindustrial economies, have led many women to seek employment abroad. As in the past, such work poses grave threats to these women's own families. Much like black women in the United States, these women are accomplishing their own tasks of domestic care by relying on an extended network of female kin and working extremely long hours. Some alternate between intense periods of work at home and abroad. Others are denied the chance of ever having a family.[15]

Access to these low-paid workers, as with the use of African American women domestic workers in the first half of the twentieth century, is prolonging existence of the gender division of labor in the United States and elsewhere around the world. By providing many women with a way of coping with the domestic tasks they still face, it relieves the pressure to devise more equitable collective strategies for accomplishing those chores. This practice is also generating strong resentment toward career women, much as they have been blamed for the breakdown of the traditional family. Once again, however, we have to step back to see the larger picture, looking beyond these women to those standing in the wings, refusing to play their part in tasks of family care. If husbands and fathers put as much time into housework and child care as wives and mothers do, the need for paid labor would shrink dramatically.

More crucially, today the vast majority of women in these service occupations are employed not by individual wives but by firms that pay low wages without health care or other benefits.[16] Further, employment practices constrain the lives of women at all levels of the workforce because they are paid less than their due and receive too little time off to properly care for their families. The most conspicuous absence, however, is that of the government—particularly in the United States, where it has failed to provide any collective arrangements for family maintenance or raise the standards of care work.

Placing the burdens of care on individual families, and primarily on mothers within them, under cover of reliance on the market, both within the United States and in the larger global economy, feeds off and fosters inequality throughout the world. We would do better to construct a new web of social policies committing employers, states, and international organizations to supporting tasks of family care in ways that would reduce inequalities of gender, race, and class.

Here, Europe offers lessons on how such funds should be utilized, as many scholars have made clear. Though more than half of employees in the United States find that they must struggle to combine their home and work lives, only a fifth of European workers report similar problems. This may be due in part to the greater persistence of the old gender division of labor, with women spending much more time on domestic tasks than on paid work. But over the course of the twentieth century, most European countries also put in place systems of social welfare that provide workers with paid leaves during pregnancy, early parenthood, and times when dependents need more care, as well as direct payments to offset the costs of raising children. Workweeks are shorter, vacations longer. Even Canada and the United Kingdom, commonly seen as the societies that most resemble the United States, have such policies. The goal of a dual earner, dual caregiver society has received much more discussion in Europe than in the United States.[17]

Though the United States is well-known as a laggard in providing welfare state benefits, even the comparatively meager programs of the New Deal did bring real gains to the male working class. Though they may never succeed in implementing policies as far-reaching as those in Europe, American women have the greatest resources of education and income in the world, and have achieved greater equality in the labor force than has been true in many social democracies. At the start of the last century they made effective, though unequally enjoyed, claims for space for the domestic realm.

Women's gains in personal autonomy in the post–World War II era, joined with recent recognition of the value of caregiving, could lead to new policies that honor the domestic realm in more equal terms than in the past. European provisions for family care are still highly gender-specific, and women in Sweden and many other European countries lag far behind men in earnings and occupational status.[18] The United States could play a vanguard role in designing ways to enable women to enjoy the fruits of family life without bearing an unfair share of the responsibility for maintaining them. The task is to frame such claims for support broadly enough that they apply to women, and men, of all backgrounds.

Surveys make clear that a substantial number of Americans would like greater government support for domestic tasks in the form of paid family leave, a standard workweek, and state-funded care for young children.[19] At present, the federal government's policies are designed primarily to free it, and employers, from the costs of family maintenance. However, we are seeing a process of over-accumulation in which much of the nation's income has ended up in a few hands. This may lead, as happened in the Great Depression, to market breakdown and a dramatic restructuring of the relationships between home, work, and state. Until that happens, however, women will continue to deal with the demands made on them by family and work in a context of great inequality.

Broader Implications for Society

This book has focused on the underlying causes of the interrelated problems that African American and white women in the United States confronted over the second half of the twentieth century, highlighting the role played by a series of encounters between home and market. In doing so, however, it contributes to our understanding of social change and inequality in general.

Gender and Established Accounts of Social Change

Once we recognize the domestic realm as an economy in its own right, we can draw out clear similarities between the market's interaction with this realm and other earlier arrangements of work. By recalling the struggles by peasants to retain their land or by handloom weavers to persist in their craft, we more fully understand why many women sought at first to fend off new demands for their labor. We also better comprehend the grave costs of such failure. The similarities between women's double burden and that of others who were held in older forms of work while forced to take on new tasks, such as peasants compelled to grow sugarcane for sale as well as rice for themselves, underscore the severe difficulties confronting African American women. Black families faced destruction not just through the loss of one parent but through the loss of life itself, as time for domestic tasks crucial to survival was devoured by the demands of the market.

Recognition of similarities in women's turn from household to wage labor and men's move from fields to factories in the nineteenth century also makes possible a more dynamic understanding of women's rise among the poor in the years after World War II. It points as well to a way out of the impasse of equality and difference that has blocked past efforts at fashioning new social policy for women. We see clearly that new policy is needed not because of women's biological difference from men but because another set of old arrangements for care collapsed as women moved from an earlier form of work into the market to support themselves.

Further, such comparison also provides a way to join the vibrant study of gender, which has grown so dramatically since the 1970s, with long-established areas of sociology.[20] It enables us to set gender in the context of the grand questions that first gave rise to classical social theory, as it considered the impact of commercial and industrial development on established ways of life and work. In widening the focus of such questions beyond one group of men, we gain a larger understanding of the varieties of economic and political development and their differing impacts.

Inequalities of Gender and Race

Once we widen our focus, we can also see some broad patterns in the ways inequalities of gender and race are affected by economic growth. In looking closely at encounters between home and market, we saw how existing arrangements of labor and power shaped such interactions in the handling of butter making or, half a century later, laundry or, later still, the reframing of divorce law. For women in general, the result was a series of moments in which a chance to accumulate some independent income or to escape sole responsibility for domestic tasks was lost. For African American women more specifically, the result was also a brutal exposure to the demands of the market in both the nineteenth and the twentieth centuries, with disastrous consequences for themselves and their families.

These results have important implications for the present. Above all, we must recognize that established arrangements of power are also shaping the latest encounter between home and market unfolding today, both in the United States and in the larger global economy. Once again, women overall are losing out; once again, some women are being left entirely at the mercy of the market.

At the same time, however, we have seen how profoundly this latest encounter has altered those old arrangements of power. In particular, women's turn from marriage to wages as their central means of support has severely undermined the very foundation of gender inequality. The main problems now facing women stem not from the persistence of men's control of their labor but rather from the collapse of this old arrangement. Though the breakdown of the gender division of labor has created great new hardships, it has also shattered the age-old base of patriarchal power. Inequities remain, in part as men have used their privileged positions to steer resources in their own direction. Yet such practices are far more vulnerable to challenge when men and women are competing on the same economic terrain and relying on their own wages, throwing into question the legitimacy of disparities in pay and in time spent in household tasks.[21]

The implications of these changes for inequalities of race are more troubling. The breakdown of the old arrangements between home and market has not leveled differences among women. Instead, despite the great changes of the past hundred years or more, we appear to be creating once again two separate and unequal relationships to the domestic realm. In part, such differences are explained by the heavy reliance on the market in the United States, giving different classes unequal access to resources for the home. Racial discrimination in the labor market then heightens those inequalities. Such inequities also result from the channeling of the new gains from the transformation of women's old ways of work toward some groups at the expense of others.

However, there is another side to this problem. The time and space necessary to care for loved ones have not yet been clearly established as rights for all, regardless of background, and are thus, again and again, withheld from those with the least power and money.[22]

Thus, once we fully understand women's problems, it becomes clear, as Nancy Fraser argues, "that justice today requires *both* redistribution *and* recognition."[23] Inequalities in individuals' relationship to home and family are tied in large part to inequalities in earnings and the lack of any collectively funded mechanism for providing care. To address these problems, the gains women have been instrumental in creating must be distributed more equally. To do so effectively, however, also requires greater recognition of groups of people, such as African American women, who have long been denied their full share of such resources.

However, it is not only groups of people that have been dismissed as not worth counting. Full resolution of the problems facing women also requires lifting an area of life long undervalued, that of the home, into full view as well. We need to acknowledge our reliance on one another as interconnected and equal beings, rather than denying such connections while exploiting them. Scholars of the welfare state point to a progression of rights claimed over time, from freedom from tyranny to democratic political representation to social and economic security, ensured by the modern welfare state.[24] Women are still fighting for their rights, as independent individuals, to such freedom and security. However, if we are to succeed, we must claim further, larger rights as well—the right to a family and the right to the time and resources needed to care for and simply enjoy those we love.

.   .   .

We cannot understand the many problems that have accompanied women's turn to the labor force unless we see clearly that a world has been lost as well as gained, and lost far more brutally and completely by some women than others. With the collapse of the old frameworks of support for women's work in the home, much of value has indeed vanished. Time for life outside the market, and for care of our own homes and families, has shrunk dramatically. However, such time was enjoyed in deeply unequal ways.

Separation of the realms of private and public has obscured such inequity, and allowed women themselves to be blamed for many of the problems they face. It has also obscured the contributions a changing domestic realm has made to the larger economy, denying women the full rewards of their labor both in the past and present.

In the largest sense, an economy is a collective pooling of efforts to address human needs. It should provide the basis upon which lives can be built, rather than the other way around. When its demands dominate, we can find real groups of people behind a seemingly faceless market, who are realizing their own interests at the expense of others.

Home is where the heart is, goes an old saying. Many of our hopes and dreams revolve around the image of a home, and time to spend with those we love. However, the means to support this realm, and the time needed to care for and enjoy those dearest to us, have been hidden goods, accrued by some and kept from others. The key problem is that the conditions necessary to sustain a family are still easily overlooked, and thus denied.

Women's lives and American homes have indeed been turned inside out over the past forty years. Mothers now spend long hours in the labor force, infants are tended by paid workers, and tasks that once took place in kitchens or behind bedroom doors make up a large portion of the national income. In many ways, these changes have been traumatic. However, one consequence is that inequities in the private realm can no longer go unnoticed. Bringing the domestic realm fully into view allows us to see what resources are needed to sustain a home and family, and differences in their possession. It also allows us to translate the needs essential to family life into clear and universal rights for women and men of all backgrounds.

NOTES

1. A World Turned Inside Out

1. These studies of pivotal issues are now huge in number. For analysis of divisions among women themselves over abortion, see, for example, Kristin Luker, *Abortion and the Politics of Motherhood*; for analysis of the Equal Rights Amendment, Jane J. Mansbridge, *Why We Lost the ERA*. For some sense of the problems faced by different groups of working mothers today and a sampling of suggestions for solutions, see Francine M. Deutsch, *Halving It All*; Kathryn Edin and Laura Lein, *Making Ends Meet*; Mindy Fried, *Taking Time*; Kathleen Gerson and Jerry A. Jacobs, "Changing the Structure and Culture of Work"; Janet C. Gornick and Marcia K. Meyers, *Families That Work*.

2. Writers who stress the loss of traditional values often draw on Robert Bellah, Richard Madsen, William M. Sullivan, Ann Swidler, and Steve M. Tipton, *Habits of the Heart*. For discussion of this approach, see Demie Kurz, *For Richer, for Poorer*, 14–15.

3. For a recent review of arguments that women's economic independence or men's employment difficulties are central to lower rates of marriage, see David T. Ellwood and Christopher Jencks, "The Spread of Single-Parent Families in the United States since 1960." Gary Becker has been key in emphasizing the role played by specialization in marriage; from this perspective, women's increased economic independence would weaken the bonds of marriage (*A Treatise on the Family*). See also, for example, Andrew Cherlin, *Marriage, Divorce, Remarriage*. The classic statement of the impact of men's employment difficulties on marriage is William Julius Wilson's *The Truly Disadvantaged*; the argument is stated

most directly in Wilson and Kathryn M. Neckerman, "Poverty and Family Structure," in this book. See also Wilson, *When Work Disappears*.

4. David T. Ellwood, "Winners and Losers in America," 2.

5. See, for example, Stephen A. Herzenberg, John A. Alic, and Howard Wial, *New Rules for a New Economy*; Martin Carnoy, *Sustaining the New Economy*; Paul Osterman, Thomas A. Kochan, Richard Locke, and Michael J. Piore, *Working in America*; Vicki Smith, *Crossing the Great Divide*.

6. Osterman et al. note, for example, that we need to "end the separation" in our discussions of home and the economy (*Working in America*, 196).

7. Pointing to such recent works as Nancy Folbre's *The Invisible Heart*, Viviana Zelizer sees a "new economics of care" as offering much-needed "bridges," or new ways of conceptualizing the relationship between the market and other realms of life ("How Care Counts," 116). Scholars focusing on the situations of women of color have been pioneers in building such bridges, paying attention to women's work both at home and for pay, and more recently emphasizing the importance of women's care work in the face of federal refusal to support such labor. See, for example, Bonnie Thornton Dill, "Our Mothers' Grief"; Evelyn Nakano Glenn, "Racial Ethnic Women's Labor"; and more recently, Glenn, *Unequal Freedom*. A large body of literature has usefully analyzed issues of gender and welfare state policy. See chapter 7 for a summary of this literature and for further analysis of women's changing relationship to home, work, and state.

8. Nancy Fraser, "From Redistribution to Recognition?" 12. See also Fraser, "Social Justice in the Age of Identity Politics."

9. The grand theorists of early sociology all thought that economic and political developments in nineteenth-century Europe would break down old social relationships. "Ties of personal dependence—of blood, education, caste, or estate—[will] fall away before the progressive pre-eminence of 'free wage labor,' " predicted Marx, an outcome also expected by Weber and Durkheim, though expressed in less economic terms. However, for women such rupturing of traditional ties did not happen, raising the question as to why not. The conventional assumption was that women were exempt from such a process, as embedded in a set of natural or biological functions or, phrased in sociological terms by Parsons, tasks of family socialization and stabilization which required their continued presence. See Karl Marx, *Grundrisse*, especially 157–64, 252–53 (quotation); Max Weber, *General Economic History*, 276–77; Emile Durkheim, *The Division of Labor in Society*; Talcott Parsons and Robert F. Bales, *Family, Socialization and Interaction Process*.

10. See Gayle Rubin, "The Traffic in Women," for an early post–World War II analysis of the social construction of difference between the sexes and of men's control over women. Heidi Hartmann usefully defined patriarchy as "a set of social relations between men . . . [which] allows men to control women's labor power, both for the purposes of serving men in many personal and sexual ways and for the purpose of rearing children" ("The Unhappy Marriage of

Marxism and Feminism," 14–15). See also Margaret Benston, "The Political Economy of Women's Liberation"; Christine Delphy, *Close to Home*; Delphy and Diana Leonard, *Familiar Exploitation*. For discussion of an early alliance between patriarchy and capitalists, see Hartmann, "Capitalism, Patriarchy, and Job Segregation by Sex."

11. Two early classics of this area of sociology are Barrington Moore's *Social Origins of Dictatorship and Democracy* and E. P. Thompson's *The Making of the English Working Class*. For insightful sociological analysis of the initial impact of industrialization on family structure in England, see Neil Smelser, *Social Change in the Industrial Revolution*. For discussion of the changing shape of historical and comparative sociology, see Julia Adams, Elisabeth S. Clemens, and Ann Shola Orloff, eds., *The Making and Unmaking of Modernity*.

12. Alice Kessler-Harris, *Out to Work*; Jacqueline Jones, *Labor of Love, Labor of Sorrow*; and Jeanne Boydston, *Home and Work*; see also Julie Matthaie, *An Economic History of Women in America*. Nancy Folbre has been key in bringing women's work in the home into discussions of the economy (see, for example, "The Unproductive Housewife"). See also Heidi Hartmann, "The Family as the Locus of Gender, Class, and Political Struggle." Feminist theorists also asked big questions about the origins of gender difference and inequality. Radical feminists helped uncover women's oppression by men, though they viewed such oppression primarily in psychological and ahistorical terms (see Kate Millett, *Sexual Politics*; Shulamith Firestone, *The Dialectic of Sex*). Other theorists drew attention to the key role played by the gender division of labor (Rubin, "The Traffic in Women"; Hartmann, "Capitalism, Patriarchy, and Job Segregation by Sex"; Christine Delphy, *Close to Home*). For a large undertaking in more recent years, see Claudia Goldin, *Understanding the Gender Gap*.

13. Heidi Hartmann, "Changes in Women's Economic and Family Roles in Post–World War II United States"; Alice Kessler-Harris and Karen Brodkin Sacks, "The Demise of Domesticity in America." See also Delphy and Leonard, *Familiar Exploitation*, and Matthaie, *Economic History of Women*.

14. Evelyn Nakano Glenn, "From Servitude to Service Work," 3; also quoted in Maxine Baca Zinn and Bonnie Thornton Dill, "Theorizing Difference from Multiracial Feminism," 325. One of the best comparative analyses of the experiences of families of color in the early United States is Dill's "Our Mothers' Grief"; see also Dill, "Fictive Kin, Paper Sons, and Compadrazgo"; Glenn, "Racial Ethnic Women's Labor"; Glenn, *Unequal Freedom*; Teresa L. Amott and Julie A. Matthaie, *Race, Gender and Work*; Dorothy E. Roberts, *Killing the Black Body*. Such studies have made clear the importance of the intersection of race and class as well as gender, and of tracing how these areas "work together in producing injustice" (Patricia Hill Collins, *Black Feminist Thought*, 18). The hardships and changes in post–World War II America surfaced earlier for poor families and families of color than for white middle-class families, have been even more dramatic, and have been more persistent (see Joyce A. Ladner, *Tomorrow's Tomorrow*;

Elaine Bell Kaplan, *Not Our Kind of Girl*). Black families also earlier created house-holds that relied on the income of both parents. See Andrew Billingsley, *Black Families in White America*; Charles Vert Willie, *A New Look at Black Families*; Billingsley, *Climbing Jacob's Ladder*; Bart Landry, *Black Working Wives*.

15. Here I draw on Maxine Baca Zinn, who notes that "we have been more successful in offering single studies of particular groups of families and women than in providing systematic comparisons of families in the same society." Thus, she has stressed, we now need to gain an understanding of diversity as "the product of forces that affect all families but affect them in different ways" ("Feminist Rethinking from Racial-Ethnic Families," 305). See also Zinn and Dill, "Theorizing Difference from Multiracial Feminism"; Patricia Hill Collins, *Fighting Words*. Collins notes also that recent studies of black women have focused more on their situation in the labor force than in the home, calling for more analyses that look at women's care of their own families and its relationship to work for pay (*Black Feminist Thought*, 46). For early research into African American women's changing position in the post–World War II workforce and the problems faced by the youngest women, see Phyllis Wallace with Linda Datcher and Julianne Malveaux, *Black Women in the Labor Force*; Wallace, *Pathways to Work*. For more recent analyses, see Elizabeth Higginbotham and Mary Romero, eds., *Women and Working*; Kathleen F. Slevin and C. Ray Wingrove, *From Stumbling Blocks to Stepping Stones*; Irene Browne, ed., *Latinas and African American Women at Work*. Studies of racial formation in general and analyses of the problems faced by African American men as well as women have also broadened our understanding of how issues of race shape those of gender. See, for example, Michael Omi and Howard Winant, *Racial Formation in the United States*; Gary Sandefur and Marta Tienda, eds., *Divided Opportunities*; Martin Carnoy, *Faded Dreams*.

16. My study thus relies on the approach of critical social theory, in that it "actively grapples with the central questions facing . . . group[s] of people in a specific political, social and historic context" (Collins, *Fighting Words*, xii).

17. Most comparative analysis seeks to explain variations in a larger process already well understood (see, for example, Charles C. Ragin, *Constructing Social Research*). For one example of excellent comparative historical analysis, see Lyn Spillman, *Nation and Commemoration*.

In some ways the approach here—in explaining why women's turn to wages over the second half of the twentieth century has been plagued with such a long stretch of problems—is similar to that of Gordon, Edwards, and Reich, who see their argument as "a connected set of detailed historical hypotheses." They continue: "Given the scope of the historical argument, our essay cannot provide . . . sufficient tests of every hypothesis. . . . [Rather, we] provide a considerable body of historical evidence that supports the general argument. . . . This evidence demonstrates, we believe, the plausibility of our set of hypotheses. We hope that our elaboration of these hypotheses will be sufficiently compelling to stimulate further historical research along the lines we suggest in this work" (*Segmented Work, Divided Workers*, 39). Thus, an argument is shown to be valid when its narrative, organized around the central threads of its theory, is able to sustain its coherence through its traversal of the evidence.

18. As several scholars have pointed out, race itself is a socially constructed and thus changing category. Yet though it is a label often imposed on groups to their disadvantage, race can also express a shared sense of experience and mistreatment, offering an identity through which to voice and protest injustice (for further discussion, see Dorothy Roberts, *Shattered Bonds*, especially 230–32). Race here therefore provides a way to trace a shared set of experiences in a realm—the domestic—itself also denied validity. Collins is among the theorists who note that race "overshadows economic class relations for Blacks" (*Fighting Words*, 209), but she, like many others, also emphasizes the importance of paying attention to the intersection of race, class, and gender. We can gain a sense of such intersections by looking at how the economic and political disruptions of the post–World War II era differed not only among African American and white women but also within each group by education, one measure of class.

19. For investigating women's experiences in the nineteenth and early twentieth centuries, I found invaluable the historical research by other scholars of gender and examinations of family life by earlier generations of sociologists, such as the rich study of Middletown by the Lynds (Robert S. Lynd and Helen Merrell Lynd, *Middletown*), as well as women's own statements about their lives drawn from a wide variety of sources. Most of the discussion of changing patterns in women's relationships to marriage, labor force participation, and motherhood is based on my own calculations using the Integrated Public Use Microdata Series, consisting of samples of the census collected by the U.S. government and standardized by a team led by Steve Ruggles in the History Department at the University of Minnesota. For further information, see *Integrated Public Use Microdata Series: Version 3.0*, ed. Steven Ruggles et al. I look at white non-Hispanic and African American women in their prime adult years, here defined as the ages between 22 and 54, with a focus on women born between 1926 and 1978 (Hispanic women are not identified in the data for 1960 and so are included in this year).

20. See Paula England, "The Impact of Feminist Thought on Sociology"; Erik O. Wright, "Explanation and Emancipation in Marxism and Feminism."

21. Nancy Fraser, *Unruly Practices*, 8. For the "stalled" state of feminist theory, see Barbara J. Risman, *Gender Vertigo*, 13–44; Kathleen Gerson, review of *Gender Vertigo*, 419.

22. See also Susan Thistle, "The Trouble with Modernity."

2. Support for Women's Domestic Economy in the Nineteenth and Early Twentieth Centuries

1. The quotation concerning women's decision not to challenge the gender division of labor is from a local newspaper report of the resolutions of an 1852 conference on women's rights in Pennsylvania, cited in Joan M. Jensen, *Loosen-*

ing the Bonds, 200. For Supreme Court rulings, see, for example, Susan Gluck Mezey, In Pursuit of Equality.

2. Marjorie G. Cohen stresses men's control of women's labor, as wives, and sometimes as sisters and mothers: "For the most part property was owned by the male head of the family. Wives and children were . . . the workers whose labour was rewarded according to the good fortune or goodwill of the owner. . . . The significance of male control over female labour has been obscured because of the conjugal relationship, their mutual dependence, and their shared standard of living" (Women's Work, 19; see also Jeanne Boydston, Home and Work). For theoretical development of the concept of the gender division of labor, see, for example, Gayle Rubin, "Traffic in Women"; Heidi Hartmann, "The Unhappy Marriage of Marxism and Feminism"; Christine Delphy, Close to Home; Delphy and Diane Leonard, Familiar Exploitation. Slavery is a notable exception to men's control and support of their wives' domestic labor. Nevertheless, black men's labor produced most of the income meeting their families' needs, though their role in the creation of such wealth, like that of black women, was denied. Moreover, research has shown that black men retained control within their own homes, and tasks were divided by gender. For discussion of the gender division of labor under slavery, see Claire Robertson, "Africa into the Americas?" especially 21, and note 22 below.

3. Scholars examining women's past and present experiences in countries around the world have found that while specific tasks vary, there is evidence of a division of labor by gender and of the organization of women's work within male kin networks in almost all agricultural societies. This arrangement persisted through the early stages of commercial and industrial development in most areas, shaping as well as being shaped by that process. In brief, while men's work has altered over time, men have remained engaged with the dominant economy and women with domestic tasks. The key to understanding women's current problems is to grasp the interaction between this earlier structure and a developing commercial and industrial economy. For a sense of how the gender division of labor shaped economic transitions in Europe, see Martha Howell, Women, Production, and Patriarchy in Late Medieval Cities; Judy Lown, Women and Industrialization. On interaction between the gender division of labor and more recent economic development, see Lourdes Beneria, ed., Women and Development; Beneria, Gender, Development, and Globalization; Christine E. Bose and Edna Acosta-Belen, eds., Women in the Latin American Development Process, especially Kathryn B. Ward and Jean Larson Pyle, "Gender, Industrialization, Corporations, and Development." See also Carmen Diana Deere, Household and Class Relations; Deere and Magdalena León, Empowering Women.

4. See Bryan Palmer, "Social and Class Formation in North America," especially 233.

5. Neil Smelser, "Toward a Theory of Modernization," 141. To put it another way, capitalism does not arise all at once, but rather "develops in the pores of a

society mainly engaged in use values . . . [t]he entire history of capitalism is the slow disintegration of this fundamentally non-market economy" (Ernest Mandel, *Marxist Economic Theory*, 31). See Julie Matthaie, *An Economic History of Women in America*, who also cites this statement by Mandel, for further discussion of the initial relationship between women's household work and capitalism.

6. Stanley B. Greenberg, *Race and State in Capitalist Development*, 66.

7. Aidan Foster-Carter, "The Modes of Production Controversy," 59. For a description of the "resistance that entrenched states and social formations imposed upon the extension of that market and, more generally, capitalist relations of production," see Elizabeth Fox-Genovese and Eugene D. Genovese, *Fruits of Merchant Capital*, 29. See also John G. Taylor, *From Modernization to Modes of Production*, 150–71, 228.

8. For key early analyses, see, for example, Bonnie Thornton Dill, "Our Mothers' Grief," and Evelyn Nakano Glenn, "Racial Ethnic Women's Labor"; for more recent studies, Glenn, *Unequal Freedom*; Dorothy E. Roberts, *Killing the Black Body*.

9. See Clifford Geertz, *Agricultural Involution*; Harold Wolpe, "Capitalism and Cheap Labour-Power in South Africa," especially 439; Wolpe, *Race, Class and the Apartheid State*.

10. Greenberg, *Race and State*, 22. In the mid-1980s, Glenn noted that explanations of women's oppression in terms of patriarchal exploitation and those of "internal colonialism," which see racism as utilized to reinforce the exploitation of labor at extremely low wages, result in two parallel but separate models and that "no satisfactory theory has been developed to analyze what happens when these systems of oppression intersect" (Glenn, "Racial Ethnic Women's Labor," 47). For analyses of such intersections, see, for example, Patricia Hill Collins, *Black Feminist Thought* and *Fighting Words*; Glenn, *Unequal Freedom*; Elizabeth Higginbotham and Mary Romero, eds., *Women and Working*.

11. Fox-Genovese and Genovese, *Fruits of Merchant Capital*, 234. Unable to reorder much of society, they argue, merchant capital used two basic strategies to draw on labor: "either reinforcing existing work arrangements or creating bastardized forms of extracting labor . . . [seen] in especially vicious form in . . . the slave-plantation systems of the Americas" (35). While they emphasize the role of merchant capital rather than women's and men's resistance to such demands, their two strategies provide a starting point for understanding the deep similarities as well as differences in the situations of African American women and white women.

12. See Boydston, *Home and Work*, especially 57; Alice Kessler-Harris, *Out to Work*, 7, 11, 2; Matthaie, *Economic History of Women*; Mary P. Ryan, *Womanhood in America*.

13. "Married persons are always more comfortable and succeed sooner . . . than single men," the writer John Howison advised prospective immigrants, "for a wife and family, so far from being a burden there, always prove sources of wealth. The wife of the new settler has many domestic duties to perform; and

the children, if at all grown up, are useful in various ways" (quoted in Cohen, *Women's Work*, 71). Though Howison's advice was based on his observations when visiting Canada, his words held true for immigrants to the United States as well.

14. Kessler-Harris, *Out to Work*, 31–36, 47; Boydston, *Home and Work*.

15. Cohen, *Women's Work*, 155. For a detailed discussion of the shift of dairy work into men's hands in Canada, see *Women's Work*, 93–113, 153–58. Jensen's summary of the diaries kept by one farm wife in Pennsylvania in the 1830s and 1840s gives a sense of the immensity of women's household tasks. Esther Forbes, her mother, and her daughters sewed all the clothes for their family, tended poultry, dried apples, made feather beds, candles, soap, and butter, and sold the surplus of these labors, while also keeping the house clean and warm and preparing meals. Jensen also stresses the importance of women's butter making in the mid-Atlantic United States in this period; Jensen, *Loosening the Bonds*, 79–91, 129–41. For women, this was a "missed" moment—the chance of accumulating some wealth went unrealized. For discussion of such moments, see Geertz, *Agricultural Involution*.

16. Mary Blewitt, "Work, Gender and the Artisan Tradition."

17. Cohen, *Women's Work*, 139; see also Boydston, *Home and Work*, 133. Though Cohen is writing of Canadian families, her observation applies to families in the United States as well. The "doctrine of separate spheres" saw the movement of men's work outside the home as leaving women with little but tasks of childbearing and nurture (Nancy F. Cott, *The Bonds of Womanhood*; Linda K. Kerber, "Separate Spheres, Female Worlds, Woman's Place"). But women's work in the household economy was never primarily to assist men. Rather, as Nancy Folbre points out, "the moral elevation of the home was accompanied by the economic devaluation of the work performed there. The growth of wage labor . . . wrought new concepts of productive labor" ("The Unproductive Housewife," 465). Moreover, it was assumed that the initial transformations of early industrial development represented the limits of what could be altered by commercial and industrial development, leaving women with only biological functions. This early division between unpaid and paid work also took rigid form in Marxist theory as production and social reproduction (see Boydston, *Home and Work*, xv; Cohen, *Women's Work*).

18. Martha Coffin Wright to Lucretia Mott, January 23, 1845; quoted in Boydston, *Home and Work*, 75. Boydston stresses that the use of hired help says more about women's need for assistance in their onerous tasks than their achievement of leisure, pointing out that these workers primarily replaced the assistance that in earlier times had been given by daughters who now were pursuing educations (78–92).

19. See, for example, Jensen, *Loosening the Bonds*, 184–204; Dolores Hayden, *The Grand Domestic Revolution*; Kessler-Harris, *Out to Work*, 71–72. "The general discontent I felt with woman's portion as wife, mother, housekeeper, physician and spiritual guide," Elizabeth Cady Stanton later wrote, led her toward political

work (*Eighty Years and More,* 147–48). However, it did not lead her to explicitly challenge that domestic role.

20. See Roger L. Ransom and Richard Sutch, *One Kind of Freedom,* 233.

21. Quoted in Octavia V. Rogers Albert, *The House of Bondage,* xv. Angela Davis was one of the first to stress black women's work for their own families as well as for plantation owners (*Women, Race and Class* and "Reflections on the Black Woman's Role in the Community of Slaves"; see also Jacqueline Jones, *Labor of Love, Labor of Sorrow,* 11–43; Deborah K. King, "Multiple Jeopardy, Multiple Consciousness," 47).

22. For acceptance of black men's authority, see Susan Mann, "Slavery, Sharecropping, and Sexual Inequality"; see also Christie Farnham, "Sapphire?"; Robert W. Fogel and Stanley L. Engerman, *Time on the Cross.* Some scholars argue that gender equality (for Davis, a "deformed equality") existed in slave families, for black men did not own property, which Marxists see as the cause of women's subordination (John Blassingame, *The Slave Community;* Davis, "The Black Woman's Role"; Eugene Genovese, *Roll, Jordan, Roll;* Jones, *Labor of Love;* Deborah Gray White, *Ar'n't I a Woman?*). More recent studies firmly refute such claims. "One must . . . debunk . . . the claim of absolute equality within slave families by considering the gender division of labor," Claire Robertson states, for example. "The evidence clearly shows . . . women slaves added the considerable burden of exclusive responsibility for domestic work to their already crushing burden of 'outside' labor" ("Africa into the Americas?" 21).

23. Blassingame, ed., *Slave Testimony,* 649; also quoted in Farnham, "Sapphire?" 80.

24. The banning of the transatlantic slave trade in 1807 and rise in slave prices in later decades increased such reliance on black women's reproductive labor. A certain minimal time was accorded women's domestic work. Women were sometimes given one half-day a week off for laundry, and pregnant women slightly higher rations and lighter workloads. Rampant sexual abuse of black women by white men provides an early example of the costs to women when some control of men's sexual desires could not be enforced by male relatives. See also Donna Franklin, *Ensuring Inequality,* especially 16; Jones, *Labor of Love,* 37–38; Mann, "Slavery, Sharecropping and Sexual Inequality"; Roberts, *Killing the Black Body,* 22–55.

25. Herbert Gutman, *The Black Family in Slavery and Freedom.* In contrast to E. Franklin Frazier and the early W. E. B. Du Bois, who saw slavery as inflicting damage on the black family structure that persisted over the next century and underlay the rise in the proportion of families headed by black women after World War II, several historians in the 1970s found strong family ties were sustained among African Americans, especially on larger plantations (see Frazier, *The Negro Family in the United States;* Du Bois, *The Philadelphia Negro;* Blassingame, *The Slave Community;* Genovese, *Roll, Jordan, Roll*). More recent studies have emphasized a much higher degree of family disruption by plantation owners, especially on small plantations (see, for example, Wilma Dunaway, *The African-American Family*

in *Slavery and Emancipation*). For discussion of much of this literature, see Franklin, *Ensuring Inequality*, especially 3–26. Recent analyses of historical census data stress that a greater share of African American than white families were headed by women throughout the nineteenth and early twentieth centuries. However, a dramatic drop in marriage rates and rise in the number of single mothers took place after World War II among both white and black families. Among African Americans, these shifts were seen mainly among those born in the North. See S. Philip Morgan, Antonio McDaniel, Andrew T. Miller, and Samuel H. Preston, "Racial Differences in Household and Family Structure at the Turn of the Century"; Steven Ruggles, "The Origins of African American Family Structure"; Stewart E. Tolnay, "The Great Migration and Changes in the Northern Black Family, 1940 to 1990." Thus, we must look to a larger underlying cause to explain the profound changes in family structure in the latter half of the twentieth century, while recognizing as well its differing impacts.

26. These strategies are outlined by Geertz in *Agricultural Involution*. See also Wolpe, "Capitalism and Cheap Labour-Power"; Wolpe, *Race, Class and the Apartheid State*. The ex-slave is quoted in Jones, *Labor of Love*, 13. Jones writes of slave women spinning; weaving and dyeing cloth; making clothes, soap, candles, and butter; growing vegetables; and preserving foods, thus carrying out a similar set of tasks as white women in the household while also spending long hours in the fields (*Labor of Love*, 29–43). See also Farnham, "Sapphire?" 82; Mann, "Slavery, Sharecropping, and Sexual Inequality," 781; Genovese, *Roll, Jordan, Roll*, 544.

27. This mother said further of her plantation owner: "He did not allow me much time to stay with my baby when I did go to nurse it" (Albert, *House of Bondage*, 14).

28. Palmer, "Social and Class Formation," 245.

29. The quote concerning the use of women's and children's labor is in Palmer, "Social and Class Formation," 261. The employer's statement is quoted in Alice Kessler-Harris, *A Woman's Wage*, 14. See also Martha May, "Bread before Roses." In 1860, only 15 percent of all women worked in the wage labor force, according to census data, and 70 percent were employed as domestic servants. Almost all were young women, 15–24 years old, working for only a few years before marriage. While census takers undercounted women's work for pay, especially in farm labor and in the taking in of boarders and laundry, the vast majority of women clearly were engaged in domestic chores for their own families.

30. For a detailed assessment of African American women's employment in the early twentieth century, see the end of this chapter and Claudia Goldin, *Understanding the Gender Gap*, 17, 43–46, 219–27.

31. Susan Strasser, *Never Done*, 88; Robert A. Lynd and Helen Lynd, *Middletown*, 97, 98.

32. Strasser, *Never Done*, 71–76, 81, 29. Less than 5 percent of homes had electricity in Middletown (i.e., Muncie, Indiana) in 1890 (Lynd and Lynd, *Middletown*, 97). Studies of twenty cities by the Bureau of Labor Statistics in 1918–19 found that two-fifths of all households had no inside toilets, and one-half had

no baths (Leila Houghteling, *The Income and Standard of Living of Unskilled Laborers in Chicago*, 109).

33. Statement in a diary kept from 1901 to 1913 by a middle-class housewife in Georgia; quoted in Molly Ladd-Taylor, *Mother-Work*, 32. On the persistence of many domestic tasks even for women able to hire someone else to do the heavy work of laundry or washing floors, see 26–34.

34. Kessler-Harris, *Out to Work*, 124. Debate over the family wage initially centered on whether it served the interests of capitalists, men, or the working class as a whole. Heidi Hartmann saw an alliance between male workers and employers ("Capitalism, Patriarchy, and Job Segregation by Sex"). Others have argued that the family wage was a working-class victory, because "biological reproduction" was jeopardized by factory labor (Joanna Brenner and Maria Ramas, "Rethinking Women's Oppression"; Jane Humphries, "The Working Class Family, Women's Liberation and Class Struggle"). However, women's domestic labor involved not just the bearing of children but other arduous tasks essential to survival whose accomplishment was threatened by the demands of the industrial economy. Kessler-Harris explains, "The nineteenth century fight for a family wage was thus simultaneously a fight for a social order in which men could support their families and receive the services of women; and women, dependent on men, could stay out of the labor force" (*A Woman's Wage*, 9). Palmer notes that working-class women themselves "found little to their liking in the new regime of waged labor," and most left it to marry ("Social and Class Formation," 251; see also Sarah Eisenstein, *Give Us Bread but Give Us Roses*, 113–45).

35. Early feminist research on the formation of social policies, noting that they served to hold women in the traditional domestic role, saw such measures as imposed on women by a patriarchy increasingly displaying a public rather than a private face (see Mimi Abramovitz, *Regulating the Lives of Women*; Zillah R. Eisenstein, *Feminism and Sexual Equality*; Hartmann, "Capitalism, Patriarchy, and Job Segregation by Sex"; Carole Pateman, "The Patriarchal Welfare State"). But a vast literature has documented how women themselves worked to achieve such programs rather than challenge their domestic role (see the essays in Linda Gordon, ed., *Women, the State, and Welfare*; Gordon, *Pitied but Not Entitled*; Hayden, *The Grand Domestic Revolution*; Ladd-Taylor, *Mother-Work*; Theda Skocpol, *Protecting Soldiers and Mothers*). The progression from Catharine Beecher, who wrote an 1841 handbook offering advice on how to best handle household tasks, to her grandniece, Charlotte Perkins Gilman, who saw such chores as imposing an unfair burden on women and called for radical alteration of this realm, shows that criticism of the gender division of labor did emerge, however (Beecher, *A Treatise on Domestic Economy*; Gilman, *Women and Economics*).

36. Jane Addams, *Twenty Years at Hull House*, 173, 174. Mothers' Aid programs were implemented primarily through the efforts of women's organizations made up mainly of older middle-class women who defined themselves strongly in terms of the traditional domestic role. They succeeded because of a "re-

markable consensus" that single mothers should be aided in such household work (Mark H. Leff, "Consensus for Reform," 408). These settlement workers, or "progressive maternalists," as Ladd-Taylor (*Mother-Work*, 8) calls them, were themselves a contradiction, as they had stepped outside the domestic role yet sought to improve the conditions of this realm for poor mothers rather than free them as well.

37. *Muller v. Oregon* (1908); the same opinion famously declared that protective legislation was justified to ensure a woman's "proper discharge of her maternal functions" (quoted in Barbara J. Nelson, "Women's Poverty and Women's Citizenship," 228–29).

38. The quotation is from Eric J. Hobsbawm, *The Age of Revolution*, 226. For discussion of the difficulties faced by women entering the professions, see Barbara Harris, *Beyond Her Sphere*; Penina Migdal Glazer and Miriam Slater, eds., *Unequal Colleagues*.

39. Stewart Tolnay, "Black Family Formation and Tenancy in the Farm South, 1900," 310. Women typically rose at 4:00 A.M. to cook breakfast outside over small fires, then interspersed the tending of gardens and poultry, the making of meals and clothes, and the care of five to six children with, during at least half the year, work in the fields (Jones, *Labor of Love*, 85–89).

40. Elizabeth Hyde Botume, *First Days amongst the Contraband*, 53; cited, for example, in Evelyn Brooks-Higginbotham, "The Problem of Race in Women's History," 122, and Genovese, *Roll, Jordan, Roll*, 494. Black men's authority in the family was legally recognized, as they were held liable for producing the cotton they had contracted for and had the right to discipline their family members to meet that obligation (see, for example, Mann, "Slavery, Sharecropping, and Sexual Inequality," 285–86; Jones, *Labor of Love*, 79–109).

41. One-quarter of black men in Atlanta in 1870, for example, were skilled workers (William Harris, "Work and the Family in Black Atlanta, 1880"). See also Claudia Goldin, "Female Labor Participation"; Beverly Guy-Sheftall, *Daughters of Sorrow*, especially 91–158.

42. A leading black settlement, the Neighborhood Union, for example, resolved to "instruct and help the mothers of the neighborhood in the proper care of themselves and their infants . . . [and to establish] clubs for cooking, sewing . . . and general homemaking" (Constitution of the Neighborhood Union, 1908; quoted in Stephanie J. Shaw, *What a Woman Ought to Be and Do*, 169). Mary Church Terrell's commendation of efforts to show women "the best way to sweep" is quoted in Deborah Gray White, *Too Heavy a Load*, 91. Brooks-Higginbotham concludes that while white racism divided women's reform efforts, their similar actions "reflected commonalities and shared interests among women regardless of race" ("The Problem of Race in Women's History," 131). One such interest was to improve the conditions of women's work in the home. See also Evelyn Brooks-Higginbotham, *Righteous Discontent*.

43. The Neighborhood Union also resolved to set up clubs for millinery and

manual training, for example. Shaw emphasizes that black professional women worked to improve their communities rather than simply extend charity to them, as white settlement workers did (*What a Woman Ought to Be*, especially 164–210). A national conference on black children led not to efforts for "mothers' pensions," as among white women, but to attempts to set up kindergartens and day care services (Jacqueline A. Rouse, "Atlanta's African American Women's Attack on Segregation, 1900–1920"; see also, for example, Rosalyn Terborg-Penn, "Discrimination against Afro-American Women in the Woman's Movement, 1830–1920"). One women's club in Indianapolis found factory jobs for black women new to its city (White, *Too Heavy a Load*, 30). Thus, black women put forth a model of womanhood that, while still viewing women as responsible for household work, might have opened possibilities for more humane integration of work at home and for pay. In fighting racial discrimination, black women's organizations faced greater difficulties and embraced broader goals than white women's organizations. White emphasizes their belief that "the progress of women marked the progress of the race" (White, *Too Heavy a Load*, 43).

44. The quotation is from Shaw, *What a Woman Ought to Be and Do*, 112; see also 111–14; Jones, *Labor of Love*, 142–46. Even Mary Church Terrell, a college graduate with ample financial resources, despite the assistance of paid domestic workers and a helpful husband, found herself torn by the conflicting demands of her maternal and household tasks and her political work. Her domestic duties left Terrell feeling, she said, like a "prisoner bound with heavy iron chains which no amount of effort or determination or yearning . . . can break" (quoted in White, *Too Heavy a Load*, 91).

45. For discussion of difficult living conditions and black women's lack of time for their own domestic chores, see Jones, *Labor of Love*, 110–41; Elizabeth H. Pleck, "The Two-Parent Household." Most black men did not receive a "family wage" sufficient to support their wives and children above the poverty level, and black single mothers were commonly denied government assistance. Even in 1931, a survey by the Department of Labor found that only 3 percent of the recipients of Mothers' Aid were African American women (Winifred Bell, *Aid to Dependent Children*, 9).

46. Guy-Sheftall, *Daughters of Sorrow*, 21; the quotation refers to the period from 1880 to 1910. In 1905 the life expectancy of white women was one and a half times that of women of color, who could expect to live only 33.5 years (U.S. Census Bureau, "Twentieth Century Statistics," in *Statistical Abstract of the United States, 1999*, table 1421). In 1910 almost 20 percent of all infants and 30 percent of infants of color died before their first birthday (Pleck, "Black Family Structure," 32).

47. City dwellers bought factory-produced bread, canned vegetables, and jams as well as clothing; for this and other savings in time spent on housework, see Joann Vanek, "Keeping Busy," 10–14, 79–85, 117–18.

48. Strasser, *Never Done*; Heidi Hartmann, "Capitalism and Women's Work in the Home, 1900–1930."

49. For close discussion of the mechanization of housework and how this process was shaped by both capitalism and the structure of home life itself, reinforcing rather than freeing women from housework, see Hartmann, "Capitalism and Women's Work"; see also Ruth Schwartz Cowan, *More Work for Mother*. Strasser (*Never Done*, xiv) was the first to note the flaw in the dates given in Siegfried Giedion's *Mechanization Takes Command*.

50. Lynd and Lynd, *Middletown*, 169. Muncie was one of the more prosperous and developed small urban areas in the United States, with a primarily white population and fewer poor than in the big cities. Conditions in Zanesville, Ohio, were similar. The Lynds found a small group of housewives with much free time, a bigger group able to attend school and civic events in the afternoons, and a somewhat larger group that struggled to accomplish all their chores each day (15–16, 97–98). Offsetting much of any savings in labor was the decreased use of servants, whose numbers dropped from 94.3 per 1,000 families in 1900 to 67.7 per 1,000 families in 1930 (Hartmann, "Capitalism and Women's Work," 170), and reduced assistance from daughters, almost all of whom were attending school or working by the mid-1920s (Claudia Goldin, *Understanding the Gender Gap*, 148). Advertisements in the *Ladies' Home Journal* began to show the housewife doing all domestic chores herself (see, for example, Ruth Schwartz Cowan, "The Industrial Revolution in the Home"). Margaret Reid, an economist writing in the mid-1930s, presents the results of a survey that shows a higher prevalence of basic services in large cities in 1926, but she notes that only certain households were included, most likely those "with incomes well above the average" (*Economics of Household Production*, 87–89).

51. For a detailed breakdown of how housewives spent their time on chores, see Lynd and Lynd, *Middletown*, 168. Definitions of women's role, by young as well as old, worked to channel women's free time within the gender division of labor. "Being a good cook and housekeeper" was the most desirable trait in a mother, children stated, followed by "Always having time to read, talk, go on picnics or play with her children" (results of a survey reported in Lynd and Lynd, *Middletown*, 524).

52. A Seattle mother of three, quoted in Ladd-Taylor, *Mother-Work*, 32. In the mid-1920s, 87 percent of unskilled workers' households in Chicago still relied on stoves for heat, more than two-fifths had only rudimentary plumbing, and almost one-third lacked electricity (Houghteling, *Unskilled Laborers*, 116); on lack of refrigeration, see Hartmann, "Capitalism and Women's Work," 162–63. In 1910, most white urban dwellers were working class or poor; only one-third of urbanites (and less than one-quarter of all whites) were middle class (Bart Landry, *The New Black Middle Class*, 21). Though baby bottles had come into use, a study of urban areas in 1925 by the Children's Bureau found that bottle-fed babies were three times as likely to die during their first month as breast-fed ones because of their greater susceptibility to bacterial infection (Ladd-Taylor, *Mother-Work*, 27). Utilities and appliances spread rapidly over the next few years. By the mid-1930s, an extensive survey by the Bureau of Labor Statistics found that

more than three-fourths of urban lower-middle- and working-class households had both hot and cold running water and used gas or electric stoves for cooking. Almost as many had central heating (cited in Hartmann, "Capitalism and Women's Work," 160–63). However, the households surveyed were in cities in the Northeast and northern Midwest, where industrialization had progressed furthest.

53. "Saving Strength" is cited in Walker and Woods, Time Use, xvii. Only 15.8 percent of farms had water inside the house and only about 10 percent had electricity in 1930 (Vanek, "Keeping Busy," 2–3), when 24.8 percent of the population still lived on farms (U.S. Bureau of the Census, Statistical Abstract of the United States, 1950, table 49, p. 42). A government survey in rural Texas found few white households with running water inside their homes at the start of the 1920s (Ladd-Taylor, Mother-Work, 28).

54. Hartmann shows how technological advances in laundry, for example, were channeled within the framings of capitalism as well as the gender division of labor, resulting in the manufacture of a multitude of appliances for individual homes ("Capitalism and Women's Work," 259–60).

55. Joe William Trotter, Jr., Coal, Class, and Color, 60–62. A government survey of a county in rural Texas found that three-fourths of black homes had no toilets and that indoor plumbing of any kind was scarce (Ladd-Taylor, Mother-Work, 28–29).

56. For a description of some of the elegant homes of blacks in Chicago and New York, see St. Clair Drake and Horace R. Cayton, Black Metropolis, 540. The survey of cities in West Virginia also found that one-tenth of African American households in Charleston had no running water in 1933, and two-thirds of their homes were in poor to fair condition. In the smaller cities surveyed, most homes had rudimentary or no plumbing. Two-thirds of homes in Wheeling, for example, lacked electricity and running water (Negro Housing Survey of Charleston, Keystone, Kimball, Wheeling and Williamson, 16, 34). A 1925 survey of Chicago stockyard, railroad, factory, and service workers, 44 percent of whom were black, found that many had only shared bathrooms and no hot water (Strasser, Never Done, 102–3). For conditions in Washington, D.C., see James Borchert, Alley Life in Washington, 88–95, 172.

57. Women of both races found it almost impossible to work at home and for pay, and turned to female relatives or friends for help. Female blue-collar workers in the South put in twelve-hour days and then did domestic chores before going to bed. A woman picking beets in the early 1920s reported rising at 2:00 A.M. to begin her domestic tasks, which she completed after returning home. "There are many nights when I do not get more than 3 hours sleep," she noted, concluding: "The work is too hard for any woman" (Ladd-Taylor, Mother-Work, 31).

58. Drake and Cayton, Black Metropolis, 583. For criticism of the "black matriarchy" thesis, see Paula Giddings, When and Where I Enter, 325–35; Franklin, Ensuring Inequality, 153–66.

59. The quotation is from 1910 census instructions defining employed persons, as presented on the IPUMS (Integrated Public Use Microdata Series) data site. Census data for 1920, adjusted to include farmwork and "work on own account" at levels similar to those in 1910, suggest that about 45 percent of black wives were employed in that year also, both on farms and in urban areas. (All employment statistics, here and later in the chapter, are based on the author's calculations using unpublished IPUMS data unless otherwise specified.) Goldin suggests that African American women's paid employment was less seriously undercounted in the census than white women's, because their 1910 census data were closer to figures reported in other decades (Goldin, *Understanding the Gender Gap*, 43–46, 219–27).

60. In urban areas, 46.3 percent of black wives ages 22–54 were engaged in work for pay, and 98.6 percent of the husbands of these women were employed. In 1910, 57.4 percent of black married women with spouses present reported no occupation or gave their occupation as housewife. Among wives "working on own account," both overall and in urban areas, 80 percent were laundresses and another sizable portion were seamstresses. Of all husbands living with black wives ages 22–54, 58 percent worked on farms, mostly their own, though about one-third worked as agricultural laborers elsewhere; 31.9 percent of these husbands were blue-collar workers.

61. No black male worker in this study earned as little as $600 a year (Houghteling, *Unskilled Laborers*, 29, 61, 62). While employment and earnings may well have been underreported, the undercount was unlikely to have been so great as to substantially alter the basic pattern of these findings.

62. For discussion of the harmful impact of slavery on economic development in the South, see Jay R. Mandle, *Not Slave, Not Free.*

63. The budget information is from "Minimum Quantity Budget Necessary to Maintain a Worker's Family of Five in Health and Decency," presented in Lynd and Lynd, *Middletown*, 518. The Lynds in fact found that 95 percent of working-class wives in Muncie had used no paid help at all during the preceding year (170; on middle-class wives, see 170). Phyllis Palmer analyzed spending on help performing household chores or laundry in six cities across the United States, using data collected by the Bureau of Labor Statistics in 1934 (*Domesticity and Dirt*, 9–10).

64. Letter from a domestic worker in Texas in 1937 to Mrs. Franklin D. Roosevelt; quoted in Phyllis Palmer, *Domesticity and Dirt*, 65. More than one-third of domestic workers were heads of households (70; see also 86). African American women did manage to gain employment by the day rather than as live-ins in the 1920s, but they still faced workdays that extended from early morning to late evening (David Katzman, *Seven Days a Week*, 89).

65. The low wages paid these workers were possible as domestic work for their own families provided part of their support. For a discussion of the difficulties in retaining very low paid workers, see Wolpe, "Capitalism and Cheap Labour-Power," 440.

66. Phyllis Palmer, *Domesticity and Dirt*, 84.

67. Phyllis Palmer argues that relief from burdensome tasks encouraged many women to continue to be housewives. Domestic workers themselves fought hard for shorter hours and higher wages. However, while the forty-hour week became the norm for many workers by the end of the 1930s, domestic workers were still struggling to limit their hours to sixty per week (Phyllis Palmer, *Domesticity and Dirt*, 111–35).

68. Here I am addressing the question raised by Glenn, that of how "internal colonialism" and gender inequality intersect (see note 10 in this chapter). First, much as holding workers in subsistence agriculture made it possible to pay them very low wages, so both black and white women's persistence in domestic tasks enabled employers to keep their wages below that necessary for survival. Second, strategies like those used to hold workers in very low paid jobs, in the United States and other areas of the world, such as discrimination and emphasis on natural attributes, were used to keep all women in household work and block their access to alternative forms of support. Finally, a similar set of strategies, framed in terms of race rather than sex, was used to exclude black women from the jobs available to white women and restrict them to extremely low paid domestic work.

69. The growing emphasis in the 1920s and 1930s on women's need to please men through specially cooked meals or sexual enticement suggests that men's need for women's household labor was dwindling. When young women moved to cities in large numbers between 1880 and 1930, efforts were made to supervise them in homelike residential settings, limiting the steps they might take outside the domestic realm (Joanne Meyerowitz, *Women Adrift*). All these changes in women's lives were accompanied by challenges to the ideological framework that legitimated women's relegation to domestic work. Charlotte Perkins Gilman's *Women and Economics* is the key work here; Rosalind Rosenberg (*Beyond Separate Spheres*) examines the beginning of such challenges within academia in the Progressive era.

70. U.S. Bureau of the Census, *Statistical Abstract*, 1950, table 49, p. 42. Electricity did expand into the countryside in the late 1930s, as part of a project set up by Franklin D. Roosevelt, reaching more than 50 percent of farmers by 1946 (Strasser, *Never Done*, 82). Gas lines were also extended and the manufacture of mechanical refrigerators doubled (U.S. Bureau of the Census, *Statistical Abstract of the United States*, 1953, tables 924, 925, pp. 776, 777). This period also saw continuous movement from the rural South to northern cities by African Americans in search of work, however (Doug McAdam, *Political Process and Black Insurgency*, 78).

71. For a discussion of women's employment in these years, see Claudia Goldin, "Life-Cycle Labor Force Participation of Married Women"; Goldin, *Understanding the Gender Gap*, 159–84. Black women in particular provided more food and clothing for their families through their own household labors (Jones, *Labor*

of *Love*, 196–231). Among white women, war workers were mainly 16–19 or over 45, with fewer domestic burdens. Black wives in their prime adult years did enter the labor force in large numbers during World War II, commencing a massive turn to paid employment more than a decade earlier than white wives (Goldin, *Understanding the Gender Gap*, 153).

3. The Breakdown of Women's Domestic Economy after World War II

1. Eric J. Hobsbawm, *Industry and Empire*, 62.

2. Claudia Goldin, *Understanding the Gender Gap*, 22, 120. Unless otherwise noted, all data are from the author's calculations based on unpublished 1960–1990 IPUMS data.

3. James Smith and Michael Ward, *Women's Wages and Work in the Twentieth Century*, 80.

4. Frank Mott, ed., *The Employment Revolution*; see also Susan Shank, "Women and the Labor Market"; Ralph E. Smith, *Women in the Labor Force in 1990*.

5. The breakdown of an earlier form of work is commonly recognized as contributing to changes in men's economic and political circumstances. The decline of the cotton industry and mechanization of its tasks, for example, reduced the need for cheap agricultural labor. Joined with northern employers' desire for new workers, this shift helped loosen the restrictive political and cultural bonds that held African Americans in the South, adding force to their challenges to these old restrictions (see McAdam, *Political Process and the Development of Black Insurgency*, especially 73–78).

6. Economists noted that the rise in women's wages had encouraged women's employment in part because market goods could increasingly be substituted for what women traditionally had produced within the home (see Glen G. Cain, *Married Women in the Labor Force*, 6–7; Clarence D. Long, *The Labor Force under Changing Income and Employment*, 120–32; Jacob Mincer, "Labor Force Participation of Married Women"; James Smith and Ward, *Women's Wages and Work*). Two sociologists, William F. Ogburn and Meyer F. Nimkoff, observed that the transfer of economic functions from the home to the factory underlay not only the rise in women's employment but the rise in the divorce rate (*Technology and the Changing Family*, 244–49.). Robert W. Smuts, in his analysis of women's work, saw industrialization as decreasing women's household work, with consequences both for the family and for women's work outside the home (*Women and Work in America*, 28–31). Their mistake was in assuming, in line with theories of modernization that were dominant in the first two decades after World War II, that social change smoothly and inevitably accompanied technological advances. They thus failed to recognize the social and political forces that could sustain older arrangements of work.

7. In her early study of housework ("Capitalism and Women's Work in the Home"), Heidi Hartmann stressed that the social relationships organizing pro-

duction in the market economy and the home resulted in developments in household technology being channeled toward individual rather than collective use in the 1920s, reinforcing women's homemaking role. Ruth Schwartz Cowan, though also stressing the dynamic relationship between technology and social relations, argues that women's domestic burdens were not lightened in the years after World War II despite the introduction of new household appliances (*More Work for Mother*).

8. Only 52.8 percent of Middletown households had both hot and cold running water (Robert S. Lynd and Helen Merrell Lynd, *Middletown in Transition*; quotation from 195; data from 557, 559, 562, 569, 558).

9. Andrew Cherlin, *Marriage, Divorce, Remarriage*, 35. A 1934 survey found that less than one-third of rural households in the Northwest had even cold running water and only a handful had "mechanical refrigerators" (Margaret Reid, *Economics of Household Production*, 88). At the start of World War II, most American households still lacked many basic appliances and utilities. Only 56 percent of urban and 44 percent of all homes had electric refrigerators in 1940, less than half (42 percent) had central heating, and just over half (54 percent) cooked using gas or electricity rather than coal, wood, or similar fuels (U.S. Bureau of the Census, *Statistical Abstract of the United States, 1953*, table 924, p. 776).

10. The number of dwelling units with refrigerators rose sharply after World War II, reaching 80 percent by 1950 (U.S. Bureau of the Census, *Statistical Abstract, 1953*, table 924, p. 776). Those with hot and cold running water increased from 70 percent in 1950 to 87 percent in 1960. By 1963, 99 percent of households had refrigerators, 96 percent had gas or electric stoves, and 50 percent had automatic washing machines, which did not come on the market until 1939. Households using wood, coal, or other alternatives to utility-provided gas or electricity for heating dropped by almost one-third, to 18 percent. Though dryers (23 percent of households) and dishwashers (7 percent of households) were still owned only by the upper middle class, by the end of the 1950s almost all households had acquired basic appliances and services (U.S. Bureau of the Census, *Statistical Abstract of the United States, 1966*, tables 1123, 1124, 1125, pp. 754–55).

11. Cherlin, *Marriage, Divorce, Remarriage*, 35.

12. Rostow, *The World Economy*, 270. According to Rostow, production of consumer durables began in 1910, with their diffusion interrupted by the Depression and World War II. Their manufacture resumed at a rapid pace in the 1950s, and demand was largely met by the late 1950s (*World Economy*, 62; see also Strasser, *Never Done*; Cowan, *More Work for Mother*). By 1960, 44.1 percent of white families and 13.4 percent of black families were middle class and 32.6 percent of white families and 25.7 percent of black families were members of the skilled working class or what some would term lower middle class (Bart Landry, *The New Black Middle Class*, 21, 68). Movement out of the rural South and into better-paying factory work in the 1940s and 1950s gave many black families ac-

cess to indoor plumbing and refrigerators (Gerald D. Jaynes and Robin M. Williams, Jr., eds., *Common Destiny*, 272).

13. Both African American and white women engaged in the dominant post–World War II pattern of early marriage and high fertility (Suzanne M. Bianchi and Daphne Spain, *American Women in Transition*, 147). Though improvements in health and nutrition greatly lessened the physical vulnerability of infants and children, a mother's presence was seen as crucial for healthy psychological development in early childhood (see, for example, Benjamin Spock, *Baby and Child Care*). In 1959, the birth-control pill was invented, followed by intrauterine devices. By 1970 half of all couples using contraception were using these new, more effective forms of birth control, enabling women to postpone or limit their pregnancies (Cherlin, *Marriage, Divorce, Remarriage*, 10). While most women born before 1910 did not begin bearing children until their late 20s and continued into their 40s, women born between 1935 and 1939 had completed most of their childbearing by their late 20s (Joann Vanek, "Keeping Busy," 29).

14. Vanek, "Keeping Busy," 187. For data, see tables 3.2, 78; pp. 93–110 (for discussion of meal preparation, see p. 98). Care of fires averaged 1 hour and 38 minutes a week in 1925. Joann Vanek's summary in *Scientific American* of her comparison of time spent in housework from 1925 to 1966 was often cited in arguments that industrialization had done little to reduce women's household work, but such arguments misrepresented this article, focusing only on its discussion of nonemployed women ("Time Spent in Housework").

15. Charlotte Adams, *Housekeeping after Office Hours*, 11. Adams goes on, "Women, they say, having acquired washing machines simply wash clothes more often than they used to." On the basis of her own experience and that of women she knew, she disagreed, concluding instead that "all the amazing and wonderful mechanical equipment that has come upon us in the past couple of decades . . . could well be part of a Great Plan to make possible the entry of women into business in overwhelming numbers . . . [and] part of the reason we've gone to work."

16. Vanek, "Keeping Busy," 107. Husbands of employed wives contributed on average 3 hours of time per week to housework, compared to 2 hours by husbands of nonemployed wives. Even when children's ages and family size were controlled for, employed wives were found to spend 18 fewer hours on housework; the great preponderance of that reduction (16 hours) came from tasks other than child care (table 4.14; pp. 138–51).

17. Kathryn E. Walker and Margaret E. Woods, *Time Use*, 43–45, 254–69. Wives employed more than 30 per week spent 3.3 hours less on such tasks. Wives' employment was more important than even the age of the youngest child, to their surprise (263). Again, husbands' contributions were small and similar. In contrast to Vanek, Walker and Woods did find some difference between employed and nonemployed women in time spent in physical

care of children. Walker and Woods compared a 1963 Cornell University survey of 1,296 households with time use studies extending back to the 1920s.

18. Time spent by all women ages 18–54 in housework dropped more than 5 hours per week over the decade, from 27 hours in 1965 to 21.7 hours in 1975. The small amount of time that men put into housework also declined by 5 percent (John P. Robinson, "Household Technology and Household Work," 61).

19. Vanek, "Keeping Busy," 192. Vanek stresses, though, that the additional time spent in housework by nonemployed women resulted in an "upgrading" of their care of their homes (192).

20. Robinson, for example, sought correlations between time spent on housework and number of appliances and found none ("Household Technology").

21. Gertrude Bancroft, "The American Labor Force," 39. James Smith and Ward noted of the period from 1940 to 1960 that "market work for women over age 35 jumped so sharply that it dwarfed the entire previous historical experience for mature women" (Women's Wages and Work, 4; see also Susan Householder Van Horn, Women, Work and Fertility). Some of these women had been among the first young wives to continue working in the 1920s and 1930s for the few years between their marriage and the birth of their first child. Declining fertility, furthered by economic hardship in the Depression and many men's absence during World War II, also lessened their domestic labor (see Goldin, Understanding the Gender Gap, 138–48). An inverse relationship between husband's income and wife's work, strong between 1930 and 1950, persisted weakly in the 1950s (Clarence D. Long, The Labor Force under Changing Income and Employment, 88). A survey of housewives in 1957 found no relation between dissatisfaction with housework and plans to enter the labor force (Alfreda P. Iglehart, Married Women and Work, 56–58).

22. Quoted in Eileen Appelbaum, Back to Work, 57. A study of women who had attended graduate school in the years immediately after World War II noted that "working out a satisfactory balance between home and job . . . frequently required that they lower their original occupational sights" (Eli Ginzberg and Alice M. Yohalem, Educated American Women, 194). For women's subordination of paid work to their role within the family in this period, see also Mirra Komarovsky, Blue-Collar Marriage; Lee Rainwater, Workingman's Wife.

23. Participation in the labor force by African American married women climbed sharply in the first decades after World War II, though assessments of change must take into account the undercounting of their work in earlier decades (see chapter 2). However, reexamination of 1910 census data suggests that there was a decline in the share of black wives taking in laundry or boarders, or working on the family farm, as such work lessened in subsequent decades, followed by a rise in black married women's participation in wage work. White women also turned to the labor force in these decades. However, while white married women who worked in World War II were mainly under

20 or over 45 years old, and thus not in their years of greatest domestic duties, a significant segment of black wives in their 20s and early 30s were employed during the war. In the 1950s, while labor force participation climbed most among older black women, as it did among older white women, employment also rose among younger black wives (Goldin, *Understanding the Gender Gap*, 152, 25). Family needs and increased employment opportunities were important factors driving this increase, but the reduced household burdens made it easier to decide to work.

24. Quoted in Jeanne L. Noble, *The Negro Woman's College Education*, 98. Another black professional woman, anticipating the complaints of later decades, observed of the career woman: "She is expected to play the subordinate role of 'female' . . . [and] to work eight hours a day and come home and keep house" (98). Only 3.8 percent of African American women 22–54 (and 6.9 percent of white women this age) had completed four or more years of college in 1960.

25. Paula Giddings, *When and Where I Enter*, 238–58. Black women's income rose from 29 percent of black men's income in 1950 to 70 percent in 1970 (Jaynes and Williams, *Common Destiny*, 535). As many white women chose to stay home, a rapidly growing group of educated black women filled the rising need for clerical and sales workers. Young black women also made gains in factory work (author's calculations, based on unpublished 1960 and 1970 IPUMS data).

26. John H. Scanzoni, *The Black Family in Modern Society*, 228–38.

27. Lillian Breslow Rubin, *Women of a Certain Age*, 38; see also Betty Friedan, *The Feminine Mystique*. These women, born in the 1920s and 1930s, were the mothers of the early baby boomers, who were now growing up. From 1968 on, middle-class women with college educations began to enter the labor force more rapidly than those with less education (Van Horn, *Women, Work and Fertility*, 184–86).

28. Diana Michener, "Catching the Sun," 154 (one in a collection of autobiographical essays by women born in the late 1930s). Educational levels among women born in 1934, for example, peaked at age 23, and then began to rise again from their mid-30s until age 50 (James Smith and Ward, *Women's Wages and Work*, 48). Satisfaction with housework dropped sharply among college-educated housewives. Though 67 percent of housewives who had attended college said they enjoyed housework in 1957, only 38 percent did in 1976 (survey by Philip E. Converse, Jean D. Dotson, Wendy J. Hoag, and William McGee III, *American Social Attitudes Data Sourcebook*, 1947–1978, 110; also discussed in Jane J. Mansbridge, *Why We Lost the ERA*, 104). By 1970 well over two-fifths of white college graduate mothers with children under eighteen and over one-third of other white mothers were employed.

29. Alice Walker, "One Child of One's Own."

30. Large numbers of the previous cohort of African American college graduates were already highly involved in the labor force, but their employment continued to rise. Their efforts contributed to the advances in occupational status and earnings achieved by the first wave of baby boomers. Black women enter-

ing the professions in the late 1960s were less likely than those before them to accept the constraints of the domestic role (Cheryl Bernadette Leggon, "Black Female Professionals"). Young African American women made great gains in education in the late 1960s and early 1970s, partly because of new civil rights legislation. About one-third of black female high school graduates went on to college in 1970, and this group grew strongly over the early 1970s (Landry, *New Black Middle Class*, 86, 205).

31. Steven D. McLaughlin et al., *The Changing Lives of American Women*, 122. Young women increasingly came to recognize that succeeding in a career required at least a postponement of the domestic role. The proportion of individuals who expected that they would be in the labor force at age 35 rose rapidly for successive cohorts born after World War II (Mott, *Employment Revolution*, 16). Kathleen Gerson's examination of women's choice of primary work role, as homemaker or career woman, provides a close look at how the instability of marital ties and opportunities in the labor force encouraged ever-greater numbers of women born after World War II to turn to wages for support (*Hard Choices*). In a survey of high school girls in 1974, only 3 percent named "housewife" as the intended focus of their adult years (National Assessment of Educational Progress survey; cited in Julie Matthaie, *An Economic History of Women in America*, 272–74).

32. For a detailed history of black women's organizations, see Deborah Gray White, *Too Heavy a Load*. The demands of African American women's organizations were more concerned with the situation of all African Americans than with the inequity of the domestic role. However, White notes that efforts to improve the situation of black women were seen as the key way to further the race as a whole at the beginning of the twentieth century but were viewed as impeding such progress in the period after World War II.

33. A founding member of NOW recalled that the organization was initially "focused on breaking through the barriers that kept woman from moving, earning and having her own voice in the advanced, rewarded work of modern society, dominated by men" (Betty Friedan, *The Second Stage*, 91).

34. "For the first decade of NOW," Friedan recalls, "it seemed as if there were only two of us really interested in doing anything about child care" (*Second Stage*, 103). For discussion of Height's views on gender roles, see White, *Too Heavy a Load*, 201. Though NOW's first president, Friedan, had exposed women's growing dissatisfaction with the domestic role in *The Feminine Mystique*, the organization still hesitated to challenge the division of labor between the sexes (see, for example, Maren Carden, *The New Feminist Movement*; Jo Freeman, *The Politics of Women's Liberation*). White (*Too Heavy a Load*) notes that the National Council of Negro Women paid little attention to poor black women through most of its history; Benita Roth (*Separate Roads to Feminism*) emphasizes that radical black feminists stressed inequalities of race and class as well as gender.

35. Dorothy Sue Cobble, whose research has brought to light the steps taken by these women, uses the term *labor feminists* because they were not all from working-class backgrounds (*The Other Women's Movement*, especially 121–44).

36. For scholarship that emphasizes women's increased resources in the rise of second-wave feminism, see Carden, *New Feminist Movement*; Myra Marx Ferree and Beth B. Hess, *Controversy and Coalition*; Freeman, *Politics of Women's Liberation*. Roth raises the question as to why feminist movements should have emerged among African American, Chicana, and white women when resources were increasing and, employing a "feminist intersectional" approach, analyzes how and why these movements developed in separate ways; see Roth, *Separate Roads to Feminism*, especially 14–17.

37. Frances Beal, quoted in Roth, *Separate Roads to Feminism*, 90.

38. "Women: Do You Know the Facts about Marriage?" 537; this two-page leaflet by the Feminists was handed out at a demonstration at the Marriage License Bureau in New York City in the winter of 1969. Feminism was most strongly espoused by women who saw and had the resources to pursue opportunities outside the domestic realm. For example, almost all members of NOW and similar women's rights organizations were college graduates or had professional degrees (Carden, *New Feminist Movement*).

39. For discussion of the role that greater access to improved methods of birth control may have played in the sharp rise in the number of women doctors, lawyers, and professors in the 1970s and 1980s, see Claudia Goldin and Lawrence F. Katz, "The Power of the Pill."

40. Russell V. Lee, paper given at California Conference on Marriage, February 1964; cited in Jessie Bernard, *Future of Marriage*, 23. In the twentieth century, a few women as well as men began to characterize women as "parasites" (see, for example, Olive Schreiner, *Woman and Labour*; Simone de Beauvoir, *The Second Sex*).

41. Barbara Ehrenreich, *The Hearts of Men*, 11–12, 121. Among couples married ten to fourteen years, marital breakdown fell among college graduates in the 1970s, while it increased dramatically among those with less education. However, the dominant pattern was that of an increase in divorce among couples of all levels of education. See James A. Sweet and Larry L. Bumpass, *American Families and Households*, 189–90. Though women, unless never married, had been more dissatisfied with marriage in the 1950s, men's disenchantment grew more rapidly over the following two decades (see Joseph Veroff, Elizabeth Douvan, and Richard Koulka, *The Inner American*, 174).

42. Two unmarried men, quoted in James L. Collier, "Husbands vs. Bachelors: Is Marriage Worth It?" 67, 109.

43. Ehrenreich also makes this point about men's reduced need for women's domestic chores before focusing on the breakdown of the ideology committing men to the male breadwinner role (*The Hearts of Men*, 1–13).

44. Rankings of men's spousal preferences are based on responses of 250 students given the same questionnaire at repeated intervals from 1939 to 2001 (Alice Eagly, "On the Flexibility of Human Mating Preferences"). For a discussion of the rise of the companionate marriage, see Steven Mintz and Susan Kel-

logg, *Domestic Revolutions*, 107–32. For changing assessments of the role of marriage, see Glenda Riley, *Divorce*.

45. Jessie Bernard, for example, predicted the increasing fragility of marriage in *Future of Marriage*, 95. For divorce rates, see Sweet and Bumpass, *American Families and Households*, 173–205. For a discussion of divorce manuals, see Riley, *Divorce*, 177.

46. For divorce rates among women with more than 16 years of education, see Alexander Plateris, "Divorces by Marriage Cohort," 11. Studies of the 1960s and 1970s found that women with secure alternative sources of support were more likely to leave a bad marriage (Heather L. Ross and Isabel V. Sawhill, *Time of Transition*; Cherlin, *Marriage, Divorce, Remarriage*, 53). For the role played by frustrations with old gender roles, see Frances K. Goldscheider and Linda J. Waite, *New Families, No Families?*

47. See, for example, Lynne Carol Halem, *Divorce Reform*; Riley, *Divorce*, 163; Herbert Jacob, *The Silent Revolution*.

48. Statement by California state legislature, quoted in Jacob, *Silent Revolution*, 60. For discussion of the negative impact of changes in divorce law, and divorce itself, on women, see, for example, Lenore Weitzman, *The Divorce Revolution*.

49. Herbert Jacob, "Women and Divorce Reform," 487. There were no women involved in the initial modification of New York divorce law in the mid-1960s. Though Herma Hill Kay was involved in the California divorce reform process, she herself has said that her advice was guided by her knowledge of family law, not feminist concerns ("Equality and Difference"). Though Alice Rossi and Jessie Bernard suggested measures representing women's interests, these were rejected (Jacob, *Silent Revolution*, 486–87). Several analysts have suggested that the man overseeing passage of the reform, undergoing a divorce himself, shaped the law to meet his own interests (Kay, "Equality and Difference," 44n13, cited in Jacob, *Silent Revolution*, 186n40).

50. Jacob, *Silent Revolution*, 60.

51. For example, a group of female legislators, learning of the hardships of divorce at a regional conference on the status of women, blocked legislation enacting no-fault divorce in Wisconsin until modifications in women's interests were added to the reform (Martha Fineman, "Implementing Equality," 800).

52. John D'Emilio and Estelle B. Freedman, *Intimate Matters*, 262–63; Jeanne J. Fleming, "Public Opinion on Change in Women's Rights and Roles," 47. In 1957, both white and black unwed mothers were "defined and treated as deviants threatening the social order" (Rickie Solinger, *Wake Up Little Susie*, 3).

53. The sociologist Ernest Groves, quoted in D'Emilio and Freedman, *Intimate Matters*, 266. For the *Newsweek* and *Time* articles, see "The Morals Revolution on the U.S. Campus"; "The Second Sexual Revolution." In the 1960s, college enrollment rose rapidly among African Americans and whites of both sexes. Rubin, *Worlds of Pain*, 60–61. For the growing numbers of black adolescents who

traveled north in the years after World War II, for example, this move allowed an escape from a "rural culture of churchy morals and racial etiquette . . . found confining" (Nell Irvin Painter, foreword to Trotter, *Coal, Class, and Color,* ix).

54. The share of young women ages 18–29 remaining single doubled between 1960 and 1980 (Bianchi and Spain, *American Women in Transition,* 12).

55. College girl, quoted in Prudence Mors Rains, *Becoming an Unwed Mother,* 28–29. Fewer than one-third of schools provided information on contraception in the mid-1970s, unreliable forms of birth control remained widespread among the young, and less than one-fifth of teenage girls always used contraception (Alan Guttmacher Institute, *11 Million Teenagers,* 16, 35).

56. Marge Piercy, "The Grand Coolie Damn"; Beauvoir, *Second Sex.* For the role of birth control in women's pursuit of professions, see Goldin and Katz, "The Power of the Pill"; for its role in lessening the pressures on men to marry, see George A. Akerlof, Janet L. Yellen, and Michael L. Katz, "An Analysis of Out-of-Wedlock Childbearing in the United States."

57. Quoted in Rubin, *Worlds of Pain,* 67. The figures on premarital conceptions and births are for women 15–29 years old at first birth (Amara Bachu, "Trends in Premarital Childbearing," 2–3). The trends were similar for all races (see also Stephanie J. Ventura and Christine A. Bachrach, "Nonmarital Childbearing in the United States, 1940–99"). Forty-four percent of the working-class couples Rubin interviewed, who had married in the early and mid-1960s, said they had done so because the woman had gotten pregnant. A national study by the Public Health Service found that from 1964 to 1966, 42.4 percent of children born to married women 15–19 years old were premaritally conceived (cited in Rubin, *Worlds of Pain,* 226n9). A study of a black southern rural community made clear the pressures to marry under such circumstances: "Once pregnancy ensues . . . individual, family, and community pressures begin to operate. It is considered the right thing for the man to marry the girl, and if he does, he is commended" (Hylan Lewis, quoted in Donna Franklin, *Ensuring Inequality,* 134).

58. For the sharp rise in premarital conceptions resulting in unwed motherhood rather than marriage, see Bachu, "Trends in Premarital Childbearing." On young women's strong reluctance to give up their babies for adoption, see Rickie Solinger, *Beggars and Choosers.*

59. See Eva Rubin, *The Supreme Court and the American Family.*

60. Joan Hoff, *Law, Gender, and Injustice,* 395; Solinger, *Wake Up Little Susie,* 212.

61. On the difficulties of obtaining an abortion, see, for example, Solinger, *Wake Up Little Susie,* 3–5. On the Supreme Court's lack of recognition of the profound implications of its decision and its retreat, once made aware of such implications, see Hoff, *Law, Gender, and Injustice,* 401; Rubin, *Supreme Court and the American Family,* 59–74. Insightful consideration of issues of race and class in the handling of abortion is offered in Marlene Gerber Fried, ed., *From Abortion to Reproductive Freedom.*

62. Rubin, *The Supreme Court and the American Family,* 27–53, 34.

63. On the "marriage bar" and its rapid abandonment in the 1950s by em-

ployers seeking a new source of labor, including quotations from employers surveyed in 1956 and 1957 by Miriam Hussey, see Goldin, *Understanding the Gender Gap*, 160–79, especially 176. The workforce grew from 57 million to 74 million workers between 1947 and 1967 (Victor R. Fuchs, *Service Economy*, 1), and married women provided the main source of new labor (Valerie Kincade Oppenheimer, *The Female Labor Force in the United States*).

64. Arthur S. Fleming, quoted in Alice Kessler-Harris, *A Woman's Wage*, 108. See also Cynthia Harrison, *On Account of Sex*. For the rise in women's wages during this period, see Goldin, *Understanding the Gender Gap*, 124–38. Goldin emphasizes the role played as well by rising levels of education over successive cohorts of women and the shift in types of occupations available.

65. The Equal Employment Opportunity Commission, though moving slowly at first, filed many class action suits against major corporations, and the courts rapidly rejected laws that had reinforced the gender division of labor (Hoff, *Law, Gender, and Injustice*, 396).

66. Brennan, writing the Supreme Court's majority opinion in *Craig v. Boren* (1976) and *Frontiero v. Richardson* (1973); quoted in Susan Gluck Mezey, *In Pursuit of Equality*, 51.

67. For discussion of *Cleveland Board of Education v. La Fleur*, see Hoff, *Law, Gender, and Injustice*, 400; see also Rubin, *Supreme Court and the American Family*, 83–87.

68. Jo Freeman, "From Protection to Equal Opportunity," 482.

4. Economic Difficulties and a Contradictory Alliance

1. Eric J. Hobsbawm, *Industry and Empire*, 66.

2. Unless otherwise noted, all data are from author's calculations based on unpublished 1960–90 IPUMS data for white non-Hispanic and African American women ages 22–54 (1960 data includes Hispanic women). By "the youngest" I mean women 22–24 years old. While focusing on this group provides only a glimpse of the larger birth cohort, it does yield some sense of the behavior of each cohort on just entering adulthood.

3. The quotation is from Mirra Komarovksy, *Blue-Collar Marriage*, 54. Studies of working-class marriages found that these wives neither seemed overworked nor complained of their husbands' failures to help with household chores, expecting them instead to be the main wage earners. See, for example, Lee Rainwater, *Workingman's Wife*; Helena Znaniecka Lopata, *Occupation: Housewife*. In interviews of fifty white working-class families, Lillian Breslow Rubin found these wives to be primarily interested in establishing a functional household unit based on traditional gender roles (*Worlds of Pain*, 93).

4. More than 40 percent of high school–educated women in their early 20s were mothers in 1970, compared to 14 percent of college graduates. Among married women 25–34, only one-third of wives who had finished high school were employed in 1970, compared to 45 percent of those with four or more years of college.

5. Though divorce rates were rising among all white women over 35, among younger women the divorce rate rose much more rapidly among those with a high school education than among college graduates. Most college graduates without spouses had never married, while most high school–educated women on their own were divorced or separated. Whether desired or not, divorce was more traumatic than the postponement of marriage. Little information exists on which spouse sought divorce in these decades, but the study mentioned found that in Florida in the early 1970s, after the passage of no-fault divorce, approximately two-thirds of divorce petitions were filed by men. Prior to such reform, 62 percent of the petitions came from women, probably because wives' claims of cruel treatment caused by infidelity was one of the few ways for either spouse to obtain a divorce (B. G. Gunter, "Notes on Divorce Filing as Role Behavior," 96).

6. Women heading families or on their own grew from 26 percent of poor adults in 1959 to 50 percent by 1973 (U.S. Bureau of the Census, *Characteristics of the Poverty Population*, figure 1).

7. Jeanne J. Fleming, "Public Opinion on Change in Women's Rights and Roles," 54. Many studies found a relationship between women's employment and attitudes toward women's issues (see, for example, Myra Ferree, "Working Class Feminism"). Others, however, did not. For discussion of these studies, see Faye D. Ginsburg, *Contested Lives*, 172.

8. Quoted in Ginsburg, *Contested Lives*, 172. Kristin Luker found that 94 percent of pro-choice activists were employed, and more than half had earnings in the upper tenth percentile of women. Almost 40 percent had some graduate school education, many had professional degrees, and more than one-third had never been married or were divorced (*Abortion and the Politics of Motherhood*, 195–96). Eighty-one percent of women on the National Right to Life Committee were housewives, compared to 28 percent of women in the National Abortion Rights Action League (Fleming, "Women's Rights and Roles," 58). But while "ordinary housewives" initially swelled the ranks of those opposing such reforms, the backgrounds of women involved in these protests shifted as the New Right took over the opposition and became made up of religious fundamentalists (Rosalind Pollack Petchesky, *Abortion and Woman's Choice*, especially 253–56).

9. Theodore S. Arrington and Patricia A. Kyle, "Equal Rights Amendment Activists in North Carolina," 673. See also Donald G. Mathews and Jane Sherron de Hart, *Sex, Gender, and the Politics of ERA*. David Brady and Kent Tedin found that 70 percent of women opposed to the ERA in one study were housewives ("Ladies in Pink," 570–71). For widening divisions between housewives and women in the labor force, see Mansbridge, *Why We Lost the ERA*, especially 212, 216–17; Mansbridge, "Organizing for the ERA," especially 323. For a constitutional amendment to be enacted, it must be ratified by three-fourths of the states after its passage by Congress; the ERA fell three states short.

10. Quoted in Mathews and de Hart, *Politics of ERA*, 156. Women opposed to the ERA spoke of their right "to be a full-time wife and mother, and to have

this right recognized by laws that obligate her husband to provide the primary financial support and a home for her and her children" (ERA opponent, quoted in Barbara Ehrenreich, "Defeating the ERA," 392). Feminists had difficulty understanding the concerns of housewives, failing initially to realize the need to construct new provisions for the domestic tasks that remained to be done.

11. Samuel Bowles, David M. Gordon, and Thomas E. Weisskopf see real after-tax pay as growing slowly throughout most of the 1970s, then falling sharply in 1978 (Beyond the Waste Land, 24–25). According to Walt W. Rostow, the economy entered serious difficulties in late 1975 (The World Economy, 297). See also Bennett Harrison and Barry Bluestone, The Great U-Turn; Robert B. Reich, The Next American Frontier.

12. Other explanations have commonly stressed growing religious involvement or the rise of a postindustrial society in which cultural issues dominate, exposing the conservative side of the working class (see Jerome L. Himmelstein, To the Right; William B. Hixson, Jr., Search for the American Right Wing). For the laissez-faire politics and conservative family values of a newly emerging middle class in Southern California, see Lisa McGirr, Suburban Warriors (see also Kirkpatrick Sale, Power Shift); for defense of traditional gender roles, see Petchesky, Abortion and Woman's Choice.

13. Frank Levy, The New Dollars and Dreams, 134. See also Bowles, Gordon, and Weisskopf, Beyond the Waste Land; Rostow, World Economy; Harrison and Bluestone, Great U-Turn; Reich, Next American Frontier.

14. The term smokestack industries is from Thomas Ferguson and Joel Rogers (Right Turn), who argue that the unions' weakness allowed the deterioration of the economy under the Democrats, who acted in the interests of multinational corporations when they permitted tax breaks encouraging overseas investment.

15. Raymond Williams, The Country and the City, 103. "For the working-class man," Rubin noted astutely in the mid-1970s, "there are few . . . rewards in the world outside the home; the family is usually the only place where he can exercise power, demand obedience to his authority" (Worlds of Pain, 99). Loss of their wives' household labor was felt more keenly because it was joined with the disappearance of well-paid work for many of these men.

16. The share of African Americans both attending and completing college rose dramatically in the 1960s. By the mid-1970s, about one-third of black as well as white high school graduates were going on to college. This change led to little growth in the black middle class, however, as any good jobs available tended to go to white men. One half of white families and one-fourth of African American families were middle class by the mid-1970s (Bart Landry, The New Black Middle Class, 75, 205).

17. Births to all married black women continued to fall in the 1970s, even more markedly than for white women. Among women 25–34 with four years of high school, almost three-fifths of African American wives were in the labor force in 1970, compared to little over one-third of white wives. Surveys have

consistently found black women expressing greater support than white women for women's rights in the public sphere; see, for example, Louis Harris and Associates, *The Virginia Slims American Women's Opinion Poll* (1972), 2, 4. Similar findings were reported when the poll was repeated in 1974, 1980, and 1985.

18. For men's drop in earnings, see Gerald D. Jaynes and Robin M. Williams, Jr., eds., *A Common Destiny*, 534. African American men had provided an important source of labor enabling the expansion of manufacturing in the mid–twentieth century. As white men moved more rapidly into white-collar jobs in the growing service sector, black men began to predominate in manufacturing jobs and they thus were hit harder when these industries faltered. They were also more likely to live in areas hurt by industrial decline. See, for example, Martin Carnoy, *Faded Dreams*, 87–89; William Julius Wilson, *The Truly Disadvantaged*; Marta Tienda and Leif Jensen, "Poverty and Minorities."

19. For African American women's contribution to family income, see Marcia Cancian, Sheldon Danziger, and Peter Gottschalk, "Working Wives and Family Income Inequality among Married Couples." In the 1970s, divorce and separation increased among all black women, as they did among white women. However, among younger black women divorce rates rose much more among high school–educated women, despite a sharp climb in the share never married, than among those with four years of college.

20. Many scholars saw such changes as due to the persistence of the destructive legacy of slavery among poor black sharecroppers who then carried such patterns northward (see, for example, E. Franklin Frazier, *The Negro Family in the United States*; St. Clair Drake and Horace R. Cayton, *Black Metropolis*; Nicholas Lemann, *The Promised Land*). In fact, such migrants were found to have higher rates of marriage and employment than those born in the North. Thus, concludes Stewart Tolnay, "the search for explanations of the dramatic change in family structure among inner-city African Americans during the last fifty years should focus on processes internal to northern cities" ("The Great Migration and Changes in the Northern Black Family," 1233). When marriage first began to break down in the 1960s, the dominant response was to stress, as Daniel P. Moynihan did, the "truly great discontinuity in family structure . . . between the white world in general and that of the Negro American" ("The Negro Family," 75). However, in arguing further that families headed by women led to ongoing poverty and marital breakdown, because young men, stripped of their positions in the labor force and at home, lost all incentive to work or marry, Moynihan was also giving early voice to men's fears of losing their power based on the gender division of labor. Early critics of Moynihan stressed instead the decline of manufacturing in the central cities, an argument developed in detail by William Julius Wilson and his colleagues as blue-collar jobs disappeared more dramatically in the following decades (see, for example, Lee Rainwater and William L. Yancy, eds., *The Moynihan Report and the Politics of Controversy*; Wilson and Kathryn M. Neckerman, "Poverty and Family Structure"; Wilson, *Truly Disadvantaged*).

21. Christopher Jencks has noted: "The stable two-parent family . . . [lost] ground throughout American society . . . not just in the underclass. . . . Single parenthood began to spread during the 1960s, when the economy was booming. It spread during the 1970s, when the economy stagnated. It spread in the early 1980s, during the worst economic downturn in a half century" (*Rethinking Social Policy*, 133–34). For the prevalence of two-parent families among African Americans throughout the nineteenth and early twentieth centuries and the dramatic increase in single-parent families from 1960 on, see chapter 2, note 25. For the limitations of black men's employment difficulties as an explanation for the breakdown of marriage, see, for example, Robert D. Mare and Christopher Winship, "Socioeconomic Change and the Decline of Marriage for Blacks and Whites." Maxine Baca Zinn has stressed that explanations of the rise of female-headed families and their increased presence among the poor failed to examine changes in women's own lives ("Family, Race, and Poverty in the Eighties").

22. See, for example, Wilson and Neckerman, "Poverty and Family Structure."

23. Nancy Folbre, for example, explains how the move to a wage economy increased the costs of children and elders while weakening family support for their care, leading to struggles over social policy at the start of the twentieth century (*Who Pays for the Kids?*, 174–95). See also Viviana Zelizer, *Pricing the Priceless Child*. The focus here is on lessened need for and interest in supporting women's household labor, leading to the dismantling of this overall framework of support by different groups.

24. Quoted in Prudence Mors Rains, *Becoming an Unwed Mother*, 39. Elliott Liebow saw poor black men's views of marriage as limiting sexuality as an effort to disguise their failure as breadwinners (*Tally's Corner*); for interest in other women even among hardworking black men valuing a stable relationship, see Elijah Anderson, *A Place on the Corner*, 100–106.

25. Manufacturing jobs began declining in New York City as early as the 1950s. The share of men in their prime adult years with no earnings doubled over the 1970s for African Americans but remained almost unchanged for whites. By the decade's end, almost one-fourth of black men ages 20–24 had no earnings (Jaynes and Williams, *Common Destiny*, 311).

26. A comparison of African American women in the early baby boom—in their early 20s in 1970 and in their early 40s in 1990—reveals a drop of 70 percent in the never married among college graduates and 50 percent among high school graduates, as these women found husbands later in life, but of less than 25 percent among those who did not complete high school.

27. The proportion of those failing to complete high school had shrunk dramatically among white women as well as African American women. Less than 20 percent of white women between the ages of 22 and 54 had not completed high school by 1980.

28. Harrison and Bluestone, *Great U-Turn*, 7.

29. For the conservative focus of those associated with the new economic growth in California and the Southwest, see McGirr, *Suburban Warriors; Sale, Power Shift.* While arguing that capital-intensive industries did not lead the turn to the right, Val Burris has found such industries in the South and West—defense, oil, agribusiness, textiles, and construction—to be very conservative ("The Political Partisanship of American Business"). For discussion of the conservative politics often associated with early development of a new region, see Franz Schurmann, *The Logic of World Power.*

30. For a blending of defense of traditional gender roles and praise of the free market, see, for example, George Gilder, *Wealth and Poverty;* Charles Murray, *Losing Ground.* For analysis of the rise of the New Right, see Himmelstein, *To the Right;* Hixson, *Search for the American Right Wing;* McGirr, *Suburban Warriors.* For women's newly visible presence and their concerns, see Rebecca E. Klatch, *Women of the New Right;* Klatch, "The Two Worlds of Women of the New Right." Klatch found that though free-market values remained central for some conservative women, many who were less educated felt that "social-conservative" support for the traditional structure of the family was key. In the mid-nineteenth-century United States, economic changes that caused widespread insecurity had led to the religious fervor known as the Great Awakening (see Mary P. Ryan, *Cradle of the Middle Class*).

31. For the emerging New Right's defense of traditional gender roles and organization around profamily issues, see Petchesky, *Abortion and Woman's Choice,* 252–59.

32. By the late 1970s, the New Right had gained access to the organizational network of Protestant fundamentalism (Petchesky, *Abortion and Woman's Choice,* 257), and most women were members of fundamentalist churches. Mansbridge herself, when participating in a pro-ERA demonstration in Springfield, Illinois, in 1980, learned in talking to women protesting the demonstration that most were fundamentalists (*Why We Lost the ERA,* 175; Brady and Tedin, "Ladies in Pink," 570–71; see also Arrington and Kyle, "Equal Rights Amendment Activists in North Carolina," 675).

33. For the compact achieved between employers and workers in some segments of manufacturing, see Thomas Ferguson, "From Normalcy to New Deal." For the breakdown of this compact, see Bowles, Gordon, and Weisskopf, *Beyond the Waste Land;* Carnoy, *Faded Dreams,* 156–58. Big corporations like Eli Lilly (a manufacturer of pharmaceuticals) began to fund the Heritage Foundation and other conservative think tanks, which in turn helped the expansion of the religious right (see Himmelstein, *To the Right*).

34. See Petchesky, *Abortion and Woman's Choice,* 264–68, 293–94.

35. Carnoy, *Faded Dreams,* 154.

36. For racism on the part of white blue-collar men and how it "decreas[ed] the ability of the working class to affect legislation which would benefit labor," see Manning Marable, *Race, Reform and Rebellion* (quotation, 119).

37. For analysis of these voting patterns, see Jeff Manza and Clem Brooks, *Social Cleavages and Political Change*.

38. About two-fifths of white married women who had completed high school but had not gone on to college were working full-time by the mid-1980s, almost twice as many as in 1960.

39. Almost three-fourths of African American wives with four years of high school were in the labor force in the mid-1980s. For comparison of percentage drops in income among African American and white families, see Tienda and Jensen, "Poverty and Minorities," 26. By the mid-1980s, two-fifths of black men and one-fifth of white men made under $10,000, the minimum deemed necessary to keep a family of four out of poverty (Jaynes and Williams, *Common Destiny*, 274). Jobs in manufacturing disappeared more rapidly for African American men from 1980 on; only one-fifth of black men worked in manufacturing by 1990 (Carnoy, *Faded Dreams*, 88–89).

40. For both white and African American couples, in the mid-1980s marital disruption was almost twice as great among the poor and unemployed as among other couples. Among African Americans, 20 percent of married couples in poverty broke up, compared to 10 percent of those not in poverty, and 22 percent of marriages in which neither spouse worked collapsed, compared to 8 percent in which both were employed. The pattern among white couples was similar, though the figures were lower (U.S. Bureau of the Census, *Studies in Household and Family Formation*, 11–14).

41. Ferguson and Rogers, *Right Turn*, 199, 200.

42. For a simple summary of these industrial cycles, see Daniel Chirot, *How Societies Change*, 84–88. See also Rostow, *World Economy*; Walt W. Rostow, *Stages of Economic Growth*.

43. Eric Hobsbawm, "The Crisis of Capitalism in Historical Perspective"; Christopher Chase-Dunn and Richard Rubinson, "Toward a Structural Perspective on the World-System." For discussion of decreases in productivity in the early post–World War II period, see Levy, *New Dollars and Dreams*, 25–56.

44. Investment declined in the 1980s below the level of the late 1970s. "For investors," notes Judith Stein, "the incentives created by Reaganomics . . . made luxury consumption, real estate, shopping malls, financial services, and speculation more attractive than steel mills" (*Running Steel, Running America*, 278). Carnoy states: "Business poured money into real estate speculation and financial schemes that aimed at short-term profits with little implications for productivity" (*Faded Dreams*, 155). Those who argue that services offer few opportunities for increased productivity draw on William Baumol's thesis that a quartet playing Beethoven could not speed up its production, though Baumol himself has pointed out that the potential for technology to increase productivity differs greatly across the service sector ("Productivity Policy and the Service Sector"; see also Victor R. Fuchs, *The Growing Importance of the Service Economy*; Barry Bluestone and Bennett Harrison, *The Deindustrialization of America*; Herbert Grubel, "Producer Services").

45. Petchesky, *Abortion and Woman's Choice*, 261–62, 276, 284, 314–15.

46. Data from the trend tables of the General Social Survey conducted by the National Opinion Research Center, questions 200 (FEWORK) and 252 (FEFAM). A 1980 Virginia Slims poll found that 64 percent of men and women said they supported efforts to strengthen and change women's status (Fleming, "Women's Rights and Roles," 48, 61). For the policy shift in Congress, see Paul Burnstein, M. R. Brichner, and Rachel Einuholer, "Policy Alternatives and Political Change."

47. One reason for the change in attitudes was the fall in the proportion of blue-collar jobs over the 1980s. For the spread of liberal attitudes among professionals, see Manza and Brooks, *Social Cleavages*.

48. By the end of the 1970s, almost 60 percent of white wives and about half of white married mothers caring for children under 18 were in the labor force, a milestone that African American married women had reached a decade earlier. The labor force participation of white wives in their late 20s and early 30s rose from about one-third to more than half in the 1980s alone, both among those who had completed only high school and overall. This rise had occurred in the 1950s and 1960s for black wives of this age.

49. A man living in an inner-city neighborhood—black and white, Mexican and Puerto Rican alike—was more likely to marry a girlfriend who became pregnant if either he or she was employed or had good job prospects (Mark Testa, Nan Marie Astone, Marilyn Krogh, and Kathryn M. Neckerman, "Employment and Marriage among Inner-City Fathers").

50. Black men were two and a half times as likely to be unemployed as white men (Jaynes and Williams, *Common Destiny*, 302–3). Those who found work were less likely to have full-time jobs, and earned less per hour, than white male workers. By 1984, the annual earnings of male high school dropouts 20–24 years old were 42 percent lower than in 1973. Barely over 10 percent earned enough to support a family of four above the poverty line in the mid-1980s (Constance W. Willard, *Black Teenage Mothers*, 3; see also Landry, *New Black Middle Class*, 68).

51. Quoted in *Child Welfare Legislative Reference Material*, 43. These policies were part of larger efforts to reinforce support of women's household work against the encroachments of industrialization (see Barbara J. Nelson, "The Origins of the Two-Channel Welfare State"; Mark H. Leff, "Consensus for Reform"). For an excellent analysis of women's roles in early social policy formation in the United States that includes close attention to women's household work, see Molly Ladd-Taylor, *Mother-Work*. See also the essays in Linda Gordon, ed., *Women, the State, and Social Welfare*; Gordon, "Black and White Visions of Welfare"; Gordon, *Pitied but Not Entitled*; Theda Skocpol, *Protecting Soldiers and Mothers*.

52. The Committee on Economic Security, (*Report to the President of the Committee on Economic Security*, 36). Katherine Lenroot, head of the Children's Bureau, won only an extension of the old mothers' pensions programs, failing to ex-

pand them. Women's efforts fared poorly, in part because, in contrast to earlier policies, in the New Deal, Roosevelt's desire to provide security "from the cradle to the grave" became focused on workers in the industrial labor force (Frances Perkins, *The Roosevelt I Knew*, 283; see also J. Craig Jenkins and Barbara G. Brents, "Social Protest, Hegemonic Competition, and Social Reform," 898–900; Ferguson, "From Normalcy to New Deal"; Jill Quadagno, "Welfare Capitalism and the Social Security Act of 1935"; Margaret Weir, Ann Orloff, and Theda Skocpol, eds., *The Politics of Social Policy Formation in the United States*). Also, the differences among women by location in household or wage labor, and sharp divisions by race, accentuated by many white women's employment of black women in paid domestic service, fragmented their interests in this era and kept them from effectively articulating their needs within the industrial economy.

53. On the common use of the term *welfare* to mean AFDC and on the easy passage of legislation in the early 1970s authorizing Supplemental Security Income to provide aid to the blind and other people with disabilities, see Rebecca Blank, *It Takes a Nation*, especially 99, 103; see also Guida West, *The National Welfare Rights Movement*; Steven M. Teles, *Whose Welfare?* For the important role played by race in growing hostility toward welfare and in limiting new policy formation, see Jill Quadagno, *The Color of Welfare*.

54. Sar Levitan and Robert Taggart, *Promise of Greatness*, 54; see also Levitan, *Programs in Aid of the Poor for the 1970s*. The programs that liberal reformers later mapped out to aid women were, by their own admission, "dismal failures," and "sorely inadequate" (Sheila B. Kamerman, "Women, Children and Poverty," 43). Basically the old consensus that women's work in the home should be supported had shattered, but the increasing view that, at least among poor black women, such domestic tasks should be integrated with labor force participation had emerged without construction of any policies effectively aiding such integration. Though African American women have never received the majority of aid, the media and politicians portrayed the typical welfare recipient as black (Martin Gilens, *Why Americans Hate Welfare*, 71–72, 102–32).

55. Teles, *Whose Welfare?*

56. On the value of AFDC payments and the minimum wage, see Blank, *It Takes a Nation*, 100, 135. Thus, staying on welfare made sense, especially if state support could be supplemented with unreported earnings, as it almost always was (see, for example, Kathryn Edin and Laura Lein, *Making Ends Meet*).

57. Teles, *Whose Welfare?* For the scapegoating of young unwed mothers, see Kristin Luker, *Dubious Conceptions*. For use of sterilization to limit births among poor women, see Solinger, *Beggars and Choosers*, 10–11.

58. Manza and Brooks, *Social Cleavages*.

59. By 1990, two-thirds of white wives and four-fifths of black wives who were employed had full-time jobs. Most women on their own were also working full-time.

60. Twenty-four percent of white women and 13 percent of black women had sixteen or more years of education. While almost all had also obtained their degrees, the census did not ask about degrees until 1990; thus trends are discussed in terms of years of education completed. For African American women especially, this marked a dramatic increase from 1960, when less than 10 percent of black women ages 22–54 had gone beyond high school.

61. African American women had turned to paid employment earlier and in greater numbers than white women in the post–World War II decades. By 1990, more than 90 percent of black college graduates, whether married, unmarried, or caring for children, were in the labor force. While somewhat more likely to combine careers with motherhood than were white women, African American graduates also married later, more often divorced, and more often remained single than white college graduates. Black college graduates in the early baby boom were almost twice as likely to be divorced or still single at 35–44 than white graduates (in 1990, 21.5 percent of black college graduates in the early baby boom were still single, compared to 12.5 percent of white baby boomer college graduates). For a detailed analysis of the employment and earnings of African American women over the 1970s and 1980s and their decline relative to those of white women, see Mary Corcoran and Sharon Parrott, "Black Women's Economic Progress"; John Bound and Laura Dresser, "Losing Ground."

62. Sixty-two percent of black women who had not graduated from college were married. Only 24 percent (and a smaller percentage of wives) were full-time year-round workers, though 47 percent were employed. Among those who completed high school, half of white women and almost two-thirds of black women were mothers by their early 20s, in sharp contrast to college graduates.

63. In the 1960s, married women who had not completed high school did not differ dramatically from other wives. All but the youngest were as likely to be in the labor force or working full-time as other married women of their race, excluding college graduates. However, as most wives turned rapidly to the labor force over the following decades, those with little education were left far behind. This gap had begun to appear among black women in the 1960s and grew substantially in the 1970s among both black and white women, widening still further in the 1980s.

64. Welfare mother, quoted in Kathryn Edin, *There's a Lot of Month Left at the End of the Money*, 21; she was discussing the outcomes of government training programs. One-fifth of white female dropouts in their early 20s could not find work.

65. Among unmarried white women, well over half of white high school dropouts in 1990 were divorced or separated, compared to one-third of college graduates. Francine D. Blau also notes the greater likelihood of less-educated women to be single parents, and provides detailed analysis of other trends in women's lives between 1970 and 1995 ("Trends in the Well-Being of American Women").

66. Almost 90 percent of high school dropouts of both races in their late 20s

and early 30s were mothers; in 1990, they were about twice as likely as college graduates to have a child.

67. Hobsbawm, "Crisis of Capitalism," 302.

5. The Formation of a Female Underclass

1. Tillmon, quoted in Guida West, *The National Welfare Rights Movement*, 46. Families headed by women grew from 20 percent to 48 percent of poor families between 1959 and 1976 (U.S. Bureau of the Census, *Characteristics of the Population below the Poverty Level*, 1976, i). See also Roger A. Wojtkiewicz, Sara S. McLanahan, and Irwin Garfinkel, "The Growth of Families Headed by Women." The phrase "feminization of poverty" was first used by Diana Pearce, who initially found that there was little concern over the growing number of women among the poor ("The Feminization of Poverty").

2. See, for example, Terry Arendell, *Mothers and Divorce*; Mary Jo Bane and David Ellwood, "One Fifth of the Nation's Children"; Irving Garfinkel and Sara McLanahan, *Single-Mother Families and Public Policy*; McLanahan, Annemette Sorensen, and Dorothy Watson, "Sex Differences in Poverty, 1950–1980"; Heather L. Ross and Isabel V. Sawhill, *Time of Transition*; Lenore Weitzman, *The Divorce Revolution*. In an early study, Bane stressed that unlike white women, most poor black women heading families were poor before setting up their own households ("Household Composition and Poverty"). Later researchers argued that Bane's methodology led her to undercount changes in household composition, such as having a child or losing a husband, compared to income changes, and they stressed instead "striking racial similarities" in female-headed family formation, movement into poverty, and relationship to the labor force (Thomas Kniesner, Marjorie McElroy, and Steven Wilcox, "Getting into Poverty without a Husband and Getting out, With or Without," especially 88; see also McLanahan, McElroy, and Wilcox, "Sex Differences in Poverty"; see as well Suzanne Bianchi, "The Changing Demographic and Socioeconomic Characteristics of Single Parent Families"; James P. Smith, "Poverty and the Family").

3. Stephan Thernstrom, "Poverty in Historical Perspective," 161. See also George Gilder, *Wealth and Poverty*; Michael Harrington, *The Other America*; Charles Murray, *Losing Ground*; William Julius Wilson, *The Truly Disadvantaged*. Though the poor are commonly viewed as entrenched in economic hardship, researchers looking at the 1970s and 1980s found a more general population moving in and out of poverty, though they also noted a small group of enduring poor, made up primarily of women (Greg J. Duncan, with Richard D. Coe et al., *Years of Poverty, Years of Plenty*; Mary Corcoran and Martha S. Hill, "The Economic Fortunes of Women"). This chapter stresses a long-term dynamic rather than persistent or cyclical patterns in women's poverty.

4. On the role played by work in the poverty of single mothers, see Arendell, *Mothers and Divorce*; Bane and Ellwood, "One Fifth of the Nation's Children"; Garfinkel and McLanahan, *Single-Mother Families*; Kniesner, McElroy, and Wilcox,

"Getting into Poverty"; Wojtkiewicz, McLanahan, and Garfinkel, "Growth of Families Headed by Women"; Leslie A. Morgan, *After Marriage Ends*. Several studies point to the importance of considering changes over time in the causes and composition of women's poverty and possible differences by race. McLanahan, Sorensen, and Watson find that the poverty gap between men and women widened between 1950 and 1980 but also stress that poverty rates actually decreased substantially for women as well as men over these decades ("Sex Differences in Poverty"). Richard Peterson found the economic situation of divorced women improved several years after divorce (*Women, Work, and Divorce*); others have found that the characteristics of the population of unmarried mothers shifted in the 1980s (Bianchi, "Single Parent Families"; Smith, "Poverty and the Family") and that the rise of poorly paying service occupations heightened difficulties for black single mothers in particular (Irene Browne, "Opportunities Lost?"; see also Corcoran, "Economic Progress of African American Women"; Linxin Hao and Mary C. Brinton, "Productive Activities and Support Systems of Single Mothers"). On average, the rise in poverty between 1970 and 1999 caused by changes in family structure was offset by women's increased labor force participation (Maria Cancian and Deborah Reed, "Changes in Family Structure").

5. Looking at women at or below 125 percent of the government poverty level allows consideration of more than the very poor. Some differences existed between poor single mothers and other women, though they were far less pronounced than thirty years later. In 1960, 96 percent of poor black unmarried mothers and 92 percent of poor white unmarried mothers had no more than a high school education, compared to 90 percent of all other African American women and over 80 percent of other white women. Though most commonly employed in the same occupations as other women, poor single mothers, especially if white, were somewhat more likely to work in service occupations than other women of their race. Rates of employment among poor single mothers and all other women were similar because childless women were most likely to be employed, offsetting the low level of employment among married mothers. Though caring for a similar number of children at home as other mothers of their race, poor single mothers had given birth to slightly more children. Unless otherwise noted, all statistics in this chapter are based on the author's calculations using unpublished 1960, 1970, 1980, and 1990 Integrated Public Use Microdata Series (IPUMS) data. *Mothers* in this chapter refers to white non-Hispanic and black women ages 22–54 with at least one child under 18 in the household; Hispanic women are included in the data for 1960.

6. Both African American and white women of all backgrounds experienced a sharp drop in income when their marriages ended (see Bianchi, "Single Parent Families"; Kniesner, McElroy, and Wilcox, "Getting into Poverty"; McLanahan, Sorensen, and Watson, "Sex Differences in Poverty"; Peterson, *Women, Work, and Divorce*; Smith, "Poverty and the Family").

7. "Nobody Tells You," 6.

8. Almost half of black single mothers and over one-third of white single mothers with some college education were in poverty in 1960. More than four-fifths of all black single mothers and well over half of all white single mothers lived in poverty (see also U.S. Department of Labor, Women's Bureau, *Women in Poverty*, especially 1). Shaken by the numbers of poor single mothers, Piven and Cloward proposed a "Strategy to End Poverty" that was embraced by the newly founded National Welfare Rights Organization, which sought to broaden women's awareness of and improve their access to government aid for single mothers (West, *National Welfare Rights Movement*).

9. The large majority of black single mothers and two-fifths of white single mothers worked at least part of the year. The simulations presented in figure 4 present probabilities for the typical mother age 22–54 of each race. In 1960, the typical white mother on average was 38 years old, had almost 11 years of education, and had two children under 18 at home; she was most commonly employed part-time in clerical or sales work and lived in the Midwest. The typical black mother, on average 37 years old, had almost 9 years of education and three children under 18 in the household; she was most commonly employed part-time or part-year in private domestic service and lived in the South. In 1960, for white unmarried women with children, full-time year-round work was slightly more effective than marriage in reducing the chances of poverty; for black, slightly less effective. For further details, see Hilarie Lieb and Susan Thistle, "The Changing Impact of Marriage, Children and Work on Women's Poverty."

10. The survey of widows who had raised their children in the 1950s is reported in Helena Znaniecka Lopata, *Women as Widows*, 60. Black college graduates were far more likely to pursue careers than were white college graduates.

11. "Divorced Woman: American Style," 66.

12. Louise Kriesberg, *Mothers in Poverty*, 144–45. Cultural pressures also played a strong role. While only 5 percent of the mothers surveyed by Kriesberg said they would think less of someone who accepted welfare benefits, approximately one-fourth expressed disapproval for mothers who worked for pay rather than focusing on their families (149–50). For the 1996 study, see U.S. Department of Labor, Women's Bureau, *Women in Poverty*, 4. Work experience of single mothers is based on author's calculations using unpublished 1967 data from the National Longitudinal Survey of Mature Women's Labor Market Experience.

13. Quoted in Sonja L. Lanehart, *Sista, Speak!* 20. Data on median earnings are from U.S. Department of Labor, Women's Bureau, *Women in Poverty*, 3. The conclusion about lack of growth in black women's wages over time is based on the author's calculations using unpublished data from the National Longitudinal Survey of Mature Women's Labor Market Experience (see Susan Thistle, "The Changing Nature of Women's Poverty").

14. Statistical details here and in later sections are drawn primarily from the author's decomposition of logistic regression analyses assessing changes in

poverty levels among white single mothers and black single mothers, 1960–70, 1970–80, 1980–90, and 1960–90, based on unpublished 1960–90 IPUMS data.

15. Quoted in Annette Grant, "After Graduation, a Job in New York?" 145.

16. Daughter of the long-term domestic worker quoted above, also quoted in Lanehart, *Sista, Speak!* 63. Mean education rose by approximately one year among both black and white single mothers over the 1960s, and employment in technical jobs also increased. The percentage of black single mothers employed in private domestic service was more than halved, to 12.7 percent in 1970. For both white and black single mothers, year-round work brought a rise in total wages beyond that tied to better-paying occupations or gains in education. See also James Cunningham and Nadja Zalokar, "The Economic Progress of Black Women, 1940–1980."

17. Heading a household is strongly associated with women's poverty. An increase in female-headed households contributed significantly to a rise in poverty among single mothers in the 1960s but was offset by gains in education and employment and by a drop in the average number of children. In other words, had headship not risen, the poverty rate among single mothers would have fallen still further in these years. Phillips Cutright argued that the formation of independent households was the primary cause of the rise in families headed by women in these years; others, who found methodological limitations in a subsequent analysis by Cutright, stressed instead a decrease in marriage (McLanahan, Sorensen, and Watson, "Sex Differences in Poverty"; Ross and Sawhill, *Time of Transition*; Cutright, "Components of Change in the Number of Female Family Heads Aged 15–44").

18. Except among college graduates, most of those without husbands were mothers. Poverty dropped only slightly for white single mothers; the decrease for black single mothers was larger (8.7 points) but still less than the fall in the previous decade.

19. The career adviser is quoted in Suzanne Seixas, "One Family's Finances," 88. Women in Transition, *Women's Survival Manual*, gave divorced women advice on how to apply for jobs.

20. "What's a Nice Girl Like You Doing in a Place Like This?" 103. For stories of single mothers in nontraditional jobs, see Brenda Payton, "Changing the Tradition: Women in Crafts Jobs," and Ruth E. Thaler, "Essence Women," *Essence*, June 1980. For the impact of gains in work, see also Cunningham and Zalokar, "Economic Progress of Black Women."

21. Unemployment rose particularly among blue-collar workers.

22. By 1980, widows made up only one-tenth of white single mothers. For whites as for blacks, most of those without husbands were mothers except among college graduates. The sheer size of the first wave of baby boomers swelled the ranks of white single mothers in their late 20s and early 30s, who had the highest rates of poverty because they were the most likely to be caring

for young children. Among black single mothers over 25, in contrast, poverty rates differed little by age, and the proportion of widows, who had never fared that much better than other unmarried black mothers, had declined earlier than among whites.

23. Poverty did not rise among black college graduates who were single mothers. Also, this rise in poverty among each educational group was offset by an overall gain in education.

24. Such difficulties finding employment had existed in earlier decades (see, for example, Phyllis Wallace, *Pathways to Work*), but they grew worse for less-educated women in the 1980s.

25. More than four-fifths of sexually active teenage girls surveyed in the mid-1970s did not always use birth control, and only half of those having sex used highly reliable methods (Alan Guttmacher Institute, *11 Million Teenagers*, 16). The government moved to limit pregnancies among poor women by providing birth control. By the late 1960s the Department of Health, Education, and Welfare and the Office of Economic Opportunity were giving substantial funds to birth-control programs. However, many young women found access to contraception difficult (Petchesky, *Abortion and Woman's Choice*, 116; see also Rickie Solinger, *Wake Up Little Susie*).

26. Joyce A. Ladner, *Tomorrow's Tomorrow*, 125; Ladner quotes the teenager, 124.

27. Young mother Erika Stone, quoted in "Seventeen's Not So Sweet When You're on Your Own—with a Baby," 55. After the passage of the Hyde Amendment, which prohibited the use of federal funds to pay for abortions, abortions plummeted among poor women (Rickie Solinger, *Beggars and Choosers*, 20). For the decrease in marriage among young women who found themselves pregnant, see Bachu, "Trends in Premarital Childbearing."

28. As in the 1970s, the increase in poverty among less-educated white and black single mothers was offset by gains in education. Poverty rose half as much for less-educated white mothers who were married than for those without husbands. It also rose less for unmarried white women without children than for those with children.

29. Quoted in Edin, *There's a Lot of Month Left*, 115.

30. See Corcoran, "Economic Progress of African American Women"; Browne, "Opportunities Lost?"

31. Only one-fifth of white single mothers in service occupations, for example, had worked full-time in the previous year, compared to one-third of those holding clerical or blue-collar jobs.

32. African American single mothers with some college education made great gains in employment overall, and the economic condition of those working full-time, year-round, also improved. However, unemployment rose as well, as a growing share of the increasing number of women looking for work could not find jobs.

33. Quoted in Edin, *There's a Lot of Month Left*, 121. This was also a difficult time

to rely on state support, as the government refused to raise benefits to keep pace with inflation even as it continued to restrict eligibility. As Edin learned, women unable to find jobs paying a living wage and providing necessary benefits such as health care often combined welfare with unreported work.

34. Only a tiny fraction of either white or black single mothers lived with male partners in the early 1970s. By 1990, roughly 13 percent of white single mothers and 6 percent of black single mothers did so (Cancian and Reed, "Changes in Family Structure," 78–79), but few of those partners had incomes that could lift the household above the poverty line. Poverty rose by a similar amount among single mothers who were not partners, and for similar reasons, though partners had, on average, the highest rates of poverty and the least education.

35. Women heading families fared increasingly poorly in comparison with other women, though these were mostly older employed mothers, in part because women's turn to the labor force raised the income of married couples. But the rise in poverty among these single mothers was offset by a drop in the share heading households.

36. Almost all white single mothers were now divorced, separated or never married rather than widowed. Single Mothers by Choice was first organized in 1981, and chapters now exist in major urban areas across the United States (see home page). See also Susan Walker, "Why I Became a Single Mother."

37. For the postponement of childbearing among more-educated women, see Spain and Bianchi, *Balancing Act*, 11–15. One result of these changes was that a shrinking percentage of single mothers had four or more years of college (see also Bianchi, "Single Parent Families"; Smith, "Poverty and the Family").

38. In 1960, the typical African American single mother in her late 20s or early 30s had a ninth-grade education. She had already had on average more than three children and would give birth to one or two more. Though employed, she worked in private domestic work and had little hope of avoiding poverty. Poverty was substantially lower, by 19.2 points, among the cohort of black women coming of age in the 1970s, primarily because these early baby boomers had significantly fewer children than their mothers. Almost all had graduated from high school and more than one-third had attended college. Three-fourths had worked in the previous year, most commonly in clerical or sales jobs; almost none were private domestic workers.

39. Black single mothers in their early 20s faced even higher unemployment than in 1970 and remained trapped in service occupations. Among white late baby boomers (ages 25–34 in 1990), one-fifth of single mothers had never married, a far greater share than in the previous cohort. These hardships continued for single mothers just entering adulthood at the end of the 1980s.

40. Behind such increased impact again lay a growth in labor force participation, especially for white women, and a move into better occupations for black women. The simulations in figure 7 are for a typical mother in each race.

The typical white mother was, on average, almost 37 years old, had one year of college, and was caring for one or two children; she most commonly was employed full-time year-round in professional, managerial, or technical work. The typical black mother was, on average, almost 36 years old, had 12.6 years of education, and was caring for two children; she was most commonly employed full-time year-round in clerical or sales work. Both were most likely to live in the South (employment in clerical and sales work was equally common for white single mothers; the impact of full-time work was slightly less in these occupations). See Daniel T. Lichter, Deborah Roempke Graefe, and J. Brian Brown, "Is Marriage a Panacea?"

41. Further, though single mothers of both races were caring for a similar number of children as other mothers, in 1990 they were more likely than the rest of women to be mothers than in 1960, given the general rise in childlessness.

42. For a discussion that attributes the appearance of an underclass to the decline of traditional manufacturing jobs, especially in central cities, and the loss of employment by less-educated black men, see Wilson, *The Truly Disadvantaged*.

6. The "New Economy" and the Transformation of Women's Work

1. Black women led women's turn to the labor force. Still, in 1960, most black women were married and were not full-time year-round workers.

2. U.S. Census Bureau, "Twentieth Century Statistics," in *Statistical Abstract of the United States*, 1999, table 1432. Data from *Statistical Abstract* is for women 16 years and older.

3. For a summary and critique of the tendency to blame the service sector for the United States' drop in productivity and rising inequality in wages, see Frank Levy, *The New Dollars and Dreams*, 25–56; Stephen A. Herzenberg, John A. Alic, and Howard Wial, *New Rules for a New Economy*.

4. Service industries made a steady and major contribution to the growth of the GDP between 1977 and 1998. They were the biggest contributor from 1977 to 1992, and were second only to manufacturing from 1992 to 1998 (Sherlene K. S. Lum, Brian C. Moyer, and Robert E. Yuskavage, "Improved Estimates of Gross Product by Industry for 1947–98"). For gains tied to new technology and expansion into new regions, see chapter 4, and Schurmann, *The Logic of World Power*.

5. Lynn E. Browne, "Taking in Each Other's Laundry—the Service Economy," 28–29.

6. Nancy Folbre and Julie A. Nelson, "For Love or Money—or Both?" 123. For women's involvement in caregiving over the past two centuries, see, for example, Emily K. Abel, "American Women Tending Sick and Disabled Children"; for insightful examination of such care today, see Carol Heimer and Lisa R. Staffen, *For the Sake of the Children*.

7. Folbre and Nelson, "For Love or Money—or Both?" For the exclusion of women's household work from the U.S. census, see Folbre, "The Unproductive Housewife." For recognition of the value of women's household work and efforts to count it, see also Margaret Reid, *Economics of Household Production*; Robert Eisner, *The Total Incomes System of Accounts*. For the undervaluation of care work in the market, see also Folbre, *The Invisible Heart*; Paula England, Michelle Budig, and Nancy Folbre, "Wages of Virtue."

8. Author's calculations, based on published data from U.S. Department of Labor, Bureau of Labor Statistics (BLS), "National Employment, Hours and Earnings (SIC), 1970–2000"; U.S. Census Bureau, "Labor Force, Employment, and Earnings," in *Statistical Abstract of the United States*, 1999, table 679. As noted earlier, the market takeover of such tasks has also involved factory production of goods once made in the home and the mechanization of household tasks (see chapters 2 and 3 for examples).

9. Julie Hatch and Angela Clinton, "Job Growth in the 1990s," 14. Computer and data processing made up only 23 percent of the jobs in business services in 1999. Though job growth in this area was dramatic from 1980 to 1999, from 221,000 to 2,079,000 workers, personnel services also grew strongly, from 235,000 to 1,066,000 workers (U.S. Census Bureau, "Labor Force, Employment, and Earnings," in *Statistical Abstract of the United States*, 2000, table 672).

10. James W. McLamore, *The Burger King*, 73, 83.

11. Herzenberg, Alic, and Wial, *New Rules for a New Economy*, 34.

12. For expenditures on prepared food, see U.S. Census Bureau, "Twentieth Century Statistics," *Statistical Abstract*, 1999, table 1424; the rise in employment is based on the author's calculations from unpublished BLS data. On the growth of franchises, see Robert L. Emerson, *Fast Food*; David Gerard Hogan, *Selling 'Em by the Sack*.

13. Whole Foods Market, for example, has grown from a small store employing fewer than 20 people in 1980 to a national chain with more than 120 stores employing 24,000 people and making $2.7 billion by 2002. While its core identity is as a provider of natural and organic foods, a large portion of its stores' profits come from the sales of a wide variety of prepared foods. "A fast, healthy lunch or easy to heat dinner can be found in our bountiful Prepared Foods department," its Bedford, Massachusetts, store advertises (http://www.wholefoodsmarket.com/bedford/tour_prepared.html [accessed January 24, 2003]).

14. Almost 2 million people worked in hotels, motels, and similar facilities in 2000. The growing trend is toward "extended-stay" facilities that offer a small home away from home—living rooms, well-stocked small kitchens, and laundry and food-shopping services (U.S. Department of Labor, Bureau of Labor Statistics, *Career Guide to Industries*, 2000–01 Edition, "Hotels and Other Accommodations").

15. Cleaning pledge from advertisement in the Ameritech Evanston, Illinois,

yellow pages (Chicago: Ameritech Publishing, 1998, 236). On the growth of cleaning services, see Phil Zinkewicz, "Cleaning and Janitorial Services." However, only 9 percent of all households paid a professional to clean their homes in 1996, 25 percent if those hiring someone "very rarely" are included (Shannon Dortch, "Maids Clean Up," 4).

16. U.S. Census Bureau, "Labor Force, Employment, and Earnings," *Statistical Abstract*, 2000, table 669. Only 1 million jobs were added in manufacturing for women and men between 1964 and 1997, compared to 6 million in health care (U.S. Department of Labor, Women's Bureau, "Women's Jobs 1964–1997," 2–3). See also U.S. Department of Labor, *Futurework*, especially chap. 4.

17. The survey is cited in Laura Freeman, "Home-sweet-home Health Care," 7.

18. Freeman, "Home-sweet-home Health Care," 4. On the growth of home health aides and care services, see also U.S. Census Bureau, "Labor Force, Employment, and Earnings," *Statistical Abstract*, 2000, table 669; Hatch and Clinton, "Job Growth in the 1990s," 14; Lynn C. Burbridge, "The Labor Market for Home Care Workers."

19. Hatch and Clinton, "Job Growth in the 1990s."

20. Quotation from U.S. Department of Labor, Bureau of Labor Statistics, "Personal and Home Care Aides."

21. U.S. Department of Labor, Women's Bureau, "Work-Related Child Care Statistics," 1–2; U.S. Department of Labor, Women's Bureau, *Facts on Working Women.*

22. U.S. Census Bureau, "Labor Force, Employment, and Earnings," *Statistical Abstract*, 2000, tables 669, 670; U.S. Department of Labor, Women's Bureau, *Facts on Working Women*, 1–12. See also U.S. Department of Labor, *Futurework*, chap. 4.

23. Author's calculations based on published BLS data from U.S. Census Bureau, "Labor Force, Employment, and Earnings," *Statistical Abstract*, 1999, table 679.

24. More precisely, the GDP grew, in current or nominal dollars, from $1,039.7 billion in 1970 to $9,268.6 billion in 1999. "Real" GDP, calculated in 1996 chained dollars, grew from $3,578.0 billion in 1970 to $8,856.5 billion—an increase of 147.5 percent, controlling for inflation (Bureau of Economic Analysis, "National Accounts Data, Current-Dollar and 'Real' GDP, 1929–2000").

25. Service industries here classified as "women's work" are care services (health, educational, social, and personal services) and private household services. The output of hotels and other lodging places, which is shown here with eating and drinking trade figures, is included in this overall estimate of the growth of women's work. The share of women's work in the overall GDP, not counting work in public education, health care, and government service agencies, has grown by almost half since 1970, and by 60 percent if the eating and drinking trade is included. Manufacturing's share of output shrank in the pri-

vate sector to 18 percent of the private sector GDP, and in the overall GDP to 15.9 percent. Overall, only the areas of finance, real estate, and insurance (commonly known as FIRE); manufacturing; and government (much of which consists of professional care services) provide larger shares of the GDP. The contribution of women's work to private GDP is one and a half times that of business services (author's calculations using detailed data tables from the Bureau of Economic Analysis, "Gross Product Originating by Industry [1972 SIC basis], Share of Gross Domestic Product, percent, 1947–1987," and "Gross Domestic Product by Industry [1987 SIC basis], Share of Gross Domestic Product [percent], 1987–2000").

26. Others have also noted this overestimation; see, for example, Lourdes Beneria, *Gender, Development, and Globalization,* 152; Folbre, *Invisible Heart,* 67. However, this point could be made of almost all areas of work. Contributions from farms, for example, are not seen as overestimates due to the value of men's earlier production of crops for family consumption. Shift of care to the market can lead to a deterioration of the treatment of the sick, elderly, or young, as pressures to realize profits lead to cost cutting at the expense of human needs, but such deterioration is not inevitable. The use of trained workers can enhance the level of care and lessen the burdens of primary caregivers. The answer, thus, is to raise the quality of care through government regulations and funding, ensuring high standards and well-paid workers. See, for example, Folbre, *Invisible Heart.*

27. These are full-time jobs (U.S. Department of Labor, Women's Bureau, "Women's Jobs 1964–1997"; see also U.S. Department of Labor, U.S. Women's Bureau, "Women at the Millennium").

28. From 1983 to 1998, 54 percent of new jobs were in professional, managerial, and technical work (4 percent of new job growth was in technical occupations). Though technicians are commonly grouped with sales and administrative support, their wages are much higher; hence they are included here among upper-tier jobs. One-third of new jobs were in low-wage service occupations and in sales and clerical jobs. Women filled two-thirds of these new upper-tier jobs and almost three-fifths of the lower-tier jobs, and they continued to hold the majority of positions in sales and administrative support. Less than 10 percent of new jobs were in manufacturing, and men took more than 90 percent of them (author's calculations based on data from U.S. Census Bureau, "Labor Force, Employment, and Earnings," *Statistical Abstract,* 1999, table 675).

29. This figure is for women in their prime adult years, 22–54, as elsewhere in the book, except when data are from *Statistical Abstracts,* when they are commonly for all female civilians, 16 years and older. Unless otherwise specified, all statistical information is drawn from the author's own calculations based on unpublished IPUMS data.

30. The increase in Ph.D.'s earned by women was particularly rapid in the

1970s among women ages 25–34, from 13 percent in 1970 to 30 percent 1980 (Suzanne M. Bianchi and Daphne Spain, "Women, Work, and Family in America" 15). Data on current degrees are from U.S. Census Bureau, "Income, Expenditures and Wealth," in *Statistical Abstract of the United States*, 2000, tables 321, 322.

31. U.S. Census Bureau, "Labor Force, Employment, and Earnings," *Statistical Abstract*, 2000, table 669. Women are concentrated in the areas of health care and teaching and are falling behind in computer science and engineering (see, for example, Department of Labor, Women's Bureau, "Women in High-Tech Jobs").

32. The eye surgeon Patricia Erna Bath, quoted in Wini Warren, *Black Women in Science*, 14. For Lynn Margulis's development of a new theory of evolution, Barbara Liskov's development of software allowing use of ultrasound to assess hearts, and the contributions of other scientists, see Martha J. Bailey, *American Women in Science, 1950 to the Present*, 238, 257–59; see also Professor Margulis's own website, http://www.geo.umass.edu/faculty/margulis/ (accessed June 1, 2005). Diane Powell Murray's work in developing the Earth Observing Satellite and Information System is discussed in Warren, *Black Women in Science*, 201–3.

33. Frances K. Conley, *Walking Out on the Boys*, 29.

34. U.S. Department of Labor, Women's Bureau, "Women at the Millennium," 2; Rita Colwell, preface to Wasserman, *The Door in the Dream*, ix. See also Henry Etzkowitz, Carol Kemelgor, and Brian Uzzi, *Athena Unbound*.

35. U.S. Census Bureau, "Labor Force, Employment, and Earnings," *Statistical Abstract*, 2000, tables 669, 670. A total of 46.2 percent of white women and 33.1 percent of black women ages 22–54 work in professional, managerial, or technical jobs.

36. Laura Katz-Najera, "Unsung Heroines," 47. See Sheila Neysmith, "Home Care Workers Discuss Their Work"; Burbridge, "Home Care Workers," 44; Steven L. Dawson and Rick Surpin, "Direct-Care Healthcare Workers," especially 28, 23; "Cheating Dignity," a report from the American Federation of State, County and Municipal Employees (AFSCME); and William Scanlon, "Nursing Workforce."

37. For discussion of government training practices, see Cynthia Negrey, Stacey Golin, Sunhwa Lee, Holly Mead, and Barbara Gault, "Working First but Working Poor," vi. Welfare recipients told of the applause that greeted those in job workshops who landed jobs at McDonald's or similar restaurants (Kathryn Edin, *There's a Lot of Month Left at the End of the Money*, 67). An analysis of ex–welfare recipients in Wisconsin found that even of the more persistent workers (employed all four quarters of both 1990 and 1998) who began in low-paid jobs at the bottom of the occupational spectrum, 30 percent were still working in those less-desirable jobs at the decade's close (Sammis B. White and Lori A. Geddes, "Economic Lessons for Welfare Mothers," 9–10, and unpublished data from this study provided by White and Geddes to the author, March 27, 2002).

Most aides at the worker-owned Cooperative Home Care Associates in the South Bronx, for example, have previously been on welfare (Paraprofessional Health-care Institute, "Cooperative Home Care Associates"). See also Herzenberg, Alic, and Wial, *New Rules for a New Economy*, 100.

38. U.S. Census Bureau, "Labor Force, Employment, and Earnings," *Statistical Abstract*, 2000, table 669. The proportion of black women among private house-hold cleaners and servants dropped by two-thirds from 1983 to 1999, but half of the top ten leading occupations for black women are still located in the lower tier of the service sector (U.S. Census Bureau, "Labor Force, Employment, and Earnings," *Statistical Abstract* 2000, table 669).

39. Quoted in Ruth Glasser and Jeremy Brecher, "We Are the Roots," 15. See also Freeman, "Home-sweet-home Healthcare," 7. For analysis of the low earn-ings of care workers, see, for example, England, Budig, and Folbre, "Wages of Virtue."

40. He continues: "Another way of looking at this is capitalists are likely to gain when the number of workers rises. Thus, the infusion of women into the market implies that total profits rose even though the profit rate remained un-changed" (David T. Ellwood, "Winners and Losers in America," 22–23).

41. This estimate of the contribution made by women's labor is conservative, as it looks only at the private sector. Private-sector GDP increased by $4,339.9 billion in chained 1996 dollars, or 176 percent. Its size in 1999 was 276 per-cent of that in 1970, again controlling for inflation (calculations are based on Bureau of Economic Analysis, "National Accounts Data, Gross Domestic Prod-uct: Current-Dollar and 'Real' GDP, 1929–01").

42. This is net increase in labor input (increase in hours worked and average skill level minus the cost of labor). Output in growth is seen as composed of three sources. Mathematically, percent change in output = percent change in multifactor productivity + SL × percent change in labor input + SK × percent change in capital input, where SL is labor's share of costs and SK is capital's share of cost, which averaged around one-third over the 1970–99 period. Multifac-tor productivity growth averaged 0.9 percent per year. Output and input growth rates were quite similar over the two periods (only after 1995 did the growth rate of output accelerate). Thus we have 3.6 = 0.9 + (0.685 × 2.0) + (0.33 × 4.03). Between 1970 and 1999, according to data from the Bureau of Economic Analysis (BEA), labor input grew 2.0 percent per year and its cost share aver-aged 0.685. Thus, labor's contribution to output growth was (0.02 × 0.685)/3.6 = 38.1. Women's share of this contribution, at its lowest bound, was 43.7 percent.

Women's contribution to output is the product of labor's share of costs, women's share of wages, and the growth rate of women's labor input. Based on BEA data, women's share of total wages from 1970 to 1999 was 26.2 percent. Women's labor growth rate from 1970 to 1999 averaged 3.3 percent, over twice that of men's. Thus, women's contribution to output was 0.685 × 0.262 ×

0.033 = 0.592, making women's contribution to private-sector output both from 1970 1999 and from 1990 to 99 equal to 0.59/3.6 (growth rate of GDP) = 16.5 percent.

While their growth rate slowed in the 1990s, to 2.7 percent (still one-third greater than that of men's wages in this period), women's wages grew in this decade, keeping their overall contribution steady. These calculations are based on hours and wage data from the March supplement to the CPS as compiled by the Office of Productivity and Technology, Bureau of Labor Statistics, on October 15, 2001 (provided to author via e-mail, November 10, 2001).

43. On the wage-lowering effects of discrimination against women, see, for example, Kimberly Bayard, Judith Hellerstein, David Neumark, and Kenneth Troske, "New Evidence on Sex Segregation and Sex Differences in Wages"; Trond Petersen and Laurie Morgan, "Separate and Unequal." Thus, women's contribution to output as calculated in note 44 is too low; it represents a lower bound. Raising women's share of wages by approximately 15 percent to give a more accurate assessment of their productivity increases women's share of wages by 31.7 percent (0.685 × 0.216 × 0.033 = 0.67) and their contribution to private-sector growth to 18.6 percent (67/3.6 = 18.6). In the most extreme case, if we see all differences in wages between the sexes as due to discrimination (since education and occupation also are shaped strongly by discrimination), and simply give women the same wages as men, we just use women's share of hours (34.4 × 0.685 × 0.033 = 0.778), raising women's contribution 21.6 percent (778/3.6 = 21.6).

44. More precisely, women's contribution, in chained 1996 dollars, can be seen as $714.0 billion, $807.3 billion, or $937.9 billion, depending on whether their contribution is taken to be 16.5 percent, 18.6 percent, or 21.6 percent of private-sector GDP (based on corrections for discrimination).

45. The economist Robert Gordon sees computer technology as explaining one-third of the growth in GDP in the late 1990s, and he attributes the rest to capital deepening and improvements in labor quality ("The United States"). See also Lum, Moyer, and Yuskavage, "Improved Estimates of Gross Product by Industry." On women's role in the growth of skilled and cheap labor, see Hatch and Clinton, "Job Growth in the 1990s," esp. 14.

46. Women's increasing labor force participation has served to redistribute income, so that consumer spending was able to grow though most men's wages did not. As Levy explains, "more paychecks were substituting for richer paychecks in supporting revenue growth" (*New Dollars and Dreams*, 45). Women's wages grew more rapidly than men's in the 1990s. See note 49.

47. In 1950, 65.8 percent of women ages 14 and over were married. By the end of the century, only 51.1 percent of women ages 15 and over were living with spouses; another 3.8 percent were married but separated (U.S. Census Bureau, "Twentieth Century Statistics," *Statistical Abstract*, 1999, table 1418; U.S. Census Bureau, "Marital Status of Persons 15 Years and Older"). The proportion of

women still single in their early 30s has tripled since 1970, and divorce rates, despite declining slightly in recent years, remain high (U.S. Census Bureau, "Population," *Statistical Abstract*, 1999, table 76). Data on childlessness are from U.S. Bureau of the Census, "Children Ever Born per 1,000 Women." Among women in their prime adult years, 18 percent of white women and 36 percent of black women are caring for children on their own.

48. In the late 1990s, 61.1 percent of white married mothers returned to work before their child was 1 year old, twice as many as in 1975, while 73.7 percent of black married mothers did so (U.S. Department of Labor, Bureau of Labor Statistics, "Employment Status of the Population"). Women now spend on average six more minutes per day in paid work than unpaid work, most of which involves tasks of family care (Liana C. Sayer, "Gender, Time and Inequality," table 3). As hours of employment are markedly higher among younger cohorts, this gap is probably greater among young women and will continue to grow.

49. The method used here is similar to that employed by others assessing married women's economic dependence on their husbands, but it is expanded in several ways. (See Annemette Sorensen and Sara McLanahan, "Married Women's Economic Dependency, 1940–1980," 659–87, for earlier insightful recognition of women's changing reliance on men's income; see also Barbara Hobson, "No Exit, No Voice," 235–50; Suzanne M. Bianchi, Lynne M. Casper, and Pia K. Peltola, "A Cross-National Look at Married Women's Earnings Dependency," 3–33.)

Here, calculations are based on unpublished 1960 and 2000 IPUMS data. Income in 1960 is reported only as income from wages, combined income from business and farms, and other income. Income in 2000 is reported in much greater detail (see figure 27 in chapter 7), but it is shown as "other personal income" here for purposes of comparison. It consists of Social Security, other retirement funds, survivor and disability payments, income from an estate or trust, dividends, interest, royalties, rents, welfare (public assistance), and Supplemental Security Income received by each woman (husband's income is a sum of all components of his income).

To illustrate, each husband's and wife's income is combined to get joint spousal income. Half of this amount is then seen as going to a wife's support (a generous assumption). The portion of a wife's support not met by her own income is then seen as the amount the husband is contributing to her support. Thus, $HS = [HI - (HI + WI)/2]/[(HI + WI)/2]$, where HS = share from husband's income, HI = husband's income, and WI = wife's income. Sorensen and McLanahan express this more simply as $DEP = HI/(HI - WI) - WI/(HI + WI)$; "Married Women's Economic Dependency," 663. The share of support coming from components of a wife's income is similarly assessed. For example, $WES = WE/[(HI + WI)/2]$, where WES = share from wife's earnings, and WE = wife's earnings.

This approach also estimates the role played by income from other family and household members, allowing an estimate of the extent to which unmarried women's support comes from men's income, and that of women overall. Here, total household income is added and the total divided similarly among all adults into shares of support. We can then see what portion of a woman's share of such support can be met by her own wages or her other income, what remains to be met by her husband's income, and then, finally, what remaining portion may be met by other men or women in the household. It can, of course, be argued that unrelated household members would not equally share income. However, these household members are also primarily family members or else cohabitating partners caring for children born out of wedlock. Also, many household expenses are collective in nature, such as utilities and rent or mortgage payments. This approach can also take into account the effect of different numbers of children, if each child under 18 is counted as half an adult, and a similar proportion of each adult's income is first seen as going to the support of children. The end result is the same as above. Although this estimate errs on the side of pooling income equally among household members, there is a long tradition of considering households in this way in anthropological and sociological studies, lending support for the use of this practice here for purposes of estimation. (However, though it was once assumed household earnings were shared equally, a closer look reveals that in general women give far more of their income to family needs, while men spend a greater amount on themselves alone. See, for example, Kathryn B. Ward and Jean Larson Pyle, "Gender, Industrialization, Corporations, and Development," 37–64, esp. 51; Susana Narotzky, "Not to Be a Burden," 70–88.)

50. In 2000, one-third of white women and two-thirds of black women between the ages of 22 and 54 were not living with husbands. Three-fourths of both white and black unmarried mothers drew mainly on their own earnings. Only a small fraction of their support came from parents, other relatives, unmarried partners, or educational assistance.

51. Also, especially among black women, both marriage and labor force participation became less closely tied to the share of support women received from men. Results from decomposition by author using unpublished 1960 and 2000 IPUMS data.

52. In 1999, the poverty level for a single individual under age 65 was $8,667, or $13,423 for an adult supporting two children ($11,483 if supporting one child; see U.S. Census Bureau, "Weighted Average Poverty Thresholds"). Approximately two-thirds of both white and black women ages 22–54 had annual earnings over $8,667, and thus their wages are here seen as able to meet their basic needs. These percentages are almost identical by race. This approach provides a slightly higher estimate of the proportion of women relying on wages than that used above to assess the share of women's support coming from their own earnings. In 1960, 28.8 percent of white women and 22.6 percent of black women could meet their own basic needs through their own wages. The capability to meet her own needs and those of one or two children gives a sense of a woman's potential to support herself and her family on her own wages.

53. Just over half of both black and white women and 43 percent of black women who were caring for children under 18 in 2000 were earning enough to meet the needs of themselves and two children.

54. Most studies focus on women's positions in the labor force in assessing inequality among women, documenting the growing gap in wages between college and high school graduates among women as well as men. Those considering the domestic realm tend to focus on one group of women, examining the problems of career women, for example, or mothers struggling to cope with the loss of government aid (see, for example, John Bound and Laura Dresser, "The Erosion of Relative Earnings"; Lisa Dodson, Don't Call Us Out of Name; Kathryn Edin and Laura Lein, Making Ends Meet; Karen Seccombe, "So You Think I Drive a Cadillac?").

55. Quoted in Carol M. Anderson, Susan Stewart, and Sona Dimidjian, Flying Solo, 218. While trends over time characterize women in terms of education completed for valid comparison over time, most women with four years of college are college graduates.

56. Quotations in, respectively, "Solving the Puzzle," 5–6; Warren, Black Women in Science, 202 (the botanist is Muriel E. Poston, born in 1950 and a recognized authority on the plants of Central and South America).

57. Even in their early 40s, more college graduates in both races are employed than are married or raising a child.

58. For white women, college graduates have shifted from being the least likely to have husbands to among the most likely, sharing this position with high school graduates; a greater share of black college graduates are married than black women with less education. The economic autonomy enjoyed by most college graduates also enables them to leave difficult relationships or have children on their own, if they wish. But only a small percentage of college graduates are in fact raising children on their own, and less than 15 percent of college graduates of either race who are single mothers are in poverty (that is, have incomes at or below 125 percent of the poverty threshold, as elsewhere in the book). For evidence that women's career success now encourages marriage among both black and white women, see Megan M. Sweeney, "Two Decades of Family Change."

59. Data on childlessness are from U.S. Bureau of the Census, "Children Ever Born per 1,000 Women." Claudia Goldin, who looked at white female college graduates between the ages of 35 and 44 in the late 1980s, has found that only 17 percent of white college graduates in the early baby boom had both moderately well-paying careers and children by their late 30s. She reports a sharp rise in the proportion never married and childless at 35–44 among those born from 1940 on ("Career and Family," 45). Elizabeth Higginbotham, interviewing black women in their late 20s who had graduated from college around 1970, found that almost all who were not married wished they were, and many also wanted children (Too Much to Ask, chap. 10).

60. June Day, "Movements," 90; Bee Lavender, "Bread and Roses," 119.

61. Herzenberg, Alic, and Wial, *New Rules for a New Economy*, xii.

62. Elga Wasserman, *The Door in the Dream*, 190. Wasserman herself earned a Ph.D. in chemistry in 1948. For increased workloads in specific professions, see Joan Norman Scott, "Watching the Changes," 29, 30 (for hours worked by women lawyers with children).

63. Dodson, *Don't Call Us Out of Name*, 39.

64. A young married woman, posting to an online discussion forum, "Motherhood, College, and Work!!!" (Working Mother Discussion website, entry posted November 1999; this website is no longer available).

65. Two-thirds of both black and white women with 12 to 15 years of education can meet their own basic needs, and more than half in each race can meet the needs of two children as well.

66. Quoted in Herzenberg, Alic, and Wial, *New Rules for a New Economy*, 54. Less than one-third of white women and one-fourth of black women who have attended but not graduated from college are in professional or managerial jobs, but most are working as teachers, as nurses, or in low-level managerial positions in fast-food outlets, motels, stores, or offices. Both black and white women with 12 to 15 years of education are most commonly employed in clerical or sales jobs or in health care.

67. White high school dropouts' climb in labor force participation was only half that of white high school graduates. Black high school dropouts were actually less likely to be employed than in 1960. Among both black and white women marriage rates dropped by about 15 points more for high school dropouts than those with four or more years of college.

68. This move was offset by a drop in employment among both black and white dropouts who were not caring for children under 18.

69. Though white dropouts still displayed a pattern of early marriage and divorce, the proportion who never married continued to increase rapidly. It also rose among African American high school dropouts, though more slowly than in the 1980s.

70. The quotation is from Jennifer Savage, "Learning to Surf," 246. For the study of disadvantaged high school girls, see Dodson, *Don't Call Us Out of Name*, 84. For the persisting importance of motherhood among poor women with low levels of education, see Kathryn Edin and Maria Kefalas, *Promises I Can Keep*.

71. Though about half of white and black women who have not finished high school are employed, little over one-third of either race can meet their own basic needs with their wages; a scant one-fourth can meet those of two children as well. For the conflict between home and work among poor single mothers and the ways in which the maternal role takes priority, see, for example, Ellen K. Scott, Kathryn Edin, Andrew S. London, and Joan Maya Mazelis, "My Children Come First."

72. While the young girl in Tracy Chapman's "Fast Car" (1988) hoped to es-

cape her poor background, she states ruefully at the song's end, "I work in a market as a checkout girl."

73. Quoted in Glasser and Brecher, "We Are the Roots," 33; see also White and Geddes, "Economic Lessons for Welfare Mothers," 9. Almost one-fifth of such workers are in poverty (Scanlon, "Nursing Workforce," 12; see also "Cheating Dignity").

74. For discussion of welfare's subsidy of low-wage businesses, see Dawson and Surpin, "Direct-Care Healthcare Workers," especially 25. A multitude of studies have shown that low-paid jobs provide little more income than welfare while forcing unmarried mothers into difficult schedules and separations from their children (Dodson, *Don't Call Us Out of Name*; Edin and Lein, *Making Ends Meet*; Sharon Hays, *Flat Broke with Children*; Seccombe, *"So You Think I Drive a Cadillac?"*).

75. Dodson, *Don't Call Us Out of Name*, 153.

76. See also, for example, Bound and Dresser, "Losing Ground."

77. Among those with four years of high school, for example, more than one-third of black women work in poorly paying service jobs, compared to little over one-fifth of white women. Black women, despite having made great gains in education, still have less education than white women: they are almost half as likely to have graduated from college and twice as likely to be high school dropouts, though few women in either race now fail to complete high school. However, the disparity in education explains little of the difference in occupations, which exist within each educational group.

78. Black single mothers are one and a half times as likely to be poor than white single mothers.

7. How and Why Mothers Have Been Shortchanged

1. Statement titled "Does anyone else feel overwhelmed?" (Working Mother Discussion website, n.d., accessed January 18, 2002; this website is no longer available).

2. These data are for mothers between the ages of 22 and 54, the group focused on throughout this study, from the author's calculations based on unpublished 1970 and 2000 Integrated Public Use Microdata Series (IPUMS) data. Unless otherwise specified, all statistical information is drawn from the author's calculations based on unpublished IPUMS data and, occasionally, unpublished Current Population Survey (CPS) data. Also, in this chapter the term *mothers* refers to those with children under 18 in the household unless otherwise stated.

3. For problems of recent Stanford graduates, and graduates from an elite Japanese university as well, see Myra H. Strober and Agnes Miling Kaneko Chan, *The Road Winds Uphill All the Way*. For lawyers' difficulties in handling home and work, see Catalyst, "Women in Law: Making the Case." See also the Sociologists for Women in Society website.

4. Statements titled "Feeling Overwhelmed," n.d., and "Working Full-time

Dilema [*sic*]", entry posted November 9, 1999, 3:01:36 A.M. (Working Mother Discussion website).

5. See, for example, essays by women who became mothers in the mid- to late 1990s, collected in Ariel Gore and Bee Lavender, eds., *Breeder*.

6. Only a small percentage of black mothers were single parents, and most lived in their fathers' homes.

7. More precisely, the share of support coming from men fell 39 percentage points for black mothers and 37 percentage points for white mothers between 1960 and 2000. The share of support from alimony and child support is based on March 2000 CPS data as such income is not separately reported in IPUMS data; the role played by other sources of support was very similar.

8. These results are based on the author's decomposition of the drop in share of support coming from income of male household members, using unpublished 1960 and 2000 IPUMS data.

9. Well-known accounts of overwork are Judith Schor, *The Overworked American*; Schor, *The Overspent American*; Arlene R. Hochschild, *The Time Bind*. For a useful summary of this literature and careful analysis of variations in overwork, stressing wives' increased employment and families' struggles to find time for the home in the face of increased demands from work, see Jerry A. Jacobs and Kathleen Gerson, "Overworked Individuals or Overworked Families?"

10. In 2000, more than two-fifths of white wives and two-thirds of black wives caring for small children were full-time workers (35 or more hours per week, full- or part-year). Each successive cohort of mothers spends longer hours in paid work as they start their families. Over half of white wives and nearly three-fourths of black wives with school-age children are employed full-time. The figures for overall workloads are based on close questioning of parents about time spent with children (Liana C. Sayer, Paula England, Michael Bitmann, and Suzanne M. Bianchi, "How Long Is the Second [Plus First] Shift?" table 6).

11. Statement titled "Not Being So Frustrated" (Working Mothers Discussion website, entry posted November 7, 1999, 2:01:20 A.M.). More than half of black mothers and about one-fifth of white mothers with children under 18 are single. In recent decades this group has grown more rapidly among white women than black women. (For hours of work in two-parent families, see Sayer, England, Bitmann, and Bianchi, "How Long Is the Second Shift?" table 6.) Recent time use studies report that single mothers spend on average much less time on housework than married mothers; the difference is mainly in time devoted to cleaning and making meals (Sayer, "Gender, Time and Inequality"). Fewer children and the absence of a husband reduce household tasks, which are likely also sharply compressed because many single mothers are working full-time (full-time workers commonly spend much less time on household chores). However, the small number of single mothers included in time use studies, together with the averaging of the experiences of nonemployed and full-time workers, makes it difficult to tell what is really happening in these homes. For

evidence that marriage increases housework, see Suzanne M. Bianchi, Melissa A. Milkie, Liana C. Sayer, and John P. Robinson, "Is Anyone Doing the House-work?"

12. Married mothers employed full-time put in 10.4 hours per day in paid and unpaid work in 1998, or 72.8 hours per week; their overall workload is very similar to that of married women employed full-time, as most of these women are mothers. Nonemployed mothers in 1965 put in 55.3 hours overall per week (Liana Sayer, "Time Use by Employment," unpublished data given to author, October 15, 2002, tables 1, 3, and personal communication, September 29, 2005). Husbands have increased their help with housework substantially over the past three decades, though their wives—even those who are working full-time—still put in many more hours at home (Sayer, "Gender, Time and Inequality," table 4).

13. This figure compares hours spent on housework by the typical (modal or most common) mother in 2000, employed full-time, with those of the typical (modal) mother in 1965, who was a full-time housewife. When all mothers are considered, on average there has been a drop of more than thirteen hours per week in household chores over those thirty-five years (Bianchi et al., "Is Anyone Doing the Housework?"). These findings contrast sharply with earlier claims that industrialization had little impact on women's household work (see, for example, Ruth Schwartz Cowan, *More Work for Mother*).

14. Over half of white mothers and more than two-thirds of black mothers were full-time workers in 2000, in sharp contrast to thirty years previously. The share of mothers employed full time was 1.9 that of 1970 for black mothers and 2.3 that of 1970 for white mothers.

15. Productivity in the wage economy has also grown, by more than half since the 1960s (Lawrence Mishel, Jared Bernstein, and Heather Boushey, *The State of Working America* 2002–03, 6). However, this gain has similarly failed to translate into more time for the home.

16. For the underlying role played by the dynamics of industrialization in welfare state formation and an excellent review of theories explaining such formation, see George Steinmetz, "The Local Welfare State." For a range of theoretical approaches establishing the parameters of the post–World War II debate, see Gosta Esping-Anderson, *The Three Worlds of Welfare Capitalism*; T. H. Marshall, *Class, Citizenship and Social Development*; Michael Shalev, "The Social Democratic Model and Beyond"; Margaret Weir, Ann Orloff, and Theda Skocpol, eds., *The Politics of Social Policy Formation*; Harold Wilensky, *The Welfare State and Equality*.

17. Wilensky, *Welfare State and Equality*, 68. The simplest form of this approach, which came to be termed the *logic of industrialism*, assumed that new programs would inevitably arise to address needs opened by industrialization. For discussion of the provision of care as a basic element of welfare state formation, see Jane Jenson, "Who Cares? Gender and Welfare Regimes." However, while Jenson sees a focus on workers and their mobilization as displacing care from the center of welfare state analysis, I am arguing that we have lost sight of a key part

of what these male workers were struggling for (see also Susan Thistle, "Gender, Class, and Welfare State Formation in the 21st Century").

18. For analysis of the New Deal, see Jill Quadagno, "Welfare Capitalism and the Social Security Act of 1935"; Weir, Orloff, and Skocpol, *Politics of Social Policy Formation*. Nancy Folbre (*Who Pays for the Kids?*) describes how the increased costs of dependent care underlay early struggles over policy (174–95).

19. Those attempting to devise policy for pregnant working mothers, for example, have grappled with the issue of equal versus special treatment (see Susan Gluck Mezey, *In Pursuit of Equality*, 132). For a range of analyses of gender and social policy stretching over several decades, see Mimi Abramovitz, *Regulating the Lives of Women*; Linda Gordon, ed., *Women, the State, and Welfare*; Gordon, *Pitied But Not Entitled*; Ladd-Taylor, *Mother-Work*; Seth Koven and Sonya Michel, eds., *Mothers of a New World*; Jane Lewis, "Gender and Welfare Regimes"; Susan Pederson, *Family, Dependence, and the Origins of the Welfare State*; Diane Sainsbury, *Gender, Equality and Welfare States*; Theda Skocpol, *Protecting Soldiers and Mothers*. For more recent analyses, see Mary Daly and Katherine Rake, *Gender and the Welfare State*; Janet C. Gornick and Marcia K. Meyer, *Families That Work*; Rianne Mahon and Sonya Michel, eds., *Child Care at the Crossroads*, especially Denise Urias Levy and Michel, "More Can Be Less"; Michel, *Children's Interests/Mothers' Rights*; Gwendolyn Mink, *Welfare's End*; Julia S. O'Connor, Ann Shola Orloff, and Sheila Shaver, *States, Markets, Families*.

20. As Dorothy D. Roberts suggests, we should "see the mothers whom the dominant society calls pathological as a source of positive insights for understanding mothers' work and for transforming social policy" ("Race, Gender, and the Value of Mothers' Work," 196). Maxine Baca Zinn and Bonnie Thornton Dill note similarly that women in "marginalized locations are well-suited for grasping social relations that remain obscure from more privileged vantage points" ("Theorizing Difference from Multiracial Feminism," 328). For concerns about poor single mothers and the importance of their having time for caregiving, see also Eva Feder Kittay, *Love's Labor*; Roberts, *Killing the Black Body*; Gwendolyn Mink, *The Wages of Motherhood*; Mink, "Wage Work, Family Work, and Welfare Politics"; Mink, *Welfare's End*. There are good reasons to worry that their needs will be ignored as in the past women of color were viewed simply as a source of labor and no attention was paid to how their own homemaking tasks would be accomplished (see Glenn, "Racial Ethnic Women's Labor"). Similarly, today businesses in the bottom tier of the service sector draw heavily on the labor of women of color while paying very low wages and providing no support for their work at home.

21. Conversely, government aid alone does not protect women from poverty. Many mothers receiving public assistance in the United States in the late 1980s and early 1990s survived by also earning income much of the year, thereby refuting images of passive welfare dependency (Kathryn Edin and Laura Lein, *Making Ends Meet*; see also Barbara Hobson, "Solo Mothers, Policy Regimes, and the Logics of Gender"; Roberta M. Spalter-Roth and Heidi I. Hartmann, "AFDC Recipients as Care-givers and Workers"; Sharon Hays, *Flat Broke with Children*).

22. Irving Garfinkle, Sara S. McLanahan, Daniel R. Meyer, and Judith A. Seltzer, introduction to *Fathers under Fire*, 2. Some time use studies show that while women still put more time into household tasks and men more hours into paid work, their overall workload, while preserving inequities in income and power, is similar (Bianchi et al., "Is Anyone Doing the Housework?"). But close scrutiny of child care tasks suggests that employed mothers, even those with full-time jobs, work on average six hours more per week than their spouses (author's calculation based on Sayer, England, Bitmann, and Bianchi, "How Long Is the Second Shift?" table 6; see also Sayer, "Time Use by Employment," table 3).

23. See Hays, *Flat Broke with Children*, for one discussion of this strategy on the part of the state. The Personal Responsibility and Work Opportunity and Reconciliation Act of 1996 gives states some funds for short-term cash relief to poor, primarily single, parents in the form of Temporary Aid to Needy Families, and for limited provision of child care services to such parents. For its inadequacies, see Levy and Michel, "More Can Be Less"; Michel, *Children's Interests/Mothers' Rights*. On the Earned Income Tax Credit and tax relief to those with dependent children, as well as useful recommendations for more effective provision of such aid, see Isabelle V. Sawhill, ed., *One Percent for the Kids*.

24. Ellwood's calculation is inclusive, representing profits *and* interest. He points out: "Since owners of capital can hold their money either in stock . . . or in bonds (and earn interest), it is best to think about capital's share as a combination of stocks and bonds" (David T. Ellwood, "Winners and Losers in America," 22). In examining who has benefited at others' expense from the growth in national income, Ellwood himself stresses not corporate profits but particular workers, namely, women and the upper third of male earners.

25. These economists state further: "The median male wage in 2000 was still below its 1979 level, even though productivity was 44.5% higher than in 1979. One reason for this divergence is increased corporate profitability, which drove a wedge between productivity and compensation growth" (Lawrence Mishel, Jared Bernstein, and Heather Boushey, *The State of Working America* 2002–03, 4–5, 6). These profits also stem from lower taxes on corporate gains (see Mishel, Bernstein, and John Schmitt, *The State of Working America* 2000/2001, 91).

26. In 1998, the lowest two-fifths of families received 14.1 percent of aggregate family income, or almost one-third less than the richest 5 percent of families, who received 20.7 percent of such income (U.S. Census Bureau, "Income, Expenditures and Wealth," in *Statistical Abstract of the United States*, 2000, table 745).

27. Quoted in Lisa Dodson, *Don't Call Us Out of Name*, 169.

28. Of the large gap that remains after controlling differences in education, work experience, and other issues, one professor states flatly, "It cannot be explained in any way except that people think that what men do is more important and more valuable than what women do." Hilary Lips, quoted in the *Chicago Tribune*, February 2, 2005. In 1999, the median hourly wage of female

workers was 76.9 percent that of male workers (Mishel, Bernstein and Schmitt, *State of Working America* 2000/2001, 127).

29. Kimberly Bayard, Judith Hellerstein, David Neumark, and Kenneth Troske, "New Evidence on Sex Segregation and Sex Differences in Wages." Until recently, most researchers have seen the gender gap in wages as stemming primarily from women's location in lower-paying occupations than men, and some still find this the more convincing explanation (see, for example, Trond Petersen and Laurie Morgan, "Separate and Unequal"; Petersen and Morgan, "The Within-Job Gender Wage Gap"). But Leslie McCall finds striking variations in the relationship between the gender wage gap and occupational segregation by sex in different labor markets in the U.S. (Leslie McCall, *Complex Inequality*).

30. Bayard et al., "New Evidence on Sex Segregation."

31. Most women, including mothers, now work full-time (35+ hours per week). The gain in wages results from raising such a woman's wages by 50 percent of the gap between her median hourly wage and that of all male workers ages 22 to 54. Here, the median wage of *all* women workers, not just white and black women workers employed 35 to 60 hours per week, with hourly wages from $2.50 to $500, in all occupations except farming, forestry, and fisheries, is used, as this is the group analyzed by Bayard et al. ("New Evidence on Sex Segregation"). Some argue that differences of education and occupation are also due to discrimination. While moving women into men's jobs would mean a loss of income for men and thus no overall gain for many families, women would clearly gain if they switched places with men. Giving women the same median hourly wage as men would result in an additional $6,500 per year in earnings or would allow a woman to work two and one-half fewer months per year while bringing home the same amount of money.

32. See Paula England, *Comparable Worth*; Peterson and Morgan, "Separate and Unequal"; Peterson and Morgan, "The Within-Job Gender Wage Gap." Forcing employers to pay higher wages in female-dominated occupations would bring gains similar to those created by the ending of within-job discrimination, though obviously not all women's wages would rise. Some economists argue that men's wages are not market based and thus that employers would pay men less if they paid women more (Emily Hoffnar and Michael Greene, "Gender Earnings Inequality in the Service and Manufacturing Industries in the U.S."). This would clearly lessen gains to families, but wages have long been set by social struggles and policies as well as "market" forces.

33. It is clear that mothers themselves pay a price for the effort they put into child rearing. For the cost to mothers in lost wages, see Jane Waldfogel, "The Effect of Children on Women's Wages"; Waldfogel, "Understanding the 'Family Gap' in Pay for Women with Children"; Michelle Budig and Paula England, "The Wage Penalty for Mothers." For the absence of much gain in family income, see Ellwood, "Winners and Losers in America." My tables are modeled on his, though I use standard educational categories, in an approach similar to

that of Barry Bluestone and Steven Rose in "Overworked and Underemployed." Those with no income or hours of paid work are included in these figures, as focus is on gains among all mothers. (Gains in income among only mothers with some earnings were markedly less.) In 1970 only interval data for hours worked in the previous week are available. Mean usual hours worked were estimated based on comparison of such interval-level data and usual hours worked for each educational and marital group.

34. Women's increased earnings kept the economy afloat as well. See, for example, Frank Levy, *The New Dollars and Dreams*, 45.

35. Women who work outside the home compress the time they spend on housework by taking advantage of new technology and by simplifying their chores. A mother working 40 hours a week for pay spends almost 20 hours less in housework than a mother who stays at home. She has thus increased her total hours of paid and unpaid work by approximately 20 hours, not 40 hours. More precisely, the overall workload of employed mothers has grown by 46 percent of the rise in their annual hours of paid work (author's calculations based on Sayer, "Trends in Parents' Paid Work," unpublished data given to author October 12, 2002). If we correct for such overwork, mothers' earnings drop to about 55 percent of their reported income. They would then be working the same number of hours as full-time housewives in the 1960s, yet now receiving wages for some of their labor. These earnings provide some sense of the increase in productivity realized by women's turn from household to paid work.

36. The loss of income from public assistance was offset somewhat by a rise in child support and retirement income. Gains in per capita income were about 6–10 percentage points more than for family income, though black single mothers and black wives with less than four years of high school saw larger gains because they experienced a greater drop in their number of children.

37. Their earnings shrink even further when the costs of going to work, estimated at $8,023 (in 2000 dollars) for families paying for child care, are counted (Timothy M. Smeeding and Joseph T. Marchand, "Family Time and Public Policy in the United States," 39n5).

38. A survey by the Women's Bureau found that by the close of the twentieth century, women's central concerns were to improve their position in the labor force through higher pay, greater respect in their jobs, and policies that would help them better balance their domestic tasks and their employment (U.S. Department of Labor, Women's Bureau, *Equal Pay*). Though women's gains have been limited, their increased training and hours of employment have brought growth in personal earnings. Each recent cohort of women has made more money than its predecessor (Daphne Spain and Suzanne M. Bianchi, *Balancing Act*, 113). For the potential utility of unions for women workers, see, for example, Dorothy Sue Cobble, ed., *Women and Unions*; Cobble, *The Other Feminists*, especially 121–44.

39. This gap was tied initially to women's rising labor force participation and more recently to their growing interest in better family policies and persisted

in the 2004 presidential election. See, for example, Jeff Manza and Clem Brooks, *Social Cleavages and Political Change*; Center for American Women and Politics, "Facts and Findings."

40. Child care is often costly and unreliable. Over half of parents needing child care found it very hard to find care they could afford; over two-fifths had great difficulty finding "high-quality" child care, and over half said lack of simply "acceptable" child care had a negative impact on their own and their partner's work (Humphrey Taylor, "Harris Poll on Child Care").

41. This married mother of three, who has worked full-time while raising her children, continues: "lets face it, we are not all lawyers that can afford nannies!" (Working Mother Discussion website, entry posted November 7, 1999, 3:20:33 A.M., signed "The REAL World").

42. Another approximately 15 percent of white mothers and 22 percent of black mothers work full-time for part of the year (some are leaving or reentering the workforce); 30 percent of white mothers and 20 percent of black mothers caring for infants and toddlers do not work outside the home at all.

43. This solution to the problem of providing adequate care for children exacts a high price from women and their families. Part-time work explains part of the lower hourly wages earned by mothers compared to other women (Waldfogel, "Effect of Children on Women's Wages"; see also Budig and England, "Wage Penalty for Mothers"). The typical (median) woman working part-time in 2000 earned only 36 percent as much per week as the typical full-time woman worker (U.S. Department of Labor, Bureau of Labor Statistics, *Highlights of Women's Earnings in 2000*, 2). In addition, both black and white women working part-time fail to realize gains in earnings over time (U.S. Department of Labor, Bureau of Labor Statistics, *Highlights of Women's Earnings in 1999*, 2; see also Marianne Ferber and Jane Waldfogel, "The Effects of Part-Time and Self-Employment on Wages and Benefits").

44. Even among high school dropouts, two-fifths of black mothers with children under 6 work full-time, compared to less than one-third of white mothers of young children. As the decrease in full-time employment among less-educated women illustrates, difficulties in finding good jobs, the burdens of single motherhood, and identification with the domestic role also shape the allocation of time between home and paid work.

45. Government aid and child support also offer a meager and unreliable amount of support to a small number of mothers. For discussion of some women's ability to stay home due to husbands' income, while the termination of AFDC has withdrawn this right from others, see, for example, Mink, *Welfare's End*, 103–31.

46. Mothers with less income also receive less support from employers. Little over one-fifth of poor mothers have the option of taking a month off with pay compared to three-fifths of middle-class mothers. For details, see Gornick and Meyers, *Families That Work*, 118.

47. Dorothy Roberts, *Shattered Bonds*, vi.

48. Louise Story, "Many Women at Elite Colleges Set Career Path to Mother-hood."

49. The data for single mothers here are for women ages 22–44, as this range best captures mothers with children under 18. Some signs, such as the faster rate of growth of single motherhood among white women, indicate that such differences may lessen in coming years. Recently, births to unmarried black women have fallen steeply while climbing among white unmarried women (Stephanie J. Ventura and Christine A. Bachrach, "Nonmarital Childbearing"). In 1960, 3 percent of white women and 9 percent of black women between the ages of 22 and 44 were raising children without help from a spouse; by 2000, 9 percent of white women and 25 percent of black women were doing so. Though the rate of growth has been slightly faster among white women, the gap between the two races has widened and inequality in this area remains great.

50. For discussion of backward- and forward-looking responses to the changes wrought by an emerging industrial economy in England, see Raymond Williams, *Culture and Society*.

51. See, for example, Jane Waldfogel, "The Family Gap for Young Women in the United States and Britain"; Folbre, *Invisible Heart*; Nancy Fraser, "After the Family Wage"; Sonya Michel and Rianne Mahon, eds., *Child Care Policy at the Crossroads*.

52. Roberts, *Shattered Bonds*, 269. The Earned Income Tax Credit (EITC) was expanded greatly in the 1990s, and again in the first years of the twenty-first century, along with the tax credit for dependent children. However, these measures are complicated, directed only at the working poor, and lack the status and level of benefits that would come with the recognition of a clear right to such support. Further, in the United States, tax exemptions for dependents have declined substantially in value since 1948 (Sheila B. Kamerman and Alfred J. Kahn, "Family Change and Family Policies," 361) and remain much lower despite the recent tax breaks. The Family and Medical Leave Act, signed into law by President Bill Clinton in 1993, mandates that businesses above a certain size allow employees twelve weeks of unpaid leave to care for a new baby or ailing family member. Clinton had originally proposed using unemployment benefits to fund paid leave for parents of newborns, a strategy that has succeeded in California, where in 2002 workers won the right to receive 55 percent of their salary for six weeks of leave to care for a new child or ailing family member. While a step forward, this approach does not clearly legitimate funding for tasks of family care. For discussion of the "care gap" between the funds and other resources that could be and actually are used for caregiving, see Francesca M. Cancian, Demie Kurz, Andrew London, Rebecca Reviere, and Mary Tuominen, eds., *Child Care and Inequality*.

53. See, for example, Ellwood, "Winners and Losers in America"; Mishel, Bernstein, and Schmitt, *State of Working America 2000/2001*; Mishel, Bernstein, and Boushey, *State of Working America 2002–03*. Isabelle V. Sawhill points out that the policies best addressing the needs of children in the United States would cost less annually than the tax cut given in 2001 to the richest 5 percent of families

(introduction to *One Percent for the Kids*, 3). Kamerman and Kahn note that the tax burden is higher for individuals, but the overall tax burden lower, in the United States than EU and OECD averages, as are government expenditures ("Family Change and Family Policies," 361).

54. Such payments include "programs targeted on families (family allowances for children, family support benefits, and one-parent cash benefits) as well as paid family leave and refundable tax credits for families" (Gornick and Meyers, *Families That Work*, 41; they note the bulk of such payments in the United States are made in the form of the EITC).

55. In the United States, Social Security is almost exclusively a financial allotment in old age to wage workers and their long-term spouses (Kamerman and Kahn, *Family Change and Family Policies*; it also offers disability benefits and support for surviving minor children). A number of scholars see social insurance as providing a feasible model for structuring new supports for women (see Folbre, *Who Pays for the Kids?*; Folbre, "Barbara, the Market, and the State"; Linda Gordon, "Thoughts on the Help for Working Parents Plan"; Heidi Hartmann and Roberta Spalter-Roth, "A Feminist Approach to Public Policy Making for Women and Families").

56. For one discussion of policies that would lessen inequality between women, see Paula England, Karen Christopher, and Lori L. Reid, "Gender, Race, Ethnicity, and Wages." For the value of affirmative action, see Barbara Reskin, *The Realities of Affirmative Action in Employment*.

57. For the role played by the minimum wage in inequality in women's earnings, see Mishel, Bernstein, and Schmitt, *State of Working America 2000/2001*, 186–92. For examples of how unions can improve the situation of service workers, see Mary C. Tuominen, "Where Teachers Can Make a Livable Wage"; Dorothy Sue Cobble, "The Prospects of Unionism in a Service Society"; Cobble, *The Other Feminists*.

58. See, for example, Fraser, "After the Family Wage"; Greg J. Duncan and Katherine Magnuson, "Promoting the Healthy Development of Young Children"; Paula England and Nancy Folbre, "Reforming the Social Contract." For discussion of the importance of considering time at home when constructing social policy, see Smeeding and Marchand, "Family Time and Public Policy."

59. Legislation like that granting up to six weeks of paid family leave for workers in California is being sought in at least twenty-seven other states. Grounding such funding in unemployment compensation, however, runs the dangers encountered in efforts to handle pregnancy within the framework of medical disability (see Jane Waldfogel, "Working Mothers Then and Now"). Duncan and Magnuson argue for a monthly allowance to parents with children under the age of 5 joined with the use of welfare as a form of full or partial family leave for poor single mothers with children under 1, through reduced work requirements ("Promoting the Healthy Development of Young Children").

60. After-school programs for teens provide one interesting way of prevent-

ing early pregnancies while at the same time providing further education, useful experience, and contact with adult mentors (see Andrea Kane and Isabel V. Sawhill, "Preventing Early Childbearing"). For the importance of adults who can broaden young adults' knowledge and access to job paths, see Carla O'Connor, "Dreamkeeping in the Inner City."

61. Some policy makers recommend that men cut their time at work almost in half during the first two years of their children's lives, as many mothers do (Gornick and Meyer, *Families That Work*, 95–97).

62. Another 20 to 25 percent of mothers would prefer to take on more hours of paid work but cannot because they must care for their children (U.S. Department of Labor, *Futurework*, chap. 3). Child care costs consume a much greater portion of a poor family's income (Levy and Michel, "More Can Be Less"). Sonya Michel notes that publicly funded child care gains support when joined with proposals for early childhood education ("Dilemmas of Child Care"). Thus, offering high-quality preschool education could aid child care while improving the life chances of young girls, especially those from disadvantaged backgrounds (see Barbara Wolfe and Scott Scrivner, "Providing Universal Preschool for Four-Year-Olds").

63. These policies could be carried further to compensate for the difficulties faced by single mothers. For example, Mink, recognizing that most mothers still rely on partial support from men during their years of child rearing, argues that all caregivers should be guaranteed a minimum level of support (*Welfare's End*, 103–31).

64. See, for example, Roberts, *Killing the Black Body*, especially 294–312; Roberts, *Shattered Bonds*, 223–76.

65. Critics point to the dismantling of AFDC and retrenchment of the welfare state in the United States and Europe. Sainsbury, for example, sees 1980 as the peak of the mature welfare state; for this point and discussion of the retrenchment of the U.S. welfare state in particular, see *Gender, Equality and Welfare States*, 198–205.

8. New Possibilities and Old Inequalities

1. Jane Lewis, "Gender and the Development of Welfare Regimes," 168–69; see also Lewis, "Gender and Welfare Regimes: Further Thoughts," and chapter 7 for further discussion.

2. For discussion of private versus state-led development in the first waves of industrialization, see Alexander Gerschenkron, *Economic Backwardness in Historical Perspective*.

3. The share of private household cleaners and servants who were Hispanic grew from 8.5 percent in 1983 to 29.3 percent in 1999; almost all these workers are female (U.S. Census Bureau, "Labor Force, Employment, and Earnings," in *Statistical Abstract of the United States*, 2000, table 669).

4. Author's calculations based on unpublished March 2001 Current Population Survey data.

5. Lourdes Beneria, while acknowledging the importance of the postmodern turn that predominated among theorists of gender in the 1990s, notes that this approach "has tended to neglect areas of social concern having to do with the material and, more concretely, the economic" (*Gender, Development, and Globalization*, 25). Perhaps because of the far greater quantity of women's domestic tasks in developing countries, women's household work there and its interactions with a changing global economy receive more recognition. "By moving reproduction to the center of analysis," observes Luz del Alba Acevedo, "we can see production and reproduction as a dialectical unit: each has relative autonomy from the other, but at the same time, their intersection shapes the whole" ("Feminist Inroads in the Study of Women's Work and Development," 84).

6. See Jane Collins, *Threads*; Ching Kwan Lee, *Gender and the South China Miracle*.

7. See Phyllis Andors, *The Unfinished Liberation of Chinese Women*, 1949–1980.

8. Shen Rong, "A New Woman Writer," 64. Her story is "At Middle Age." "At work they shoulder a heavy load, at home they have all the housework," Shen Rong observed of women like the doctor in her story ("A New Woman Writer," 68). Even before the Communists came to power, this burden was anticipated by the writer Ding Ling in her insightful essay "Thoughts on March 8 (Women's Day)."

9. Li Xiaojiang, "Economic Reform and the Awakening of Chinese Women's Collective Consciousness," 374.

10. "No question about it, a successful woman must be a good deal stronger than a man since she must always contend with two worlds at once," Zhang Jie writes ("The Ark," 188).

11. "Single Chinese Mothers Beset with Troubles," *China Daily* (Xinhua), December 12, 2004.

12. Li, "Resisting While Holding the Tradition," 114.

13. Lee, *Gender and the South China Miracle*, 1–5, 67–106.

14. See, for example, Nicole Constable, *Maid to Order in Hong Kong*; Pei-chia Lan, "Global Divisions, Local Identities"; Rhacel Salazar Parreñas, *Servants of Globalization*, especially 61–115.

15. For reliance on an extended network of kin, or even other paid domestic workers, and the loss of a chance to have a family, see Lan, "Global Divisions, Local Identities"; Parreñas, *Servants of Globalization*. On women who spend part of the year working abroad and the other part working at home, see Deborah Barndt, *Tangled Routes*.

16. For better regulation of the working conditions of private domestic workers as crucial to improving their situation, see Pierrette Hondagneu-Sotelo, *Doméstica*, 210–43.

17. The survey information, from the Families and Work Institute, is presented in Janet C. Gornick and Marcia K. Meyer, *Families That Work*, 79, joined with comparison of family policy in the U.S. with that of other countries.

18. For a cross-national assessment of variations of economic and political gender equality, see Erik O. Wright, *Class Counts*.

19. Gornick and Meyer, *Families That Work*, 19.

20. Barbara L. Marshall sees the "marginalization of gender" as "due in no small part, to the lingering hold of the public/private dualism as grounding the analysis of gender" (*Configuring Gender*, esp. 189, 29).

21. Suzanne Bianchi and Daphne Spain stress a "profound movement towards gender equality" among younger women in the last decades of the twentieth century—seen, for example, in a substantial narrowing of the wage gap in the 1980s and the "remarkable change" in the index of occupational dissimilarity compared to the period before 1970 (*Women, Work, and Family in America*, 24, 22; see also Claudia Goldin, "The Rising [and then Declining] Significance of Gender"). For an introductory overview of the ways in which gender inequality is being sustained among men and women in the labor force, see Barbara F. Reskin and Irene Padavic, *Women and Men at Work*. For detailed examination of ways such inequality has been sustained, see Robert L. Nelson and William P. Bridges, *Legalizing Gender Inequality*; Jennifer L. Pierce, *Gender Trials*.

22. For discussion of the concealed, yet crucial, importance of care work in the functioning of our society, see Nancy Folbre, *The Invisible Heart*; for the importance of translating needs into rights, see Nancy Fraser, "Struggle over Needs."

23. Nancy Fraser, "Social Justice in the Age of Identity Politics: Redistribution, Recognition, and Participation," 9.

24. For the progressive gains in rights of citizenship, see T. H. Marshall, *Class, Citizenship and Social Development*.

BIBLIOGRAPHY

Abel, Emily K. "American Women Tending Sick and Disabled Children." In *Child Care and Inequality: Rethinking Carework for Children and Youth*, edited by Francesca M. Cancian, Demie Kurz, Andrew London, Rebecca Reviere, and Mary Tuominen, 11–22. New York: Routledge, 2002.

Abramovitz, Mimi. *Regulating the Lives of Women: Social Welfare Policy from Colonial Times to the Present*. Rev. ed. Boston: South End Press, 1996.

Acevedo, Luz del Alba. "Feminist Inroads in the Study of Women's Work and Development." In *Women in the Latin American Development Process*, edited by Christine E. Bose and Edna Acosta-Belen, 65–98. Philadelphia: Temple University Press, 1995.

Adams, Charlotte. *Housekeeping after Office Hours: A Home-Making Guide for the Working Woman*. New York: Harper, [1953].

Adams, Julia, Elisabeth S. Clemens, and Ann Shola Orloff, eds. *The Making and Unmaking of Modernity: Politics and Processes in Historical Sociology*. Durham, NC: Duke University Press, 2005.

Addams, Jane. *Twenty Years at Hull House*. New York: Macmillan, 1910.

Akerlof, George A., Janet L. Yellen, and Michael L. Katz. "An Analysis of Out-of-Wedlock Childbearing in the United States." *Quarterly Journal of Economics* 111 (May 1996): 277–317.

Alan Guttmacher Institute. *11 Million Teenagers: What Can Be Done about the Epidemic of Adolescent Pregnancies in the United States*. New York: Alan Guttmacher Institute, 1976.

Albert, Octavia V. Rogers. *The House of Bondage*. New York: Hunt and Eaton, 1890. Electronic edition, http://docsouth.unc.edu/neh/albert/albert.html#albert1 (accessed November 10, 2002). This work is the property of the University of North Carolina at Chapel Hill. It may be used freely by individuals for research, teaching, and personal use as long as this statement of availability is included in the text.

Amott, Teresa L., and Julie A. Matthaei. *Race, Gender and Work: A Multicultural History of Women in the United States*. Boston: South End Press, 1991.

Anderson, Carol M., Susan Stewart, and Sona Dimidjian. *Flying Solo: Single Women in Midlife*. New York: Norton, 1994.

Anderson, Elijah. *A Place on the Corner*. Chicago: University of Chicago Press, 1978.

Andors, Phyllis. *The Unfinished Liberation of Chinese Women, 1949–1980*. Bloomington: Indiana University Press; Brighton, Sussex: Wheatsheaf Books, 1983.

Appelbaum, Eileen. *Back to Work: Determinants of Women's Successful Re-entry*. Boston: Auburn House, 1981.

Arendell, Terry. *Mothers and Divorce: Legal, Economic, and Social Dilemmas*. Berkeley: University of California Press, 1986.

Arrington, Theodore S., and Patricia A. Kyle. "Equal Rights Amendment Activists in North Carolina." *Signs: Journal of Women and Culture* 3 (Spring 1978): 666–80.

Bachu, Amara. "Trends in Premarital Childbearing: 1930 to 1994." *Current Population Reports* P23–197. Washington, DC: U.S. Census Bureau, 1999. http://www.census.gov/prod/99pubs/p23-197.pdf (accessed November 9, 2003).

Bailey, Martha J. *American Women in Science, 1950 to the Present: A Biographical Dictionary*. Santa Barbara, CA: ABC-CLIO, 1998.

Bancroft, Gertrude. *The American Labor Force: Its Growth and Changing Composition*. New York: Wiley, 1958.

Bane, Mary Jo. "Household Composition and Poverty." In *Fighting Poverty: What Works and What Doesn't*, edited by Sheldon H. Danziger and Daniel H. Weinberg, 206–31. Cambridge, MA: Harvard University Press, 1986.

Bane, Mary Jo, and David Ellwood. "One Fifth of the Nation's Children: Why Are They Poor?" *Science* 245 (September 1989): 1047–53.

Barndt, Deborah. *Tangled Routes: Women, Work, and Globalization on the Tomato Trail*. Lanham, MD: Rowman and Littlefield, 2002.

Baumol, William. "Productivity Policy and the Service Sector." Fishman-Davidson Center for the Study of the Service Sector, discussion paper no. 1. April 1987.

Bayard, Kimberly, Judith Hellerstein, David Neumark, and Kenneth Troske. "New Evidence on Sex Segregation and Sex Differences in Wages from

Matched Employee-Employer Data." *Journal of Labor Economics* 21 (October 2003): 887–923.

Beauvoir, Simone de. *The Second Sex.* Translated and edited by H. M. Parshley. New York: Knopf, 1952.

Becker, Gary. *A Treatise on the Family.* Cambridge, MA: Harvard University Press, 1991.

Beecher, Catherine E. *A Treatise on Domestic Economy.* 1841. Reprint, New York: Source Book Press, 1970.

Bell, Winifred. *Aid to Dependent Children.* New York: Columbia University Press, 1965.

Bellah, Robert, Richard Madsen, William M. Sullivan, Ann Swidler, and Steve M. Tipton. *Habits of the Heart: Individualism and Commitment in American Life.* Berkeley: University of California Press, 1985.

Beneria, Lourdes. *Gender, Development, and Globalization: Economics As If All People Mattered.* New York: Routledge, 2003.

———, ed. *Women and Development: The Sexual Division of Labor in Rural Societies.* New York: Praeger, 1982.

Benston, Margaret. "The Political Economy of Women's Liberation." *Monthly Review* 21 (September 1969): 13–25.

Bernard, Jessie. *Future of Marriage.* 2nd ed. New York: Yale University Press, 1982.

Bianchi, Suzanne M. "The Changing Demographic and Socioeconomic Characteristics of Single Parent Families." *Marriage and Family Review* 20 (Spring 1995): 71–97.

Bianchi, Suzanne M., Lynne M. Casper, and Pia K. Peltola. "A Cross-National Look at Married Women's Earnings Dependency." *Gender Issues* 17 (Summer 1999): 3–33.

Bianchi, Suzanne M., Melissa A. Milkie, Liana C. Sayer, and John P. Robinson. "Is Anyone Doing the Housework? Trends in the Gender Division of Household Labor." *Social Forces* 79 (September 2000): 191–228.

Bianchi, Suzanne M., and Daphne Spain. *American Women in Transition.* New York: Russell Sage Foundation, 1986.

———. *Women, Work, and Family in America.* Population Bulletin 51. Washington, DC: Population Reference Bureau, 1996.

Billingsley, Andrew. *Black Families in White America.* New York: Prentice-Hall, 1968.

———. *Climbing Jacob's Ladder: The Enduring Legacy of African American Families.* New York: Simon and Schuster, 1992.

Blank, Rebecca. *It Takes a Nation: A New Agenda for Fighting Poverty.* New York: Russell Sage Foundation; Princeton, NJ: Princeton University Press, 1994.

Blassingame, John. *The Slave Community: Plantation Life in the Antebellum South.* New York: Oxford University Press, 1972.

————, ed. *Slave Testimony: Two Centuries of Letters, Speeches, Interviews, and Autobiographies.* Baton Rouge: Louisiana State University Press, 1977.

Blau, Francine D. "Trends in the Well-Being of American Women, 1970–1995." *Journal of Economic Literature* 36 (March 1998): 112–65.

Blewitt, Mary. "Work, Gender and the Artisal Tradition." *New England Shoemaking* 17 (Winter 1983): 221–48.

Bluestone, Barry, and Bennett Harrison. *The Deindustrialization of America.* New York: Basic Books, 1982.

Bluestone, Barry, and Steven Rose. "Overworked and Underemployed: Unraveling an Economic Enigma." *American Prospect* 8, no. 31 (March/April 1997): 58–69.

Borchert, James. *Alley Life in Washington: Family, Community, Religion, and Folklife in the City, 1850–1970.* Urbana: University of Illinois Press, 1980.

Bose, Christine E. *Women in 1900: Gateway to the Political Economy of the 20th Century.* Philadelphia: Temple University Press, 2001.

Bose, Christine E., and Edna Acosta-Belen, eds. *Women in the Latin American Development Process.* Philadelphia: Temple University Press, 1995.

Botume, Elizabeth Hyde. *First Days amongst the Contraband.* Boston: Lee and Shepard, 1893.

Bound, John, and Laura Dresser. "Losing Ground: The Erosion of the Relative Earnings of African American Women during the 1980s." In *Latinas and African American Women at Work: Race, Gender, and Economic Inequality,* edited by Irene Browne, 61–104. New York: Russell Sage Foundation, 1999.

Bowles, Samuel, David M. Gordon, and Thomas E. Weisskopf. *Beyond the Waste Land: A Democratic Alternative to Economic Decline.* Garden City, NY: Doubleday, 1983.

Boydston, Jeanne. *Home and Work: Housework, Wages, and the Ideology of Labor in the Early Republic.* New York: Oxford University Press, 1990.

Brady, David, and Kent Tedin. "Ladies in Pink: Religion and Political Ideology in the Anti-ERA Movement." *Social Science Quarterly* 56 (March 1976): 564–75.

Brenner, Joanna, and Maria Ramas. "Rethinking Women's Oppression." *New Left Review,* no. 144 (March–April 1984): 33–71.

Brooks-Higginbotham, Evelyn. "The Problem of Race in Women's History." In *Coming to Terms: Feminism, Theory, Politics,* edited by Elizabeth Weed, 122–33. New York: Routledge, 1989.

————. *Righteous Discontent: The Women's Movement in the Black Baptist Church, 1880–1920.* Cambridge, MA: Harvard University Press, 1993.

Browne, Irene. "Opportunities Lost? Race, Industrial Restructuring, and Employment among Young Women Heading Households." *Social Forces* 78 (March 2000): 907–29.

————, ed. *Latinas and African American Women at Work: Race, Gender, and Economic Inequality.* New York: Russell Sage Foundation, 1999.

Browne, Lynn E. "Taking in Each Other's Laundry—The Service Economy." *New England Economic Review,* July/August 1986, pp. 20–31.

Budig, Michelle, and Paula England. "The Wage Penalty for Mothers." *American Sociological Review* 66 (April 2001): 204–25.

Burbridge, Lynn C. "The Labor Market for Home Care Workers: Demand, Supply, and Institutional Barriers." *Gerontologist* 33 (February 1993): 41–46.

Bureau of Economic Analysis. National Income and Product Accounts Tables, table 6.4B, last revised February 13, 2004. http://www.bea.gov/bea/dn/nipaweb/TableView.asp (accessed April 26, 2005).

———. "Gross Domestic Product by Industry (1987 SIC basis), Share of Gross Domestic Product (percent), 1987–2000." http://www.bea.doc.gov/bea/dn2/gpo.htm (accessed February 15, 2002).

———. "Gross Product Originating by Industry (1972 SIC basis), Share of Gross Domestic Product, percent, 1947–1987." http://www.bea.doc.gov/bea/dn2/gpo.htm (accessed February 15, 2002).

———. "National Accounts Data, Current-Dollar and 'Real' GDP, 1929–2000." http://www.bea.doc.gov/bea/dn1.htm (accessed March 20, 2002).

———. "National Accounts Data, Gross Domestic Product: Current-Dollar and 'Real' GDP, 1929–01." http://www.bea.doc.gov/bea/dn1.htm (accessed November 14, 2001).

———. "National Income by Type of Income," table 1.14, published November 1, 2002. http://www.bea.doc.gov/bea/nipaweb/SelectTable.asp (accessed November 11, 2002).

Burris, Val. "The Political Partisanship of American Business: A Study of Corporate Political Action Committees." *American Sociological Review* 52 (December 1987): 732–44.

Cain, Glen G. *Married Women in the Labor Force: An Economic Analysis.* Chicago: University of Chicago Press, 1966.

Cancia, Francesca M., et al., eds. *Child Care and Inequality: Re-thinking Carework for Children and Youth.* New York: Routledge, 2002.

Cancian, Maria, Sheldon Danziger, and Peter Gottschalk. "Working Wives and Family Income Inequality among Married Couples." In *Uneven Tides: Rising Inequality in America,* edited by Sheldon Danziger and Peter Gottschalk, 195–221. New York: Russell Sage Foundation, 1992.

Cancian, Maria, and Deborah Reed. "Changes in Family Structure: Implications for Poverty and Related Policy." In *Understanding Poverty,* edited by Sheldon H. Danziger and Robert H. Haveman, 69–96. New York: Russell Sage Foundation, 2001.

Carden, Maren. *The New Feminist Movement.* New York: Russell Sage Foundation, 1974.

Carnoy, Martin. *Faded Dreams: The Politics and Economics of Race in America.* Cambridge: Cambridge University Press, 1994.

————. *Sustaining the New Economy: Work, Family and Community in the Information Age.* New York: Russell Sage Foundation; Cambridge, MA: Harvard University Press, 2000.

Catalyst. "Women in Law: Making the Case." January 30, 2001. www.catalyst women.org/pressroom/press_releases/women_in_law.htm (accessed May 25, 2005).

Center for American Women and Politics. "Facts and Findings." http://www .cawp.rutgers.edu/Facts5.html (accessed January 9, 2006).

Chase-Dunn, Christopher, and Richard Rubinson. "Toward a Structural Perspective on the World-System." *Politics and Society* 7, no. 4 (1977): 453–76.

"Cheating Dignity: The Direct-Care Wage Crisis in America." A report from the American Federation of State, County and Municipal Employees. http://www.afscme.org/pol-leg/cdtc.htm (accessed July 9, 2003).

Cherlin, Andrew. *Marriage, Divorce, Remarriage.* 2nd ed. Cambridge, MA: Harvard University Press, 1992.

Child Welfare Legislative Reference Material. Compiled by the American Legion, National Child Welfare Division. Indianapolis: American Legion, n.d.

Chirot, Daniel. *How Societies Change.* Thousand Oaks, [CA]: Pine Forge Press, 1994.

Cobble, Dorothy Sue. *The Other Women's Movement: Workplace Justice and Social Rights in Modern America.* Princeton, NJ: Princeton University Press, 2004.

————. "The Prospects of Unionism in a Service Society." In *Working in the Service Society*, edited by Cameron Lynne Macdonald and Carmen Sirianni, 333–58. Philadelphia: Temple University Press, 1996.

————, ed. *Women and Unions: Forging a Partnership.* Ithaca, NY: ILR Press, 1993.

Cohen, Marjorie G. *Women's Work, Markets, and Economic Development in Nineteenth-century Ontario.* Toronto: University of Toronto Press, 1988.

Collier, James L. "Husbands vs. Bachelors: Is Marriage Worth It?" *Redbook*, July 1968, pp. 66–109.

Collins, Jane. *Threads: Gender, Labor, and Power in the Global Apparel Industry.* Chicago: University of Chicago Press, 2003.

Collins, Patricia Hill. *Black Feminist Thought: Knowledge, Consciousness, and the Politics of Empowerment.* Rev. ed. New York: Routledge, 2000.

————. *Fighting Words: Black Women and the Search for Justice.* Minneapolis: University of Minnesota Press, 1998.

Colwell, Rita. Preface to *A Door in the Dream: Conversations with Eminent Women in Science* by Elga Wasserman, ix–xii. Washington, D.C.: Joseph Henry Press, 2000.

Committee on Economic Security. *Report to the President of the Committee on Economic Security.* Washington, DC: U.S. Government Printing Office, 1935.

Conley, Frances K. *Walking Out on the Boys.* New York: Farrar, Straus and Giroux, 1998.

Constable, Nicole. *Maid to Order in Hong Kong: Stories of Filipina Workers.* Ithaca, NY: Cornell University Press, 1997.

Converse, Philip E., Jean D. Dotson, Wendy J. Hoag, and William McGee III. *American Social Attitudes Data Sourcebook, 1947–1978.* Cambridge, MA: Harvard University Press, 1980.

Corcoran, Mary, and Martha S. Hill. "The Economic Fortunes of Women." In *Women and Poverty,* edited by Barbara C. Gelpi, Nancy C. M. Hartsock, Clare C. Novak, and Myra H. Strober, 7–23. Chicago: University of Chicago Press, 1986.

Corcoran, Mary, and Sharon Parrott. "Black Women's Economic Progress." Unpublished manuscript, Institute for Policy Research, University of Michigan, Ann Arbor.

Cott, Nancy F. *The Bonds of Womanhood: "Woman's Sphere" in New England, 1780–1835.* 2nd ed. New Haven: Yale University Press, 1997.

Cowan, Ruth Schwartz. "The Industrial Revolution in the Home: Household Technology and Social Change in the 20th Century." *Technology and Culture* 17 (January 1976): 1–24.

———. *More Work for Mother: The Ironies of Household Technology from the Open Hearth to the Microwave.* New York: Basic Books, 1983.

Cunningham, James, and Nadja Zalokar. "The Economic Progress of Black Women, 1940–1980: Occupational Distribution and Relative Wages." *Industrial and Labor Relations* 45 (April 1992): 540–55.

Cutright, Phillips. "Components of Change in the Number of Female Family Heads Aged 15–44: United States, 1940–1970." *Journal of Marriage and the Family* 36 (November 1974): 714–21.

Daly, Mary, and Katherine Rake. *Gender and the Welfare State: Care, Work and Welfare in Europe and the USA.* London: Polity Press, 2003.

Davis, Angela. "Reflections on the Black Woman's Role in the Community of Slaves." *Black Scholar* 3 (December 1971): 3–14.

———. *Women, Race and Class.* New York: Random House, 1981.

Dawson, Steven L., and Rick Surpin. "Direct-Care Healthcare Workers: You Get What You Pay For." *Generations* 25 (Spring 2001): 23–28.

Day, June. "Movements." In *Breeder: Real-Life Stories from the New Generation of Mothers,* edited by Ariel Gore and Bee Lavender, 86–91. Seattle: Seal Press, 2001.

Deere, Carmen Diana. *Household and Class Relations: Peasants and Landlords in Northern Peru.* Berkeley: University of California Press, 1990.

Deere, Carmen Diana, and Magdalena León. *Empowering Women: Land and Property Rights in Latin America.* Pittsburgh: University of Pittsburgh Press, 2001.

Delphy, Christine. *Close to Home: A Materialist Analysis of Women's Oppression.* London: Hutchinson, 1984.

Delphy, Christine, and Diana Leonard. *Familiar Exploitation: A New Analysis of Marriage in Contemporary Western Societies.* Cambridge, MA: Polity Press, 1992.

D'Emilio, John, and Estelle B. Freedman. *Intimate Matters: A History of Sexuality in America.* New York: Harper and Row, 1988.

Deutsch, Francine M. *Halving It All: How Equally Shared Parenting Works.* Cambridge, MA: Harvard University Press, 1999.

Dill, Bonnie Thornton. "Fictive Kin, Paper Sons, and Compadrazgo: Women of Color and the Struggle for Family Survival." In *Women of Color in U.S. Society,* edited by Maxine Baca Zinn and Bonnie Thornton, 149–69. Philadelphia: Temple University Press, 1994.

———. "Our Mothers' Grief: Racial Ethnic Women and the Maintenance of Families." *Journal of Family History* 13, no. 4 (1988): 415–31.

Ding Ling. "Thoughts on March 8 (Women's Day)," translated by Gregor Benton. *New Left Review,* no. 92 (July–August 1975): 102–3. Originally published in *Jiefang ribao* (Liberation Daily), March 9, 1942.

"Divorced Woman: American Style." *Newsweek,* February 13, 1967, pp. 64–67.

Dodson, Lisa. *Don't Call Us Out of Name: The Untold Lives of Women and Girls in Poor America.* Boston: Beacon Press, 1998.

Dortch, Shannon. "Maids Clean Up." *American Demographics,* November 1996, pp. 4–9.

Drake, St. Clair, and Horace R. Cayton. *Black Metropolis: A Study of Negro Life in a Northern City.* Vol. 2. New York: Harcourt, Brace, 1945.

Du Bois, W. E. B. *The Philadelphia Negro: A Social Study.* 1899. Reprint, Philadelphia: University of Pennsylvania Press, 1996.

Dunaway, Wilma. *The African-American Family in Slavery and Emancipation.* Cambridge: Cambridge University Press, 2003.

Duncan, Greg J., with Richard D. Coe et al. *Years of Poverty, Years of Plenty: The Changing Economic Fortunes of American Workers and Families.* Ann Arbor: Survey Research Center, Institute for Social Research, University of Michigan, 1984.

Duncan, Greg J., and Katherine Magnuson. "Promoting the Healthy Development of Young Children." In *One Percent for the Kids: New Policies, Brighter Futures for America's Children,* edited by Isabel V. Sawhill, 16–39. Washington, DC: Brookings Institution Press, 2003.

Durkheim, Emile. *The Division of Labor in Society.* Translated by W. D. Halls. 1933. Reprint, New York: Free Press, 1984.

Eagly, Alice. "On the Flexibility of Human Mating Preferences." Invited address, Midwestern Psychological Association, Chicago, April 2004.

Edin, Kathryn. *There's a Lot of Month Left at the End of the Money: How Welfare Recipients Make Ends Meet in Chicago.* New York: Garfield, 1993.

Edin, Kathryn, and Maria Kefalas. *Promises I Can Keep: Why Poor Women Put Motherhood before Marriage.* Berkeley: University of California Press, 2005

Edin, Kathryn, and Laura Lein. *Making Ends Meet: How Single Mothers Survive Welfare and Low-Wage Work.* New York: Russell Sage Foundation, 1997.

Ehrenreich, Barbara. "Defeating the ERA: A Right-Wing Mobilization of Women." *Journal of Sociology and Social Welfare* 9 (September 1982): 391–98.

————. *The Hearts of Men: American Dreams and the Flight from Commitment.* Garden City, NY: Anchor Press, 1984.

Eisenstein, Sarah. *Give Us Bread but Give Us Roses: Working Women's Consciousness in the United States, 1890 to the First World War.* London: Routledge and K. Paul, 1983.

Eisenstein, Zillah R. *Feminism and Sexual Equality.* New York: Monthly Review Press, 1984.

Eisner, Robert. *The Total Incomes System of Accounts.* Chicago: University of Chicago Press, 1989.

Ellwood, David T. "Winners and Losers in America: Taking the Measure of the New Economic Realities." In *A Working Nation: Workers, Work, and Government in the New Economy,* edited by David T. Ellwood, Rebecca M. Blank, Joseph Blasi, Douglas Kruse, William A. Niskanen, and Karen Lynn-Dyson, 1–41. New York: Russell Sage Foundation, 2000.

Ellwood, David T., and Christopher Jencks. "The Spread of Single-Parent Families in the United States since 1960." In *The Future of the Family,* edited by Daniel P. Moynihan, Timothy P. Smeeding, and Lee Rainwater, 25–65. New York: Russell Sage Foundation, 2004.

Emerson, Robert L. *Fast Food: The Endless Shakeout.* New York: Chain Store Publishing, 1982.

England, Paula. *Comparable Worth: Theories and Evidence.* New York: Aldine de Gruyter, 1992.

————. "The Impact of Feminist Thought on Sociology." *Contemporary Sociology* 28 (May 1999): 263–68.

England, Paula, Michelle Budig, and Nancy Folbre. "Wages of Virtue: The Relative Pay of Care Work." *Social Problems* 49 (November 2002): 455–73.

England, Paula, Karen Christopher, and Lori L. Reid. "Gender, Race, Ethnicity, and Wages." In *Latinas and African American Women at Work: Race, Gender, and Economic Inequality,* edited by Irene Browne, 139–182. New York: Russell Sage Foundation, 1999.

England, Paula, and Nancy Folbre. "Reforming the Social Contract: Public Support for Childrearing in the U.S." In *For Better and For Worse: Welfare Reform and the Well-Being of Children and Families,* edited by Greg J. Duncan and P. Lindsay Chase-Lansdale, 290–306. New York: Russell Sage Foundation, 2001.

Esping-Anderson, Gosta. *The Three Worlds of Welfare Capitalism*. Princeton, NJ: Princeton University Press, 1990.

Etzkowitz, Henry, Carol Kemelgor, and Brian Uzzi. *Athena Unbound: The Advancement of Women in Science and Technology*. Cambridge: Cambridge University Press, 2000.

Farnham, Christie. "Sapphire? The Issue of Dominance in the Slave Family, 1830–1865." In *"To Toil the Livelong Day": America's Women at Work, 1780–1980*, edited by Carol Groneman and Mary Beth Norton, 68–83. Ithaca, NY: Cornell University Press, 1987.

Ferber, Marianne, and Jane Waldfogel. "The Effects of Part-Time and Self-Employment on Wages and Benefits: Differences by Race/Ethnicity and Gender." In *Nonstandard Work: The Nature and Challenges of Changing Employment Arrangements*, edited by Francoise Carre, Marianne Ferber, Lonnie Golden, and Steve Herzenberg, 213–34. Ithaca, NY: Industrial Relations Research Association, 2000.

Ferguson, Thomas. "From Normalcy to New Deal: Industrial Structure, Party Competition and American Public Policy in the Great Depression." *International Organization* 38 (Winter 1984): 41–94.

Ferguson, Thomas, and Joel Rogers. *Right Turn: The Decline of the Democrats and the Future of American Politics*. New York: Hill and Wang, 1986.

Ferree, Myra Marx. "Working Class Feminism: A Consideration of the Consequences of Employment." *Sociological Quarterly* 21, no. 2 (1980): 173–84.

Ferree, Myra Marx, and Beth B. Hess. *Controversy and Coalition: The New Feminist Movement across Three Decades of Change*. New York: Twayne, 1994.

Fineman, Martha. "Implementing Equality: Ideology, Contradiction, and Social Change." *Wisconsin Law Review* (July/August 1983): 789–886.

Firestone, Shulamith. *The Dialectic of Sex: The Case for Feminist Revolution*. New York: Morrow, 1970.

Fleming, Jeanne J. "Public Opinion on Change in Women's Rights and Roles." In *Feminism, Children, and the New Families*, edited by Sanford M. Dornbusch and Myra Strober, 47–66. New York: Guilford Press, 1988.

Fogel, Robert W., and Stanley L. Engerman. *Time on the Cross*. Boston: Little, Brown, 1974.

Folbre, Nancy. "Barbara, the Market, and the State." *Feminist Economics* 4 (November 1998): 159–68.

———. *The Invisible Heart: Economics and Family Values*. New York: New Press, 2001.

———. "The Unproductive Housewife: Her Evolution in Nineteenth-century Economic Thought." *Signs: Journal of Women in Culture and Society* 16 (Spring 1991): 463–84.

———. *Who Pays for the Kids? Gender and the Structures of Constraint*. New York: Routledge, 1994.

Folbre, Nancy, and Julie A. Nelson. "For Love or Money—or Both?" *Journal of Economic Perspectives* 14 (Autumn 2000): 123–40.

Foster-Carter, Aidan. "The Modes of Production Controversy." *New Left Review*, no. 107 (January–February 1978): 47–77.

Fox-Genovese, Elizabeth, and Eugene D. Genovese. *Fruits of Merchant Capital: Slavery and Bourgeois Property in the Rise and Expansion of Capitalism.* New York: Oxford University Press, 1983.

Franklin, Donna. *Ensuring Inequality: The Structural Transformation of the African-American Family.* New York: Oxford University Press, 1997.

Franklin, John Hope, and Alfred A. Moss, Jr. *From Slavery to Freedom: A History of African Americans.* 7th ed. New York: McGraw-Hill, 1994.

Fraser, Nancy. "After the Family Wage: A Postindustrial Thought Experiment." In *Justice Interruptus: Critical Reflections on the "Postsocialist" Condition,* 41–68. New York: Routledge, 1997.

———. "From Redistribution to Recognition: Dilemmas of Justice in a 'Postsocialist' Age." In *Justice Interruptus: Critical Reflections on the "Postsocialist" Condition,* 11–40. New York: Routledge, 1997.

———. "Social Justice in the Age of Identity Politics: Redistribution, Recognition, and Participation." In *Redistribution or Recognition? A Political-Philosophical Exchange,* edited by Nancy Fraser and Axel Honneth, 7–109. Translated by Joel Golb, James Ingram, and Christiane Wilke. New York: Verso, 2003.

———. "Struggle over Needs: Outline of a Socialist-Feminist Critical Theory of Late-Capitalist Political Culture." In *Women, the State, and Welfare,* edited by Linda Gordon, 199–225. Madison: University of Wisconsin Press, 1990.

———. *Unruly Practices: Power, Discourse, and Gender in Contemporary Social Theory.* Minneapolis: University of Minnesota Press, 1989.

Fraser, Nancy, and Axel Honneth. *Redistribution or Recognition? A Political-Philosophical Exchange.* Translated by Joel Golb, James Ingram, and Christiane Wilke. New York: Verso, 2003.

Frazier, E. Franklin. *The Negro Family in the United States.* 1939. Reprint, Chicago: University of Chicago Press, 1966.

Freeman, Jo. "From Protection to Equal Opportunity: The Revolution in Women's Legal Status." In *Women, Politics and Change,* edited by Louise A. Tilly and Patricia Gurin, 457–82. New York: Russell Sage Foundation, 1990.

———. *The Politics of Women's Liberation: A Case Study of an Emerging Social Movement and Its Relation to the Policy Process.* New York: Longman, 1975.

Freeman, Laura. "Home-sweet-home Health Care." *Monthly Labor Review* 118 (March 1995): 3–11.

Fried, Marlene Gerber, ed. *From Abortion to Reproductive Freedom: Transforming a Movement.* Boston: South End Press, 1990.

Fried, Mindy. *Taking Time: Parental Leave Policy and Corporate Culture*. Philadelphia: Temple University Press, 1998.

Friedan, Betty. *The Feminine Mystique*. New York: Norton, 1963.

———. *The Second Stage*. New York: Summit Books, 1981.

Fuchs, Victor R. *Service Economy*. New York: National Bureau of Economic Research. General series, number 87. New York: Columbia University Press, 1968.

Garfinkel, Irving. Introduction to *Fathers under Fire: The Revolution in Child Support Enforcement*, edited by Irving Garfinkel, Sara S. McLanahan, Daniel R. Meyer, and Judith A. Seltzer, 1–10. New York: Russell Sage Foundation, 1998.

Garfinkel, Irving, and Sara McLanahan. *Single-Mother Families and Public Policy: A New American Dilemma*. Washington, DC: Urban Institute, 1986.

Geertz, Clifford. *Agricultural Involution: The Pressures of Ecological Change in Indonesia*. Berkeley: University of California Press, 1963.

General Social Survey, 1972–2000 Cumulative Codebook. http://www.icpsr.umich.edu/GSS (accessed July 17, 2005).

Genovese, Eugene. *Roll, Jordan, Roll: The World the Slaves Made*. New York: Pantheon, 1974.

Gerschenkron, Alexander. *Economic Backwardness in Historical Perspective: A Book of Essays*. Cambridge, MA: Belknap Press of Harvard University Press, 1966.

Gerson, Kathleen. *Hard Choices: How Women Decide about Work, Career, and Motherhood*. Berkeley: University of California Press, 1986.

———. Review of *Gender Vertigo: American Families in Transition*, by Barbara Risman. *Contemporary Sociology* 28 (July 1999): 419–20.

Gerson, Kathleen, and Jerry A. Jacobs. "Changing the Structure and Culture of Work." In *Working Families: The Transformation of the American Home*, edited by Rosanna Hertz and Nancy L. Marshall, 207–26. Berkeley: University of California Press, 2001.

Giddings, Paula. *When and Where I Enter: The Impact of Black Women on Race and Sex in America*. New York: Morrow, 1984.

Giedion, Siegfried. *Mechanization Takes Command: A Contribution to Anonymous History*. New York: Oxford University Press, 1948.

Gilder, George. *Wealth and Poverty*. New York: Basic Books, 1981.

Gilens, Martin. *Why Americans Hate Welfare: Race, Media, and the Politics of Antipoverty Policy*. Chicago: University of Chicago Press, 1999.

Gilman, Charlotte Perkins. *Women and Economics*. 1898. Reprint, New York: Source Book Press, 1970.

Ginsburg, Faye D. *Contested Lives: The Abortion Debate in an American Community*. Berkeley: University of California Press, 1989.

Ginzberg, Eli, and Alice M. Yohalem. *Educated American Women: Self-Portraits*. New York: Columbia University Press, 1966.

Glass, Jennifer, and Valerie Camarigg. "Gender, Parenthood and Job-Family Compatibility." *American Journal of Sociology* 98 (July 1992): 131–51.

Glasser, Ruth, and Jeremy Brecher. "We Are the Roots: The Culture of Home Health Aides." *New England Journal of Public Policy* 13 (Fall/Winter 1997). http://www.paraprofessional.org/publications/wearetheroots_exrpt.pdf (accessed March 28, 2002).

Glazer, Penina Migdal, and Miriam Slater, eds. *Unequal Colleagues: The Entrance of Women into the Professions, 1890–1940*. New Brunswick, NJ: Rutgers University Press, 1987.

Glenn, Evelyn Nakano. "From Servitude to Service Work: Historical Continuities in the Racial Division of Paid Reproductive Labor." *Signs: Journal of Women in Culture and Society* 18 (Autumn 1992): 1–43.

———. "Racial Ethnic Women's Labor: The Intersection of Race, Gender, and Class Oppression." In *Hidden Aspects of Women's Work*, edited by Christine Bose, Roslyn Feldberg, and Natalie Sokoloff, 46–73. New York: Praeger, 1987.

———. *Unequal Freedom: How Race and Gender Shaped American Citizenship and Labor*. Cambridge, MA: Harvard University Press, 2002.

Goldin, Claudia. "Career and Family: College Women Look to the Past." In *Gender and Family Issues in the Workplace*, edited by Francine D. Blau and Ronald G. Ehrenberg, 20–58. New York: Russell Sage Foundation, 1997.

———. "Female Labor Participation: The Origin of Black and White Differences, 1870–1880." *Journal of Economic History* 37 (March 1977): 87–108.

———. "Life-Cycle Labor Force Participation of Married Women: Historical Evidence and Implications." *Journal of Labor Economics* 7 (January 1989): 20–47.

———. "The Rising (and Then Declining) Significance of Gender." NBER Working Paper no. 8915 (April 2002). http://kuznets.fas.harvard.edu/~goldin/papers.html (accessed May 15, 2003).

———. *Understanding the Gender Gap: An Economic History of American Women*. New York: Oxford University Press, 1990.

Goldin, Claudia, and Lawrence F. Katz. "The Power of the Pill: Oral Contraceptives and Women's Career and Marriage Decisions." *Journal of Political Economy* 110 (August 2002). http://www.economics.harvard.edu/~goldin/papers/pillpaper.pdf (accessed April 21, 2004).

Goldscheider, Frances K., and Linda J. Waite. *New Families, No Families? The Transformation of the American Home*. Berkeley: University of California Press, 1991.

Gordon, David M., Richard Edwards, and Michael Reich. *Segmented Work, Divided Workers: The Historical Transformation of Labor in the States*. Cambridge: Cambridge University Press, 1982.

Gordon, Linda. "Black and White Visions of Welfare: Women's Welfare Activism, 1890–1945." *Journal of American History* 78 (September 1991): 559–90.

———. *Pitied but Not Entitled: Single Mothers and the History of Welfare, 1890–1935.* New York: Free Press, 1994.

———. "Thoughts on the Help for Working Parents Plan." *Feminist Economics* 1 (January 1995): 91–94.

———, ed. *Women, the State, and Welfare.* Madison: University of Wisconsin Press, 1990.

Gordon, Robert. "The United States." In *Technological Innovation and Economic Performance,* edited by Benn Steil, David G. Victor, and Richard R. Nelson, 49–73. Princeton, NJ: Princeton University Press, 2002.

Gore, Ariel, and Bee Lavender, eds. *Breeder: Real-Life Stories from the New Generation of Mothers.* Seattle: Seal Press, 2001.

Gornick, Janet C., and Marcia K. Meyer. *Families That Work: Policies for Reconciling Parenthood and Employment.* New York: Russell Sage Foundation, 2003.

Grant, Annette. "After Graduation, a Job in New York?" *Mademoiselle,* June 1967, pp. 144–45.

Greenberg, Stanley B. *Race and State in Capitalist Development: Comparative Perspectives.* New Haven: Yale University Press, 1980.

Grubel, Herbert. "Producer Services: Their Important Role in Growing Economies." In *The Service Sector: Productivity and Growth,* edited by Ernesto Felli, Furio C. Rosati, and Giovanni Tria, 11–42. Heidelberg: Physica-Verlag, 1995.

Gunter, B. G. "Notes on Divorce Filing as Role Behavior." *Journal of Marriage and the Family* 39 (February 1977): 95–98.

Gutman, Herbert. *The Black Family in Slavery and Freedom: 1750–1925.* New York: Pantheon, 1976.

Guy-Sheftall, Beverly. *Daughters of Sorrow: Attitudes toward Black Women, 1880–1920.* Vol. 11 of *Black Women in United States History,* edited by Darlene Hine. Brooklyn, NY: Carlson, 1990.

Halem, Lynne Carol. *Divorce Reform: Changing Legal and Social Perspectives.* New York: Free Press, 1980.

Hao, Linxin, and Mary C. Brinton. "Productive Activities and Support Systems of Single Mothers." *American Journal of Sociology* 102 (March 1997): 1305–44.

Harrington, Michael. *The Other America: Poverty in the United States.* New York: Macmillan, 1962.

Harris, Barbara. *Beyond Her Sphere: Women and Professions in American History.* Westport, CT: Greenwood Press, 1978.

Harris, William. "Work and the Family in Black Atlanta, 1880." In *Black Women in United States History: From Colonial Times through the Nineteenth Century,* edited by Darlene Hine, 2:591–602. Brooklyn, NY: Carlson, 1990.

Harrison, Bennett, and Barry Bluestone. *The Great U-Turn: Corporate Restructuring and the Polarizing of America*. New York: Basic Books, 1988.

Harrison, Cynthia. *On Account of Sex: The Politics of Women's Issues, 1945–1968*. Berkeley: University of California Press, 1988.

Hartmann, Heidi. "Capitalism and Women's Work in the Home, 1900–1930." Ph.D. diss., Yale University, 1974.

———. "Capitalism, Patriarchy, and Job Segregation by Sex." In *Capitalist Patriarchy and the Case for Socialist Feminism*, edited by Zillah Eisenstein, 206–47. New York: Monthly Review Press, 1979.

———. "Changes in Women's Economic and Family Roles in Post–World War II United States." In *Women, Households and the Economy*, edited by Catherine R. Stimpson and Lourdes Beneria, 33–64. New Brunswick, NJ: Rutgers University Press, 1987.

———. "The Family as the Locus of Gender, Class, and Political Struggle: The Example of Housework." *Signs* 6 (Spring 1981): 366–94.

———. "The Unhappy Marriage of Marxism and Feminism: Towards a More Progressive Union." In *Women and Revolution*, edited by Linda Sargent, 1–41. Boston: South End Press, 1981.

Hartmann, Heidi, and Roberta Spalter-Roth. "A Feminist Approach to Public Policy Making for Women and Families." *Current Perspectives in Social Theory* 16 (1996): 33–51.

Hatch, Julie, and Angela Clinton. "Job Growth in the 1990s: A Retrospect." *Monthly Labor Review* 123 (December 2000): 3–18.

Hayden, Dolores. *The Grand Domestic Revolution: A History of Feminist Designs for American Homes, Neighborhoods, and Cities*. Cambridge, MA: MIT Press, 1981.

Hays, Sharon. *Flat Broke with Children: Women in the Age of Welfare Reform*. Oxford: Oxford University Press, 2003.

Heimer, Carol, and Lisa R. Staffen. *For the Sake of the Children: The Social Organization of Responsibility in the Hospital and the Home*. Chicago: University of Chicago Press, 1998.

Herzenberg, Stephen A., John A. Alic, and Howard Wial. *New Rules for a New Economy: Employment and Opportunity in Postindustrial America*. Ithaca, NY: ILR Press, 1998.

Higginbotham, Elizabeth. *Too Much to Ask: Black Women in the Era of Integration*. Chapel Hill: University of North Carolina Press, 2001.

Higginbotham, Elizabeth, and Mary Romero, eds. *Women and Working: Exploring Race, Ethnicity, and Class*. Thousand Oaks, CA: Sage, 1997.

Himmelstein, Jerome L. *To the Right: The Transformation of American Conservatism*. Berkeley: University of California Press, 1990.

Hixson, William B., Jr. *Search for the American Right Wing: An Analysis of the Social Science Record, 1955–1987*. Princeton, NJ: Princeton University Press, 1992.

Hobsbawm, Eric J. *The Age of Revolution: 1789–1848*. New York: Mentor, 1962.

————. "The Crisis of Capitalism in Historical Perspective." *Marxism Today* 19 (October 1975): 300–308.

————. *Industry and Empire: An Economic History of Britain since 1750.* London: Weidenfeld and Nicolson, 1968.

Hobson, Barbara. "No Exit, No Voice: Women's Economic Dependency and the Welfare State." *Acta Sociologica* 33, no. 3 (1990): 235–50.

————. "Solo Mothers, Policy Regimes, and the Logics of Gender." In *Gendering Welfare States*, edited by Diane Sainsbury, 170–87. London: Sage, 1994.

Hochschild, Arlene R. *The Time Bind: When Work Becomes Home and Home Becomes Work.* New York: Metropolitan, 1997.

Hoff, Joan. *Law, Gender, and Injustice: A Legal History of U.S. Women.* New York: New York University Press, 1991.

Hoffnar, Emily, and Michael Greene. "Gender Earnings Inequality in the Service and Manufacturing Industries in the U.S." *Feminist Economics* 1 (November 1993): 82–95.

Hogan, David Gerard. *Selling 'Em by the Sack: White Castle and the Creation of American Food.* New York: New York University Press, 1997.

Hondagneu-Sotelo, Pierrette. *Doméstica: Immigrant Workers Cleaning and Caring in the Shadows of Affluence.* Berkeley: University of California Press, 2001.

hooks, bell. *Ain't I a Woman? Black Women and Feminism.* Boston: South End Press, 1981.

Houghteling, Leila. *The Income and Standard of Living of Unskilled Laborers in Chicago.* Chicago: University of Chicago Press, 1927.

Howell, Martha. *Women, Production, and Patriarchy in Late Medieval Cities.* Chicago: University of Chicago Press, 1986.

Humphries, Jane. "The Working Class Family, Women's Liberation and Class Struggle: The Case of Nineteenth-century British History." *Review of Radical Political Economics* 9 (Fall 1977): 25–42.

Iglehart, Alfreda P. *Married Women and Work: 1957 and 1976.* Lexington, MA: Lexington Books, 1979.

Integrated Public Use Microdata Series: Version 3.0 (machine-readable database), edited by Steven Ruggles, Matthew Sobek, Trent Alexander, Catherine A. Fitch, Ronald Goeken, Patricia Kelly Hall, Miriam King, and Chad Ronnander. Minneapolis: Minnesota Population Center (producer and distributor), 2004. http://www.ipums.org (last accessed January 9, 2005).

Jacob, Herbert. *The Silent Revolution: The Transformation of Divorce Law in the United States.* Chicago: University of Chicago Press, 1988.

————. "Women and Divorce Reform." In *Women, Politics and Change*, edited by Louise A. Tilly and Patricia Gurin, 482–502. New York: Russell Sage Foundation, 1990.

Jacobs, Jerry A., and Kathleen Gerson. "Overworked Individuals or Overworked Families? Explaining Trends in Work, Leisure, and Family Time." *Work and Occupations* 28 (November 2001): 40–63.

Jaynes, Gerald D., and Robin M. Williams, Jr., eds. *A Common Destiny: Blacks and American Society.* Committee on the Status of Black Americans, Commission on Behavioral and Social Sciences and Education, National Research Council. Washington, DC: National Academy Press, 1989.

Jencks, Christopher. *Rethinking Social Policy: Race, Poverty and the Underclass.* Cambridge, MA: Harvard University Press, 1992.

Jenkins, J. Craig, and Barbara G. Brents. "Social Protest, Hegemonic Competition, and Social Reform: A Political Struggle Interpretation of the Origins of the American Welfare State." *American Sociological Review* 54 (December 1989): 891–909.

Jensen, Joan M. *Loosening the Bonds: Mid-Atlantic Farm Women, 1750–1850.* New Haven: Yale University Press, 1986.

Jenson, Jane. "Who Cares? Gender and Welfare Regimes." *Social Politics* 4 (September 1997): 182–87.

Jones, Jacqueline. *Labor of Love, Labor of Sorrow: Black Women, Work, and the Family from Slavery to the Present.* New York: Basic Books, 1987.

Kamerman, Sheila B. "Women, Children and Poverty: Public Policies and Female-Headed Families in Industrialized Countries." In *Women and Poverty,* edited by Barbara C. Gelpi, Nancy C. M. Hartsock, Clare C. Novak, and Myra H. Strober, 41–64. Chicago: University of Chicago Press, 1986.

Kamerman, Sheila B., and Alfred J. Kahn. "Family Change and Family Policies: United States." In *Family Change and Family Policies in Great Britain, Canada, New Zealand, and the United States,* edited by Sheila B. Kamerman and Alfred J. Kahn, 350–76. Oxford: Clarendon Press; New York: Oxford University Press, 1997.

Kane, Andrea, and Isabel V. Sawhill. "Preventing Early Childbearing." In *One Percent for the Kids: New Policies, Brighter Futures for America's Children,* edited by Isabel V. Sawhill. 56–75. Washington, DC: Brookings Institution Press, 2003.

Kaplan, Elaine Bell. *Not Our Kind of Girl: Unraveling the Myths of Black Teenage Motherhood.* Berkeley: University of California Press, 1997.

Katz-Najera, Laura. "Unsung Heroines: A Vision of Home Care." *Nursing Management* 27 (December 1996): 47–49.

Katzman, David. *Seven Days a Week: Women and Domestic Service in Industrializing America.* New York: Oxford University Press, 1978.

Kay, Herma Hill. "Equality and Difference." *Cincinnati Law Review* 56 (1987): 1–90.

Kerber, Linda K. "Separate Spheres, Female Worlds, Woman's Place: The Rhetoric of Women's History." *Journal of American History* 75 (June 1988): 9–39.

Kessler-Harris, Alice. *Out to Work: A History of Wage-Earning Women in the United States.* New York: Oxford University Press, 1982.

———. *A Woman's Wage: Historical Meanings and Social Consequences.* Lexington: University Press of Kentucky, 1990.

Kessler-Harris, Alice, and Karen Brodkin Sacks. "The Demise of Domesticity in America." In *Women, Households and the Economy,* edited by Catherine R. Stimpson and Lourdes Beneria, 65–84. New Brunswick, NJ: Rutgers University Press, 1987.

King, Deborah K. "Multiple Jeopardy, Multiple Consciousness: The Context of a Black Feminist Ideology." *Signs: Journal of Women in Culture and Society* 14 (Autumn 1988): 42–72.

Kittay, Eva Feder. *Love's Labor: Essays on Women, Equality, and Dependency.* New York: Routledge, 1999.

Klatch, Rebecca E. "The Two Worlds of Women of the New Right." In *Women, Politics and Change,* edited by Louise A. Tilly and Patricia Gurin, 529–52. New York: Russell Sage Foundation, 1990.

———. *Women of the New Right.* Philadelphia: Temple University Press, 1987.

Kniesner, Thomas, Marjorie McElroy, and Steven Wilcox. "Getting into Poverty without a Husband and Getting out, With or Without." *American Economic Review* 78 (May 1988): 86–90.

Komarovsky, Mirra. *Blue-Collar Marriage.* New York: Vintage Books, 1967.

Koven, Seth, and Sonya Michel, eds. *Mothers of a New World: Maternalist Politics and the Origins of Welfare States.* New York: Routledge, 1993.

Kriesberg, Louise. *Mothers in Poverty: A Study of Fatherless Families.* Chicago: Aldine, 1970.

Kurz, Demie. *For Richer, for Poorer: Mothers Confront Divorce.* New York: Routledge, 1995.

Ladd-Taylor, Molly. *Mother-Work: Women, Child Welfare, and the State, 1890–1930.* Urbana: University of Illinois Press, 1994.

Ladner, Joyce A. *Tomorrow's Tomorrow: The Black Woman.* Garden City, NY: Doubleday, 1971.

Lan, Pei-chia. "Global Divisions, Local Identities: Filipina Migrant Domestic Workers and Taiwanese Employers." Ph.D. diss., Northwestern University, 2000.

Landry, Bart. *Black Working Wives: Pioneers of the American Family Revolution.* Berkeley: University of California Press, 2000.

———. *The New Black Middle Class.* Berkeley: University of California Press, 1987.

Lanehart, Sonja L. *Sista, Speak! Black Women Kinfolk Talk about Language and Literacy.* Austin: University of Texas Press, 2002.

Lavender, Bee. "Bread and Roses." In *Breeder: Real-Life Stories from the New Generation of Mothers,* edited by Ariel Gore and Bee Lavender, 115–21. Seattle: Seal Press, 2001.

Lee, Ching Kwan. *Gender and the South China Miracle: Two Worlds of Factory Women.* Berkeley: University of California Press, 1998.

Leff, Mark H. "Consensus for Reform: The Mothers' Pension Movement in the Progressive Era." *Social Service Review* 47 (1973): 397–429.

Leggon, Cheryl Bernadette. "Black Female Professionals: Dilemmas and Contradictions of Status." In *The Black Woman,* edited by La Frances Rodgers-Rose, 189–202. Newbury Park, CA: Sage, 1980.

Lemann, Nicholas. *The Promised Land: The Great Black Migration and How It Changed America.* New York: Knopf, 1991.

Levitan, Sar. *Programs in Aid of the Poor for the 1970s.* Baltimore: Johns Hopkins Press, 1969.

Levitan, Sar, and Robert Taggart. *Promise of Greatness.* Cambridge, MA: Harvard University Press, 1976.

Levy, Denise Urias, and Sonya Michel. "More Can Be Less: Child Care and Welfare Reform in the United States." In *Child Care at the Crossroads: Gender and Welfare State Restructuring,* edited by Rianne Mahon and Sonya Michel, 239–63. New York: Routledge, 2002.

Levy, Frank. *The New Dollars and Dreams: American Incomes and Economic Change.* New York: Russell Sage Foundation, 1998.

Lewis, Hylan. *Blackways of Kent.* 1955. Reprint, Chapel Hill: University of North Carolina Press, 1964.

Lewis, Jane. "Gender and the Development of Welfare Regimes." *Journal of European Social Policy* 2, no. 3 (1992): 159–73.

———. "Gender and Welfare Regimes: Further Thoughts." *Social Politics* 4 (September 1997): 160–77.

Li, Xiaojiang. "Economic Reform and the Awakening of Chinese Women's Collective Consciousness." In *Engendering China: Women, Culture, and the State,* edited by Christina K. Gilmartin, Gail Hershatter, Lisa Rofel, and Tyrene White, 360–84. Cambridge, MA: Harvard University Press, 1994.

———. "Resisting While Holding the Tradition—Claims for Right Raised in Literature by Chinese Women Writers in the New Period." In *Feminism/Femininity in Chinese Literature,* edited by Peng-hsiang Chen and Whitney Crothers Dilley, 109–16. Critical Studies 18. Amsterdam: Rodopi, 2002.

Lichter, Daniel T., Deborah Roempke Graefe, and J. Brian Brown. "Is Marriage a Panacea? Union Formation among Economically Disadvantaged Mothers." *Social Problems* 50 (February 2003): 60–86.

Lieb, Hilarie, and Susan Thistle. "The Changing Impact of Marriage, Motherhood and Work on Women's Poverty." *Journal of Women, Politics, and Policy,* vol. 27, nos. 3/4 (2006): 5–22.

Liebow, Elliott. *Tally's Corner: A Study of Negro Streetcorner Men.* Boston: Little, Brown, 1967.

Long, Clarence D. *The Labor Force under Changing Income and Employment.* Princeton, NJ: Princeton University Press for the NBER, 1958.

Lopata, Helena Znaniecka. *Occupation: Housewife.* New York: Oxford University Press, 1971.

———. *Women as Widows: Support Systems.* New York: Elsevier, 1979.

Louis Harris and Associates. *The Virginia Slims American Women's Opinion Poll: A Survey of the Attitudes of Women on Their Roles in Politics and the Economy.* Polls taken 1971–85.

Lown, Judy. *Women and Industrialization: Gender at Work in Nineteenth-century England.* Minneapolis: University of Minnesota Press, 1990.

Luker, Kristin. *Abortion and the Politics of Motherhood.* Berkeley: University of California Press, 1984.

———. *Dubious Conceptions: The Politics of Teenage Pregnancy.* Cambridge, MA: Harvard University Press, 1996.

Lum, Sherlene K. S., Brian C. Moyer, and Robert E. Yuskavage. "Improved Estimates of Gross Product by Industry for 1947–98." *Survey of Current Business,* June 2000, pp. 24–54.

Lynd, Robert S., and Helen Merrell Lynd. *Middletown: A Study in Contemporary American Culture.* New York: Harcourt, Brace, 1929.

———. *Middletown in Transition: A Study in Cultural Conflicts.* London: Harcourt, 1937.

Mahon, Rianne, and Sonya Michel, eds. *Child Care at the Crossroads: Gender and Welfare State Restructuring.* New York: Routledge, 2002.

Mandel, Ernest. *Marxist Economic Theory.* Vol. 1. Translated by Brian Pearce. New York: Monthly Review Press, 1968.

Mandle, Jay R. *Not Slave, Not Free: The African American Economic Experience since the Civil War.* Durham, NC: Duke University Press, 1992.

Mann, Susan. "Slavery, Sharecropping, and Sexual Inequality." In *We Specialize in the Wholly Impossible: A Reader in Black Women's History,* edited by Darlene Clark Hine, Wilma King, and Linda Reed, 281–302. Brooklyn, NY: Carlson, 1995.

Mansbridge, Jane J. "Organizing for the ERA: Cracks in the Facade of Unity." In *Women, Politics, and Change,* edited by Louise A. Tilly and Patricia Gurin, 323–28. New York: Russell Sage Foundation, 1990.

———. *Why We Lost the ERA.* Chicago: University of Chicago Press, 1986.

Manza, Jeff, and Clem Brooks. *Social Cleavages and Political Change: Voter Alignments and U.S. Party Coalitions.* New York: Oxford University Press, 1999.

Marable, Manning. *Race, Reform and Rebellion: The Second Reconstruction in Black America, 1945–1990.* 2nd ed. Jackson: University Press of Mississippi, 1991.

Mare, Robert D., and Christopher Winship. "Socioeconomic Change and the Decline of Marriage for Blacks and Whites." In *The Urban Underclass,* edited by

Christopher Jencks and Paul E. Peterson, 175–203. Washington, DC: Brookings Institution, 1991.

Marshall, Barbara L. *Configuring Gender: Explorations in Theory and Politics*. Orchard Park, NY: Broadview Press, 2000.

Marshall, T. H. *Class, Citizenship and Social Development*. Garden City, NY: Doubleday, 1964.

Marx, Karl. *Grundrisse: Foundations of the Critique of Political Economy*. Translated by Martin Nicolaus. New York: Vintage Books, 1973.

Mathews, Donald G., and Jane Sherron de Hart. *Sex, Gender, and the Politics of ERA: A State and the Nation*. New York: Oxford University Press, 1990.

Matthaie, Julie. *An Economic History of Women in America*. New York: Schocken Books, 1984.

May, Martha. "Bread before Roses: American Workingmen, Labor Unions, and the Family Wage." In *Women, Work, and Protest*, edited by Ruth Milkman, 1–21. Boston: Routledge and Kegan Paul, 1985.

McAdam, Doug. *Political Process and the Development of Black Insurgency, 1930–1970*. Chicago: University of Chicago Press, 1982.

McCall, Leslie. *Complex Inequality*. New York: Routledge, 2001.

McGirr, Lisa. *Suburban Warriors: The Origins of the New American Right*. Princeton, NJ: Princeton University Press, 2001.

McLamore, James W. *The Burger King: Jim McLamore and the Building of an Empire*. New York: McGraw-Hill, 1998.

McLanahan, Sara, Annemette Sorensen, and Dorothy Watson. "Sex Differences in Poverty, 1950–1980." *Signs: Journal of Women and Culture in Society* 15 (Autumn 1989): 102–22.

McLaughlin, Steven D., et al. *The Changing Lives of American Women*. Chapel Hill: University of North Carolina Press, 1988.

Meyerowitz, Joanne. *Women Adrift: Independent Wage Earners in Chicago, 1880–1930*. Chicago: University of Chicago Press, 1988.

Mezey, Susan Gluck. *In Pursuit of Equality: Women, Public Policy, and the Federal Courts*. New York: St. Martin's, 1992.

Michel, Sonya. *Children's Interests/Mothers' Rights: The Shaping of America's Child Care Policy*. New Haven: Yale University Press, 1999.

———. "Dilemmas of Child Care." In *Child Care Policy at the Crossroads: Gender and Welfare State Restructuring*, edited by Sonya Michel and Rianne Mahon, 333–38. New York: Routledge, 2002.

Michel, Sonya, and Rianne Mahon, eds. *Child Care Policy at the Crossroads: Gender and Welfare State Restructuring*. New York: Routledge, 2002.

Michener, Diana. "Catching the Sun." In *Working It Out: 23 Women Writers, Artists,*

Scientists, and Scholars Talk about Their Lives and Work, edited by Sara Ruddick and Pamela Daniels, 147–61. New York: Pantheon, 1977.

Millett, Kate. *Sexual Politics.* New York: Avon, 1971.

Mincer, Jacob. "Labor Force Participation of Married Women: A Study of Labor Supply." In *Aspects of Labor Economics,* edited by National Bureau Committee for Economic Research Conference, 63–105. Princeton, NJ: Princeton University Press, 1962.

Mink, Gwendolyn. *The Wages of Motherhood: Inequality in the Welfare State, 1917–1942.* Ithaca, NY: Cornell University Press, 1995.

———. "Wage Work, Family Work, and Welfare Politics." *Feminist Economics* 1 (Summer 1995): 95–98.

———. *Welfare's End.* Ithaca, NY: Cornell University Press, 2002.

Mintz, Steven, and Susan Kellogg. *Domestic Revolutions: A Social History of American Family Life.* New York: Free Press, 1988.

Mishel, Lawrence, Jared Bernstein, and Heather Boushey. *The State of Working America 2002–03.* Economic Policy Institute, January 2003, executive summary. http://www.epinet.org/books/swa2002itntro.html (accessed November 21, 2002).

Mishel, Lawrence, Jared Bernstein, and John Schmitt. *The State of Working America 2000/2001.* Ithaca, NY: ILR Press, 2001.

Moore, Barrington. *Social Origins of Dictatorship and Democracy: Lord and Peasant in the Making of the Modern World.* Boston: Beacon Press, 1966.

Morgan, Leslie A. *After Marriage Ends: Economic Consequences for Midlife Women.* New York: Sage, 1991.

Morgan, Robin, ed. *Sisterhood Is Powerful: An Anthology of Writings from the Women's Liberation Movement.* New York: Vintage Books, 1970.

Morgan, S. Philip, Antonio McDaniel, Andrew T. Miller, and Samuel H. Preston. "Racial Differences in Household and Family Structure at the Turn of the Century." *American Journal of Sociology* 98 (January 1993): 798–828.

Mott, Frank, ed. *The Employment Revolution: Young American Women in the 1970s.* Cambridge, MA: MIT Press, 1982.

Moynihan, Daniel P. "The Negro Family: The Case for National Action." In *The Moynihan Report and the Politics of Controversy,* edited by Lee Rainwater and William L. Yancy, 39–132. Cambridge, MA: MIT Press, 1967.

Murray, Charles. *Losing Ground: American Social Policy, 1950–1980.* New York: Basic Books, 1984.

Narotsky, Susana. " 'Not to Be a Burden': Ideologies of the Domestic Group and Women's Work In Rural Catalonia." In *Work without Wages,* edited by Jane L. Collins and Martha Gimenez, 70–88. Albany: State University of New York Press, 1990.

Negrey, Cynthia, Stacey Golin, Sunhwa Lee, Holly Mead, and Barbara Gault. "Working First but Working Poor: The Need for Education and Training Following Welfare Reform." Institute for Women's Policy Research, 2001. http://www.iwpr.org/ (accessed February 12, 2002).

Negro Housing Survey of Charleston, Keystone, Kimball, Wheeling and Williamson. Prepared and Issued by Bureau of Negro Welfare and Statistics of the State of West Virginia. [Charleston: Jarrett Printing Company,] 1938.

Nelson, Barbara J. "The Origins of the Two-Channel Welfare State: Workmen's Compensation and Mothers' Aid." In *Women, the State, and Welfare,* edited by Linda Gordon, 123–51. Madison: University of Wisconsin Press, 1990.

———. "Women's Poverty and Women's Citizenship: Some Political Consequences of Economic Marginality." In *Women and Poverty,* edited by Barbara C. Gelpi, Nancy C. M. Hartsock, Clare C. Novak, and Myra H. Strober, 209–31. Chicago: University of Chicago Press, 1986.

Nelson, Robert L., and William P. Bridges. *Legalizing Gender Inequality: Courts, Markets, and Unequal Pay for Women in America.* Cambridge: Cambridge University Press, 1999.

Neysmith, Sheila. "Home Care Workers Discuss Their Work: The Skills Required to 'Use Your Common Sense.' " *Journal of Aging Studies* 10 (Spring 1996): 1–14.

Noble, Jeanne L. *The Negro Woman's College Education.* 1956. Reprint, New York: Garland, 1987.

"Nobody Tells You." *Woman's Home Companion,* January 1951, pp. 4–6.

O'Connor, Carla. "Dreamkeeping in the Inner City: Diminishing the Divide between Aspirations and Expectations." In *Coping with Poverty: The Social Contexts of Neighborhood, Work and Family in the African-American Community,* edited by Sheldon Danziger and Ann Chih Lin, 49–73. Ann Arbor: University of Michigan Press, 2000.

O'Connor, Julia S., Ann Shola Orloff, and Sheila Shaver. *States, Markets, Families: Gender, Liberalism, and Social Policy in Australia, Canada, Great Britain, and the United States.* Cambridge: Cambridge University Press, 1999.

Ogburn, William F., and Meyer F. Nimkoff. *Technology and the Changing Family.* Boston: Houghton Mifflin, 1955.

Omi, Michael, and Howard Winant. *Racial Formation in the United States: From the 1960s to the 1990s.* 2nd ed. New York: Routledge, 1994.

Oppenheimer, Valerie Kincade. *The Female Labor Force in the United States: Demographic and Economic Factors Governing Its Growth and Changing Composition.* Berkeley: Institute of International Studies, University of California, 1970.

Osterman, Paul, Thomas A. Kochan, Richard Locke, and Michael J. Piore. *Working in America: A Blueprint for the New Labor Market.* Cambridge, MA: MIT Press, 2001.

Painter, Nell Irvin. Foreword to *Coal, Class, and Color: Blacks in Southern West Virginia, 1915–32,* by Joe William Trotter, Jr., xiii–xx. Urbana: University of Illinois Press, 1990.

Palmer, Bryan. "Social and Class Formation in North America, 1800–1900." In *Proletarianization and Family History*, edited by David Levine, 229–309. Orlando, FL: Academic Press, 1984.

Palmer, Phyllis. *Domesticity and Dirt: Housewives and Domestic Servants in the United States, 1920–1945*. Philadelphia: Temple University Press, 1989.

Paraprofessional Healthcare Institute. "Cooperative Home Care Associates." http://www.paraprofessional.org/Sections/chca.htm (accessed March 13, 2002).

Parreñas, Rhacel Salazar. *Servants of Globalization: Women, Migration and Domestic Work.* Stanford, CA: Stanford University Press, 2001.

Parsons, Talcott, and Robert F. Bales. *Family, Socialization and Interaction Process.* Glencoe, IL: Free Press, 1954.

Pateman, Carole. "The Patriarchal Welfare State." In *Democracy and the Welfare State*, edited by Amy Gutmann, 231–36. Princeton, NJ: Princeton University Press, 1988.

Payton, Brenda. "Changing the Tradition: Women in Crafts Jobs." *Essence*, June 1980, pp. 36–38.

Pearce, Diana. "The Feminization of Poverty: Women, Work and Welfare." *Urban and Social Change Review* 11 (February 1978): 28–36.

Pederson, Susan. *Family, Dependence, and the Origins of the Welfare State: Britain and France, 1914–1945.* Cambridge: Cambridge University Press, 1993.

Perkins, Frances. *The Roosevelt I Knew.* New York: Viking Press, 1946.

Petchesky, Rosalind Pollack. *Abortion and Woman's Choice: The State, Sexuality, and Reproductive Freedom.* Rev. ed. Boston: Northeastern University Press, 1990.

Petersen, Trond, and Laurie Morgan. "Separate and Unequal: Occupation-Establishment Sex Segregation and the Gender Wage Gap." *American Journal of Sociology* 101 (September 1995): 329–65.

———. "The Within-Job Gender Wage Gap." In *Social Stratification: Class, Race, and Gender in Sociological Perspective*, edited by David B. Grusky, 734–42. 2nd ed. Boulder, CO: Westview, 1994.

Peterson, Richard. *Women, Work, and Divorce.* Albany: State University of New York Press, 1989.

Pierce, Jennifer L. *Gender Trials: Emotional Lives in Contemporary Law Firms.* Berkeley: University of California Press, 1995.

Piercy, Marge. "The Grand Coolie Damn." In *Sisterhood Is Powerful: An Anthology of Writings from the Women's Liberation Movement*, edited by Robin Morgan, 421–38. New York: Vintage Books, 1970.

Plateris, Alexander. *Divorces by Marriage Cohort.* Vital and Health Statistics, series 21, no. 24. Hyattsville, MD: U.S. Department of Health, Education and Welfare, 1979.

Pleck, Elizabeth H. "The Two-Parent Household: Black Family Structure in Late–Nineteenth Century Boston." *Journal of Social History* (Fall 1972): 3–36.

Quadagno, Jill. *The Color of Welfare: How Racism Undermined the War on Poverty.* New York: Oxford University Press, 1994.

———. "Welfare Capitalism and the Social Security Act of 1935." *American Sociological Review* 49 (October 1984): 632–47.

Ragin, Charles C. *Constructing Social Research: The Unity and Diversity of Method.* Thousand Oaks, [CA]: Pine Forge Press, 1994.

Rains, Prudence Mors. *Becoming an Unwed Mother: A Sociological Account.* Chicago: Aldine, Atherton, 1971.

Rainwater, Lee. *Workingman's Wife: Her Personality, World, and Lifestyle.* New York: Oceana Publications, 1959.

Rainwater, Lee, and William L. Yancy, eds. *The Moynihan Report and the Politics of Controversy.* Cambridge, MA: MIT Press, 1967.

Ransom, Roger L., and Richard Sutch. *One Kind of Freedom: The Economic Consequences of Emancipation.* Cambridge: Cambridge University Press, 1977.

Reich, Robert B. *The Next American Frontier.* New York: Times Books, 1983.

Reid, Margaret. *Economics of Household Production.* New York: J. Wiley and Sons, 1934.

Reskin, Barbara. *The Realities of Affirmative Action in Employment.* Washington, DC: American Sociological Association, 1998.

Reskin, Barbara F., and Irene Padavic. *Women and Men at Work.* Thousand Oaks, [CA]: Pine Forge Press, 1994.

Riley, Glenda. *Divorce: An American Tradition.* New York: Oxford University Press, 1991.

Risman, Barbara J. *Gender Vertigo: American Families in Transition.* New Haven: Yale University Press, 1998.

Roberts, Dorothy E. *Killing the Black Body: Race, Reproduction, and the Meaning of Liberty.* New York: Pantheon, 1997.

———. "Race, Gender, and the Value of Mothers' Work." *Social Politics* 2 (Summer 1995): 195–207.

———. *Shattered Bonds: The Color of Child Welfare.* New York: Basic Books, 2002.

Robertson, Claire. "Africa into the Americas? Slavery and Women, the Family, and the Gender Division of Labor." In *More Than Chattel: Black Women and Slavery in the Americas,* edited by David Barry Gaspar and Darlene Clark Hine, 3–40. Bloomington: Indiana University Press, 1996.

Robinson, John P. "Household Technology and Household Work." In *Women and Household Labor,* edited by Sarah Fenstermaker Berk, 53–68. Beverly Hills, [CA]: Sage, 1980.

Rosenberg, Rosalind. *Beyond Separate Spheres: Intellectual Roots of Modern Feminism*. New Haven: Yale University Press, 1982.

Ross, Heather L., and Isabel V. Sawhill. *Time of Transition: Growth of Families Headed by Women*. Washington, DC: Urban Institute, 1975.

Rostow, Walt W. *The Stages of Economic Growth: A Non-Communist Manifesto*. 3rd ed. Cambridge: Cambridge University Press, 1990.

————. *The World Economy: History and Prospect*. Austin: University of Texas Press, 1978.

Roth, Benita. *Separate Roads to Feminism: Black, Chicana, and White Feminist Movements in America's Second Wave*. Cambridge: Cambridge University Press, 2004.

Rouse, Jacqueline A. "Atlanta's African American Women's Attack on Segregation, 1900–1920." In *Gender, Class, Race and Reform in the Progressive Era*, edited by Noralee Frankel and Nancy S. Dye, 10–23. Lexington: University Press of Kentucky, 1991.

Rubin, Eva. *The Supreme Court and the American Family: Ideology and Issues*. Westport, CT: Greenwood, 1986.

Rubin, Gayle. "The Traffic in Women: Notes on the 'Political Economy' of Sex." In *Toward an Anthropology of Women*, edited by Rayna Reiter, 157–210. New York: Monthly Review Press, 1975.

Rubin, Lillian B. *Women of a Certain Age: The Mid-life Search for Self*. New York: Harper and Row, 1979.

————. *Worlds of Pain: Life in the Working-Class Family*. New York: Basic Books, 1976.

Ruggles, Steven. "The Origins of African American Family Structure." *American Sociological Review* 59 (February 1994): 136–51.

Ryan, Mary P. *Cradle of the Middle Class: The Family in Oneida County, New York, 1790–1865*. Cambridge: Cambridge University Press, 1981.

————. *Womanhood in America, from Colonial Times to the Present*. 3rd ed. New York: F. Watts, 1983.

Sainsbury, Diane. *Gender, Equality and Welfare States*. Cambridge: Cambridge University Press, 1996.

Sale, Kirkpatrick. *Power Shift: The Rise of the Southern Rim and Its Challenge to the Eastern Establishment*. New York: Random House, 1975.

Sandefur, Gary, and Marta Tienda, eds. *Divided Opportunities: Minorities, Poverty and Social Policy*. New York: Plenum Press, 1988.

Savage, Jennifer. "Learning to Surf." In *Breeder: Real-Life Stories from the New Generation of Mothers*, edited by Ariel Gore and Bee Lavender, 244–54. Seattle: Seal Press, 2001.

Sawhill, Isabel. "Discrimination and Poverty among Women Who Head Families." *Signs: Journal of Women and Culture in Society* 3 (Spring 1976): 201–11.

————. Introduction to *One Percent for the Kids: New Policies, Brighter Futures for America's Children*, edited by Isabel V. Sawhill, 1–15. Washington, DC: Brookings Institution Press, 2003.

————, ed. *One Percent for the Kids: New Policies, Brighter Futures for America's Children*. Washington, DC: Brookings Institution Press, 2003.

Sayer, Liana C. "Gender, Time and Inequality: Trends in Women's and Men's Paid Work, Unpaid Work and Free Time." Paper presented at the annual meeting of the Population Association of America, Atlanta, GA, May 2002.

Sayer, Liana C., Paula England, Michael Bittman, and Suzanne Bianchi. "How Long Is the Second (Plus First) Shift? Gender Differences in Paid, Unpaid, and Total Work Time in Australia and the United States." Unpublished manuscript.

Scanlon, William J. "Nursing Workforce: Recruitment and Retention of Nurses and Nurse Aides Is a Growing Concern." Testimony before the U.S. Senate Committee on Health, Education, Labor and Pensions. May 17, 2001. http://www.gao.gov/new.items/do1750t.pdf (accessed April 10, 2003).

Scanzoni, John H. *The Black Family in Modern Society*. Boston: Allyn and Bacon, 1971.

Schor, Judith. *The Overspent American: Upscaling, Downshifting, and the New Consumer*. New York: Basic Books, 1998.

————. *The Overworked American: The Unexpected Decline of Leisure*. New York: Basic Books, 1991.

Schreiner, Olive. *Woman and Labour*. 1911. Reprint, London: Virago, 1985.

Schurmann, Franz. *The Logic of World Power: An Inquiry into the Origins, Currents, and Contradictions of World Politics*. New York: Pantheon, 1974.

Scott, Ellen K., Kathryn Edin, Andrew S. London, and Joan Maya Mazelis. "My Children Come First: Welfare Reliant Women's Post-TANF Views of Work-Family Trade-offs and Marriage." In *For Better and for Worse: Welfare Reform and the Well-Being of Children and Families*, edited by Greg J. Duncan and P. Lindsay Chase-Lansdale, 132–53. New York: Russell Sage Foundation, 2001.

Scott, Joan Norman. "Watching the Changes." In *Women and Minorities in American Professions*, edited by Joyce Tang and Earl Smith, 19–42. Albany: State University of New York Press, 1996.

Scott, Wilbur J. "The Equal Rights Amendment and Status Politics." *Social Forces* 64 (December 1985): 499–506.

Seccombe, Karen. *"So You Think I Drive a Cadillac?": Welfare Recipients' Perspectives on the System and Its Reform*. Boston: Allyn and Bacon, 1998.

"The Second Sexual Revolution." *Time*, January 24, 1964, p. 57.

Seixas, Suzanne. "One Family's Finances: A Divorced Mother's Fears for Tomorrow." *Money*, July 1978, pp. 85–88.

Shalev, Michael. "The Social Democratic Model and Beyond: Two Generations of Comparative Research on the Welfare State." *Comparative Social Research* 6 (1983): 315–51.

Shank, Susan. "Women and the Labor Market: The Link Grows Stronger." *Monthly Labor Review* 111 (March 1988): 3–8.

Shaw, Stephanie J. *What a Woman Ought to Be and Do: Black Professional Women Workers during the Jim Crow Era.* Chicago: University of Chicago Press, 1996.

Shen, Rong. "At Middle Age." In *Seven Contemporary Chinese Women Writers,* edited by Gladys Yang, 117–204. Beijing: Chinese Literature, 1982.

———. "A New Woman Writer: Shen Rong and Her Story 'At Middle Age.' " Interview by Gladys Yang. *Chinese Literature* 10 (1980): 64–70.

"Single Chinese Mothers Beset with Troubles." *China Daily* (Xinhua). December 12, 2004. http://www.chinadaily.com.en/english/doc/2004-12/18/content_401364.htm.

Single Mothers by Choice. Home page. http://mattes.home.pipeline.com (accessed November 25, 2003).

Skocpol, Theda. *Protecting Soldiers and Mothers: The Political Origins of Social Policy in the United States.* Cambridge, MA: Belknap Press of Harvard University Press, 1992.

Slevin, Kathleen F., and C. Ray Wingrove. *From Stumbling Blocks to Stepping Stones: The Life Experiences of Fifty Professional African American Women.* New York: New York University Press, 1998.

Smeeding, Timothy M., and Joseph T. Marchand. "Family Time and Public Policy in the United States." In *Family Time: The Social Organization of Care,* edited by Nancy Folbre and Michael Bittman, 25–48. New York: Routledge, 2004.

Smelser, Neil. *Social Change in the Industrial Revolution: An Application of Theory to the Lancashire Cotton Industry, 1770–1840.* London: Routledge and Paul, 1959.

———. "Toward a Theory of Modernization." In *Essays in Sociological Explanation,* 125–46. Englewood Cliffs, NJ: Prentice-Hall, 1968.

Smith, James. "Poverty and the Family." In *Divided Opportunities: Minorities, Poverty and Social Policy,* edited by Gary Sandefur and Marta Tienda, 141–72. New York: Plenum Press, 1988.

Smith, James, and Michael Ward. *Women's Wages and Work in the Twentieth Century.* Santa Monica, CA: Rand Corporation, 1984.

Smith, Ralph E. *Women in the Labor Force in 1990.* Washington, DC: Urban Institute, 1979.

Smith, Vicki. *Crossing the Great Divide: Worker Risk and Opportunity in the New Economy.* Ithaca, NY: ILR Press, 2001.

Smuts, Robert W. *Women and Work in America.* New York: Schocken, 1959.

Sociologists for Women in Society. Home page. http://newmedia.colorado.edu/~socwomen/index.html#facts (accessed March 13, 2003).

Solinger, Rickie. *Beggars and Choosers: How the Politics of Choice Shapes Adoption, Abortion, and Welfare in the United States.* New York: Hill and Wang, 2001.

———. *Wake Up Little Susie: Single Pregnancy and Race before Roe v. Wade.* New York: Routledge, 1992.

"Solving the Puzzle: Researchers Collaborate in the Struggle to Understand and Treat Alzheimer's Disease." *Pilot* (Publication of the Office of Public Relations, Evanston Northwestern Healthcare) 65 (Summer 2001): 4–6.

Sorensen, Annemette, and Sara McLanahan. "Married Women's Economic Dependency, 1940–1980." *American Journal of Sociology* 93 (1987): 659–87.

Spain, Daphne, and Suzanne M. Bianchi. *Balancing Act: Motherhood, Marriage, and Employment among American Women.* New York: Russell Sage Foundation, 1996.

Spalter-Roth, Roberta M., and Heidi I. Hartmann. "AFDC Recipients as Care-Givers and Workers: A Feminist Approach to Income Security Policy for American Women." *Social Politics* 1 (Summer 1994): 190–210.

Spillman, Lyn. *Nation and Commemoration: Creating National Identities in the United States and Australia.* New York: Cambridge University Press, 1997.

Spock, Benjamin. *Baby and Child Care.* New York: Duell, Sloan and Pearce, 1946.

Stanton, Elizabeth Cady. *Eighty Years and More.* New York: European Publishing, 1898.

Stein, Judith. *Running Steel, Running America: Race, Economic Policy, and the Decline of Liberalism.* Chapel Hill: University of North Carolina Press, 1998.

Steinmetz, George. "The Local Welfare State: Two Strategies for Social Domination in Urban Imperial Germany." *American Sociological Review* 55 (December 1991): 891–911.

Stone, Erika. "Seventeen's Not So Sweet When You're on Your Own—with a Baby." *Parents' Magazine,* October 1977, p. 55.

Story, Louise. "Many Women at Elite Colleges Set Career Path to Motherhood." *New York Times,* September 20, 2005.

Strasser, Susan. *Never Done: A History of American Housework.* New York: Pantheon, 1982.

Strober, Myra H., and Agnes Miling Kaneko Chan. *The Road Winds Uphill All the Way: Gender, Work, and Family in the United States and Japan.* Cambridge, MA: MIT Press, 1999.

Sweeney, Megan M. "Two Decades of Family Change: The Shifting Economic Foundations of Marriage." *American Sociological Review* 67 (February 2002): 132–47.

Sweet, James A., and Larry L. Bumpass. *American Families and Households: The Population of the United States in the 1980s.* New York: Russell Sage Foundation, 1987.

Taylor, Humprey. "Harris Poll on Child Care." The Harris Poll, January 28, 1998. http://www.harrisinteractive.com/harris-poll/index.asp?PID-200 (accessed January 12, 2006).

Taylor, John G. *From Modernization to Modes of Production: A Critique of the Sociologies of Development and Underdevelopment.* London: Macmillan, 1979.

Teles, Steven M. *Whose Welfare? AFDC and Elite Politics.* Lawrence: University Press of Kansas, 1996.

Terborg-Penn, Rosalyn. "Discrimination against Afro-American Women in the Woman's Movement, 1830–1920." In *The Afro-American Woman: Struggles and Images,* edited by Sharon Harley and Rosalyn Terborg-Penn, 17–27. Port Washington, NY: Kennikat Press, 1978.

Testa, Mark, Nan Marie Astone, Marilyn Krogh, and Kathryn M. Neckerman. "Employment and Marriage among Inner-City Fathers." In *The Ghetto Underclass: Social Science Perspectives,* edited by William J. Wilson, 79–91. Newbury Park, CA: Sage, 1989.

Thaler, Ruth E. "Essence Women." *Essence,* June 1980, p. 45.

Thernstrom, Stephan. "Poverty in Historical Perspective." In *On Understanding Poverty: Perspectives from the Social Sciences,* edited by Daniel P. Moynihan, 160–86. New York: Basic Books, 1968.

Thistle, Susan. "The Changing Nature of Women's Poverty: An Analysis of Two Cohorts of African-American and White Women." Working Paper 98–22. Institute for Policy Research, Northwestern University, 1998.

———. "Gender, Class, and Welfare State Formation in the 21st Century." *Current Perspectives in Social Theory,* edited by Jennifer Lehmann, 21 (2002): 115–42.

———. "The Trouble with Modernity: Gender and the Remaking of Social Theory." *Sociological Theory* 18 (July 2000): 275–89.

Thompson, E. P. *The Making of the English Working Class.* London: Gollancz, 1963.

Tienda, Marta, and Leif Jensen. "Poverty and Minorities: A Quarter-Century Profile of Color and Socioeconomic Disadvantage." In *Divided Opportunities: Minorities, Poverty and Social Policy,* edited by Gary Sandefur and Marta Tienda, 23–62. New York: Plenum Press, 1988.

Tolnay, Stewart E. "Black Family Formation and Tenancy in the Farm South, 1900." *American Journal of Sociology* 90 (September 1984): 305–25.

———. "The Great Migration and Changes in the Northern Black Family, 1940 to 1990." *Social Forces* 75 (June 1997): 1213–38.

Trotter, Joe William, Jr. *Coal, Class, and Color: Blacks in Southern West Virginia, 1915–32.* Urbana: University of Illinois Press, 1990.

Tuominen, Mary C. "Where Teachers Can Make a Livable Wage: Organizing to Address Gender and Racial Inequalities in Paid Child Care Work." In *Child Care and Inequality: Rethinking Carework for Children and Youth,* edited by Francesca M. Cancian, Demie Kurz, Andrew London, Rebecca Reviere, and Mary Tuominen, 193–206. New York: Routledge, 2002.

U.S. Bureau of the Census. *Characteristics of the Population below the Poverty Level: 1976.*

Current Population Survey Reports, series P-60, no. 115. Washington, DC: U.S. Government Printing Office, 1978.

———. *Characteristics of the Poverty Population.* Current Population Survey Reports, series P-60, no. 98. Washington, DC: U.S. Government Printing Office, 1975.

———. "Children Ever Born per 1,000 Women and Percent Childless, by Selected Characteristics: June 2002." (Internet release date October 23, 2003.) http://www.census.gov/population/www/socdemo/fertility/cps2002/tab03.pdf (accessed January 20, 2006).

———. "Education." In *Statistical Abstract of the United States,* 2000. http://www.census.gov/prod/2001pubs/statab/sec04.pdf (accessed August 27, 2005).

———. *Historical Statistics of the United States: Colonial Times to 1970.* Washington, DC: U.S. Government Printing Office, 1970.

———. "Income, Expenditures and Wealth." In *Statistical Abstract of the United States,* 2000. http://www.census.gov/prod/2001pubs/statab/sec13.pdf (accessed August 27, 2005).

———. "Labor Force, Employment, and Earnings." In *Statistical Abstract of the United States,* 1999. http://www.census.gov/prod/99pubs/99statab/sec13.pdf (accessed August 27, 2005).

———. "Labor Force, Employment, and Earnings." In *Statistical Abstract of the United States,* 2000. http://www.census.gov/prod/2001pubs/statab/sec13.pdf (accessed August 27, 2005).

———. "Marital Status of Persons 15 Years and Older, by Age, Sex, Race, Hispanic Origin, Metropolitan Residence, and Region: 1998." Detailed tables, table 1 in *Marital Status and Living Arrangements: March 1998 (Update).* Current Population Survey Reports, series P20-514. http://www.census.gov/prod/www/abs/marital.html (accessed January 19, 2005).

———. "Population." In *Statistical Abstract of the United States:* 1999. http://www.census.gov/prod/99pubs/99statab/sec01.pdf (accessed August 27, 2005).

———. *Statistical Abstract of the United States: 1950.* 71st ed. Washington, DC: U.S. Government Printing Office, 1950.

———. *Statistical Abstract of the United States: 1953.* 74th ed. Washington, DC: U.S. Government Printing Office, 1950.

———. *Statistical Abstract of the United States: 1966.* 87th ed. Washington, DC: U.S. Government Printing Office, 1966.

———. *Studies in Household and Family Formation.* Current Population Reports, series P23–179. Washington, DC: U.S. Government Printing Office, 1992.

———. "Twentieth Century Statistics." In *Statistical Abstract of the United States:* 1999. http://www.census.gov/prod/99pubs/99statab/sec31.pdf (accessed August 26, 2005).

————. "Weighted Average Poverty Thresholds for Families of Specified Size 1959 to 2000." Table 1 in *Historical Poverty Tables*. http://www.census.gov/hhes/poverty/histpov/hstpov1.html (accessed April 2, 2001).

U.S. Department of Labor. *Futurework: Trends and Challenges for Work in the 21st Century.* September 1999. http://www.dol.gov/asp/programs/history/herman/reports/futurework/report.htm (accessed October 4, 2003).

U.S. Department of Labor, Bureau of Labor Statistics. *Career Guide to Industries, 2000–01 Edition,* "Hotels and Other Accommodations." http://stats.bls.gov/oco/cg/cgs036.htm (accessed July 17, 2005).

————. *Career Guide to Industries, 2001–02 Edition.* http://www.bls.gov/oco/cg/cgs036.htm#outlook (accessed January 29, 2003).

————. "Employment Status of the Population by Sex, Marital Status, and Presence and Age of Own Children under 18, 1998–99 Annual Averages" (last modified 6/19/2000). Table 5 of *Labor Force Statistics from the Current Population Survey, BLS.* http://stats.bls.gov/news.release/famee.to5.htm (accessed August 3, 2000).

————. *Highlights of Women's Earnings in 1999.* Report 943 (May 2000). http://www.bls.gov/cps/cpswom99.pdf (accessed July 10, 2000).

————. *Highlights of Women's Earnings in 2000.* Report 952 (August 2001). http://www.bls.gov/cps/cpswom2000.pdf (accessed September 3, 2001).

————. "National Employment, Hours and Earnings (SIC), 1970–2000." http://www.bls.gov/cesoldces/sic.htm (accessed April 26, 2005).

————. *National Longitudinal Survey of Mature Women's Labor Market Experience,* 1967–2000. http://www.bls.gov/nls/nlsdata.htm (accessed October 1, 2005).

————. "Personal and Home Care Aides." In *Occupational Outlook Handbook, 2000–2001 Edition.* http://stats.bls.gov/oco/pdf/ocos173.pdf (accessed July 17, 2005).

U.S. Department of Labor, Women's Bureau. *Equal Pay: A Thirty-Five Year Perspective.* Washington, DC: U.S. Government Printing Office, 1998.

————. *Facts on Working Women* 97–3 (May 1997). Washington, DC: U.S. Government Printing Office.

————. "Women at the Millennium, Accomplishments and Challenges Ahead." *Facts on Working Women* 00–02 (March 2000). http://permanent.access.gpo.gov/lps5585/millennium52000.htm (accessed May 15, 2005).

————. "Women in High-Tech Jobs." *Facts on Working Women* 02–01 (July 2002). http://www.dol.gov/wb/factsheets/hitecho2.htm (accessed April 9, 2003).

————. *Women in Poverty: Jobs and the Need for Jobs.* 68–161 (April 1968). Washington, DC: Department of Labor, Wage and Labor Standards Administration; U.S. Government Printing.

————. "Women's Jobs 1964–1997: More Than 30 Years of Progress." http://www.wb/public/jobs6496 (accessed May 20, 1999).

————. "Work-Related Child Care Statistics." www.dol.gov/wb/childcare/ ccstats.htm (accessed July 29, 2001).

Vanek, Joann. "Keeping Busy: Time Spent in Housework, United States, 1920–1970." Ph.D. diss., University of Michigan, 1973.

————. "Time Spent in Housework." *Scientific American* 231 (November 1974): 116–20.

Van Horn, Susan Householder. *Women, Work and Fertility, 1900–1986.* New York: New York University Press, 1988.

Ventura, Stephanie J., and Christine A. Bachrach. "Nonmarital Childbearing in the United States, 1940–99." *National Vital Statistics Reports* 48, no. 16 (revised) (October 2000). Hyattsville, MD: National Center for Health Statistics. http://www.cdc.gov/nchs/data/nvsr/nvsr48/nvs48_16.pdf (accessed November 9, 2003).

Veroff, Joseph, Elizabeth Douvan, and Richard Koulka. *The Inner American: A Self-Portrait from 1957 to 1976.* New York: Basic Books, 1981.

Waldfogel, Jane. "The Effect of Children on Women's Wages." *American Sociological Review* 62 (1997): 209–17.

————. "The Family Gap for Young Women in the United States and Britain: Can Maternity Leave Make a Difference?" *Journal of Labor Economics* 16 (July 1998): 505–45.

————. "Understanding the 'Family Gap' in Pay for Women with Children." *Journal of Economic Perspectives* 12 (Winter 1998): 137–56.

————. "Working Mothers Then and Now: A Cross-Cohort Analysis of the Effects of Maternity Leave on Women's Pay." In *Gender and Family Issues in the Workplace,* edited by Francine D. Blau and Ronald G. Ehrenberg, 92–126. New York: Russell Sage Foundation, 1997.

Walker, Alice. "*One Child of One's Own: A Meaningful Digression within the Work(s).*" In *The Writer on Her Work,* edited by Janet Sternburg, 121–40. New York: Norton, 1981.

Walker, Kathryn E., and Margaret E. Woods. *Time Use: A Measure of Household Production of Family Goods and Services.* Washington, DC: American Home Economics Association, 1976.

Walker, Susan. "Why I Became a Single Mother." *Ladies' Home Journal,* March 1985, pp. 22–24.

Wallace, Phyllis. *Pathways to Work: Unemployment among Black Teenage Females.* Lexington, MA: Lexington Books, 1974.

Wallace, Phyllis, with Linda Datcher and Julianne Malveaux. *Black Women in the Labor Force.* Cambridge, MA: MIT Press, 1980.

Ward, Kathryn B., and Jean Larson Pyle. "Gender, Industrialization, Corporations, and Development." In *Women in the Latin American Development Process,* edited by Christine E. Bose and Edna Acosta-Belen, 37–64. Philadelphia: Temple University Press, 1995.

Waring, Marilyn. *If Women Counted: A New Feminist Economics.* New York: Harper and Row, 1988.

Warren, Wini. *Black Women in Science.* Bloomington: Indiana University Press, 1999.

Wasserman, Elga. *The Door in the Dream: Conversations with Eminent Women in Science.* Washington, DC: Joseph Henry Press, 2000.

Weber, Max. *General Economic History.* Translated by Frank H. Knight. New York: Greenberg, 1927.

Weir, Margaret, Ann Orloff, and Theda Skocpol, eds. *The Politics of Social Policy Formation in the United States.* Princeton, NJ: Princeton University Press, 1988.

Weitzman, Lenore. *The Divorce Revolution: The Unexpected Social and Economic Consequences for Women and Children in America.* New York: Free Press, 1985.

West, Guida. *The National Welfare Rights Movement: The Social Protest of Poor Women.* New York: Praeger, 1981.

"What's a Nice Girl Like You Doing in a Place Like This?" *Ebony,* June 1977, pp. 103–10.

White, Deborah Gray. *Ar'n't I a Woman? Female Slaves in the Plantation South.* New York: Norton, 1985.

———. *Too Heavy a Load: Black Women in Defense of Themselves, 1894–1994.* New York: Norton, 1999.

White, Sammis B., and Lori A. Geddes. "Economic Lessons for Welfare Mothers." Wisconsin Policy Research Institute Report 14, February 2001. http://www.wpri.org/Reports/Volume14/Vol14no1.pdf (accessed May 5, 2005).

Wilensky, Harold. *The Welfare State and Equality: Structural and Ideological Roots of Public Expenditure.* Berkeley: University of California Press, 1975.

Willard, Constance W. *Black Teenage Mothers: Pregnancy and Child Rearing from Their Perspective.* Lexington, MA: Lexington Books, 1991.

Williams, Joan. *Unbending Gender: Why Family and Work Conflict and What to Do about It.* Oxford: Oxford University Press, 2000.

Williams, Raymond. *The Country and the City.* New York: Oxford University Press, 1973.

———. *Culture and Society: 1780–1950.* New York: Columbia University Press, 1983.

Willie, Charles Vert. *A New Look at Black Families.* 2nd ed. Bayside, NY: General Hall, 1981.

Wilson, William Julius, ed. *The Truly Disadvantaged: The Inner City, the Underclass and Public Policy.* Chicago: University of Chicago Press, 1987.

———. *When Work Disappears: The World of the New Urban Poor.* New York: Knopf, 1996.

Wilson, William Julius, and Kathryn M. Neckerman. "Poverty and Family Structure: The Widening Gap between Evidence and Public Policy Issues." In *The Truly Disadvantaged: The Inner City, the Underclass and Public Policy,* edited by William Julius Wilson, 63–92. Chicago: University of Chicago Press, 1987.

Witte, Edwin. *The Development of the Social Security Act.* Madison: University of Wisconsin Press, 1962.

Wojtkiewicz, Roger A., Sara S. McLanahan, and Irwin Garfinkel. "The Growth of Families Headed by Women: 1950–1980." *Demography* 27 (February 1990): 19–30.

Wolfe, Barbara, and Scott Scrivner. "Providing Universal Pre-school for Four-Year-Olds." In *One Percent for the Kids: New Policies, Brighter Futures for America's Children,* edited by Isabel V. Sawhill, 113–35. Washington, DC: Brookings Institution Press, 2003.

Wolpe, Harold. "Capitalism and Cheap Labour-Power in South Africa: From Segregation to Apartheid." *Economy and Society* 1 (Autumn 1972): 425–56.

———. *Race, Class and the Apartheid State.* London: James Currey, 1988.

"Women: Do You Know the Facts about Marriage?" In *Sisterhood Is Powerful: An Anthology of Writings from the Women's Liberation Movement,* edited by Robin Morgan, 536–37. New York: Vintage Books, 1970.

Women in Transition. *Women's Survival Manual: A Feminist Handbook on Separation and Divorce.* Philadelphia: Women in Transition, 1972.

Working Mother Discussion. Home page. http://fleury.coastalw.com/default _disc1.htm (last accessed January 18, 2002).

Wright, Erik O. *Class Counts: Comparative Studies in Class Analysis.* Cambridge: Cambridge University Press, 1998.

———. "Explanation and Emancipation in Marxism and Feminism." *Sociological Theory* 11 (March 1993): 39–54.

Zelizer, Viviana. "How Care Counts." *Contemporary Sociology* 31 (March 2002): 115–19.

———. *Pricing the Priceless Child: The Changing Social Value of Children.* Princeton, NJ.: Princeton University Press, 1994.

Zhang, Jie. "The Ark." In *Love Must Not Be Forgotten,* 113–201. San Francisco: China Books and Periodicals; Beijing: Panda Books, 1986.

Zinkewicz, Phil. "Cleaning and Janitorial Services: A Growing Market." *Rough Notes,* no. 136 (September 1993): 39–40.

Zinn, Maxine Baca. "Family, Race, and Poverty in the Eighties." *Signs: Journal of Women in Culture and Society* 14 (Summer 1989): 856–74.

———. "Feminist Rethinking from Racial-Ethnic Families." In *Women of Color in U.S. Society*, edited by Maxine Baca Zinn and Bonnie Thornton Dill, 303–14. Philadelphia. Temple University Press, 1994.

Zinn, Maxine Baca, and Bonnie Thornton Dill. "Theorizing Difference from Multiracial Feminism." *Feminist Studies* 22 (Summer 1996): 321–31.

INDEX

abortion, 50–51, 130; and politics, 57–58, 64–65, 69. *See also under* poverty of single mothers

Abramovitz, Mimi, 195n35

Addams, Jane, 25

AFDC. *See* Aid to Families with Dependent Children

affirmative action, 87

African American men: education, 60, 213n16; family wage, 197n45; marriage, changing attitudes toward 61–62; need of women's domestic labor, 22, 26; sharecropping, 26; slavery, 22–23; unemployment 61, 62, 66; wage employment, 26, 30–31, 70, 196n41, 200n59, 214n18. *See also* support, women's changing sources of

African American women: changing relationship to marriage, motherhood and labor force, by education, 73–78, 123–32; changing sources of support, by marital status, 30–31, 67, 115–22, 136–38; college graduates, 44, 60, 70, 73–74, 123–26, 131; comparison with Latina women, 175; comparison with recent immigrants, 179; divorce, 61, 63, 67, 125; domestic realm, lack of time for, 22–23, 26, 27, 31–32, 43, 155–60; double burden, 18–19, 22–23, 26, 27, 32, 33; and gender division of labor 7, 18–19, 21–23, 26–27, 29–32, 43; gender equality, support for, 45–46, 60–61, 196n43, 213n17; high school dropouts, 62–63, 67, 70, 76–78, 129–31; high school graduates, 62–63, 67, 74–77, 126–28, 129, 130; in private domestic work, 31–32; in sharecropping, 26; in slavery, 21–23; wage employment, 29–32, 37, 67, 70. *See also under* housework: African American women; poverty of single mothers; professional women; women's organizations

agricultural involution, 18–19, 201n68. *See also* double burden, compared to other arrangements of labor

Aid to Families with Dependent Children (AFDC), 66, 71–72, 91–92

Anderson, Elijah 215n24

baby boomers, 44, 93–94, 109, 167
Bane, Mary Jane, 221n2
Beauvoir, Simone de, 50
Becker, Gary, 185n3
Beecher, Catherine, 195n35
Benería, Lourdes, 190n3
Bernstein, Jared, 144
Bianchi, Suzanne, 239nn10,11,
    240n13, 242n22, 244n38
birth control, 39, 50, 51, 204n13,
    208n39
Black Women's Liberation Committee, 45
Blank, Rebecca, 219n53
Boushey, Heather, 144
Boydston, Jeanne, 6, 192nn17,18
Brennan, Justice William Joseph, 53
Brooks-Higginbotham, Evelyn, 196n42
Browne, Irene, 222n4

capitalism, 7, 10, 18, 114, 190n5,
    198n49
caregiving. See care work
care work, 5, 139, 106, 110; market
    takeover of care of sick, 105; and
    social policy, 140–43, 162, 164,
    175. See also health care
census data: in 1910, 30, 200n59; Inte-
    grated Public Use Microdata Series
    (IPUMS), 8–9
Cherlin, Andrew, 38, 185n3, 204n13
child care: market takeover of, 106; and
    new social policy, 165, 207n34. See
    also under poverty of single mothers
childlessness, 114. See also under college
    graduates
child support, 143–44, 163
citizenship, and new social policy, 163–
    64
Civil Rights Act (1964), 52–53
cleaning, market takeover of, 105
Cloward, Richard, 82
Cobble, Dorothy Sue, 45
cohabitation, 92
Cohen, Marjorie Griffin, 20, 21, 190n2,
    192nn15,17
cohorts, of women, 9. See also under
    poverty of single mothers

college graduates: childlessness, 56,
    124; differences, by race, 74, 131,
    220n61; divorce, 56, 57, 60, 75,
    124; employment, 44, 56, 73,
    123 26, 206n28; feminism,
    208n38; marriage, 56, 60, 70, 73,
    123–26; motherhood, 56, 60, 63,
    73, 123–26; in People's Republic
    of China 178; single mothers, 92,
    236n58; as source of skilled labor
    109–10; as sources of support,
    129; wages and basic needs 128.
    See also under African American
    women; poverty of single mothers;
    white women
Collins, Patricia Hill, 187n14, 188n15
comparable worth, 146
comparative method, 8
Conley, Frances, 110
contraception. See birth control
cooking, market takeover of, 104–5
Cott, Nancy, 192n17

Davis, Angela, 193nn21,22
differences by class among women: in
    labor force participation, 73–78,
    110–11, 123–31, 155–57; in mar-
    riage and motherhood, 73–78,
    123–31; in mothers' income, 146–
    53, 157; in relationship to domes-
    tic realm, 24, 154–57, 160, 183–
    84
differences by gender: in family care,
    40, 143; in gains from transforma-
    tion of women's tasks and labor,
    143–53; in wages, 30–31, 145–46
differences by race among women: in
    current time and resources for fam-
    ily care, 155–60, 172–73, 182–84;
    in goals of women's organizations,
    27; in labor force participation, 7,
    11, 43, 73–78, 110–11, 131–32;
    in marriage and motherhood, 73–
    78, 131–32; in mothers' income,
    146–53, 157; in past relationship
    to domestic realm, 7, 11, 19, 24,
    31–32, 60; in sources of support,

mothers, before 1960: lessened need for physical presence, 39; overwork, 21, 23, 24, 25, 26, 27, 44

mothers, from 1960 on: changing sources of support, by race, 136–38, 158; differences by race, 157–58; difficulties combining work at home and for pay, 42–44, 133–39; full-time employment, 138–40, 154–57, 159; inequalities in time and support for families, 154–60; part-time employment, 155–56; trends in income and work by race and marital status, 146–50; withdrawal from labor force, 151–57. *See also* college graduates; high school dropouts; high school graduates; poverty of single mothers; single mothers

Mothers' Aid. *See* Mothers' Pensions

Mothers' Pensions, 25; and African American women 71, 197n45

Muller v. Oregon, 196n37

Muncie, Indiana. *See* Middletown, Indiana

National Association of Colored Women (NACW), 26–27

National Council of Negro Women, 45

National Organization of Women (NOW), 45, 79

National Welfare Rights Organization, 223n8

Neighborhood Union, 196nn42,43

Nelson, Julie, 102

never-married mothers, 50, 88. *See also* high school dropouts: never-married mothers; unwed mothers

new economy, 4–5, 13, 99, 141; and transformation of women's work, 99–113

New Right, 64–65, 69

Nimkoff, Meyer F., 202n6

occupational segregation, by sex, 146

Ogburn, William F., 202n6

Osterman, Paul, 186n6

Palmer, Phyllis, 32, 200n63, 201n67

Parsons, Talcott, 186n9

patriarchy, 10, 182–83, 186n10, 191n10, 195n35. *See also* employers; men

Pearce, Diana, 87

personal care, market takeover of, 106

Petcheskey, Rosalind, 212n8, 216nn31,32

Piercy, Marge, 50

Piven, Frances, 82

politics of representation, 183

poverty of single mothers, 1960–2000, 13, 79–98, 171; changing causes of, 79–81, 82–84, 94–95; changing characteristics of, 80–81, 96–97; childcare, 80, 83, 85, 87; children, 80, 83, 85, 87, 93–94; cohabitation, 91; by cohort, 88, 93–94; college graduates, 81, 84, 85, 90, 92–93; differences by race, 82–83, 84, 85, 97–98, 131; divorce, 82, 83, 85, 93; education, 80, 84, 85, 96; employment, 80–98; heading families, 84, 85, 92; less-educated, 87–88, 89–93, 128–30; marriage, 82–83, 87, 89, 91, 93, 94–95; maternal role, 88; never-married motherhood, 88, 91, 92–94; occupations, 80–98; pregnancy, 88; private domestic work, 80, 83, 84, 85, 87; and theories of, 79–80; trends by age and race, 85–88, 89, 130; trends by education and race, 87–93, 128; unemployment, 87, 89, 97; wages, 84, 91, 94; welfare, 89, 91–92, 94; widows, 84, 87

pregnancy 129; premarital, 50, 88, 130, 210nn57,58; welfare policy, 141, 241n19

professional women, 73, 75, 109, 125–27, 135; African American, 27, 43, 109–10, 125–27, 196n43, 206n24; in China, 178; white, 43, 44, 125–27, 205n22

protective labor legislation, 25, 52

Puerto Rican women, 176

Quadagno, Jill, 219n53

Ragin, Charles, 188n17
Reagan, Ronald, 66, 72
Reid, Margaret, 198n50
rights, 5; and new social policy, 166; to support a family, 183–84
Roberts, Dorothy, 157, 158–59, 161, 189n18, 241n20
Robertson, Claire, 193n22
Robinson, John P., 205n18
Rogers, Joel, 213n14
Rostow, Walt W., 39, 203n12, 213n11
Roth, Benita, 207n34, 208n36
Rubin, Gayle, 186n10
Rubin, Lillian, 44, 49, 213n15
Ruggles, Steve, 194n25

Sawhill, Isabel, 224n17, 242n23, 246n53, 247n60
Sayer, Liana, 239nn10,11, 240n12, 244n35
service occupations, 75, 77, 89, 95–96, 110–11, 130
service sector, 69, 100–101, 103, 106–8, 110–12, 217n44
sexual division of labor. See gender division of labor
sexual revolution, 49–50
sharecropping, 26–27
Shen, Rong, 177
single mothers: changing sources of support, 118–20, 136; differences by race, 131, 157, 160; in People's Republic of China, 178; overwork 138, 150; and social policy, 142–43, 165; trends in family income, by race, 150–53. See also college graduates; high school dropouts; high school graduates; poverty of single mothers
Single Mothers by Choice, 92
Smelser, Neil, 190n5
social policy: 164, 195n35; cross-national comparisons, 173, 180–81; divisions among women, 154, 159; divisions by race, 218n52;

and dynamics of industrialization, 173; in Europe, 173; and gender, 71, 163–64, 218n52; and single mothers, 71 166; and unions, 155; women's new resources for, 153–54. See also social policy proposals
social policy proposals: family income, 164; family leave, 163; new definitions of adulthood, 163–64; new definitions of citizenship and rights, 165–66; single mothers, 166; unions, 162–63; wages, 162–63
Solinger, Rickie, 209n52, 225n27
Sorensen, Annemette, 222n4, 224n17, 234n49
Stanton, Elizabeth Cady, 192n19
state, 57, 67; and aid to families 71; dismantling of gender division of labor, 57, 72; as employer of women, 177; in People's Republic of China, 177–78
Strasser, Susan, 198n49, 199n56, 201n70
support, women's changing sources of: all women, by race and marital status, 115–23; married women, by race, 115–16; mothers, by race, 135–38, 158
Supreme Court, 51, 53, 57, 69, 69, 114

Terrell, Mary Church, 196n42, 197n44
theories: classical sociological, 5–6, 169; critical social, 188n16; of cultural representation, 5, 183; feminist, 6, 187n12; of gender, 9; of gender division of labor and market, 17–19; of intersection of race, class, and gender, 7, 33, 187n14, 189n18, 191n10, 201n68; of social change and gender, 5–7, 169, 181–82
Tillmon, Johnnie, 79
time use studies, of housework, 28, 39–41, 138–40, 143, 149
Tolnay, Stewart, 26, 214n20

7823

transformation, of women's work: consequences for women, by education and race, 73–78; and new economy, 171; unequal distribution of gains, 11, 143, 150–51, 159–60, 172, 175

unemployment: African American women, 62, 70, 77, 129; white women, 63, 70, 73, 129. See also under African American men

unions, 68; and new social policy, 162–63; and paid family leave 155; and women's new resources, 154

unmarried mothers. See never-married mothers; single mothers; unwed mothers

unwed mothers, 49, 50, 51, 129. See also never-married mothers

Vanek, Joann, 39–41, 197n47; 204n14, 205n19

wages, of women. See women's wages
Walker, Alice, 44
Wallace, Phyllis, 188n15, 225n24
War on Poverty, 71, 82, 219n54
Weber, Max, 186n9
welfare, 66, 71–72, 88, 91–92, 110–11, 129, 130. See also under poverty of single mothers
welfare state formation: comparative analysis, 180–81; in Europe, 180; and gender, 140–43; and single mothers, 142
White, Deborah Gray, 207n32
white women: changing relationship to marriage, motherhood, and labor force participation, by education, 73–78, 123–32; changing sources of support, by marital status, 67, 115–22, 136–38; college graduates, 44, 56, 57, 60, 124–27, 131; comparison with Latina women, 175; divorce, 56–57, 60, 63, 125; and gender division of labor, 18–19, 19–20, 24–26, 28–29, 170;

high school dropouts, 63, 70, 76–78; high school graduates, 56–57, 60, 67, 74–77, 126–28, 129, 130; use of private domestic workers, 31–32; wage employment, after 1950, 37, 42–43, 56, 60, 67, 70; wage employment, before 1950, 20, 23–24, 199n57. See also college graduates; high school dropouts; high school graduates; housewives; housework; poverty of single mothers; professional women; white women; women's organizations

Williams, Raymond, 60, 213n15
Wilson, William Julius, 61, 185n3, 214n20, 227n42
Wolpe, Harold, 191n9, 194n26, 200n65
women's challenges to gender division of labor, 37, 42–44; defense of gender division of labor, 21, 57–58; in Europe 173; and global economy 179–80; in industrialized countries 173; in newly industrialized countries, 176–79; in People's Republic of China, 177–78; and state, 177; and unions 154–55. See also African American women; college graduates; high school dropouts; high school graduates; white women
women's organizations: 15–16, 21, 49, 154, 163–64; African-American, 26–27, 44–46, 154; differences by race, 197n43; white, 25, 44–46
women's wages, 33, 52, 112–13; of African American women, 31, 43, 200n65; gender gap in, 145–46; and paid family leave, 145–46; role in mother's support, 135–38; role in women's support, 115–23; and social policy 162–63; trends among mothers, by marital status and race, 146–53; and women's basic needs, 123; and women's poverty 119–22

women's work: definition of, 102; and growth of service sector, 106; and growth of GDP, 106–8; and job growth, 103; and new economy, 11, 113, 171; and prosperity of the 1990s, 113; unequal distribution of gains from transformation, 143, 159–60

working class, 68, 69, 78; black male, 26, 30–31, 70; divisions by race and gender, 32, 64, 66; families, 59–62, 67; and New Right 64, 66; women, 25, 31–32, 45; white male, 24–25, 60, 63–64. *See also* high school dropouts; high school graduates

working-class formation, comparisons by gender, 58, 78, 140–42, 169, 172, 181–82

Zelizer, Viviana, 186n7
Zhang, Jie, 178
Zinn, Maxine Baca, 188n15, 241n20

Text: 10/13 Joanna
Display: Joanna, Syntax
Compositor: Binghamton Valley Composition, LLC
Printer and binder: Maple-Vail Manufacturing Group